The Blueprint for AI Adoption and Societal Transformation

This book analyses artificial intelligence (AI) and its impact on sustainability, ethics, security, and society. It provides actionable strategies for eco-friendly AI, navigating legal frameworks and implementing ethical practices. It examines security challenges from AI misuse, outlining necessary cybersecurity enhancements. Real-world case studies bridge theory and practice. Guidance is provided for aligning AI adoption with societal and environmental goals, promoting responsible AI development for a sustainable future.

This comprehensive study of AI begins by looking at AI's role in environmental sustainability, providing actionable strategies for eco-friendly AI development and deployment. This includes understanding the complex relationship between AI and the environment to minimise its footprint and promote AI solutions that contribute to environmental goals. The authors extend into an insightful discussion on navigating the intricate legal frameworks and implementing ethical AI practices. This guidance reduces the risk of legal challenges and reputational damage, leading to increased trust and responsible AI development and use. Bridging the gap between theory and practice is another important feature in this book. With real-world case studies, the reader gains a practical understanding of how AI is being used in different contexts. This enhances the accelerated adoption and increased innovation of AI solutions in different fields. This book provides a clear roadmap for responsible and sustainable AI integration, aligning AI initiatives with broader societal and environmental objectives.

The primary audience for this book includes business leaders, professionals, policymakers, technologists, and AI practitioners.

The Blueprint for AI Adoption and Societal Transformation

Sandeep Bhalekar and Amit Tiwary

CRC Press
Taylor & Francis Group
Boca Raton London New York

CRC Press is an imprint of the
Taylor & Francis Group, an **informa** business

Designed cover image: Shutterstock

First edition published 2026
by CRC Press
2385 NW Executive Center Drive, Suite 320, Boca Raton FL 33431

and by CRC Press
4 Park Square, Milton Park, Abingdon, Oxon, OX14 4RN

CRC Press is an imprint of Taylor & Francis Group, LLC

© 2026 Sandeep Bhalekar and Amit Tiwary

ISBN: 978-1-041-04031-6 (hbk)
ISBN: 978-1-041-04030-9 (pbk)
ISBN: 978-1-003-62650-3 (ebk)

DOI: 10.1201/9781003626503

Typeset in Palatino
by codeMantra

I dedicate this work with love and gratitude to my parents, **Shalan and Bapurao**, *whose values and support have been my foundation. To my family—***Shubhangi, Eva, and Rudra***—for being my strength and inspiration every step of the way.*

(Sandeep Bhalekar)

And to **Renu, Aneesh, Ayesha, Ayush, Ayansh, and Ayaana**—
for their love, encouragement, and unwavering belief in this journey.

(Amit Tiwary)

Contents

Note to Readers and Educators

Each chapter in this book concludes with reflective and practical questions designed to help readers think critically, connect theory with practice, and explore the real-world implications of Artificial Intelligence adoption. These questions are not merely academic—they are meant to inspire meaningful dialogue, deeper inquiry, and purposeful action.

To enhance your learning experience, comprehensive answers and detailed explanations to all chapter-end questions are available at www.sandeepb-halekar.com. The website also includes extended frameworks, structured methodologies, and practical rules to further support your journey through AI adoption and implementation.

For educators, trainers, and facilitators, the website offers additional resources such as teaching frameworks, assessment rubrics, case studies, and discussion prompts to enable structured learning and classroom integration.

This digital companion is a living resource, continuously updated with new insights, examples, and research as the AI landscape evolves. By combining this book with the online resources, readers and educators can engage in a dynamic and up-to-date exploration of how Artificial Intelligence is reshaping industries, education, and society at large.

Let us continue learning, questioning, and advancing together—building a future where technology empowers humanity through knowledge, ethics, and innovation.

Authors

Sandeep Bhalekar is a visionary leader, technologist, and mentor with over two decades of experience in driving digital transformation through artificial intelligence and data engineering. As the Founder and CEO of the Global Institute of Artificial Intelligence (GIofAI) and the Managing Director of Bhalekar Consulting, Sandeep has empowered individuals and organisations alike to embrace the future of work with confidence, clarity, and capability. With a rich background that includes leadership roles at global financial institutions such as Bank of America, HSBC, and NAB, Sandeep blends deep fintech knowledge with a passion for ethical, scalable, and human-centred AI solutions. He holds a master's (research) in AI and machine learning from Liverpool John Moores University, London, UK, and a Postgraduate Certification from IIIT Bangalore, alongside a BTech from NIT Allahabad. An educator at heart, Sandeep has mentored hundreds of professionals in transitioning to successful careers in data and AI. His work has made waves across industries, particularly in bridging the gap between AI innovation and practical business impact. This book represents not only his expertise but also his enduring belief in the power of mentorship, resilience, and purposeful innovation.

Amit Tiwary is a highly experienced leader with over 40 years in enterprise architecture across various industries, including manufacturing, utilities, government, and finance. He specialises in developing pragmatic architecture solutions that align with current business needs while anticipating future challenges.

His innovative and collaborative approach has been key to transforming numerous organisations and government departments. He employs a capability-based framework that enhances stakeholder communication and drives organisational success.

In recent years, Amit has focused on the adoption of artificial intelligence (AI), developing comprehensive strategies that address both opportunities and ethical considerations. He has played a significant role in guiding organisations through their AI journeys, ensuring responsible use of technology.

His published works include key titles on business architecture and government efficiency, alongside presentations at international conferences that focus on advancing industry standards. Amit is dedicated to promoting sustainability through architectural frameworks and has contributed to numerous prestigious journals. His ongoing commitment to education and leadership in enterprise architecture positions him as a vital figure in the field.

Acknowledgements

Writing this book has been one of the most transformative journeys of my life. It was born out of a deep desire to democratise knowledge and inspire those navigating the ever-changing landscape of artificial intelligence and technology. Balancing this endeavour while running two startups—Global Institute of Artificial Intelligence (GIofAI) and Bhalekar Consulting—demanded discipline, resilience, and above all, purpose.

I am forever grateful to my wife, Shubhangi, whose unshakeable support and quiet strength have anchored me throughout this demanding path, and to my children, Rudra and Eva, who are the heart of my inspiration, reminding me each day of the future we're building.

I honestly want to thank my father for challenging me and believing in my potential even before I saw it in myself.

I am grateful to my closest friend, Harshal Kolambe, who has walked beside me through every challenge. His loyalty and presence mean more than words can express.

I am also deeply indebted to the mentors who shaped my professional journey, for their wisdom and guidance: Umakant Wadiyar, Mark Miller, Kedar Joshi, Chris Gelea, and Judy Smith.

My heartfelt appreciation to the incredible teams at GIofAI, a global initiative committed to AI education and innovation, and Bhalekar Consulting, where we solve real-world business problems through data and AI. I also extend gratitude to my trusted advisors—Vinit Jha, Ameet Nandlaskar, Amit Kumar Das, Kendall Eilo, and Lawrence Sticca —whose belief in this mission has been invaluable.

I also wish to thank my former colleagues, who influenced my career across institutions, for their collaboration, friendship, and shared vision: from Bank of America: Siva, Srini, Jo, Dinesh, Shubhendu, Sanil, and Sandesh; from HSBC: Avinash, Mani, and Manoj; and from NAB: Kiran, Viraj, and J. Viney.

I would especially like to thank my co-author, Amit Tiwary. His mentorship, clarity, and creativity made this journey intellectually fulfilling and personally meaningful.

Lastly, I dedicate this work to my parents, Shalan and Bapurao.

May this book spark thought, courage, and transformation in its readers—just as writing it has in me.

Sandeep Bhalekar

1

The AI Adoption Landscape

📌 **SIDEBAR: UNDERSTANDING CAIF—COLLABORATIVE AI FRAMEWORK**

Core Components of CAIF

- Service-Oriented Architecture (SOA)
- Cloud and Mobile Integration
- Secure Data Handling
- Green ICT Principles
- Outcome-Driven Collaboration
- Sustainability Metrics

CAIF aims to streamline operations by integrating SOA, cloud computing, mobile technology, and enhanced security measures. Key components of the CAIF are outlined, focusing on optimising resource utilisation and promoting a culture of continuous learning and knowledge-sharing. Ultimately, this chapter underscores the importance of organisational change management in aligning AI initiatives with strategic business goals to thrive in the modern digital economy.

📌 **SIDEBAR: WHAT MAKES AI A BUSINESS NECESSITY?**

- Reduces cost and manual effort
- Enables fast data-driven decisions
- Supports scalability through automation
- Unlocks innovation through analytics and insight

Key Points

- **Necessity of AI:** AI is essential for businesses to maintain a competitive edge by automating tasks, driving efficiency, and fostering innovation.

DOI: 10.1201/9781003626503-1

- **Impact on Personal and Business Life:** AI enhances convenience and efficiency in people's personal lives through applications like virtual assistants; it also drives operational effectiveness in businesses through data-driven decision-making.

? **DID YOU KNOW:** *More than 77% of smartphone users already use AI-powered services daily—often without realising it.*

- **Collaborative AI Framework (CAIF):** This chapter introduces CAIF as a solution for integrating AI into existing Enterprise Architecture Frameworks, promoting collaboration and eco-friendly practices.
- **Organisational Change Management:** Successfully integrating AI with business capabilities requires effective change management to align strategic goals with actionable strategies.
- **Key Artefacts and Concepts:** Identifying and clarifying key CAIF artefacts is crucial for ensuring effective business and IT alignment.
- **AI Architecture (AIA):** A robust AIA program is vital for tracking CAIF's success and providing insightful growth metrics.
- **Knowledge-Sharing and Continuous Learning:** Promoting a culture of knowledge-sharing fosters collaboration and underpins a thriving environment of continuous learning within organisations.
- **Transforming Traditional Frameworks:** The integration of AI has the potential to significantly transform traditional, silo organisational structures, specifically in government services like immigration and health.

♀ **QUICK NOTE:** *Many government services still rely on legacy systems. AI is key to unlocking interoperability and digital access.*

- **Predictive Analytics and Decision-Making:** AI enables companies to utilise predictive analytics to anticipate trends and make informed, data-driven decisions.
- **Overall Business Advantage:** Leveraging AI transforms businesses to not just survive but lead in today's digital economy, emphasising the importance of adaptation and acceleration with AI technologies.

Artificial Intelligence (AI) has evolved into a critical tool for businesses aiming to succeed in today's rapidly changing marketplace. By automating repetitive tasks, AI streamlines operations, reduces costs, and improves overall productivity. Additionally, AI serves as a catalyst for innovation, facilitating the development of new business models, enhancing customer experiences, and refining product development processes. It contributes to a company's competitive edge, equipping organisations with tools to swiftly adapt to market changes and derive insights into their operations.

Through sophisticated predictive analytics, businesses can identify emerging trends, optimise operations, and make data-driven decisions. AI also impacts personal daily life by increasing convenience and efficiency through applications such as virtual assistants, personalised shopping recommendations, and smart home devices. These technologies help streamline routine activities, improve decision-making, and customise experiences according to individual preferences. In enterprise architecture, traditional frameworks have often been influenced by siloed organisational structures. However, with the integration of AI into various operations, there is potential for significant transformation of these frameworks. An example of this transformation can be observed in government functions, such as immigration and health services, collaborating to improve service delivery and citizen experiences. This chapter explores the development and implementation of a Collaborative AI Framework (CAIF), focusing on overcoming challenges within business architecture. CAIF emphasises achieving business outcomes through collaboration, enhancing organisational capabilities and facilitating results. The creation and application of CAIF involve necessary changes, along with methods to assess impact. Change Management will be discussed as a critical aspect of this process, including metrics and evaluation techniques to measure the effectiveness of collaborative strategies and their positive effects across organisations. The focus is on leveraging AI to enhance business operations and improve various aspects of life. Each initiative in this direction aims to contribute to a more interconnected and efficient future.

Architecture Challenges in Adopting AI

Artificial intelligence (AI) has transitioned from being a luxury to an essential component for businesses in today's competitive landscape. It increases efficiency by automating repetitive tasks, streamlining operations, reducing costs, and improving productivity. Additionally, AI acts as a driver for innovation, enabling new business models, enhancing customer experiences, and advancing product development. AI also contributes to competitiveness by allowing organisations to adapt to market changes and extract insights from complex data. Through predictive analytics, AI provides companies with tools to anticipate trends, refine operations, and make data-driven strategic decisions. In the current digital economy, organisations that integrate AI are positioned to not only navigate challenges but also take advantage of future opportunities. The advancement of civilisation is linked to the transfer of knowledge across generations. Innovations in various fields are cumulative, with each generation building upon previous achievements.

The emergence of AI and digital transformation supports this evolution, making knowledge more accessible. The progress of society relies on the capacity to preserve, share, and innovate upon knowledge, potentially ensuring improvements for future generations. Historically, major transitions are based on foundational developments made by prior generations. Much like the industrial revolution benefited from mass production technology, today's digital age benefits from historical advancements in computing, engineering, and AI. AI adoption aims to create solutions that enhance inclusivity in knowledge-sharing. AI tools such as voice recognition and real-time translation help eliminate language barriers and improve communication, particularly for individuals with disabilities and those in multilingual contexts. In education, AI-driven platforms offer personalised learning experiences tailored to the varying needs of students. Adaptive learning systems adjust content to individual learning speeds, enhancing accessibility and effectiveness. In healthcare, AI is transforming patient care through innovations like predictive diagnostics and remote health monitoring, which can provide crucial medical attention to underserved populations. AI is significantly changing day-to-day activities by simplifying tasks, personalising experiences, and expanding educational opportunities. Virtual assistants like Alexa, Google Assistant, and Siri automate reminders and manage smart home systems. In entertainment, AI algorithms used by platforms like Netflix and Spotify suggest personalised content. Educational tools like Duolingo and Coursera leverage AI to customise lessons according to individual learning preferences, enhancing accessibility. Health and fitness applications such as Fitbit and MyFitnessPal provide tailored health insights for personal wellness goals. The integration of AI enables individuals to improve efficiency, navigate tasks more effectively, and ultimately fosters a more convenient and productive environment.

The CAIF provides a clear and insightful overview of an organisation's information technology (IT) system assets. It delineates strategic directions for innovation, guides the prioritisation of IT investments, and offers an integrated methodology to align these components with broader business objectives, thereby enhancing overall performance. By employing CAIF, organisations establish a robust mechanism for defining their business and IT policies, identifying needs, and setting goals. These foundational components drive organisational priorities and create a solid basis for services that promote maturity and growth. As a result, this framework fosters improved efficiency and effectiveness within the organisation, ultimately supporting long-term sustainability. A carefully designed CAIF quantifies the Total Sustainability Value of both internal and external IT assets, emphasising the interconnection between technology and sustainability. The successful implementation of a value-driven CAIF model can facilitate significant positive transformations within an organisation, greatly impacting its sustainability initiatives and adaptability in the dynamic landscape of AI. The returns on strategic IT investments manifest as increased profitability, reduced operational costs through enhanced efficiency, and the cultivation of competitive advantages that strategically position the organisation within the marketplace. Nevertheless, the development and implementation of coherent business architecture present several challenges. Recognising and addressing these obstacles is essential for the creation and ongoing maintenance of an effective CAIF. The forthcoming sections examine these challenges in detail, covering various aspects of both development and execution.

Lack of Use of Standards

Building AI from the ground up presents one of the most formidable challenges for organisations. This foundational approach necessitates widespread consultation and consensus across all levels of the organisation regarding the definition of AI capabilities. The endeavour demands a substantial investment of time, patience, and resources to arrive at a definition that is widely accepted within the enterprise. Often, this process can devolve into a theoretical discussion, straying away from practical applications. The aim of this book is to provide actionable, pragmatic frameworks and methodologies that organisations can easily adopt to foster successful AI implementation. To navigate these complexities effectively, organisations are encouraged to embrace industry-wide standards, particularly concerning capability dimensions like process definitions. The absence of such standards when implementing AI can significantly undermine the potential business value. Here are some critical considerations to bear in mind:

- **Increased Complexity and Inefficiency:** When organisations try to use AI without any clear guidelines or standards, they often face a lot of confusion. This confusing situation can lead to many problems, as complicated and inconsistent methods make it hard to work together and manage these projects effectively. Without a clear structure, teams may struggle to collaborate and come up with new ideas, making it difficult to make the most of the available AI tools. As a result, organisations might find it challenging to fully tap into the capabilities of AI.

- **Lack of Interoperability:** AI systems that do not adhere to established industry standards encounter notable obstacles regarding transportability and comprehensibility across different organisations. This lack of interoperability poses a significant barrier, impeding effective collaboration and communication with external partners. Consequently, this limitation can stifle opportunities for innovation and joint ventures, ultimately constraining the potential for transformative advancements and collaborative growth within the field.

- **Resource Misallocation:** In the absence of well-defined standards, organisations risk misallocating critical resources towards short-term solutions rather than addressing the root cause of underlying inefficiencies. This diversion not only escalates operational costs but also compromises the organisation's capacity to implement sustainable, long-term solutions. By prioritising temporary fixes, companies may unintentionally perpetuate a cycle of inefficiency, blocking efforts to optimise processes effectively. Consequently, this undermines the overall impact of AI initiatives, as inadequate foundational strategies can obstruct significant advancements and innovation in AI. Establishing robust standards is essential to create a structured framework that promotes enduring success and leverages the full potential of AI.

- **Increased Costs:** Non-standardised systems and processes often lead to unpredictable costs and create substantial managerial challenges for organisations. The lack of consistency in operational procedures can result in inefficiencies, consuming both time and resources on duplicative tasks. Furthermore, legacy systems that do not align with current operational demands can misallocate valuable resources that could otherwise drive innovation and growth initiatives. These outdated systems not only obstruct productivity but also impede an organisation's agility in responding to market fluctuations and shifting customer needs, ultimately diminishing its competitive advantage in a rapidly evolving landscape. By neglecting to modernise and standardise their systems, organisations risk becoming inflexible and less responsive, which complicates the implementation of necessary changes in a dynamic environment.

- **Poor Governance and Communication:** When organisations don't have clear guidelines to follow, they often end up using different management methods that might not work well. This lack of clarity can lead to poor communication between teams, creating a mix of approaches and solutions that don't fit together smoothly. As a result, team members may have a hard time working together, which can hold the organisation back from achieving its goals. Without a common strategy and straightforward rules, productivity can drop, new ideas may not develop, and the organisation might struggle to react effectively to challenges and opportunities in the market.

- **Challenges in Measuring Impact:** In today's rapidly evolving business landscape, harnessing AI is crucial for success. However, one significant challenge organisations face is accurately assessing how AI impacts their overall performance. This uncertainty can prevent companies from fully grasping the effectiveness of their AI initiatives, hindering their ability to make informed strategic decisions. Consequently, they risk missing out on the transformative benefits that these groundbreaking technologies can provide, placing them at a competitive disadvantage in an increasingly tough market. Embracing a clear understanding of AI's impact is essential for any organisation aiming to thrive in this dynamic environment.

Organisations can lay a robust foundation for achieving more effective and impactful AI implementations by tackling these challenges head-on and embracing standardised practices. This strategic approach not only enhances their operational capabilities but also fortifies their competitive edge in the market. Adopting industry-wide standards is instrumental in unlocking AI's true potential, enabling businesses to harness its power to drive substantial value. Implementing these standards in AI projects is vital for fostering efficiency, ensuring interoperability, and supporting long-term success. To navigate this journey adeptly, here are several key steps to consider:

1. **Adopt a CAIF:** This framework highlights the importance of achieving tangible business outcomes through effective collaboration among teams. It provides a comprehensive overview of IT system assets, detailing how these resources can be leveraged. Additionally, it outlines strategic direction for innovation and establishes a systematic approach to prioritising IT-related investments. By employing the CAIF, organisations can align these critical components with overarching business goals, ultimately driving improved performance and fostering long-term sustainability.

2. **Develop a Robust AI Architecture (AIA):** An effective and thoughtfully designed program for AI not only monitors performance but also provides essential insights that pinpoint areas ripe for improvement. Creating a vibrant atmosphere of knowledge-sharing and collaboration encourages participants to express their unique perspectives and lend support to one another. This initiative goes beyond mere tracking; it nurtures a culture of continuous learning, where individuals are inspired to expand their skills and remain informed about the latest breakthroughs and trends in the ever-evolving world of technology. Through this dynamic environment, participants can grow both personally and professionally, fostering innovation and creativity in the field.

3. **Embrace Organisational Change Management:** Bringing AI into a business requires a significant change in how the organisation handles adjustments and improvements. It's crucial to ensure that big goals align with practical, doable plans. By accepting this approach, companies can better manage the challenges that come with change, ensuring that new ideas and technologies are smoothly adopted and lead to real, positive results that contribute to company success.

4. **Measure and Assess Impact:** The development and use of CAIF requires significant changes within organisations and assessing the impact of the changes is important to determine success. To do this, it is necessary to establish clear measures and new ways to track the success of their collaborative efforts. This evaluation helps

organisations understand what has changed and how effective those changes are within their organisation.

5. **Ensure Good Governance and Communication:** Successful organisations rely heavily on good communication at all levels. When communication channels are weak or filled with misunderstandings, it can create serious problems. These issues often result in poor planning and design, leading to disjointed efforts that don't work well together. To make informed and united decisions about goals and plans, it is crucial to encourage open discussions and clear information sharing throughout the organisation.

6. **Address Challenges in Developing AI**: Understanding and addressing challenges such as lack of standards, increased complexity, inefficiency, and poor governance are vital for developing and maintaining a good CAIF.

By following these steps, organisations can effectively implement standards in AI projects and realise their full potential in driving business value.

Consolidation without Understanding the Outcomes

AI has the potential to significantly enhance the consolidation of systems by integrating diverse processes and platforms to create seamless functionality. This optimisation is important to keep resource use within the needs of the organisation.

Effectively managing complex processes can lead to better utilisation of larger servers, infrastructure, and personnel, all working towards a common goal. By streamlining operations and adopting a cohesive solution, organisations can gain vital clarity on their objectives and facilitate smooth information flow within a centralised infrastructure. This proactive approach not only bolsters operational efficiency but also lays a strong foundation for future success.

That said, it is essential to approach system consolidation with a comprehensive vision of the outcomes to avoid potential pitfalls. Transitioning to a single platform offers great opportunities but requires careful management to prevent bottlenecks. By establishing clear expectations and identifying the desired outcomes, organisations can minimise challenges such as increased complexity, inefficiencies, and resource misallocation. Utilising a strategic focus helps avoid unplanned costs, reduce management overhead, and ensure alignment with current organisational needs. Furthermore, fostering robust governance and effective communication promotes consistent methodologies and unified solutions, ultimately enhancing the organisation's capacity to meet and exceed its goals.

Architecture as a Solution to a Problem. When focusing exclusively on immediate needs, there is a risk of misusing valuable resources, which ultimately hampers effective architectural practice. Tackling symptoms instead of addressing the root causes of challenges leads to inefficiencies and wasted effort.

Architecture should be embraced as a robust framework to navigate multiple issues rather than a solution to a single problem. Architecture isn't just about technology; it is about fostering a deeper comprehension of the complexities and interdependencies that span the entire enterprise.

Focusing on short-term fixes can create redundant capabilities across various projects, causing conflicts and disruptions within departments that share the same value chain. Moreover, prioritising immediate demands over a comprehensive architectural strategy can lead to significant inefficiencies and waste. It is essential to approach architecture as a solid foundation that enables effective management of a variety of challenges. Adopting a more strategic, integrated mindset fosters greater collaboration and innovation, paving the way for sustained success.

Architecture without Process Management

Architecture plays a crucial role in re-engineering processes, often more effectively than mere automation. When re-engineering is absent and architectures remain suboptimal, organisations face significant process inefficiencies that hinder automation. This situation creates unnecessary complexity within organisational systems and processes. The prevalence of undocumented, outdated, and redundant practices—often defended with the phrase "we have always done it this way"—represents a major challenge, particularly in the context of leveraging AI.

Without effective process management, architecture can lead to serious inefficiencies and complexities. The failure to optimise and re-engineer processes results in architectures that simply do not fit organisational needs, creating a cycle of inefficiency and automation hurdles. Poorly designed, nonstandard processes add layers of complexity that complicate integration and management.

Consider the impact of legacy systems that are no longer aligned with current demands. These systems consume vital resources and restrict an organisation's capacity for transformation. For example, an outdated billing system may utilise considerable resources, including servers and specialised staff, to remain operational. This dependence on legacy infrastructure can consume a large portion of the IT budget, diverting funds away from necessary advancements and innovations.

In conclusion, neglecting process management within the architecture framework leads to inefficiencies, heightened complexity, and inefficient resource use. To foster organisational efficiency and effectiveness, it is essential to re-engineer processes to align with a well-structured architectural framework. Consider the following strategies to enact effective process management within the architecture:

1. **Re-engineer and Optimise Processes:** Focus on re-engineering current processes to eliminate inefficiencies. Analyse existing workflows and redesign them to meet organisational objectives, rather than simply applying automation.

2. **Document and Standardise Processes:** Ensure that all processes are thoroughly documented, consistently applied, and kept current across the organisation. This approach enhances consistency, simplifies integration, and improves manageability.

3. **Align Processes with Organisational Needs:** Processes should be aligned with both the current and future requirements of the organisation. This alignment ensures optimal resource utilisation and a supportive architecture that enables strategic goals.

4. **Implement Strong Governance and Communication:** Establish clear governance structures and effective communication throughout the organisation. Good governance ensures accountability and oversight, while effective communication aligns all stakeholders with common objectives.

5. **Adopt a CAIF:** Utilising frameworks like CAIF can ensure that IT assets, innovations, and investments align with business goals. CAIF provides a structured methodology for process management, optimising processes in line with organisational ambitions.

6. **Measure and Assess Impact:** Continuously measure and evaluate the outcomes of process management initiatives. Employ metrics to assess the effectiveness of re-engineered processes, facilitating informed decision-making.

By implementing these strategies, organisations can transform their process management approaches, leading to enhanced efficiency, reduced complexity, and better alignment with their organisational goals.

Effective Communication across the Organisation

Effective communication constitutes the foundation of successful architectural design within an organisation, creating an environment conducive to collaboration and clarity. When communication is strong, it enriches the architectural framework and ensures all team members are aligned with common objectives. Conversely, ineffective communication can result in fragmented designs and inefficiencies. For instance, when similar capabilities are developed across various projects without proper coordination, inconsistencies emerge, leading to isolated solutions that fail to contribute to a cohesive architectural structure.

Inefficient communication may also hinder the successful adoption and integration of AI technologies. When teams encounter challenges in sharing information, the impact can extend throughout the architecture, resulting in redundant capabilities appearing across different projects. This misalignment disrupts collaboration among departments that are interconnected and share the same value chain. Furthermore, a deficiency in clear communication can lead to wasted resources, as teams may inadvertently duplicate efforts or devise their own strategies without considering insights and support from centralised IT departments.

Moreover, inadequate communication can establish barriers to aligning AI initiatives with the organisation's overarching goals. Establishing a coherent dialogue is essential for ensuring that these projects are strategically grounded, thus preventing misallocation of resources, costs escalating, and AI's transformative potential remains underutilised.

The ramifications of poor communication can manifest as inconsistent practices, overlapping capabilities, resource wastage, and a disconnect between AI projects and organisational objectives. Establishing transparent and effective communication channels should be a priority to ensure the successful implementation and enhancement of AI initiatives.

- **Establish Clear Communication Channels:** Effective architectural design requires robust communication, which streamlines integration and management processes. Essential elements of robust communication are regular meetings, collaborative tools, and a culture of open dialogue. These practices enable teams to work collaboratively and navigate challenges with confidence and clarity.

- **Promote Knowledge-Sharing:** Nurturing a knowledge-sharing culture across all departments is essential for driving collaboration and continuous learning. This can be accomplished through regular meetings, engaging workshops, and comprehensive training sessions. By promoting knowledge exchange, every team member remains current with the latest advancements and best practices in AI, ultimately leading to more impactful implementations.

- **Align AI Initiatives with Organisational Goals:** Ensuring that AI projects correspond with organisational strategic objectives is crucial for maximising effectiveness. Continuous and clear communication is vital in the alignment process, as it aids in defining specific objectives for AI initiatives while keeping all stakeholders informed regarding progress and outcomes.

- **Avoid Redundancy and Conflicts:** Maintaining transparent communication channels is vital to prevent overlaps and conflicts within projects, particularly in organisations where departments share a common value chain. By ensuring that projects are well-coordinated and aligned with a holistic strategy, redundancy can be minimised, thus facilitating smoother collaboration and efficiency.

- **Centralise IT Strategies and Architectures:** It is important to acknowledge that different business units may pursue their own strategies and architectures independently of centralised IT guidance. By establishing a framework for centralised IT governance, organisations can ensure that all teams align their efforts with shared objectives and a strategic vision, thereby promoting collaboration and coherence across the organisation.
- **Implement Good Governance:** Establishing clear governance models is essential for ensuring that oversight and accountability remain prioritised. Effective governance structures enhance communication efficacy and ensure that AI initiatives remain continuously aligned with organisational goals. This involves assembling representatives from relevant departments and conducting regular reviews of AI projects to monitor progress and ensure alignment with objectives.

By adopting these strategies, organisations can significantly enhance communication, which facilitates the successful adoption and execution of AI initiatives. Collectively harnessing the power of effective communication unlocks new opportunities.

The Importance of Holistic Leadership for AI Adoption

? **DID YOU KNOW:** *Organisations with clear AI leadership are 2.5×x more likely to report significant value from AI initiatives (source: MIT Sloan Management Review).*

The absence of comprehensive and integrated leadership in an organisation can lead to significant challenges in AI adoption. Without holistic leadership, the results are substantial expenditures with minimal realisation of organisational benefits, leading to frustrations regarding the implementation and management of increasingly complex technology.

One of the primary issues is that IT departments are perceived as unable to produce value-added deliverables. This perception is exacerbated by a growing imperative for change, driven by audit recommendations, legacy systems, and emerging trends that impact business outcomes. Without strong leadership, there is a lack of direction and coordination, leading to fragmented efforts and inefficiencies.

Moreover, the absence of holistic leadership can result in poor architecture and governance. When business units and their owners lack trust and confidence in each other, it leads to inadequate measurement controls, lack of scope, and clear communication issues. This lack of trust and coordination often results in wasted resources and duplicate efforts, as many business units develop their strategies and architectures independently of centralised IT departments.

It is crucial to establish strong leadership across business units to guide the organisation through the complexities of AI adoption and ensure alignment with strategic goals.

1. **Integrated Leadership Approach:** Holistic leadership involves a comprehensive and integrated approach that aligns all departments and stakeholders towards common goals. This approach ensures that AI initiatives are not fragmented, and the organisation has a clear direction and coordination.

2. **Building Trust and Confidence:** Building trust and confidence among business units and owners is essential. A lack of trust leads to poor architecture, inadequate measurement controls, and apparent communication issues. Establishing strong leadership helps foster trust and ensures that all stakeholders are aligned.

3. **Clear Governance and Communication:** Establishing explicit governance models and effective communication channels is vital for maintaining oversight and accountability. Good governance ensures that AI initiatives are aligned with organisational goals and that progress is continuously monitored and evaluated.

4. **Centralised IT Strategies and Architectures:** Different business units may develop their strategies and architectures independently of centralised IT departments. By consolidating IT strategies and architectures, organisations can ensure that all teams are working towards common objectives and provide coherence across the organisation.

5. **Promoting Knowledge-Sharing and Collaboration:** Encouraging knowledge-sharing and collaboration across departments fosters a culture of continuous learning and innovation. This can be achieved through regular meetings, workshops, and training sessions.

By following these strategies, organisations can establish holistic leadership for AI adoption, leading to better alignment with strategic goals, improved efficiency, and realisation of the full potential of AI.

Lack of Trust amongst Key Stakeholders

When key stakeholders in an organisation lack trust and confidence in each other, it can significantly impact the adoption of AI. This lack of trust often results in poor architecture and governance, leading to several challenges discussed in this chapter.

Without trust, inadequate controls on measurements, lack of scope, and clear communication issues arise. These problems can cause wasted resources and duplicate efforts, as many business units develop their own strategies and architectures independently of centralised IT departments.

This phenomenon, often referred to as "shadow architectures," happens without the knowledge and participation of centralised IT departments, leading to fragmented and inefficient systems.

Moreover, the absence of trust among stakeholders can hinder collaboration and coordination, which are essential for successful AI adoption. When business units do not trust each other, they are less likely to share information and work together towards common goals. This lack of collaboration can result in siloed efforts, where different departments pursue their own AI initiatives without considering the broader organisational objectives.

It is crucial to build trust and confidence among stakeholders to ensure the successful adoption and implementation of AI in the organisation.

Building trust among stakeholders is crucial for the successful adoption of AI in an organisation. Here are some strategies to help foster trust and confidence:

1. **Integrated Leadership Approach:** Holistic leadership involves a comprehensive and integrated approach that aligns all departments and stakeholders towards common goals. This approach ensures that AI initiatives are not fragmented and there is a clear direction and coordination across the organisation.

2. **Building Trust and Confidence:** Building trust and confidence among business units and their owners is essential. A lack of trust leads to poor architecture, inadequate measurement controls, and clear communication issues. Establishing strong leadership helps foster trust and ensure that all stakeholders are aligned.

3. **Clear Governance and Communication:** Establishing clear governance models and effective communication channels is vital for maintaining oversight and accountability. Good governance ensures that AI initiatives are aligned with organisational goals and that progress is continuously monitored and evaluated.

4. **Centralised IT Strategies and Architectures:** Different business units may develop their own strategies and architectures independently of centralised IT departments. By centralising IT strategies and architectures, organisations can ensure that all teams are working towards common objectives and that there is coherence across the organisation.

5. **Promoting Knowledge-Sharing and Collaboration:** Encouraging knowledge-sharing and collaboration across departments fosters a culture of continuous learning and innovation. This can be achieved through regular meetings, workshops, and training sessions.

By following these strategies, organisations can build trust among stakeholders, leading to better alignment with strategic goals, improved efficiency, and realisation of the full potential of AI.

Chapter Questions

- Why is AI considered a necessity for businesses in today's digital economy?
- How does AI enhance convenience and efficiency in personal life?
- What are some common applications of AI in the business realm?
- How does the CAIF propose to integrate AI into existing Enterprise Architecture Frameworks?
- What challenges do organisations face when integrating AI into their operations?
- In what ways can predictive analytics help businesses make better decisions?
- How does organisational change management facilitate the successful adoption of AI?
- What role does knowledge-sharing play in promoting a culture of continuous learning within organisations?
- How can AI transform traditional organisational structures, particularly in government services?
- What are some key components of the CAIF?
- Why is identifying key CAIF artefacts important for business and IT alignment?
- How can businesses utilise AI to enhance customer interactions and service delivery?
- What metrics can be used to track the success of AI initiatives within an organisation?
- How does AI foster innovation through new business models?
- What are the implications of failing to adapt to AI technologies in today's market?

Note to Readers and Educators

Comprehensive answers and explanations to these chapter-end questions are available at www.sandeepbhalekar.com. The website also provides supplementary frameworks, teaching guidelines, and reference materials to support deeper understanding and classroom discussion.

Educators and facilitators can access additional resources, including presentation frameworks, assessment rubrics, and discussion prompts, to help integrate the concepts from this chapter into academic or professional learning environments.

2

The AI Adoption Framework— Business Perspective

Key Points

- Embracing organisational change management is vital for seamlessly integrating with AI and business capabilities. Leveraging CAIF aligns goals with actionable strategies.
- Identifying the key artefacts of CAIF and ensuring clarity around concepts like business IT alignment.
- A robust AI Architecture program tracks CAIF's success and delivers insightful growth metrics. Promoting knowledge-sharing ignites collaboration and nurtures a thriving culture of continuous learning!

This chapter provides an in-depth exploration of the development and implementation of a Collaborative AI Framework. At its core, CAIF consists of two intertwined layers: a business layer that outlines strategic objectives and a technology layer that aligns innovative technological solutions with these objectives. The chapter begins by examining the various business components associated with targeting specific business outcomes, particularly those that arise from distinct business strategies and the actions taken to realise them. While CAIF can be classified as a form of enterprise architecture with multiple layers, it distinctly prioritises the achievement of organisational goals through an emphasis on collaboration and teamwork. This outcome-driven perspective not only focuses on the end results but also on enhancing the capabilities and skills within the organisation. By fostering a culture of cooperation and mutual support, CAIF aims to drive significant improvements in both performance and adaptability, enabling organisations to navigate complexities and seize opportunities in an ever-evolving business landscape.

The development and application of CAIF necessitate significant changes and the ability to effectively measure the impact of those changes. Therefore, change management becomes a vital component in this chapter's discussions. Furthermore, it introduces metrics and measurement techniques for assessing the effectiveness of collaborative approaches and the resultant changes within the organisation.

DOI: 10.1201/9781003626503-2

✂ SIDEBAR: LAYERS OF CAIF—QUICK OVERVIEW

Business Layer:

- Defines strategic objectives
- Maps business capabilities
- Guides planning and prioritisation

Technology Layer:

- Aligns tools to business goals
- Integrates cloud, security, and data governance
- Enables cross-functional collaboration

The CAIF Framework

The architectural view of an organisation provides a big-picture look at how everything fits together over the long term rather than just focusing on quick fixes or immediate solutions. This overall perspective helps organisations ensure that their structures and processes align with their main objectives and goals. When an organisation designs this architecture carefully to reach its desired outcomes, it is known as CAIF or Collaborative Artificial Intelligence Framework.

? DID YOU KNOW: *CAIF is not just for enterprises—governments are applying CAIF models to integrate healthcare, immigration, and social services.*

CAIF highlights the importance of having a single, trustworthy source of information that everyone in the organisation can rely on. It also acknowledges an important truth: not every project or activity, even if well-intentioned, contributes to the organisation's goals. Without properly exploring all options, organisations can end up with poor planning, ineffective resource management, and incorrect assessments of potential impacts. By adopting CAIF, organisations can create a clear path towards their goals.

This framework helps eliminate overlapping efforts and ensures that activities are closely aligned with business objectives, leading to greater efficiency and effectiveness throughout the organisation. CAIF prepares organisations to handle challenges more effectively, ensuring that every effort genuinely supports the long-term vision. The outcome-driven business architecture framework provides the following:

TABLE 2.1

Establishing a CAIF

Activity	Rationale
Establish CAIF Framework	Provide a structure to manage outcomes and the key capabilities required to support the organisation's decision-making process. The CAIF is pragmatic and serves the organisation's goals. Developing this framework is an iterative process. The outcome from the business architecture framework enables strategic investment and resource allocation activities. The framework considers the company's culture, and the flexibility required for future changes. Senior executives communicate this framework across the organisation.
Populate the CAIF Framework	Provide a single source of truth for architectural information with an appropriate governance plan and ensure decisions are based on accurate and appropriate information. The information mapped to the business architecture framework includes applications, systems, processes, policies, organisational risks, and information exchanges. The framework is agile to support any other dimensions, such as the costs of maintaining the capabilities.
Use the CAIF as a Business-as-Usual tool	All relevant and available facts are considered for decision-making. Access to the right information promotes easy decision-making and increased understanding of the impact on the organisation's operations. Solutions are compliant and aligned with the vision, principles, and standards defined.

- **Business Capabilities Mapping for Enhanced Outcomes:** Creating a clear Business Capabilities map is essential in today's rapidly evolving business landscape, as it serves as an organisation-wide accepted business architecture framework. Developing a CAIF has three phases, detailed in Table 2.1.

📌 SIDEBAR: KEY PHASES OF BUILDING CAIF

1. Establish the Framework
2. Populate it with trusted organisational data
3. Use it for Business-as-Usual decisions

"CAIF isn't a static plan—it's a living business alignment tool."

Business capabilities are the foundation for business outcome-based architecture. The capabilities are layered based on the organisational appetite for the capability-based framework. The capability-based framework implementation is a well-defined program of work with key dimensions. Two examples of dimensions are as follows: the scope of the program is defined to achieve the organisational strategies and linked to projects, and the selection and prioritisation of business capabilities are based on the organisational value chain analysis. Table 2.2 defines the elements of the Business layer of CAIF:

TABLE 2.2

Elements of the Business Layer That Are Extended and Applied to CAIF

Elements	CAIF Focus
Scope	CAIF takes a holistic approach by emphasising the comprehensive performance of the entire business and its operational outcomes, rather than isolating its focus solely on the IT components. This means that CAIF recognises the interplay between all facets of the organisation, ensuring that IT functions are seamlessly integrated and aligned with broader business objectives to drive overall success.
Direction	The focus of the organisation is firmly rooted in strategic planning, emphasising comprehensive initiatives such as business transformation and strategic change programs. This approach prioritises long-term vision and overarching goals, rather than getting bogged down in tactical operational changes that may provide only short-term gains. By concentrating on transformative strategies, the organisation aims to drive significant progress and innovation, ensuring sustainable growth and adaptability in a constantly evolving landscape.
Timeline	Planning involves a strategic consideration of future scenarios, considering long-term objectives and anticipated developments, rather than merely focusing on the present situation. It encompasses a broad vision that seeks to prepare an organisation for the challenges and opportunities that lie ahead. Conversely, business architecture plays a crucial role by outlining a comprehensive roadmap that details the evolution of an organisation's capabilities. This roadmap serves as a guiding framework for implementing necessary changes, ensuring that the organisation can adapt effectively and thrive in a dynamic business landscape.
Value Chain	The business layer emphasises a comprehensive view of the entire enterprise organisation, delving into the intricate web of interactions within the value chain it provides. This perspective goes beyond the confines of a single delivery project, revealing how various components work together harmoniously to support the overall mission and objectives of the organisation. It explores the essential relationships and processes that drive value, ensuring a holistic understanding of how the enterprise operates as a cohesive unit.
Stakeholders	The needs and concerns of the executive management team, encompassing both the overarching organisation and its various divisions and departments, are carefully considered. These considerations transform them into vital stakeholders in the planning and implementation of business architecture. By integrating their insights and priorities, we ensure that the architecture aligns with both strategic goals and operational realities, fostering a cohesive approach that drives success at every level of the organisation.

Business Capabilities and CAIF

? **DID YOU KNOW:** *APQC's Process Classification Framework (PCF) is one of the most widely used global standards for defining business capabilities.*

The business layer of CAIF is essential in creating a map of the organisation's capabilities, which helps in its growth and development. Identifying specific skills and functions a company needs can be a challenging task that requires a lot of teamwork and communication among various people within the organisation. For example, figuring out how to "plan for and acquire resources" means that different stakeholders, such as human resources (HR), information technology (IT), and business teams, need to work together and agree on a shared approach.

Having a widely accepted definition for business capabilities can make it much easier to use the CAIF. A visual representation of business capabilities, shown in a map like in Figure 2.1, helps everyone in the organisation understand what those capabilities are. This map follows a well-established framework (the APQC Process Classification Framework, or PCF) that helps create a common understanding across all areas of the organisation.

The capability map not only outlines the different skills and functions the business already possesses but also considers other important factors like personnel, processes, technology, finance, and how information is managed. The CAIF map, illustrated in Figure 2.1, contains detailed information about these factors. This helps in visualising key insights such as areas of strength, potential risks, and opportunities, giving a clearer picture of the organisation's overall situation.

CAIF incorporates an organisation's operational capability map. This map defines capabilities required across the organisation for effective and efficient operations. This map enables the business to understand how its

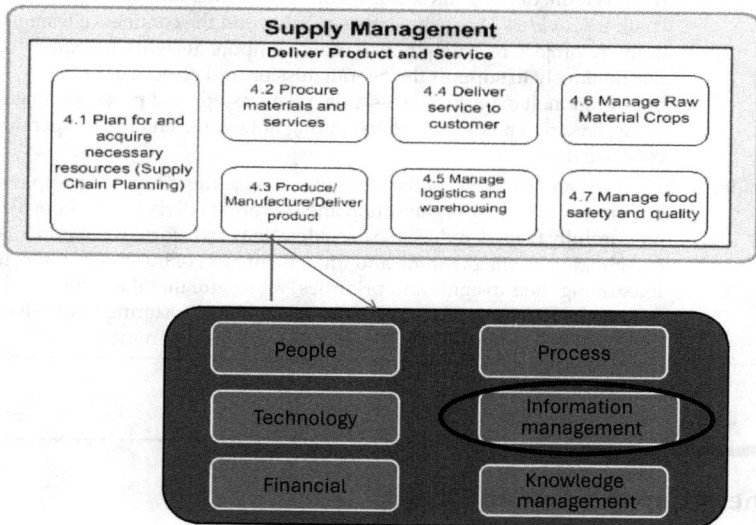

FIGURE 2.1

Further details of the business layer map (based on the APQC Process Classification Framework).

capabilities map to the desired outcomes. The capability map represents an understanding of the business needs, its existing capabilities, and represents those needs to the cross-functional community of business users and developers of solutions.

Business units (BUs) comprise users with different contexts of business capabilities based on their roles, and the architects collaborate with the project managers to enable them to develop capabilities needed by the users. The CAIF ensures both business and enterprise architecture decisions are made in alignment and consideration of BU-specific capability needs and enterprise standards. The business analysis program guides and influences IT strategy initiatives within the BU. An important part is ensuring there is adequate representation of BU in all relevant forums to shape the initiatives during the assess and select phase and influence solutions and program architects during the development and execution phases (Figure 2.2).

Organisational capabilities can be categorised in different ways. Some capabilities are essential, while others are more supportive; some are related to big-picture strategies, while others focus on everyday tasks. The main idea behind CAIF is to develop the key strengths and skills that help the organisation achieve its main goals and desired results. By focusing on these foundational strengths, the organisation can improve its overall performance and stay competitive in its industry.

Identifying core strengths varies based on company goals and size and identifying these strengths is important for making strategic decisions, especially when a company is looking to merge or acquire another business. By analysing the core abilities of potential partners, a company can determine

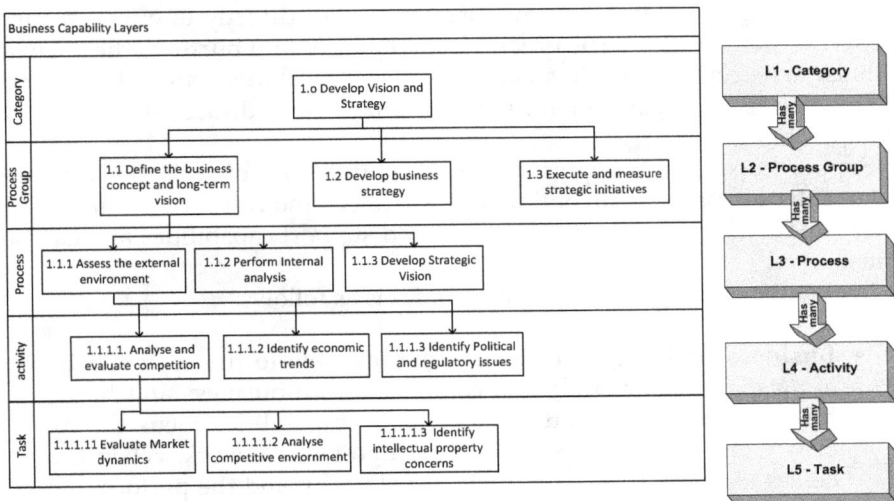

FIGURE 2.2
Business capability layers.

which organisation excels in certain areas and which skills may need more development to reach its overall goals. This evaluation can also reveal any overlapping skills between companies, which can then be streamlined or eliminated.

Determining capability maturity, meaning how well-established and effective they are an important consideration when joining forces. Another scenario to consider is when companies choose to outsource certain functions. In this case, it's crucial to identify which skills should stay in-house and which ones could be effectively developed by external partners. A common approach is to keep the essential functions in-house while outsourcing supporting roles instead.

Overall, categorising these capabilities can be broken down into two main areas:

- **Business advantage capabilities** are strategic and directly contribute to the customer's value proposition and have a high impact on the company financials. Value contribution is assured when performance is amongst the best in peer organisations and at an acceptable cost.
- **Business support capabilities** directly support advantage capabilities. Value contribution is assured when performance is above industry parity at a competitive cost.

Advantage capabilities are the organisation's core differentiators in achieving market or product leadership. For example, if an organisation is dealing with goods (like phones, laptops, and other electronic personal computing devices), then its strategic capabilities are related directly to effective supply chain management. The organisation develops and nurtures these capabilities to be competitive. In some cases, these capabilities are valuable and rare, making an organisation's position unique and difficult to mimic by competitors.

Support capabilities support the core capabilities. An organisation can outsource these capabilities to optimise its processes and resource utilisation. In many industries, IT and HR are considered support capabilities and can be outsourced.

Yet another way of looking at capabilities is as follows:

- **Business basic capabilities** may be invisible to the customer but are a major contributor to a company's core business and have a huge impact on its bottom line. These capabilities focus on efficiency improvements, especially in high-volume work. When processes are performed at industry-level parity and the performance is above the competitors', then the business capability value contribution increases.

- **Business needs capabilities** as value contribution is assured when performed at industry parity performance below competitors' cost. These can be candidates for alternate sourcing.

  Business capabilities are defined clearly across the organisation and shared with business partners when providing or requesting services. Business capabilities are defined in the organisational language for all operational functions. It adapts to various dimensions such as process, people skills, information, and knowledge management. A capability management framework that defines a complete picture of the capabilities is the enterprise capability model. It is a blueprint for the business, connoted in terms of the necessary capabilities for execution of strategy, including delivery of services.

Business Capability Layers

The multiple levels and types of business capabilities are summarised in Figure 2.1. Many organisations define business capabilities based on the structure of their process development frameworks, such as eTOM[1] or APQC.

Each layer of the capability definition provides enough detail to measure organisational outcomes and aggregate to a higher level. The definition at any layer provides clarity to the organisation and assigns an owner of the capability or sub-capability. The definition is not tailored to fit the current organisation's roles and responsibilities. Roles are assigned based on fit and reassigned when the organisation structure changes.

The definition of business capabilities at level one helps the organisation prioritise goals and outcomes. Prioritising these capabilities allows for clearer mapping of projects and activities to specific capabilities. To organise this effectively, level two defines sub-capabilities, level three focuses on activities, and level four breaks down activities to tasks. This ensures better alignment of projects, systems, and activities and assigns clear ownership.

For example, Figure 2.1 depicts APQC©-defined PCF. This framework defines a five-layered approach where level one is the category of the business capabilities such as "1.0 Develop Vision and Strategy." Layer two defines the process group "1.3 Manage strategic initiatives." The organisation, based on its available resources, adopts a standard framework or develops its own.

Vision and Strategy for Business Capability

Capabilities define what an organisation can achieve, without specifying how these achievements are realised. For instance, consider the capabilities related to AI. "Predictive analytics" would be a capability because it outlines what is being done—using AI to forecast future trends based on historical data. However, "using Python to implement a predictive model" is not a capability; it describes the method or tool used to fulfil that capability.

Another example is "automating customer service responses" as a capability. This defines the objective of improving customer engagement through AI chatbots or automated systems. In contrast, "deploying a specific chatbot technology" is not a capability, as it focuses on how the "automating customer service response" objective is achieved.

In most organisations, each department tends to define its own vision and strategy surrounding capabilities, such as a marketing department focusing on "enhancing customer segmentation through machine learning" while the sales department adopting a strategy of "leveraging AI for lead scoring." This siloed approach can lead to competing strategies that may conflict with one another, potentially undermining the overall organisational goals.

A well-defined framework of business capabilities aims to create a cohesive structure that is usable and repeatable throughout the organisation. For instance, if the capabilities were aligned, the marketing and sales departments could collaborate on a unified AI-driven customer relationship management (CRM) system that enhances both departments' strategies.

A capability-based outcome, such as "improving operational efficiency through data-driven decision-making," ensures that all processes are backed by accurate information, reinforcing data integrity across the organisation. As organisations develop lower-level capabilities—like "optimising inventory levels using AI algorithms"—these have specific outcomes that align with the broader goals of their parent capabilities, ensuring consistency and coherence in achieving organisational objectives.

The framework depicted in Figure 2.3 illustrates a comprehensive approach to identifying and enhancing capabilities across different levels of an organisation, while also highlighting its adaptability. One key capability is the ability to understand market dynamics and customer preferences. This means grasping what customers truly need and desire so that the organisation can tailor its products and services accordingly.

To effectively develop this capability, a fundamental activity is to analyse customer requirements. This process not only clarifies the specific needs of the market but also defines the expected results of these activities. For instance, when the discussion is "understanding market and customer," or "developing vision and strategy," an organisation is essentially outlining the desired outcomes that stem from these capabilities. Additionally, this involves establishing measures and governance practices to assess whether the organisation is meeting its goals.

As an example, consider the "developing vision and strategy" capability, an essential function that helps to shape the organisation's overall direction and determine its financial success. The outcome of this capability is a clear vision that guides the company towards its future objectives.

Take Netflix, for instance; their ability to develop a customer-focused strategy has heavily relied on AI algorithms that analyse user preferences and behaviours. By understanding what their audience is watching and suggesting personalised content, they have not only enhanced customer satisfaction

4.1 Plan for and acquire necessary resources (Supply Chain Planning)

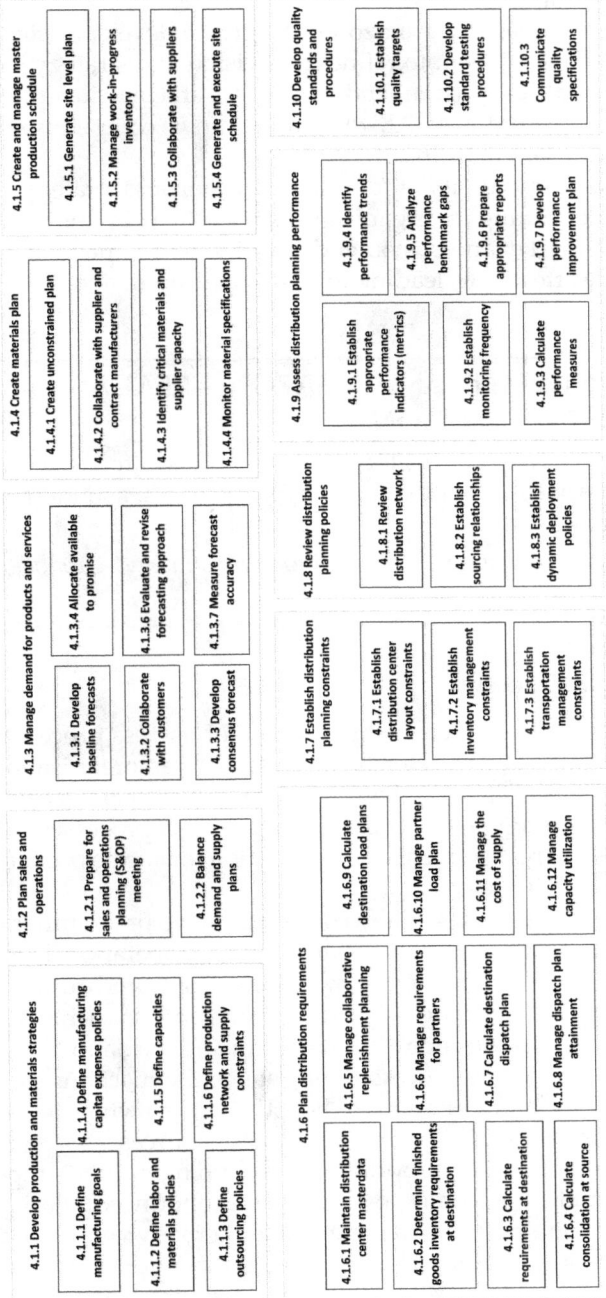

4.1.1 Develop production and materials strategies
- 4.1.1.1 Define manufacturing goals
- 4.1.1.2 Define labor and materials policies
- 4.1.1.3 Define outsourcing policies
- 4.1.1.4 Define manufacturing capital expense policies
- 4.1.1.5 Define capacities
- 4.1.1.6 Define production network and supply constraints

4.1.2 Plan sales and operations
- 4.1.2.1 Prepare for sales and operations planning (S&OP) meeting
- 4.1.2.2 Balance demand and supply plans

4.1.3 Manage demand for products and services
- 4.1.3.1 Develop baseline forecasts
- 4.1.3.2 Collaborate with customers
- 4.1.3.3 Develop consensus forecast
- 4.1.3.4 Allocate available to promise
- 4.1.3.6 Evaluate and revise forecasting approach
- 4.1.3.7 Measure forecast accuracy

4.1.4 Create materials plan
- 4.1.4.1 Create unconstrained plan
- 4.1.4.2 Collaborate with supplier and contract manufacturers
- 4.1.4.3 Identify critical materials and supplier capacity
- 4.1.4.4 Monitor material specifications

4.1.5 Create and manage master production schedule
- 4.1.5.1 Generate site level plan
- 4.1.5.2 Manage work-in-progress inventory
- 4.1.5.3 Collaborate with suppliers
- 4.1.5.4 Generate and execute site schedule

4.1.6 Plan distribution requirements
- 4.1.6.1 Maintain distribution center masterdata
- 4.1.6.2 Determine finished goods inventory requirements at destination
- 4.1.6.3 Calculate requirements at destination
- 4.1.6.4 Calculate consolidation at source
- 4.1.6.5 Manage collaborative replenishment planning
- 4.1.6.6 Manage requirements for partners
- 4.1.6.7 Calculate destination dispatch plan
- 4.1.6.8 Manage dispatch plan attainment
- 4.1.6.9 Calculate destination load plans
- 4.1.6.10 Manage partner load plan
- 4.1.6.11 Manage the cost of supply
- 4.1.6.12 Manage capacity utilization

4.1.7 Establish distribution planning constraints
- 4.1.7.1 Establish distribution center layout constraints
- 4.1.7.2 Establish inventory management constraints
- 4.1.7.3 Establish transportation management constraints

4.1.8 Review distribution planning policies
- 4.1.8.1 Review distribution network
- 4.1.8.2 Establish sourcing relationships
- 4.1.8.3 Establish dynamic deployment policies

4.1.9 Assess distribution planning performance
- 4.1.9.1 Establish appropriate performance indicators (metrics)
- 4.1.9.2 Establish monitoring frequency
- 4.1.9.3 Calculate performance measures
- 4.1.9.4 Identify performance trends
- 4.1.9.5 Analyze performance benchmark gaps
- 4.1.9.6 Prepare appropriate reports
- 4.1.9.7 Develop performance improvement plan

4.1.10 Develop quality standards and procedures
- 4.1.10.1 Establish quality targets
- 4.1.10.2 Develop standard testing procedures
- 4.1.10.3 Communicate quality specifications

FIGURE 2.3
Developing vision and strategy in the business capability.[2]

but also driven up subscription numbers significantly, ultimately resulting in higher financial gains.

Similarly, companies like Amazon utilise AI to develop insights into customer habits, enabling them to refine their vision and strategy continuously. Through personalised recommendations and efficient inventory management practices powered by AI, they maintain a competitive edge while increasing their profit margins.

In summary, the capability of "developing vision and strategy" plays a pivotal role in determining an organisation's trajectory. By integrating AI into understanding market and customer dynamics, companies can achieve their objectives more effectively, leading to financial growth and a solidified market position.

📌 SIDEBAR: NETFLIX AND AMAZON—REAL AI CAPABILITY IN ACTION

- **Netflix:** Uses AI to personalise viewer experience, reduce churn.
- **Amazon:** Applies AI for customer insight, logistics, and inventory optimisation.

These companies operationalise their "vision and strategy" capability using data-driven insights.

Capabilities and Processes

The differences between a capability map and business processes are a key concept for businesses to understand, especially as organisations increasingly explore the role of AI in their operations. At its core, a capability map outlines "what" an organisation can achieve, while processes detail "how" those outcomes are realised. This differentiation forms the backbone of effective organisational strategy.

Over the past two decades, many companies have predominantly focused on processes, viewing them as essential for driving operational efficiency and effectiveness. Processes dictate the workflow, tasks, and resources needed to carry out activities creating a dynamic framework for achieving business objectives. However, a common pitfall is confusing the definitions of capabilities and processes. While processes may shape the mechanics of an organisation, capabilities represent a more holistic view of what the organisation can offer based on its skills, technologies, and resources.

As businesses consider adopting AI technologies, the importance of defining capabilities becomes even more pronounced. For instance, a retail company looking to enhance its customer service might develop an AI-driven chatbot capability. Here, the capability represents the organisation's potential to provide 24/7 customer assistance, leveraging advanced natural language processing. The underlying processes might include data collection, machine learning, and user interaction design, which define how the chatbot operates effectively.

Before launching any AI initiatives, it's vital for senior management to establish a shared understanding of what capabilities the organisation needs. This foundational agreement leads to a comprehensive definition of the organisation's capabilities, which can be leveraged across different departments and business units. For example, a healthcare provider might identify a capability in predictive analytics to anticipate patient needs, utilising AI algorithms to analyse historical data for better resource allocation.

The scope of capabilities that an organisation identifies often correlates with its size and the complexity of its operational structure. Larger organisations may oversee numerous capabilities, while smaller firms may start with a few foundational capabilities. The key is to begin with commonly agreed-upon definitions and examples that fit the organisation's specific context.

Typically, the first level of capability hierarchy delineates the major categories of organisational activities without merely mimicking existing structures. For instance, a manufacturing company might identify capabilities related to automation, quality control, and supply chain management. Each of these capabilities can then be linked to specific processes enhanced by AI, such as predictive maintenance or real-time inventory tracking.

More broadly, some well-known business capabilities that weave through various organisational processes include CRM, inventory optimisation, and data analytics. In each of these areas, AI can play a transformative role. For instance, implementing AI-powered analytics tools can enable a finance department to identify spending patterns, thereby enhancing budget accuracy and forecasting.

In summary, recognising the distinction between capabilities and processes is fundamental for organisations as they navigate the integration of AI. By clearly defining what capabilities they need, companies can position themselves to utilise AI effectively, drive innovation, and adapt to the demands of an ever-changing market landscape. The following capabilities are required for utilising AI in a customer-centric organisation:

- **Define Market and Customer:** An organisation needs to understand the market and customers to provide products based on customer needs or wants. A key activity for this customer-centric organisation is meeting customers' requirements. This is the driving capability for the rest of the organisation and is a short-term focus based on market dynamics. Examples are threats from competitors and first-mover advantage.
- **Develop Vision and Strategy:** Most organisations have different departments creating their own vision and strategy. Disparate visions prevent the organisation from moving forward as one entity. A single shared vision across the enterprise ensures each department

is focused on activities that contribute to the achievement of the goal and the organisation's success.

- **Design Products and Services:** Every commercial organisation exists to sell some product and/or service and design the products or services should be uniform across the enterprise. The organisational vision, strategy, and understanding of the market determine the design of products and services. When an organisation is heavily siloed, the design and services may be duplicated for each product offered by the organisation, which impacts total sustainability.

- **Market and Sell Products and Services:** Like products and services, sales and marketing functions are separate departments. It is not uncommon for an organisation to have conflicting marketing efforts where one unit adopts sustainability efforts while another department operates in ways that contradict or undermine those efforts. In addition, lack of alignment might increase manual processes or paperwork due to the lack of cross-functional coordination. The total impact of these activities on the organisation should be identified throughout the entire organisation.

- **Maintain and Support Products and Services:** In any organisation, resources are devoted to maintaining and supporting products and services. The product life cycle defines the maintenance stages, and AI could assist in maintaining the product life cycle and suggesting the maintenance and retirement of products and services.

- **Retire Products and Services:** Product disposition is planned after its life validity expires. Organisations usually ignore this capability and do not give it enough thought. Although these capabilities are often considered to be of least importance when designing the products, they could have a huge effect on the environment. For example, garbage tips across the world are overflowing with the previous models of PC, laptops, printers, and printer cartridges from the computing industry. Retirement of products requires a strategy and is aligned with the product design, development, and marketing to maximise the resource usage.

- **Management Support Processes:** This function requires optimising resources used by the organisation during the total life cycle of the products and services. Financial management, skills management, HR, and vendor management activities all contribute to either optimising or wasting resources due to duplication, varying, or uncoordinated demands on resources.

Steps to Define Capabilities

Capabilities play a crucial role in supporting and enhancing business processes, and it is essential to take a structured, step-by-step approach to effectively develop these capabilities. Business capability management aligns organisations with strategic goals, ultimately accelerating the achievement of desired results. This section describes the process in detail, particularly from the perspective of the adoption of AI and real-world examples.

- **Clarifying Business Outcomes:** The first step is to define the desired business outcomes clearly. This involves ensuring that the business architecture is strategically aligned to facilitate these outcomes. Think of business architecture as the bridge connecting business strategy with IT initiatives. For instance, a company aiming to leverage AI might define an outcome such as improving customer service response times through AI-driven chatbots. This aligns the business capability of customer service with the technological tools needed to reach that goal.

- **Incorporating Risk-Adjusted Value:** Next, it is crucial to incorporate risk-adjusted value into the governance framework for business architecture. This means looking at the risks linked with the business capabilities being developed and measuring the value of the capability after implementation. For example, if an organisation shifts from a traditional goods-based model to a service-driven model bolstered by AI, it may face risks regarding customer expectation management. If their data management systems cannot handle the increasing volume of information generated by customer interactions, it exposes the business to potential failure in meeting service-level agreements. Companies like Netflix utilise AI to analyse vast amounts of viewer data, managing risks by adapting their content offerings to meet changing audience preferences.

- **Aligning Governance with Organisational Culture:** Finally, the governance around business architecture must resonate with the organisation's culture and operational maturity. This means that all levels of the organisation need to embrace a capability-based governance approach for it to succeed. For example, in a technology company where individual achievements are prioritised over collaborative capability-building, initiatives might focus on quick wins rather than long-term investments in capability development, such as advanced AI projects. If an organisation opts for tactical solutions—say, deploying a rudimentary AI tool for immediate analysis rather than developing sophisticated predictive analytics capabilities—this can undermine the overall architecture and diminish potential benefits.

To illustrate a successful integration of these principles, consider how Google implemented its AI-powered tools. Google defined the business outcome of improving the user experience across all services. This involved creating an agile governance structure that supported capabilities in machine learning while also being mindful of risks associated with data privacy. As a result, Google has been able to adapt and innovate continuously, setting a high benchmark in leveraging AI for strategic success.

By taking a systematic approach to develop business capabilities aligned with the organisation's strategic intent, incorporating risk assessment, and fostering a supportive culture, businesses can thrive in the age of AI and harness its full potential.

Embedding Business Capabilities in CAIF

Business capability maps serve as essential tools in helping organisations seamlessly align their capabilities with desired outcomes. Capability maps are sophisticated blueprints that layer various elements of an organisation: IT systems, information management requirements, processes, policies, and the stakeholders responsible for managing information. All this needs to be strategically aligned to achieve significant business outcomes.

The CAIF leverages capability maps to guide organisations in innovating and optimising resources. By dynamically managing risks associated with information and technology, it empowers organisations to remain adaptable in a continuously evolving landscape. In this context, the capability maps not only provide crucial insights but also offer the flexibility necessary to navigate the complexities of today's IT environment.

○ **QUICK NOTE:** *A capability map shows what the organisation can do, not how. It's strategic, not operational.*

Just as geographical maps contain various overlays that highlight different features, business capability maps serve a similar purpose in the business layer of CAIF. They can illustrate the maturity of capabilities and the state of information management, and identify gaps that may hinder achieving business goals. This layered approach allows for a comprehensive view, facilitating better decision-making.

For example, consider a company contemplating a merger with another firm. The business architecture framework utilises the capability maps to evaluate each organisation's capabilities and maturity levels. By doing this, leadership can make informed decisions about whether to consolidate certain capabilities or select the more mature ones. This analysis can be critical to ensuring a smooth integration process and maximising the potential benefits of the merger.

AI adoption plays a significant role in enhancing the effectiveness of these capability maps. For instance, organisations can use AI algorithms to analyse vast datasets concerning their operations, identifying patterns and trends that may not be readily apparent. In one case, a retail company implemented AI-driven analytics to map its supply chain capabilities. By overlaying these insights with the organisation's existing systems and processes, it was able to streamline inventory management, resulting in reduced costs and improved customer satisfaction.

Moreover, AI can help pinpoint common business capabilities across different departments or even across various subsidiaries of a larger organisation. Through natural language processing and machine learning, organisations can assess existing capabilities, identifying areas that are underdeveloped or require enhancement. For example, a healthcare provider may use AI to analyse patient care processes within various departments, identifying common inefficiencies that could be addressed through data-driven improvements.

Business capability maps are invaluable in aligning organisational capabilities with outcomes, particularly as AI technologies become more deeply integrated into business processes. By utilising these maps, businesses can better navigate mergers, identify areas for improvement, and respond agilely to the ever-changing demands of the market. Whether through optimising supply chains, enhancing customer service, or consolidating systems, the application of AI in conjunction with these capability maps promises to drive efficiency and innovation within organisations.

CAIF Business Layer Context and Outcomes

CAIF business layer provides valuable context at the solution or project level, and it has significant value in the strategic decision-making process across the organisation. Organisational leadership is supported by CAIF as the decisions are based on facts and knowledge bases (business services repository) delivered by the business layer function. The decision-making process *will* be compromised unless there is an end-to-end and interdepartmental view of the organisation. Business architecture enables informed, effective, and controlled changes in a planned and efficient manner and provides:

- Views based on change context to understand and guide appropriate decision-making;
- The capability that monitors coherence and completeness of the enterprise and its strategic change agenda/portfolio;
- The opportunity to manage an increasingly complex technology landscape;
- Ensure that the information/data provided is contextually appropriate;
- Format, determine, and regulate decision-making associated with change; and
- Understand the impact of decisions and transformation on organisational operations.

Table 2.3 depicts the outcome-driven business architecture benefits to the organisation. The business layer-based prioritisation of projects and investment provides a path to transparent and objective investment decisions, avoiding any favourite project mentality. Table 2.3 illustrates the business outcomes achieved by a mature business architecture.

TABLE 2.3

The Context Provided by Business Architecture in Business Outcomes

Outcomes	Business Layer Context
Establishing and aligning initiative prioritisation	CAIF business layer is a framework that helps organisations navigate their priorities and growth strategies by establishing a layered understanding of their capabilities. Think of it as a blueprint that outlines how different parts of a company work together to achieve their goals. To effectively prioritise initiatives, businesses consider how each one enhances their existing capabilities, much like how a software update can improve the functionality of an app. This is where governance comes into play—by streamlining decision-making processes, organisations can clearly define criteria for prioritising their initiatives. This structured approach ensures that everyone in the organisation has a shared understanding of what is most important to focus on. One relevant example of AI adoption in this context is how companies are increasingly utilising AI-driven analytics to determine which initiatives to pursue. For instance, an e-commerce platform might implement a machine learning algorithm that analyses customer purchasing patterns. By doing so, they can prioritise the development of new features or services based on what will most effectively enhance their customer experience and revenue—essentially a clearer view of the maturity each initiative will bring to their capabilities. Another example is in the healthcare sector, where AI can help streamline processes such as patient triage or appointment scheduling. Hospitals using AI systems to triage patients can prioritise initiatives that enhance their operational efficiency, ensuring that they allocate resources to the most impactful areas, such as improving patient outcomes or reducing waiting times. In summary, business layer and AI work hand in hand to help organisations prioritise their initiatives wisely, ensuring that each step taken contributes meaningfully to their capabilities and overall mission.
Comparing options to validate ideas and solutions	Business capability maturity refers to an organisation's ability to consistently improve and expand its operational capabilities to achieve better business outcomes. This concept emphasises the importance of carefully selecting projects that align with the organisation's strategic goals and priorities. By focusing on projects that enhance these capabilities, businesses can eliminate those initiatives that do not contribute significantly to their growth or operational efficiency. For example, consider a retail company looking to improve its inventory management. By adopting an AI-powered analytics platform, the company can gain insights into consumer purchasing patterns and optimise stock levels accordingly. This project is a prime example of maximising business outcomes through capability enhancement, as it not only streamlines operations but also improves customer satisfaction by ensuring the right products are available at the right time.

(Continued)

TABLE 2.3 (*Continued*)

The Context Provided by Business Architecture in Business Outcomes

Outcomes	Business Layer Context
	On the other hand, if the same company were to invest in a project centered around building a virtual reality shopping experience without having a solid foundation in e-commerce or real-time inventory management, it may not yield the desired results. Such a project could divert resources from more pressing needs and not align with the current priorities of the organisation.
	AI adoption provides numerous examples of how businesses can enhance their capabilities effectively. For instance, a healthcare provider implementing AI-driven diagnostic tools can significantly accelerate the identification of diseases, improving patient outcomes. By concentrating on such transformative projects, organisations can ensure they are continuously evolving and enhancing their capabilities in a manner that directly contributes to their overall mission and success.
	In summary, focusing on the right projects is crucial for building and refining business capabilities. By leveraging AI technologies strategically, organisations can drive growth, streamline operations, and ultimately achieve superior business outcomes.
Assessing and prioritising possible solutions Providing structure to support appropriate assessment, comparison, and decisions	In today's rapidly evolving business landscape, organisations are increasingly turning to artificial intelligence (AI) to enhance decision-making and streamline operations. A crucial aspect of this transformation involves establishing a set of predefined criteria that helps prioritise potential solutions. By adopting a structured approach, businesses can effectively evaluate various AI applications and determine which ones align best with their strategic goals.
	For instance, a retail company might set criteria focused on improving customer experience and operational efficiency. This could lead to the adoption of an AI-powered chatbot for customer service, which can handle inquiries and assist shoppers 24/7, thus freeing up human employees for more complex tasks.
	As organisations mature in their understanding of business architecture, the integration of AI frameworks can significantly reduce the demands placed on IT projects by various business units. When AI is woven into the fabric of business operations, it allows for a more streamlined process where technology solutions emerge from a clear understanding of business needs rather than urgent, reactive requests.
	For example, in a manufacturing setting, AI can analyse production data in real time, identifying inefficiencies and suggesting preventative maintenance schedules. This proactive approach not only addresses immediate concerns but also aligns with long-term strategic objectives, thereby minimising the strain on IT resources.
	Ultimately, defining an IT project based on strategic results becomes more effective when organisations have a well-established AI strategy. By clearly articulating their vision and goals, companies can leverage AI technologies—such as predictive analytics for market trends or machine learning for optimising supply chains—to drive meaningful results and support sustained growth. This ensures that every AI initiative is purposeful and contributes to the broader mission of the organisation.

(Continued)

TABLE 2.3 (*Continued*)

The Context Provided by Business Architecture in Business Outcomes

Outcomes	Business Layer Context
Presenting complex information to targeted stakeholder groups Enabling impact and scenario analysis	Understanding the outcomes of various projects can often be a challenge, especially in a business context. This is where a well-defined business architecture becomes essential. It serves as a framework that translates complex project results into clear, relatable business language, making it easier for everyone involved to grasp the bigger picture.
	Imagine a company looking to adopt AI to enhance its customer service. By using a business architecture, the organisation can map out the capabilities it needs—such as natural language processing to understand customer inquiries or machine learning to predict customer preferences. This mapping helps visualise how each AI capability layers onto existing business functions, clarifying how these enhancements will ultimately improve customer satisfaction and drive sales.
	Additionally, whenever new technologies like AI are introduced, understanding potential risks is crucial. For example, while AI can significantly streamline operations, it also raises concerns about data privacy and bias in decision-making. By layering risk assessments onto the business capability maps, stakeholders can see not just the benefits but also the potential pitfalls, allowing them to make informed decisions.
	In another example, consider an e-commerce company implementing AI for personalised marketing. Through business architecture, the various capabilities—like data analytics for consumer behaviour and automated recommendation systems—are communicated clearly. Stakeholders can easily visualise how these capabilities interplay and contribute to a targeted approach, ultimately leading to increased engagement and higher conversion rates.
	By presenting complex information in an easily digestible format, the business layer helps ensure that all stakeholders, from executives to team members, understand the impact of AI adoption on the organisation. It transforms abstract outcomes into a strategic narrative, illuminating the path forward while addressing any challenges along the way.
Guiding technology selection	The choice of technology and vendors is fundamentally driven by clearly defined outcomes. A rigorous evaluation of innovative concepts, paired with a thorough assessment of the organisation's readiness for change, is essential in this process. By strategically aligning these factors, we empower ourselves to make informed decisions that not only enhance operational efficiency but also ensure we partner with vendors who can truly drive our vision forward. This approach not only fosters adaptability but also positions us for long-term success in a rapidly evolving landscape.
Supporting financial management (investment and benefit) of the portfolio	Business architecture consolidates projects and invests in technologies at an organisational level, reducing proliferating tactical solutions for capabilities. The project selection and investment management framework include business capabilities-based investment processes and procedures.

(Continued)

TABLE 2.3 (*Continued*)

The Context Provided by Business Architecture in Business Outcomes

Outcomes	Business Layer Context
Informing release planning and optimisation of release of change portfolio	Business architecture provides optimised information and knowledge management dimensions to the business capabilities. The reporting, information release, and information planning are anchored by the business capabilities, and key performance indicators are managed by the information collection, planning. The business capability-based governance, risk management, and compliance provides an information exchange framework based on context-based information sharing using business capabilities.

Measuring Business layer maturity is done annually and utilises the industry standard maturity model. This evaluation enables the organisation to review rates of progress, determine the achievability of target rates, and modify organisational plans to facilitate further improvement.

Approach to Developing CAIF

QUICK NOTE: *CAIF isn't a tool just for architects—it's for leadership, product owners, IT, and business units alike.*

Since CAIF impacts decision-making in an organisation, its development is necessarily consensus-based. CAIF also supports strategic investment decisions across the organisation within the constraints of the fiscal realities of organisation. This requires the involvement of multiple non-technical disciplines of the organisation.

CAIF development starts with workshops with subject matter experts about goals, visions, and objectives from the requirements of business architecture. The workshops explore the strengths and weaknesses of the organisation. The following results come from a workshop:

1. Identifying which business capabilities are at risk by defining and assessing current capabilities and assessing maturity level and their mapping to business outcomes.
2. Undertaking a gap analysis (both qualitative and quantitative) to evaluate and prioritise which business capabilities require investment. This requires an understanding of the organisation's current state and its desired future state.
3. Aligning new IT initiatives to business capabilities.
4. Highlighting gaps, overlaps, and interdependencies within planned projects.
5. Establishing a roadmap (with 5-year rolling investment plan) and an annual prioritised investment plan for information management and technology.

Chapter Questions

1. What does it mean to develop a comprehensive end-to-end view of an organisation's business capabilities?
2. Why is it important to have a holistic understanding of operational processes within an organisation?
3. How can mapping out interconnections between various functions improve overall organisational performance?
4. What strategies can be employed to cultivate a deep understanding of an organisation's business capabilities?
5. In what ways can understanding the synergy between different operational processes benefit decision-making within a company?
6. What are some potential challenges in creating an intricate map of an organisation's functions?
7. How can organisations ensure that all functions are aligned and working towards common performance goals?
8. What role does communication play in enhancing the interconnections between various operational processes?
9. How can technology assist in developing a comprehensive view of business capabilities and processes?
10. What are the key outcomes to expect from establishing a well-defined end-to-end view of an organisation's operations?

Note to Readers and Educators

Comprehensive answers and explanations to these chapter-end questions are available at www.sandeepbhalekar.com. The website also provides supplementary frameworks, teaching guidelines, and reference materials to support deeper understanding and classroom discussion.

Educators and facilitators can access additional resources, including presentation frameworks, assessment rubrics, and discussion prompts, to help integrate the concepts from this chapter into academic or professional learning environments.

Notes

1 https://en.wikipedia.org/wiki/Business_Process_Framework_(eTOM).
2 Using on APQC capability PCF.

3

The AI Adoption Framework—
Technology Perspective

QUICK NOTE: *Organisational change management (OCM) is not a soft skill—it's a hard requirement for successful AI integration.*

CAIF tackles long-standing inefficiencies in siloed systems by enabling shared services and standardised data platforms. Through real-world examples—such as health, social security, and immigration departments—the chapter illustrates how CAIF facilitates secure, context-aware data sharing without compromising individual departmental responsibilities or legislative compliance. The integration of emerging technologies, including AI-powered analytics, cloud computing, and mobile access, fosters the creation of responsive and intelligent service ecosystems.

The framework's technology architecture is articulated through five layers:

- The Presentation Layer ensures user-friendly access to relevant information.
- The Information Layer manages data as a strategic asset, ensuring accuracy and accessibility.
- The Services Layer transforms data into actionable insights and services.
- The Governance Layer defines policies for accountability and collaboration.
- The Security Layer embeds robust protection across systems, supported by AI for threat detection and prevention.

Additionally, the chapter introduces an Information Collection Framework to tackle the ethical and operational considerations of data use in AI-enabled environments, such as smart cities and digital service platforms. It explores the balance between personalisation and privacy, advocating for transparent data governance to maintain public trust while realising the benefits of AI technologies.

In conclusion, CAIF is positioned as a forward-looking architecture that empowers Australian organisations and governments to modernise their operations.

DOI: 10.1201/9781003626503-3

By promoting sustainable, AI-driven collaboration and enhancing service responsiveness, CAIF serves as a strategic enabler of digital transformation in both the public and private sectors.

Key Points

- Embracing organisational change management is vital for seamlessly integrating it with AI and business capabilities. By leveraging CAIF, we can brilliantly align our goals with actionable strategies.
- It's exciting to identify the key artifacts of CAIF and ensure clarity around concepts like business IT alignment.
- A robust AI Architecture program tracks CAIF's success and delivers insightful growth metrics. Promoting knowledge-sharing ignites collaboration and nurtures a thriving culture of continuous learning!

This chapter delves into developing and implementing a Collaborative AI Framework (CAIF) technology layer. The technology layer strongly emphasises achieving the organisation's business outcomes through collaboration and must be based on the business layer discussed in the business layer chapter. This outcome-driven perspective is guided by the enhancement of capabilities within the organisation.

The development and application of CAIF necessitate significant changes and the ability to measure the impact of those changes effectively. Therefore, change management becomes a vital component in this chapter's discussions. Furthermore, it introduces metrics and measurement techniques for assessing the effectiveness of collaborative approaches and the resultant changes within the organisation.

Introduction

In today's rapidly evolving digital landscape, organisations are striving to integrate artificial intelligence (AI) into their operations in ways that enhance efficiency, promote innovation, and align with strategic objectives. The CAIF is a pivotal enabler in this transformation. This chapter introduces the CAIF technology layer, focusing on its ability to support smart, integrated service delivery by fostering collaboration between departments while preserving organisational autonomy and legislative compliance.

Why Collaboration Matters in the Digital Age

From Siloed Systems to Integrated Ecosystems

For decades, many organisations—especially within the public sector—have operated in functional silos. Departments such as health, education, transportation, and social services built and managed their own information systems, databases, and service channels independently. While this approach may have been suitable in the past, it has led to duplication of effort, fragmented service delivery, poor data interoperability, and significant inefficiencies.

Siloed systems are characterised by isolated decision-making, redundant processes, and restricted data sharing. For example, a citizen seeking government assistance may need to interact separately with multiple departments—each requesting the same documentation repeatedly. This disjointed experience leads to delays, user frustration, and increased administrative burden.

In contrast, integrated, collaborative ecosystems enable seamless interaction across departments, using shared platforms, common data standards, and interoperable services. These ecosystems allow agencies to deliver services in a more coordinated and efficient manner, drawing on shared data and resources while respecting the autonomy of individual entities. Such collaboration is not only beneficial internally but also enhances public trust and satisfaction through simplified and transparent service delivery.

Global Trends Driving the Need for Collaboration

Across the globe, a wave of digital transformation is reshaping how governments and businesses operate. Several key trends are fuelling this change:

- **Smart Services:** Countries are moving towards smart services that use real-time data, automation, and AI to deliver personalised and efficient experiences. In cities, this manifests in smart traffic management, waste collection, and emergency response systems that adapt dynamically to community needs.

- **E-Government Initiatives:** Governments in Australia, Singapore, Estonia, and the United Kingdom, among others, are pioneering digital government strategies that unify services through citizen-centric portals. These efforts aim to reduce red tape, improve access, and drive better policy outcomes through integrated systems.

- **AI Integration:** AI is being embedded in core operations to support predictive analytics, automate routine decisions, and enable adaptive service delivery. From fraud detection in finance to early intervention in healthcare, AI is becoming a key enabler of operational agility and informed decision-making.

- **Cloud Adoption and Data Sharing:** The rise of secure, scalable cloud platforms is facilitating the centralisation of data and applications, enabling cross-agency collaboration and resource optimisation. Interconnected systems can now operate in real time, improving responsiveness and reducing data inconsistencies.

These global shifts demonstrate that the future lies in connected, collaborative, and intelligent systems that can adapt to evolving user expectations and complex service environments.

Why CAIF Is Essential in This Context

In light of these trends and challenges, the need for a structured, scalable, and collaborative digital framework has never been more urgent. The CAIF provides the architectural and strategic foundation necessary for organisations to move beyond legacy silos and embrace connected ecosystems.

💡 **QUICK NOTE:** *Interoperability is the foundation. Without it, AI is just a patch, not a platform.*

CAIF serves several key purposes:

- It enables interoperability across systems and departments, ensuring that data flows securely and meaningfully between different parts of the organisation.
- It aligns AI capabilities with business outcomes, transforming data into actionable insights and driving more strategic, informed decisions.
- It promotes resource optimisation by reducing redundancy, enhancing agility, and leveraging shared infrastructure through cloud and mobile technologies.
- It supports governance and accountability, providing robust mechanisms for data privacy, ethical AI use, and compliance with regulations like Australia's Privacy Act.

Without a framework like CAIF, organisations risk falling behind in their digital transformation journeys, struggling with incompatible systems, fragmented services, and missed opportunities for innovation. CAIF offers a pathway to not only modernise technology infrastructure but also transform organisational culture, operational efficiency, and service quality.

Overview of CAIF

? **DID YOU KNOW:** *Estonia's e-Government platform allows 99% of public services to be accessed online—enabled by shared architecture frameworks like CAIF.*

The modern business era is particularly adept at using information and communication technologies (ICT) to capitalise on global opportunities to collaborate, rather than compete. This chapter intends to give readers an understanding of the need for a CAIF as organisations move towards smart services concepts or service-based approaches.

Smart services are revolutionising how businesses and governments design and deliver their products and services. Traditionally, many businesses and public services have been developed by individual departments, each focusing solely on their specific area, be it transportation, health, social security, or immigration. This siloed approach often leads to inefficiencies, especially when departments attempt to collaborate.

To address these challenges, a new approach called CAIF is emerging. Think of CAIF as a network that allows different business entities (business and government departments) to work together more effectively while still maintaining their own unique roles and responsibilities. For instance, imagine a scenario where the health department needs to share information with the Social Security and immigration services. CAIF facilitates this by enabling departments to share essential data and processes without compromising their individual legislative requirements.

One method illustrating this concept is through the integration of various information systems. An example is when an individual applies for social security benefits. Currently, the Social Security Department may need to verify the applicant's health status and immigration status through separate systems. With CAIF, these departments can share a common platform where resident information is accessible and standardised. This means an applicant's health details could be verified through a secure portal that both the health department and social services can access, streamlining the process significantly.

Further, CAIF supports the development of shared services that can be accessed from a single portal. This initiative not only enhances efficiency but also reduces costs. For example, using emerging technologies like cloud computing, departments can easily deposit and withdraw shareable information. When data is stored once in a secure cloud system rather than replicated across various departmental databases, it ensures that everyone is working with the same, most up-to-date information.

? **DID YOU KNOW:** *Cloud-first strategies are mandated across many OECD countries for all new government ICT projects.*

It is crucial to address issues like incompatible data formats and the absence of unique identifiers that can connect different pieces of information to make data sharing effective. CAIF aims to create a common framework where departments can share crucial insights about residents, locations, and other datasets in a coherent manner. By doing so, it paves the way for a more collaborative, transparent, and efficient government service landscape that truly prioritises the needs of the community.

The Collaborative Architecture Integration layer stands at the forefront of technological advancement, offering significant advantages in communication, security, and cloud computing. In today's evolving digital landscape, it is essential to refine the Enterprise Architecture Framework to foster effective collaboration across all levels of an organisation.

One of the primary benefits of CAIF is its ability to optimise resources, particularly in reducing the physical footprint of servers and client devices. For instance, by leveraging AI-driven analytics, organisations can better manage their server loads, dynamically allocating resources based on real-time demand. This not only streamlines operations but also dramatically cuts down on power consumption, paving the way for greener ICT practices.

Moreover, CAIF introduces high-level strategies that urge organisations to embrace sustainable technologies. For instance, by utilising machine learning algorithms, businesses can analyse energy usage across their infrastructures and identify areas for improvement, ultimately leading to a lower carbon footprint.

This chapter delves into the ways CAIF integrates critical components of modern systems development. For example, incorporating Service-Oriented Architecture (SOA) allows different services to communicate seamlessly, enabling organisations to publish and subscribe to vital data, information, and intelligence services. In a retail context, an AI-driven SOA could facilitate real-time inventory management, where stock levels are automatically updated and shared across various departments, enhancing responsiveness to customer needs.

Additionally, with the incorporation of mobile technology, CAIF empowers employees to access and contribute to collaborative platforms from anywhere, anytime. Imagine a scenario where a remote project team can leverage AI-powered tools to brainstorm and develop solutions, providing insights based on data trends and customer feedback gathered in real-time.

Enhanced security measures are integral to CAIF as well. AI can play a pivotal role here by monitoring network traffic and identifying potential threats faster than traditional methods. For example, financial institutions can utilise AI systems to detect unusual transaction patterns, automatically alerting security teams to investigate potential fraud.

⤤ SIDEBAR: THE 5-LAYER TECHNOLOGY STACK OF CAIF

CAIF Technology Stack

- **Presentation Layer:** User-centric access to data
- **Information Layer:** Treats data as a strategic asset
- **Services Layer:** Converts data into actionable services
- **Governance Layer:** Ensures policies and collaboration
- **Security Layer:** Embedded protection and AI-based threat detection

These layers form the technical backbone of CAIF's smart service ecosystem.

Technical Layers of CAIF

The CAIF promotes collaboration and actively harnesses the power of AI technologies. This results in smarter decision-making, optimised resource usage, and robust security measures that ultimately transform how organisations operate and innovate.

The layers of the organisation that need to be aligned with all existing and future IT systems are described as follows:

- **The Presentation Layer** is crucial for delivering information directly to users in an accessible and intuitive manner. Past methods of information access involved accessing multiple databases, each with a different purpose, creating a slow-reacting process to develop reports or assist customers. Instead of navigating a complex web of outdated systems, a modern employee portal streamlines access, providing the necessary information based on the specific needs of each employee. For instance, if an employee is tasked with handling housing applications, their portal could prioritise documents and resources pertinent to housing, without exposing them to irrelevant systems. This tailored access, driven by user profiles, ensures efficiency and security, as information access is authenticated and authorised centrally.

- **The Information Layer** serves as the backbone of the organisation's data management, ensuring that information is treated as an asset. By employing standardised rules, this layer guarantees that the data is accurate, timely, and relevant. For example, consider how smart cities use real-time data to manage traffic. The information layer might aggregate data from sensors on roads, public transport schedules, and even social media trends, helping city planners make informed decisions on public transport routes. However, as some systems may be outdated, strategic realignment is necessary to harmonise these aged infrastructures with cutting-edge technology. The implementation of the common architecture information layer can provide a structured modernisation plan, ensuring that various agencies can enhance their information systems through effective funding allocation.

- **The Services Layer** is where the magic happens—transforming raw data into actionable insights through a range of services designed for various users. For example, citizens can access a single portal to apply for permits, report issues, or seek information about their rights. This layer acts as the bridge connecting information to services, ensuring consistency and ease of use. For instance, if a local business needs to apply for a grant, the services layer could automatically pull relevant data from existing systems to populate their application, making the process smoother and more efficient. AI plays a significant role here by providing context-aware services; it can learn from user interactions to offer personalised recommendations, significantly enhancing user experience.

- **Governance and Security Layers:** These are the two foundational pillars that support the other three layers. Governance ensures that there are clear policies and procedures that guide the management of information systems, allowing for accountability and enhancing collaboration across agencies. For example, a governance framework might dictate how data is shared between health and social services, ensuring compliance with privacy standards. Security is seamlessly integrated across all layers, reinforcing the architecture with consistent protections that adhere to statutory requirements. This is especially vital in collaborative environments, where multiple stakeholders interact with sensitive information. By leveraging AI, organisations can implement advanced security measures, such as predictive analytics, to identify potential threats before they occur, ensuring that data remains safe and secure.

Modern systems development incorporates AI strategically across layers to enhance user experiences, streamline processes, and ensure a robust governance and security framework—ultimately creating a more efficient and responsive organisational infrastructure. The new collaborative architecture requires consideration of the following key principles.

💡 **QUICK NOTE:** *Governance=structure; Security=trust. Both must be baked into every layer, not bolted on.*

Single Data Entry Collection Methods Are Used for Information Exchange

The success of the CAIF largely hinges on effective information management. This means collecting data in a way that is not only efficient but also tailored to the specific context. For instance, imagine a healthcare system where patient data is gathered seamlessly during appointments. Instead of requiring multiple forms and repeated entries, patients could simply verify their information once. This creates a smoother experience for them while ensuring that data accuracy is maintained.

Once this data is entered, advanced AI systems come into play. Advanced systems synthesise the information, analysing it to extract valuable insights and trends. For example, AI might identify patterns in patient visits and suggest optimised scheduling to reduce waiting times. The synthesised data would then be distributed to various systems automatically, using a method often referred to as "Publish and Subscribe." This means that different departments can access the information they need without unnecessary duplication or delay.

Additionally, managing the sheer volume and speed at which information is generated is crucial. Consider how social media platforms process millions of posts every minute. AI algorithms can quickly filter through this data to highlight relevant content or flag significant trends, ensuring that the right information reaches decision-makers in real time. By leveraging AI in these ways, the CAIF can enhance efficiency, reduce information overload, and provide timely insights for better decision-making across various sectors (Figure 3.1).

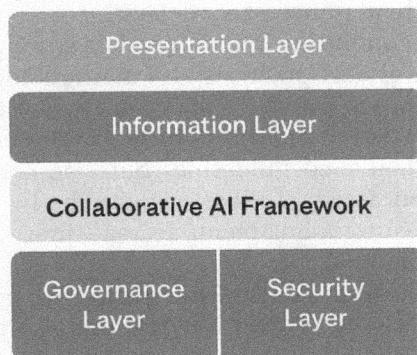

FIGURE 3.1
Collaborative Enterprise Architecture Framework.

The success of the CAIF relies heavily on how well organisations work together to contribute to and utilise the services available through its platform. There's a global effort to refine the framework, allowing governments to create shared services accessible from a single portal.

This initiative aligns with a broader trend seen across Asia, India, Europe, and America, where governments are increasingly adopting cloud computing solutions. For instance, cloud technology is transforming e-government services, fundamentally changing how citizens interact with governmental systems. For example, a citizen could fill out an online form with personal information once. From there, a single registration number retrieves the data for multiple uses or for different services and departments. This streamlined process not only simplifies things for citizens but also saves time and resources for government agencies.

CAIF plays a vital role in ensuring that personal information is transmitted securely while adhering to privacy regulations. One of its key benefits is reducing redundancy; instead of each department developing its own applications, CAIF enables them to share vital information efficiently. For example, if a citizen updates their address with one department, that update is automatically reflected across all relevant agencies, eliminating the necessity of repeated paperwork.

To ensure this information is useful and easily shared, it is crucial that it is formatted consistently and can be accessed by various applications. In this context, AI has a significant role to play. AI could analyse patterns in data usage, identify potential areas of improvement, and automate data sharing processes between different departments. For instance, AI algorithms could prioritise data requests, ensuring that departments receive the most pertinent information without unnecessary delays.

Investing in cloud computing and robust data sharing practices requires a strong foundation of best practices and methodologies. Projects utilising the CAIF framework will be subject to review by committees that adhere to industry-wide standards. These evaluations not only ensure compliance with established guidelines but also encourage continuous improvement. AI can assist in these evaluations by monitoring project outcomes and suggesting adjustments in real-time, helping to maintain adherence to best practices.

By embracing these standards and integrating AI, governments can not only enhance the efficiency of their services but also rethink their investments and strategies to ensure they align with industry standards. In essence, CAIF and AI together pave the way for a modernised government experience that is more responsive to citizens' needs and future-ready.

📌 SIDEBAR: SMART CITIES AND ETHICAL AI—BALANCING TECH AND TRUST

AI enables smart mobility, health monitoring, and urban planning—but privacy, consent, and bias must be carefully managed.

Regulatory Touchpoints:
- Australia's Privacy Act 1988
- AI Ethics Framework (Australia)
- Consumer Data Right (CDR)

Ethical data governance is the backbone of smart city trust.

Information Collection Framework

As cities evolve into smart ecosystems, a significant concern for residents is how their personal information is handled, especially regarding data protection and privacy. Smart cities thrive on the collection and analysis of data to provide better services, but this reliance on data can lead to some serious privacy issues.

Cities use AI to analyse traffic patterns and collect data from various sources, such as GPS data from cars and public transportation schedules, in order to optimise traffic signals and reduce congestion. This personalisation improves commuting times for everyone. However, the same data that makes these improvements possible can also reveal personal details about individuals, like their travel habits and daily routines. This raises a critical question: What is the balance between the benefits of these personalised services with the need to protect individual privacy?

Additionally, think of smart public services like community health monitoring systems. These systems can use AI to analyse health data from various sources to respond to public health crises more effectively. For example, during an outbreak of flu, AI can track symptoms reported online or in healthcare facilities, allowing the city to allocate resources efficiently. However, if this data isn't managed properly, it risks breaching the privacy of the individuals whose information is being analysed.

This is where the idea of a robust data governance model comes into play. Such a model would outline strict guidelines on how personal data is collected, stored, and used, ensuring transparency and protecting citizens' rights. Without these safeguards, discussions about the value of data can quickly become misguided, focusing more on fears rather than the real benefits that data can provide.

Moreover, retail businesses often tap into social media data for marketing strategies. While there's immense potential for creating targeted ads that resonate with consumers, it can feel invasive if people aren't informed about how their data is being used. For example, if someone likes a local café on social media, an AI-powered system could potentially deliver coupons or advertisements for that café directly to their phone. However, if consumers do not know how their preferences are being tracked and utilised, they may view this as a violation of their privacy.

Overall, while the integration of AI into smart city operations offers exciting opportunities for improved services and enhanced citizen experience, it's crucial that clear, transparent data governance frameworks are established to ensure that individual privacy is respected and protected. Otherwise, public trust is at risk and undermines the very benefits these technologies promise to deliver (Figure 3.2).

The use of AI and large-scale data collection raises significant ethical concerns, particularly regarding consent, surveillance, algorithmic bias, and the potential for discrimination. Organisations must ensure that data is collected responsibly, with full transparency, and used in a way that respects individual rights and public trust.

For smart cities and government environments, robust data governance models are essential. These models should define clear roles, data stewardship responsibilities, privacy safeguards, and compliance measures. Approaches such as federated data sharing, role-based access controls, and data classification policies support secure and ethical data use.

In Australia, frameworks must align with the Privacy Act 1988, the Australian Privacy Principles, and recent updates to the Consumer Data Right. These regulations govern how personal data is collected, stored, and shared, ensuring citizens' privacy is protected while enabling responsible innovation.

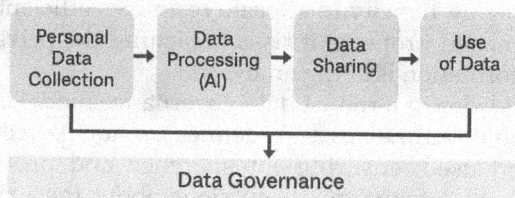

FIGURE 3.2
Information Collection Framework.

CAIF Implementation: Best Practices and Challenges

Implementation Steps

- **Assessment:** Evaluate existing systems, data maturity, and organisational readiness.
- **Pilot Projects:** Launch small-scale implementations to test interoperability and stakeholder engagement.
- **Scale-Up:** Gradually expand integration, standardisation, and change management across departments.

Common Challenges

- **Data Silos:** Inconsistent or isolated data systems hinder collaboration.
- **Legacy Infrastructure:** Outdated technologies resist modernisation.
- **Stakeholder Resistance:** Cultural inertia and fear of change can delay progress.

Recommendations for Success

- Foster cross-functional leadership and early stakeholder buy-in.
- Establish strong governance and change management structures.
- Adopt modular, scalable architectures to ease integration and future growth.

? DID YOU KNOW: *According to Gartner, by 2026, 80% of government digital transformation initiatives will involve cross-agency data sharing.*

CAIF aligns with international shifts towards cloud-first, AI-ready governance frameworks. Across Australia, Asia, Europe, and North America, governments are prioritising digital platforms that are interoperable, citizen-centric, and privacy-conscious.

Australia's Digital Transformation Strategy and New Zealand's Digital Government Partnership highlight regional commitment to shared services and data integration. Similarly, the EU's AI Act and Singapore's Smart Nation initiative provide roadmaps for the ethical adoption of AI.

CAIF is highly scalable and adaptable, making it suitable for both local governments and large federal agencies. Its modular structure supports ongoing innovation, aligning with global trends in platform governance and intelligent public services.

The CAIF is a blueprint for building more innovative, more agile, and ethically responsible digital ecosystems. It supports organisations in overcoming legacy inefficiencies, enabling cross-sector collaboration, and delivering citizen-centric outcomes.

By integrating strong governance, data ethics, and AI technologies, CAIF transforms how services are designed, delivered, and scaled.

Chapter Questions

1. What is the CAIF, and how does it differ from traditional enterprise architecture approaches?
2. Why is organisational change management critical for the successful implementation of CAIF?
3. Explain the role of AI in transforming siloed systems into collaborative digital ecosystems.
4. Describe the five key layers of the CAIF technology stack and how they interact with each other.
5. What role does the Information Layer play in enabling smart city or government services?
6. How do the Governance and Security Layers contribute to ethical and secure data sharing across departments?
7. Provide an example of how CAIF could streamline service delivery between multiple government departments (e.g., health and social services).
8. How does CAIF enable shared services through cloud platforms? Mention at least one real-world scenario.
9. What are some practical applications of AI in the Services Layer of CAIF?
10. What are the major ethical implications of using AI in data-driven public services?
11. How does Australia's Privacy Act 1988 guide the responsible use of citizen data?
12. Why is data governance essential in the context of smart cities and digital government transformation?
13. Outline the three major steps in implementing CAIF across an organisation.
14. What are the common challenges organisations face when transitioning to a collaborative AI framework?
15. How does CAIF align with global trends in digital governance, and why is this alignment important?
16. If you were leading a CAIF implementation in a mid-sized city council, what would be your top three priorities and why?
17. Discuss how CAIF can contribute to reducing Australia's digital divide and improving equity in public service delivery.
18. What strategies would you propose to overcome resistance from legacy system stakeholders during a CAIF rollout?

Note to Readers and Educators

Comprehensive answers and explanations to these chapter-end questions are available at www.sandeepbhalekar.com. The website also provides supplementary frameworks, teaching guidelines, and reference materials to support deeper understanding and classroom discussion.

Educators and facilitators can access additional resources, including presentation frameworks, assessment rubrics, and discussion prompts, to help integrate the concepts from this chapter into academic or professional learning environments.

Bibliography

Australian Government. (1988). *Privacy Act 1988*. Canberra: Australian Government. https://www.legislation.gov.au/Details/C2023C00225

Australian Government. (2023). *Digital Government Strategy*. Canberra: Digital Transformation Agency. https://www.digital.gov.au/strategy-policy/digital-government-strategy

Commonwealth of Australia. (2021). *Australia's AI Ethics Framework*. Canberra: Department of Industry, Science and Resources. https://www.industry.gov.au/publications/australias-artificial-intelligence-ethics-framework

Digital Transformation Agency. (2023). *Cloud Hosting Strategy*. Canberra: Digital Transformation Agency.

European Commission. (2021). *Proposal for a Regulation Laying Down Harmonised Rules on Artificial Intelligence (Artificial Intelligence Act)*. Brussels: European Commission. https://eur-lex.europa.eu/legal-content/EN/TXT/?uri=CELEX%3A52021PC0206

Gartner. (2023). *Hype Cycle for Artificial Intelligence*. Stamford: Gartner Research. https://www.gartner.com/en/research/methodologies/gartner-hype-cycle

IBM. (2022). *AI Governance and Trust*. New York: IBM Corporation. https://www.ibm.com/cloud/learn/ai-governance

National Institute of Standards and Technology (NIST). (2023). *AI Risk Management Framework (AI RMF 1.0)*. Gaithersburg: NIST. https://www.nist.gov/itl/ai-risk-management-framework

OECD. (2022). *OECD Digital Government Index 2022*. Paris: Organisation for Economic Co-operation and Development. https://www.oecd.org/governance/oecd-digital-government-index.htm

Open Group. (2018). *The TOGAF® Standard, Version 9.2*. San Francisco: The Open Group. https://pubs.opengroup.org/architecture/togaf9-doc/arch/

Singapore Government. (2022). *Smart Nation Strategy Overview*. Singapore: Smart Nation and Digital Government Office. https://www.smartnation.gov.sg/

World Economic Forum. (2023). *Global AI Governance Frameworks: Shaping the Future of AI*. Geneva: World Economic Forum. https://www.weforum.org/reports/

Zuboff, S. (2019). *The Age of Surveillance Capitalism: The Fight for a Human Future at the New Frontier of Power*. New York: PublicAffairs.

4

AI and Crisis Management

Crisis management involves carefully planned strategies, methods, and technologies to prepare for, respond to, and recover from events that impact people and place. Crisis events are disruptive and can jeopardise human lives and economic stability as well as institutional integrity. Crisis can take many different forms such as natural disasters like earthquakes or wildfires, health events like pandemics or outbreaks, cyberattacks, financial collapses, and political conflicts.

In today's world, characterised by interconnectivity and digitalisation, crises unfold more quickly and information, both factual and false, spreads rapidly, introducing further complications. Conventional crisis management methods, which rely on manual data collection, human judgement, and reactive strategies, often struggle to keep up with the scale and complexity of modern crises. As a result, there is a growing need to integrate advanced technologies, such as artificial intelligence (AI), to make crisis management efficient, accurate, and responsive. AI is revolutionising crisis management by enabling proactive and data-driven responses. AI-powered systems can process vast amounts of real-time data, detect patterns, predict outcomes, and provide actionable insights, allowing governments, organisations, and emergency responders to make quicker, more informed decisions. AI in crisis management improves the following:

- **Predictive Analysis:** Prevent crisis escalation by forecasting disasters, detecting cybersecurity threats, and identifying disease outbreaks.

- **Real-Time Monitoring:** Provide early warning through AI-driven surveillance systems and sensors to track environmental changes, social unrest, and economic shifts.

- **Simulation:** AI algorithms simulate crisis scenarios and can assist decision-makers by recommending actions and optimising resource allocation.

- **Enhance Communication:** AI-driven fact-checking tools help verify information, preventing panic and confusion from the spread of false narratives. AI-powered chatbots, virtual assistants, and automated messaging systems provide relief for overworked emergency responders and ensure timely and accurate information reaches affected populations.

DOI: 10.1201/9781003626503-4

Utilising AI capabilities to analyse data in real time and identify needed actions transforms crisis response from a reactive process into a proactive, strategic approach. This reduces casualties, minimises economic damage, and improves the ability to keep functioning during or after a crisis.

This chapter examines AI's role in crisis management through these concepts.

- **AI's Potential in Crisis Scenarios**
  AI technologies such as machine learning (ML), natural language processing (NLP), and computer vision are reshaping emergency preparedness and response. Examples are provided for various crises, including pandemic management, disaster relief, and cybersecurity defence.
- **Challenges and Ethical Considerations**
  Challenges include the potential for over-reliance on AI in high-stakes scenarios and striking a balance between human expertise and AI automation during the decision-making process. Ethical concerns include bias in AI decision-making, data privacy issues, and managing misinformation.
- **Best Practices for AI Deployment in Crisis Management**
  Best practices include responsible integration of AI and collaborative efforts between government, tech, and humanitarian organisations for preparation and response. In addition, a strategic plan for future innovations in AI-driven crisis mitigation is examined.

By the end of this chapter, readers will understand how AI is transforming crisis management, its advantages and challenges, and strategies to fully utilise AI while minimising risks.

The Role of AI in Crisis Management

Understanding Crisis Management

Crises can take many forms, ranging from natural disasters to economic collapses, each with its own unique challenges. In this section, some of the most critical crisis categories are described, along with some challenges specific to the crisis.

- **Natural Disasters**
  Natural disasters, such as earthquakes, hurricanes, floods, and wildfires, cause large-scale devastation, often displacing communities and overwhelming emergency response teams. Because of the

unpredictability, early detection systems are critical. The severity of these events requires efficient relief distribution and real-time situational awareness.

- **Public Health Crises**

  Global health crises, such as the COVID-19 pandemic, Ebola outbreaks, and seasonal flu epidemics, put immense pressure on healthcare systems and governments. Mitigation strategies include using AI for the timely detection of outbreaks, using data to drive decisions, and ensuring effective communication with the public.

- **Cybersecurity Threats**

  Critical threats have increased with the rising use of digital dependence and the accompanying risks of cyberattacks, data breaches, ransomware, and misinformation campaigns. Real-time threat detection with AI can prevent sensitive data compromises, infrastructure disruptions, and financial losses.

- **Economic Crises**

  Economic crises, including financial meltdowns and supply chain disruptions, have widespread implications for the public. AI provides resources through predictive analytics and data-driven risk assessments to effectively respond.

Each crisis type demands a structured approach to mitigation, preparedness, response, and recovery. Traditionally, crisis management has relied on manual coordination, human decision-making, and established protocols. However, AI transforms crisis management by making responses faster and more efficient, and with a more innovative approach (Figure 4.1).

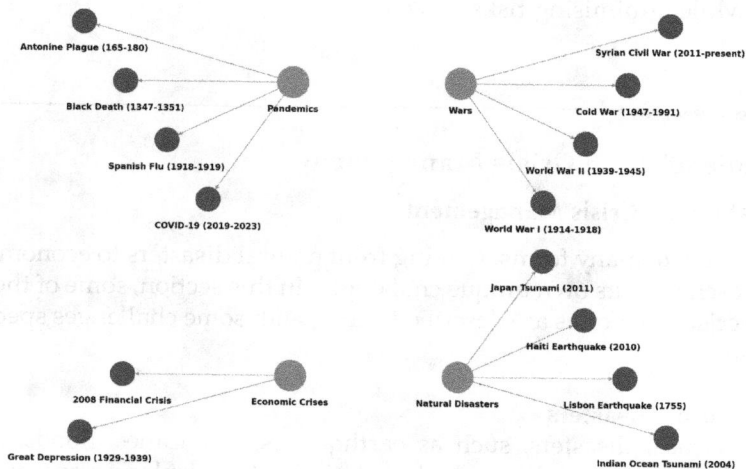

FIGURE 4.1
World crisis.

Traditional Crisis Management vs. AI-Driven Approaches

Traditional Crisis Management

Traditional crisis management relies heavily on human expertise, predefined response plans, and historical data. While effective in many cases, these methods have significant limitations, particularly in dealing with complex, large-scale crises that require real-time decision-making.

Key Characteristics of Traditional Crisis Management

- **Reactive Approach:** Crisis response is often initiated after an event, limiting preventive measures.
- **Manual Data Processing:** Information is gathered through reports, surveys, and news sources, leading to delays and potential inaccuracies.
- **Human-Centric Decision-Making:** Experts analyse situations and determine appropriate actions, which can be slow and influenced by cognitive biases.
- **One-Size-Fits-All Solutions:** Many crises plan provide general guidelines, making plans less adaptable to unique, evolving situations.

While traditional methods have served well, modern crises increasing complexity and urgency require more dynamic and technology-driven solutions.

AI-Driven Crisis Management: A Paradigm Shift

AI revolutionises crisis management by introducing capabilities that enhance every crisis response phase, from early warning systems to recovery efforts.

Key Advancements of AI in Crisis Management

- **Early Warning through Predictive Analytics**
  AI-powered algorithms analyse historical data, real-time environmental conditions, and social trends to predict potential crises before they occur. For example, AI models forecast natural disasters like hurricanes with higher accuracy, allowing for early evacuation. In the COVID-19 outbreak, AI analysed global health reports to detect the outbreak before the World Health Organization (WHO)'s official announcement of the pandemic.
- **Real-Time Monitoring and Data Processing**
  Real-time insights are provided by AI's ability to process massive amounts of data from various sources, including social media,

satellite imagery, sensors, and news reports. Two examples include how satellite imagery tracks wildfires or floods to aid in relief efforts, and the use of cybersecurity tools to quickly prevent data breaches.

- **Simulations**
  Simulating a variety of scenarios with AI helps decision-makers customise response strategies. Simulations include everything from pandemic containment strategies to building chatbots that can provide support for emergency call centres during a crisis.

- **Managing Public Communication**
  AI-powered fact-checking tools and NLP algorithms can detect and counter false information, preventing panic and confusion. During COVID-19, AI flagged false claims on social media. Communication with the public during a crisis can be disseminated more quickly and accurately using chatbots.

⚲ SIDEBAR: THE FOUR PILLARS OF AI-DRIVEN CRISIS MANAGEMENT

- **Predictive Analytics**—Anticipates disasters and outbreaks
- **Real-Time Monitoring**—Provides situational awareness
- **Decision Support and Simulation**—Recommends optimal actions
- **Automated Communication**—Keeps the public informed and calm

Optimising Response and Resource Allocation

During an emergency, it is essential that rescue personnel, medical supplies, and other types of aid effectively reach those impacted. AI optimised responses during COVID-19 to provide medical equipment to high-risk areas first; in other disasters, AI-powered drones deliver food and medical aid to impacted areas.

The Future of AI in Crisis Management

While AI offers unprecedented capabilities in crisis response, challenges remain. Ethical concerns, including bias in AI models, data privacy issues, and the need for human oversight, must be addressed to ensure the responsible deployment of AI. However, as AI continues to evolve, its role in crisis management will expand, leading to faster, more thoughtful, and more coordinated responses to global emergencies.

There are many benefits to integrating AI with traditional crisis management frameworks operated by governments, organisations, and emergency response teams. AI has the potential to strengthen preparedness, minimise damage, and save lives. AI-driven crisis management marks a fundamental shift in how humanity confronts uncertainty and disaster.

AI Technologies in Crisis Management

There are many different types of AI technology that help drive the transformation of use in crisis management. Thus far, this chapter has illustrated how AI is replacing traditional methods of emergency management and enhancing human decision-making capabilities. AI technologies such as ML, NLP, computer vision, and automation are revolutionising how governments, organisations, and emergency responders tackle crises. This section examines different AI technologies and how they are applied in crisis management.

Machine Learning and Predictive Analytics

ML enables robust predictive analytics, allowing organisations to anticipate crises before they occur. ML models identify patterns and predict potential threats by analysing historical data, sensor inputs, and real-time events, giving authorities time to act.

Applications in Crisis Management

- **Predicting Natural Disasters:**
  - AI-driven weather forecasting models predict hurricanes, floods, and wildfires, helping authorities take preventive action. Earthquake prediction models analyse seismic data to estimate the likelihood of future tremors.
- **Forecasting in Disease Outbreaks:**
  - ML-powered epidemiological models track disease spread, detect early outbreaks, and help form public health strategies.
  - Predictive analytics helped identify the COVID-19 outbreak before official reports, using AI-driven monitoring of health-related searches and news.
- **Detecting Cybersecurity Threats:**
  - AI detects anomalies in network traffic, identifying cyber threats such as malware, phishing attacks, and data breaches before threats escalate.

Natural Language Processing for Communication

Enhancing Communication during Crises

Accurate and timely communication is critical in high-stakes situations. NLP, a branch of AI, can extract information from large amounts of text, categorise the content, and produce summaries of the data to aid in developing crisis-related messages. It is essential that these messages are transparent, trustworthy, and relevant to the audience.

Applications in Crisis Management

- **AI-Powered Chatbots and Virtual Assistants:**
  - Governments and emergency response agencies deploy AI chatbots to provide real-time updates on disasters, public health measures, and emergency guidelines.
  - Chatbots, like the WHO's COVID-19 information bot, responded to millions of queries, reducing strain on helplines.
- **Misinformation Detection and Fact-Checking:**
  - AI-driven NLP models analyse social media, news, and online platforms to detect false or misleading information.
  - Google's Fact Check Tools and Facebook's AI-driven misinformation filters helped combat COVID-19 falsehoods by flagging misleading content.
- **Public Sentiment Analysis:**
  - NLP evaluates public sentiment on social media and news platforms to gauge public perception and emotional responses during crises.
  - NLP sentiment analysis alerts authorities to misinformation-driven panic or discontent, allowing appropriate intervention.

By leveraging NLP, AI promotes efficient and transparent communication so that misinformation does not exacerbate a challenging situation.

💡 **QUICK NOTE:** *NLP not only decodes meaning but also tracks public sentiment—crucial for determining the tone of government responses.*

Computer Vision for Assessment and Planning

Computer vision, a subset of AI that processes and analyses visual data, is crucial in disaster assessment. It enables responders to assess damage and swiftly prioritise relief efforts. AI-powered image recognition and remote sensing technologies help analyse images from satellites, drones, and surveillance cameras to amplify crisis response.

Applications in Crisis Management

- **Damage Assessment and Post-Disaster Analysis:**
  - AI-driven satellite imagery analysis helps assess infrastructure damage after hurricanes, floods, and earthquakes.
  - To optimise relief distribution, computer vision tools identify destroyed roads, collapsed buildings, or other infrastructure impacts.
- **Wildfire and Flood Monitoring:**
  - AI-powered drones with computer vision track wildfire spread and flood progression, assisting emergency teams.
  - Real-time mapping of affected areas ensures efficient evacuation planning.
- **Search and Rescue Operations:**
  - AI-driven facial recognition and thermal imaging help locate missing persons in disaster-struck areas.
  - Autonomous drones with AI-powered vision assist in scanning large areas that are unsafe for human responders.

Computer vision provides another tool to increase situational awareness, ensuring rapid and informed decision-making during disaster response and recovery.

AI-Driven Automation for Emergency Response

AI-driven automation accelerates emergency response by enabling faster, more informed decision-making and optimising resources and operations. This is accomplished by reducing human workload and automating critical tasks. Automation ensures swift execution of crisis protocols, allowing first responders to focus on life-saving actions.

Applications in Crisis Management

- **Automated Resource Allocation and Logistics:**
  - AI systems predict which areas need the most resources, optimising the distribution of medical supplies, food, and relief aid.
  - AI-powered drones and autonomous vehicles deliver medical supplies and emergency aid to remote or inaccessible areas.
- **AI in Healthcare Crisis Management:**
  - AI-driven diagnostic tools detect and monitor disease outbreaks, enabling early intervention.
  - Robotic process automation reduces hospital administrative burdens, automating patient record management and triage systems.

- **Cybersecurity and Automated Threat Response:**
  - AI-based cybersecurity tools autonomously detect, analyse, and neutralise cyber threats in real time, protecting critical infrastructure.
  - Automated security protocols help businesses and governments defend against large-scale cyberattacks during crises.

AI-driven automation supports efficiency, accuracy, and adaptability during crisis response. In turn, this can reduce human error and create faster response times.

AI technologies are reshaping crisis management to better anticipate, prepare for, and respond to crisis. Using predictive analytics to analyse historic trends and external factors can help identify the potential for natural disasters, financial crises, or health crises, before they escalate. Real-time monitoring through data, enables faster response times and can also detect misinformation to the public.

While AI offers remarkable advancements in crisis response, it must be implemented ethically, ensuring human oversight, transparency, and data privacy. As AI continues to evolve, its integration into crisis management will further enhance resilience, save lives, and mitigate damage in an increasingly unpredictable world.

Leveraging AI to Combat Misinformation and Enhance Communication

The Challenge of Misinformation in Crises

During a crisis, not all the information shared is accurate or helpful. There are two main types of false information that can cause harm:

- Misinformation is when someone shares something untrue without realising it's false—there's no intent to mislead.
- Disinformation, on the other hand, is intentionally created to deceive or cause harm.

Both can be dangerous, especially in emergencies. When false information spreads quickly—especially on social media—it can lead to confusion, fear, and a breakdown in trust in official sources. What's usually a strength during a crisis—fast communication—can become a weakness when bad information goes viral. This can slow down rescue efforts, delay the delivery of help, and even stop people from taking actions that could save lives.

How people make sense of competing stories or explanations during a crisis often shapes their behaviour. If conspiracy theories aren't addressed, they can easily drown out expert advice. That's why it's crucial that clear, accurate, and trustworthy information is available and easy to access when people need it most.

The Impact of Misinformation on Crisis Response

False information during a crisis can do serious damage. When people are misled—whether by mistake (misinformation) or on purpose (disinformation)—it can break down trust in the very agencies trying to help. If communities start doubting emergency services or government advice, they may make poor choices that put themselves and others at risk.

Not only does misinformation cause confusion, but it can also pull attention and resources away from where they're truly needed. Disinformation—deliberately false content—makes it even harder for people to tell what's true. In fast-moving situations like bushfires, that confusion can literally cost lives.

On top of that, disinformation often fuels fear and panic. When anxiety rises, people may start hoarding essentials like food, water, and fuel—creating shortages and making it even harder to respond to the crisis effectively.

Case Studies of Misinformation Spread in Past Crises (COVID-19, Natural Disasters)

- **COVID-19:** During the COVID-19 pandemic, misinformation about the virus's origin, transmission, and treatment spread rapidly online. False claims about masks being ineffective or even harmful, or that the Centers for Disease Control and Prevention (CDC) reported that the majority of those infected with COVID-19 always wore masks, led to confusion and resistance to public health measures. Conspiracy theories about the virus being a hoax or a bioweapon fuelled distrust in government and healthcare professionals.

Natural Disasters

False stories can make a bad situation worse—and real-life examples show just how damaging they can be. After Hurricane Helene, misleading narratives spread quickly, fuelling confusion and weakening public trust in the very agencies trying to help.

During the 2018 Kerala floods in India, fake videos went viral and disrupted rescue operations, wasting precious time and resources. Similarly, after Hurricane Irma in 2017, a bizarre but widely shared story claimed sharks were swimming on a flooded Florida highway—false, but enough to distract and mislead.

In Australia's devastating 2019/2020 bushfires, the hashtag #arsonemergency was used to spread disinformation, falsely blaming arson for the fires instead of climate conditions. This not only shifted public focus away from the real issues but also stirred division and confusion at a time when unity and clear communication were most needed.

AI Tools to Detect and Prevent Misinformation

AI provides a diverse set of tools for combating misinformation during crises, enabling faster and more accurate responses. These tools are broadly categorised as follows:

- **Fact-Checking Tools:**
    Fact-checking tools powered by AI help verify information quickly by comparing it against trusted sources. Using NLP, these tools can understand the context of a statement and flag anything that doesn't quite add up. They look at the words being used, check where the information is coming from, and judge how credible those sources are.

    Some tools go even further by using ML to spot common warning signs of misinformation—like overly emotional language or conspiracy-style messaging. When they flag something as false or misleading, they can also explain why, such as pointing out a lack of scientific evidence, unclear sourcing, or manipulative wording.

- **Social Media Monitoring:**
    NLP makes it possible to scan social media in real time and spot misinformation as it spreads. These systems can pick up on specific keywords, hashtags, and phrases linked to false stories, helping authorities track how misinformation is moving through the digital space.

    They also use sentiment analysis to understand how people feel about different claims—whether they're scared, angry, or confused—which helps identify which groups might be more vulnerable to false information. On top of that, AI tools can detect and flag fake accounts or bots that are actively pushing misinformation, making it easier to shut them down before they cause more harm.

- **Bots and Digital Assistants for Crisis Communication:**
    AI-powered chatbots and digital assistants are valuable tools for keeping the public informed during a crisis. They can answer common questions, offer safety tips, and guide people to essential services and resources—all in real time. Because they can be used across platforms like social media, messaging apps, and websites, they help ensure accurate information reaches as many people as possible.

Chatbots also play a key role in fighting misinformation. When someone asks about a false claim, the chatbot can respond with facts and point them to reliable sources. Plus, these tools can track what people are asking about most. That information helps authorities fine-tune their messaging and quickly address new or growing concerns in the community.

The Role of AI Agents in Misinformation Detection and Prevention

AI agents are intelligent systems designed to analyse, detect, and combat misinformation autonomously across various digital platforms. These agents work in real time, continuously learning from evolving patterns of misinformation and improving accuracy over time. Below are different ways AI agents contribute to managing misinformation:

- **Real-Time Misinformation Detection**
  - AI agents use NLP and ML to scan vast amounts of digital content and identify misleading or false information. One method uses semantic analysis, where agents analyse the context, tone, and structure of online articles, social media posts, and news to detect misinformation patterns. Fact-checking automation, mentioned above, can flag potentially false claims by cross-referencing statements with verified databases such as government reports, trusted news sources, and scientific studies. A third method is multilingual processing where AI agents can detect misinformation in multiple languages, addressing disinformation on a global scale.
  Example:
  During the COVID-19 pandemic, AI-driven tools like Google's Fact Check Tools and Facebook's AI moderation systems helped detect and limit the spread of false claims about vaccines and treatments.
- **Identifying Deepfake and Synthetic Media**

? **DID YOU KNOW:** *Over 90% of deepfakes online are undetectable by the human eye. AI is our best line of defence.*

Deepfake technology creates highly realistic but entirely fake videos, images, and audio that can be used to spread false narratives. There are several methods, using computer vision and audio forensics, to analyse media content and detect synthetic alterations.

- **Facial and Voice Recognition:** AI agents compare videos with original content to identify digital alterations.

- **Pixel and Metadata Analysis:** AI tools analyse image inconsistencies, shadows, and metadata to detect manipulated media.
- **Generative Adversarial Networks Detection:** AI models are trained to identify deepfake content by distinguishing AI-generated patterns from authentic media.
  Example:
  Deepfake detection tools developed by Microsoft and DARPA have been used to identify altered videos in political campaigns and social media misinformation.

- **Social Media Monitoring and Trend Analysis**
  AI agents continuously monitor social media platforms, online forums, and news websites to detect misinformation trends before they escalate.
  - **Network Analysis:** AI maps how misinformation spreads by analysing user interactions, hashtags, and retweets.
  - **Bot and Troll Detection:** AI agents use behavioural pattern analysis to identify inauthentic accounts that magnify misinformation.
  - **Sentiment Analysis:** AI assesses public reactions to misinformation, detecting emotional triggers used in viral disinformation campaigns.
  Example:
  Twitter's AI-driven moderation system detects and limits the spread of harmful misinformation by analysing trending discussions and flagging misleading content.

- **Automated Response and Counter-Misinformation Strategies**
  AI agents detect misinformation and actively engage with users, debunk false claims, and promote factual content.
  - **AI Chatbots for Fact-Checking:** Automated AI-powered chatbots provide real-time, accurate responses to users' misinformation-related queries.
  - **Algorithmic Content Prioritisation:** AI agents adjust search rankings and recommendation algorithms to promote credible sources over misleading ones.
  - **Automated Alerts and Warnings:** AI tools generate instant alerts to warn users about flagged misinformation.
  Example:
  WhatsApp's AI-powered chatbot, developed in partnership with fact-checking organisations, allowed users to verify forwarded messages during the COVID-19 pandemic.

AI in Public Communication and Awareness

AI-Driven Chatbots for Real-Time Crisis Updates

🔖 SIDEBAR: CRISIS COMMUNICATION—CHATBOTS VS. HUMAN HELPLINES

Feature	AI Chatbot	Human Helpline
Availability	24/7	Business hours
Simultaneous Responses	Unlimited	Limited by staff availability
Response Time	Instant	May experience long wait times
Empathy and Judgement	Limited	High

AI-powered chatbots provide instant, automated, and interactive responses to public queries, ensuring real-time information dissemination during emergencies. Unlike traditional call centres, which may be overwhelmed during crises, AI chatbots operate 24/7 and handle millions of simultaneous interactions, reducing wait times and the spread of misinformation.

Key Features of AI-Driven Crisis Chatbots

1. **Real-Time Information Sharing**
   AI chatbots provide up-to-date information on disasters, public health guidelines, evacuation procedures, and government announcements.
   - Chatbots integrate with official data sources like WHO, CDC, and national disaster agencies to deliver verified updates.
   - Example: During COVID-19, chatbots, such as the WHO's AI chatbot on WhatsApp, provided real-time information on symptoms, vaccination, and preventive measures.

2. **Multilingual Support for Diverse Audiences**
   - AI chatbots use NLP to interact in multiple languages, ensuring accessibility for diverse populations.
   - Example: The FEMA chatbot in the US provides crisis assistance in English and Spanish to reach wider audiences.

3. **Interactive Emergency Assistance**
   - Chatbots answer frequently asked questions; assist impacted populations in finding shelters, hospitals, or food distribution centres; and guide people through emergency steps.

- Use of geolocation to **redirect users to local emergency services** based on location.

4. **Reducing Misinformation Spread**
   - AI chatbots cross-verify user queries against reliable databases to prevent the spread of false or misleading information.
   - Example: Google's Fact-Checking AI Bot helps debunk misinformation by referencing verified sources.

There are multiple positive impacts of AI chatbots during a crisis response, including reducing strain on human emergency responders and operating 24/7 to ensure constant communication with the public. Chatbots also provide instant, reliable information and help prevent the spread of misinformation.

💡 **QUICK NOTE:** *Multilingual NLP lets chatbots deliver life-saving instructions in multiple languages instantly.*

✔ **Personalised AI-Driven Public Alerts and Warnings**
AI systems analyse geospatial, environmental, and social media data to generate personalised alerts for individuals based on their location and risk factors. Unlike traditional mass notifications, which may be generic or irrelevant to some recipients, AI-driven alerts are context-aware and personalised for each recipient.

Using Enhancing Public Alerts

1. **Real-Time Disaster Warnings**
   AI models **predict natural disasters** like hurricanes, wildfires, and earthquakes and send **timely alerts** to at-risk populations.
   - Example: **Google's AI-Powered Flood Forecasting System** provides hyper-local alerts to residents in flood-prone areas.

2. **Custom Alerts Based on Individual Risk**
   AI integrates historical data, location tracking, and behavioural analysis to send personalised evacuation warnings and risk assessments.
   - Example: AI-driven systems in Japan's earthquake alert network notify users based on their proximity to the epicentre.

3. **Traffic and Evacuation Route Optimisation**
   AI analyses real-time traffic data to provide optimised evacuation routes, ensuring faster and safer evacuations.
   - Example: Waze Crisis Response AI provides alternate routes to avoid blocked roads during disasters.

4. Health and Pandemic-Related Alerts

AI alerts individuals about virus exposure risks, quarantine guidelines, and vaccination centres during public health emergencies.

- For example, Apple and Google's AI-based COVID-19 Exposure Notification System alerted users about potential virus exposure through Bluetooth tracking.

Benefits of AI-Driven Alerts

- **Faster, localised warnings** that reach individuals at risk.
- **Customised notifications** based on personal safety concerns.
- **Prevents congestion** by optimising evacuation routes.
- **Enhances public safety** by reducing exposure to hazards.

Managing Public Sentiment and Misinformation Control

Misinformation spreads rapidly during crises, fuelling panic, confusion, and anxiety. AI-driven sentiment analysis and misinformation detection tools are crucial in correcting misleading narratives before they escalate.

How AI Monitors and Controls Misinformation

1. **Sentiment Analysis for Crisis Monitoring**
   - AI analyses millions of social media posts and news articles to detect public sentiment and emotional responses to crises.
   - Governments and organisations use sentiment tracking to gauge public perception and adjust their messaging strategies accordingly.
   - Example: IBM Watson AI analyses global social media trends during crises to detect shifts in public sentiment.

2. **Real-Time Misinformation Detection and Fact-Checking**
   - AI-powered tools scan online content, detect fake news, and flag misleading posts.
   - NLP algorithms compare claims against verified sources to determine accuracy.
   - Example: Facebook's AI-driven misinformation detection system flagged COVID-19 conspiracy theories before they gained traction.

3. **Automated Content Moderation**
   - AI moderates online discussions by detecting harmful content, hate speech, and fake news.

- Example: YouTube's AI-powered moderation system automatically removes misleading medical information during pandemics.

4. **AI-Generated Counter-Misinformation Responses**
   - AI agents auto-generate fact-checked responses to counter viral misinformation.
   - Example: Twitter's Birdwatch AI system allows users to add fact-checking notes to misleading tweets.

Impact of AI on Public Sentiment and Misinformation Control

- **Prevents misinformation-driven panic** by promoting factual content.
- **Provides real-time tracking** of public emotions to guide crisis communication strategies.
- **Detects and removes harmful content** before it spreads widely.
- **Improves public trust** by ensuring crisis-related information is accurate and transparent.

By leveraging AI for the public, AI-driven public communication tools transform how authorities and organisations engage with the public during crises. AI-powered chatbots provide instant, reliable updates, while personalised AI alerts ensure targeted crisis warnings, and AI-based misinformation detection tools help maintain trust and prevent panic.

As AI evolves, its role in public crisis communication will become crucial to a safer, more informed society. Through awareness and crisis communication, governments and institutions reduce the impact of misinformation and ensure that people receive timely and accurate crisis-related information.

Case Studies of AI in Global Crisis Management

Case Study: COVID-19 Pandemic Response

The COVID-19 pandemic stands as a defining global crisis of the 21st century—one that has tested the resilience of governments, overwhelmed healthcare systems, and disrupted economies worldwide. The speed, scale, and complexity of the outbreak revealed critical gaps in traditional crisis response mechanisms. In the face of such a challenge, AI emerged as a powerful ally, enabling faster decision-making, more targeted interventions, and effective public engagement.

? **DID YOU KNOW:** *BlueDot flagged the COVID-19 outbreak 9 days before WHO's official statement—using only AI-driven analysis.*

AI technologies were used across several key areas of the pandemic response, making a measurable difference in how the world detected, managed, and recovered from the crisis:

AI-Driven Epidemiological Modelling and Outbreak Prediction

AI models were instrumental in predicting COVID-19 outbreaks, enabling early interventions.

- BlueDot, a Canadian AI startup, identified early signs of the COVID-19 outbreak in Wuhan, China, 9 days before the WHO issued an official statement. It used ML and NLP to scan news reports, airline ticketing data, and health records to predict outbreaks.
- AI-powered models from Johns Hopkins University and MIT used real-time data analytics to forecast virus transmission rates, helping governments allocate healthcare resources efficiently.
- Google's DeepMind AI analysed global health data to detect emerging hotspots and provide outbreak trends.

AI-Assisted Drug Discovery and Vaccine Development

AI significantly accelerated drug discovery by identifying potential treatments and vaccine candidates.

- DeepMind's AlphaFold accurately predicted protein structures, helping researchers understand the virus's behaviour and identify possible drug targets.
- Moderna and BioNTech/Pfizer used AI-driven algorithms to speed up mRNA vaccine development, reducing the traditional timeline from years to months.
- AI tools analysed thousands of existing drugs to identify existing treatments or medicines, including Remdesivir, for treating COVID-19.

Chatbots and Virtual Assistants for Public Health Communication

To handle the overwhelming volume of public inquiries, AI-driven chatbots and virtual assistants played a key role in crisis communication.

- WHO partnered with WhatsApp and Facebook to launch AI-powered chatbots, providing real-time information about COVID-19 symptoms and preventive measures.

- Countries like India, the United States, and the United Kingdom deployed AI chatbots to reduce call centre congestion, allowing health authorities to focus on critical cases.
- AI-powered virtual assistants helped track COVID-19 symptoms and schedule vaccination appointments, reducing the burden on healthcare staff.

Utilising AI in all these areas during the pandemic enabled a much more efficient and effective response, and at a faster pace than had been experienced in any prior health crisis.

Case Study: Natural Disaster Management

Natural disaster management is transforming through AI with improvements seen in early warnings and assessing impacts. AI in disaster response helps optimise resource allocation after a disaster and through AI assessments of impact helps determine what resources are needed. ML and computer vision technologies enable real-time analysis, ensuring faster and more effective emergency responses.

Satellite Imagery and AI for Disaster Impact Assessment

AI-powered satellite imagery analysis helps responders assess disaster damage quickly and efficiently.

- NASA and Google's AI-driven satellite imaging technology helped track wildfires in California, providing real-time updates on fire progression.
- The United Nations and IBM used AI-based image analysis to assess flood damage in Southeast Asia, helping relief agencies prioritise affected areas.
- AI models analysed post-earthquake satellite images in Haiti and Nepal, providing a damage severity index that guided emergency aid distribution.

AI-Powered Early Warning Systems

AI has enhanced early disaster warnings by analysing climate data, geological activity, and weather patterns to predict potential catastrophes.

- Japan's AI-powered earthquake warning system integrates seismic data and ML to provide seconds to minutes of advanced warning, allowing residents to seek shelter.

- Google's Flood Forecasting Initiative uses AI to predict river flooding up to 48 hours in advance, significantly improving evacuation planning in flood-prone regions.
- AI models developed by the National Oceanic and Atmospheric Administration (NOAA) forecast hurricanes with 30% greater accuracy than traditional meteorological models.

📌 SIDEBAR: CASE IN POINT—JAPAN'S EARTHQUAKE ALERT SYSTEM

- Japan's AI-powered early warning system uses seismic data and ML to provide alerts within seconds of tremors, buying critical time for evacuation and infrastructure safety.

Predictive Analytics for Resource Allocation and Response Optimisation

AI ensures that relief supplies, medical aid, and emergency teams are deployed efficiently during disasters.

- The Red Cross and IBM Watson use AI to analyse real-time reports from disaster zones, ensuring that aid is delivered to the most affected areas first.
- AI-driven logistics platforms optimise supply chain routes, ensuring emergency supplies reach disaster-hit areas faster.
- Predictive models help governments pre-position emergency response teams based on AI-generated disaster risk assessments.

By leveraging AI for disaster prediction, damage assessment, and optimised response, emergency agencies can reduce casualties, minimise economic losses, and improve resilience to natural disasters.

Case Study: Cybersecurity Crisis Management

As cyber threats become increasingly sophisticated, AI has become a vital tool for detecting and mitigating cybersecurity crises, protecting sensitive data, and preventing financial and reputational damage.

AI-Driven Threat Detection and Response

AI-powered cybersecurity solutions provide real-time detection and automated responses to cyberattacks.

- Darktrace's AI-driven cybersecurity system detects network anomalies, identifying potential breaches before they occur.

- Google's Chronicle AI platform continuously scans enterprise networks for threats, using ML to predict and neutralise cyberattacks.
- AI-based fraud detection systems in financial institutions monitor transactional patterns to detect potential fraud, preventing major economic crises.

Automated Security Monitoring and Anomaly Detection

AI enhances cybersecurity monitoring by analysing millions of data points in real time to detect suspicious activity.

- IBM's Watson for Cybersecurity processes large datasets, detecting patterns of cyber threats and providing automated insights for IT teams.
- AI-powered intrusion detection systems identify unusual login patterns and block potential hacking attempts in real time.
- ML models detect malware and ransomware threats before they execute, reducing the risk of large-scale data breaches.

AI-Powered Risk Assessment and Mitigation Strategies

? DID YOU KNOW: *Cybercrime surged by over 600% during the COVID-19 pandemic—AI-driven threat detection tools helped prevent billions in losses.*

AI provides predictive analytics for cybersecurity risk assessments, helping organisations proactively defend against threats.

- AI tools analyse historical cyberattack patterns to predict which industries or organisations are at the highest risk.
- AI-powered phishing detection systems flag malicious emails and prevent users from interacting with fraudulent links.
- Banking institutions use AI-driven fraud detection algorithms to monitor transactions, blocking real-time fraudulent activities.

Case Study: AI in Protecting the 2020 US Elections

During the 2020 US elections, AI cybersecurity systems monitored voting infrastructure and detected attempts at misinformation campaigns, cyberattacks, and voter data breaches.

- Microsoft's Election Guard AI secured digital voting systems, preventing hacking attempts.

- AI-based social media monitoring tools flagged disinformation campaigns and fake news designed to manipulate voters.

By integrating AI in cybersecurity, organisations and governments can enhance digital defence mechanisms, detect cyber threats faster, and mitigate risks before they escalate into full-scale crises.

The case studies in this section demonstrate how AI is revolutionising crisis management across various domains. AI-driven solutions have significantly improved preparedness, detection, and mitigation strategies, from epidemiological modelling during pandemics to disaster response and cybersecurity defence. AI continues to evolve, promising even more advanced, real-time, and efficient crisis management solutions in the future. Governments, organisations, and humanitarian agencies must invest in AI-driven crisis management to enhance resilience, save lives, and protect critical infrastructure in an increasingly uncertain world.

AI Deployment Best Practices in Crisis Management

The deployment of AI in crisis management offers transformative benefits, through higher accuracy in predicting crises, faster decision-making during crises, and more efficient response times after crises. However, given the high stakes involved, AI must be deployed ethically, responsibly, and transparently. This section examines the ethical challenges and best practices for ensuring that AI is a reliable tool in crisis response.

Ethical Considerations in AI for Crisis Management

Bias and Fairness in AI Crisis Response Systems

AI systems are only as unbiased as the data on which they are trained. Bias in AI crisis management can lead to unequal treatment of affected populations, disproportionately impacting marginalised communities.

- **Incident Description:** During the COVID-19 pandemic, early AI-based diagnostic models performed better on populations with better representation in the training dataset, leading to disparities in healthcare access and risk assessment.
- **Impact and Consequences:** AI must be trained on diverse datasets representing regions, socioeconomic groups, and demographics to prevent biased decision-making in crisis scenarios.

- **Mitigation and Prevention:** To ensure equitable assistance, regular audits, fairness checks, and diverse data representation should be mandated in AI crisis systems.

Privacy Concerns in AI-Driven Surveillance and Data Collection

AI in crisis management often relies on large-scale data collection, including social media monitoring, GPS tracking, facial recognition, and health records. While these tools improve crisis response, they also pose serious privacy risks.

- **Incident Description:** During the COVID-19 pandemic, some governments implemented AI-powered contact tracing, raising concerns about surveillance overreach and citizen privacy violations.
- **Impact and Consequences:** AI systems should adhere to strict data governance policies, ensuring that personal data collection is transparent, consensual, and limited to crisis-specific use cases.
- **Mitigation and Prevention:** Implementing privacy-preserving AI techniques, such as federated learning and data anonymisation, can balance effectiveness and privacy protection.

Transparency and Accountability in AI Decision-Making

AI must be explainable, auditable, and accountable when it is used for crisis management decision-making due to the critical nature of crises. Lack of transparency in AI-driven crisis decision-making can lead to public distrust and resistance to AI adoption.

- **Incident Description:** AI-powered predictive policing systems have faced criticism for making opaque, unexplainable decisions, leading to unjustified arrests and racial profiling.
- **Impact and Consequences:** Crisis management AI must be designed with explainable AI (XAI) frameworks, which allow decision-makers to understand why and how AI makes specific recommendations.
- **Mitigation and Prevention:** Crisis management agencies should enforce AI accountability frameworks, ensuring human oversight in AI-driven crisis interventions.

Challenges and Limitations of AI in Crisis Management

Data reliability and Access Issues

AI systems depend on high-quality data to function effectively. However, data may be scarce, inaccurate, or rapidly changing during a crisis, affecting AI's reliability.

- **Incident Description:** Network failures and infrastructural damage in disaster-struck regions may delay data collection, making AI predictions less accurate.
- **Impact and Consequences:** Real-time crisis data often comes from multiple sources, including social media, news, and satellite imagery, increasing the risk of data inconsistency and misinformation.
- **Mitigation and Prevention:** AI models should incorporate data validation mechanisms to filter out noise, misinformation, and outdated insights while leveraging trusted data sources.

Dependence on AI vs. Human Decision-Making in High-Risk Scenarios

AI should support rather than replace human decision-makers in crisis response. Over-reliance on AI can be dangerous in unpredictable or novel situations, where human expertise is irreplaceable.

- **Incident Description:** AI-driven earthquake prediction systems can forecast aftershocks, but evacuation and emergency response decisions require human judgement based on real-world conditions.
- **Impact and Consequences:** AI should act as an augmentative tool, providing decision support while allowing crisis managers to override AI recommendations when necessary.
- **Mitigation and Prevention:** AI crisis systems should include fail-safe mechanisms that allow human intervention in critical scenarios, ensuring human judgement prevails when AI is uncertain.

The Need for Continuous Model Training and Adaptation

Crises are dynamic, and AI models must continuously adapt to evolving data patterns. However, most AI models are trained on historical data, making them less effective in never-before-seen crises.

- **Incident Description:** Early COVID-19 AI models trained on Severe Acute Respiratory Syndrome (SARS) and Middle East Respiratory Syndrome (MERS) data struggled to adapt to the unique characteristics of COVID-19, requiring frequent retraining.
- **Impact and Consequences:** AI crisis management systems must be continuously updated with real-time data to improve predictive accuracy and relevance.
- **Mitigation and Prevention:** AI teams should establish continuous learning pipelines, where models ingest new crisis data and self-improve in real time.

Guidelines for Implementing AI Responsibly in Crisis Response

Best Practices for AI Governance and Policy

To ensure ethical AI deployment, governments and organisations must establish clear AI governance policies for crisis response.

- **Mandate AI Ethics Audits:** Conduct regular ethical reviews of AI models to detect bias, privacy risks, and moral concerns.
- **Define AI Accountability Measures:** Assign clear responsibility to human operators for AI-generated decisions in crisis scenarios.
- **Ensure Compliance with Global AI Ethics Standards:** Align AI crisis management practices with frameworks such as the OECD AI Principles, EU AI Act, and IEEE Ethically Aligned Design.

Collaboration Between AI Developers, Policymakers, and Crisis Management Teams

AI's effectiveness in crisis response depends on multidisciplinary collaboration.

- AI developers must collaborate closely with policymakers, emergency responders, healthcare professionals, and disaster relief agencies to design AI tools that meet real-world needs.
- Governments must invest in AI training for crisis responders, ensuring emergency teams can effectively interpret and act on AI recommendations.

Future Directions and Improvements in AI for Crisis Management

AI is still evolving, and its role in crisis management will continue to expand. Future improvements include the following:

- **XAI:** Increasing transparency in AI decision-making to ensure public trust.
- **Decentralised AI and Blockchain Integration:** Enhancing data security, privacy, and transparency in AI-driven crisis communication.
- **Autonomous AI Systems for Faster Response:** AI-powered drones, robotic rescue systems, and intelligent traffic routing to enhance disaster response.
- **Federated Learning for Privacy-Preserving AI:** Enabling AI to train on decentralised data sources without compromising individual privacy.

AI has the potential to revolutionise crisis management, but ethical and responsible deployment is crucial to maximise its benefits while minimising risks.

Addressing bias, privacy concerns, transparency, and governance challenges can help AI become a trusted ally in disaster response, public health management, and cybersecurity defence. However, human oversight, collaboration between stakeholders, and continuous AI adaptation are essential to ensuring AI remains a force for good in high-stakes crisis scenarios.

Organisations, governments, and AI researchers must collaborate to establish ethical AI frameworks, ensure responsible deployment, and continuously refine AI technologies. This will ultimately help the world be more prepared and resilient in future crises.

Conclusion

Summary of AI's Role in Crisis Management

AI has emerged as a transformative force in crisis management, revolutionising how governments, organisations, and emergency responders prepare for, respond to, and recover from crises. Through predictive analytics, real-time monitoring, decision automation, misinformation detection, and enhanced communication systems, AI has demonstrated its ability to improve crisis response effectiveness, minimise damage, and save lives.

- **Key Contributions of AI in Crisis Management Include:**
  - **Predictive Analytics and Early Warning Systems:** AI-driven models anticipate disasters, detect cybersecurity threats, and identify disease outbreaks before they escalate.
  - **Real-Time Monitoring and Situational Awareness:** AI leverages satellite imagery, Internet of Things sensors, and social media data to track disasters, environmental changes, and public sentiment.
  - **Automated Decision Support and Resource Optimisation:** AI recommends optimal strategies for response efforts, ensuring efficient allocation of emergency resources.
  - **Misinformation Detection and Fact-Checking:** AI-powered tools combat the spread of false information, ensuring public trust and accurate decision-making.
  - **AI-Driven Public Communication and Awareness:** AI-powered chatbots, digital assistants, and automated alert systems enhance crisis communication and ensure people receive timely, reliable updates.

AI has proven instrumental in enhancing resilience, reducing human workload, and enabling proactive, data-driven decision-making in high-risk situations across multiple domains, including pandemic response, natural disaster management, and cybersecurity defence.

The Future of AI-Driven Crisis Response and Resilience

As AI technology evolves, its role in crisis management will expand, making responses more accurate, efficient, and adaptive. Future advancements will likely include the following:

- **XAI:** Increasing transparency and trust in AI-driven decisions by making AI models interpretable and auditable.
- **AI-Powered Autonomous Systems:** Using drones, robotics, and intelligent automation to deliver aid, conduct search-and-rescue missions, and manage disaster logistics.
- **Decentralised AI and Blockchain Integration:** Strengthening data privacy and security in AI-driven decision-making.
- **Federated Learning and Privacy-Preserving AI:** Allowing AI to train on decentralised datasets without compromising personal privacy, ensuring responsible AI deployment.
- **Multimodal AI for Crisis Simulation and Preparedness:** AI-driven simulations will help train emergency responders and policymakers to better prepare for multiple types of crises.

While AI continues to drive speed, accuracy, and efficiency in crisis management, ensuring ethical implementation, human oversight, and governance frameworks are critical to maintaining public trust and effectiveness.

The Importance of Human–AI Collaboration in Managing Global Crises

? DID YOU KNOW: *85% of public safety agencies in developed countries plan to use AI-powered chatbots by 2027 for emergency alerts and citizen guidance.*

Despite AI's potential, crisis management cannot be fully automated—human expertise remains indispensable in high-stakes decision-making. AI must function as an augmentative tool, enhancing but not replacing human judgement. The most effective crisis response strategies involve collaboration between AI systems and human decision-makers.

To maximise AI's impact in crisis management, organisations must:

- **Ensure Human Oversight in AI Decision-Making:** AI should serve as a decision-support system, with final judgements made by human experts who can evaluate ethical, social, and contextual factors.

- **Invest in AI Training for Crisis Responders:** Emergency personnel, policymakers, and first responders should be trained in AI tools and analytics to effectively interpret and leverage AI insights.
- **Develop Ethical AI Governance Frameworks:** AI-driven crisis management must align with global ethical standards, such as transparency, fairness, and privacy protection.
- **Encourage Multi-Stakeholder Collaboration:** Governments, tech companies, humanitarian organisations, and researchers must collaborate to co-develop AI solutions that address real-world crisis challenges.

In an increasingly unpredictable world, AI and human collaboration are the key to building a global ability to cope with, recover from, and adapt to crises. An agile, informed, and effective response mitigates risks in future crises. By embracing AI responsibly, crisis management is better able to safeguard communities and reduce casualties.

Finally, AI in crisis management represents not just a technological evolution but a paradigm shift in how people predict, respond to, and recover from global crises. By integrating AI-driven efficiency with human intelligence, empathy, and ethical oversight, a future emerges where crises are managed with remarkable foresight and accuracy.

Chapter Questions

1. What is crisis management, and why is it essential in today's interconnected world?
2. How does AI improve traditional crisis management approaches?
3. What are the key types of crises AI can help manage?
4. How is machine learning used in predicting natural disasters and pandemics?
5. What role does real-time monitoring play in AI-driven crisis response?
6. How does simulation using AI assist in decision-making during a crisis?
7. What are the advantages of using AI for resource allocation during emergencies?
8. How does natural language processing help combat misinformation?
9. What is the difference between misinformation and disinformation?
10. How do AI-powered chatbots support public health communication?
11. What was AI's role in the early detection of the COVID-19 outbreak?
12. How has AI been applied in disaster damage assessment using satellite imagery?

13. How does AI enhance cybersecurity crisis management?
14. What ethical issues arise when using AI in crises?
15. Why is human oversight important in AI-based crisis decision-making?
16. What are some future innovations in AI for improving crisis resilience?

Note to Readers and Educators

Comprehensive answers and explanations to these chapter-end questions are available at www.sandeepbhalekar.com. The website also provides supplementary frameworks, teaching guidelines, and reference materials to support deeper understanding and classroom discussion.

Educators and facilitators can access additional resources, including presentation frameworks, assessment rubrics, and discussion prompts, to help integrate the concepts from this chapter into academic or professional learning environments.

Bibliography

BMJ Global Health. (2020). *Crisis Communication and Health Misinformation*. London: BMJ Publishing Group.

Brookings Institution. (2024). *Fighting Hurricane Misinformation Requires Aggressive Pushback*. Washington, DC: Brookings. https://www.brookings.edu/articles/fighting-hurricane-misinformation-requires-aggressive-pushback/

Bryghtpath LLC. (2023). *Misinformation during a Crisis*. Minneapolis: Bryghtpath. https://bryghtpath.com/misinformation-during-a-crisis/

Carnegie Endowment for International Peace. (2024). *FEMA, Helene Milton, and the $750 Misinformation Incident*. Washington, DC: Carnegie Endowment. https://carnegieendowment.org/posts/2024/10/fema-helene-milton-disaster-rumors-misinformation-750-dollars-why?lang=en

Central Washington University Libraries. (2022). *Fake News and Disinformation Research Guide*. Ellensburg: CWU. https://libguides.lib.cwu.edu/c.php?g=625394&p=4391900

DergiPark. (2024). *Understanding Crisis Rumours and Misinformation*. Istanbul: DergiPark.

European Journal of Public Health. (2024). *The Role of Communication in Crisis Events*. Oxford: Oxford University Press.

Homeland Security Today. (2023). *Confronting Misinformation during Disasters: Strategies for Crisis Communicators*. Washington, DC: Homeland Security Today. https://www.hstoday.us/featured/column-confronting-misinformation-during-disasters-strategies-for-crisis-communicators/

Journal of Health Communication. (2019). *Understanding Misinformation in Crisis Contexts*. London: Taylor & Francis.

Journal of Health Communication. (2023). *Combating Health Misinformation: Strategies and Challenges*. London: Taylor & Francis.

Mayo Clinic. (2024). *COVID-19 Myths and Facts*. Rochester: Mayo Foundation for Medical Education and Research. https://www.mayoclinic.org/diseases-conditions/coronavirus/in-depth/coronavirus-myths/art-20485720

MDPI. (2024). *Societies Journal: Tackling Misinformation during Disasters*. Basel: MDPI.

National Center for Biotechnology Information. (2023). *Social Media and Risk Perception in Disasters*. Bethesda: NCBI.

National Institutes of Health. (2021). *The COVID-19 Infodemic: Navigating a Flood of Misinformation*. Bethesda: NIH.

National Institutes of Health. (2022). *Crisis Misinformation during COVID-19: A Public Health Challenge*. Bethesda: NIH.

Nature Humanities and Social Sciences Communications. (2024). *Digital Misinformation in Disaster Events*. London: Nature Publishing Group.

Journal of Medical Internet Research. (2024). *Public Health Messaging and Crisis Misinformation During COVID-19*. Toronto: JMIR Publications.

SOAS University of London. (2022). *Disinformation during Natural Disasters: An Emerging Vulnerability*. London: SOAS. https://www.soas.ac.uk/about/blogs/disinformation-during-natural-disasters-emerging-vulnerability

START Center, University of Maryland. (2023). *A Process View of Crisis Misinformation: How Public Relations Professionals Detect and Manage Misinformation*. College Park: National Consortium for the Study of Terrorism and Responses to Terrorism. https://www.start.umd.edu/publication/process-view-crisis-misinformation-how-public-relations-professionals-detect-manage-and

United Nations Development Programme. (2023). *Misinformation in Times of Crisis*. New York: UNDP Eurasia. https://www.undp.org/eurasia/dis/misinformation

University of Melbourne. (2022). *Fake News in the Age of COVID-19*. Melbourne: Faculty of Business and Economics. https://fbe.unimelb.edu.au/newsroom/fake-news-in-the-age-of-covid-19

University of Melbourne. (2023). *Australia Isn't Immune to Disaster Disinformation*. Melbourne: Pursuit. https://pursuit.unimelb.edu.au/articles/australia-isnt-immune-to-disaster-disinformation

U.S. Department of Homeland Security. (2018). *Countering False Information on Social Media during Disasters and Emergencies*. Washington, DC: DHS. https://www.dhs.gov/sites/default/files/publications/SMWG_Countering-False-Info-Social-Media-Disasters-Emergencies_Mar2018-508.pdf

World Health Organization. (2022). *Infodemics and Misinformation Negatively Affect People's Health Behaviours—New WHO Review Finds*. Copenhagen: WHO Europe. https://www.who.int/europe/news-room/01-09-2022-infodemics-and-misinformation-negatively-affect-people-s-health-behaviours-new-who-review-finds

World Health Organization. (2023). *Chatbots in Crisis Communication: A Case Study*. Geneva: WHO. https://cdn.who.int/media/docs/default-source/science-translation/case-studies-1/cs7_chatbots.pdf?sfvrsn=4fa08841_4

World Organisation for Animal Health. (2023). *Tackling Misinformation to Enforce Efforts in Global Disaster Risk Reduction*. Paris: WOAH. https://www.woah.org/en/article/tackling-misinformation-to-enforce-efforts-in-global-disaster-risk-reduction/

5

AI and Workforce Transformation

As organisations navigate the evolving work landscape in 2025, artificial intelligence (AI) has transitioned from a peripheral innovation to a fundamental force reshaping multiple industries. The integration of AI into the workforce marks a shift in job roles, the emergence of new skill requirements, and a heightened emphasis on human–AI collaboration. While concerns over job displacement persist, research indicates that AI is more likely to transform and augment jobs rather than replace them, creating new opportunities in sectors such as healthcare, finance, and technology.

This chapter explores the myths and realities surrounding AI's impact on employment, highlighting its role as a tool for augmentation rather than replacement. AI boosts workforce productivity by automating repetitive tasks, enabling employees to concentrate on innovation and strategy. As industries adopt AI-driven solutions, workforce expectations are shifting, necessitating new skill sets that combine technical proficiency—such as AI literacy, programming, and data analysis—with essential soft skills like adaptability, critical thinking, and emotional intelligence.

The chapter further explores corporate reskilling initiatives, highlighting how organisations invest in training programs, micro-credentialing, and online learning platforms to prepare employees for AI-driven roles. Case studies from leading companies, such as Amazon and IBM, illustrate the effectiveness of structured reskilling strategies in empowering employees to thrive in an AI-augmented environment.

The role of educational institutions is further explored, highlighting the necessity for AI-integrated curricula, collaboration between industry and academia, and lifelong learning to adequately prepare future professionals for an AI-driven future economy.

The final section explores the implications of AI-driven workforce transformation, including ethical considerations, workforce policy interventions, and the evolving collaboration between humans and AI. By embracing these changes, organisations can harness AI's potential to boost productivity, innovation, and economic growth while ensuring a fair transition for workers. Continuous learning, adaptability, and human–machine synergy will define career success in this AI-driven future.

DOI: 10.1201/9781003626503-5

✏ **SIDEBAR: UNDERSTANDING AUGMENTATION VS. AUTOMATION**

- **Augmentation:** AI supports humans by automating tasks, enabling creativity, decision-making, and problem-solving.
- **Automation:** AI fully replaces tasks previously performed by humans.
- **Example:** In customer service, AI chatbots handlefrequently asked questions (FAQs) (automation), while human agents resolve complex issues (augmentation).

Introduction to Workforce Transformation through AI

Integrating AI into the workforce is not just a trend but a significant transformation in the evolving landscape of work. The redefinition of job roles marks the emergence of new skills and a fundamental change in how organisations operate. The narrative surrounding AI often swings between fears of job displacement and excitement about its potential to enhance human capabilities. Dissecting the myths and the realities of AI's impact on jobs, recognising its role as a tool for augmentation rather than replacement, and examining how it reshapes industry skills are required to process this transformation.

💡 **QUICK NOTE:** *AI augments human talent—organisations that embrace both will lead the future of work.*

The Impact of AI on Jobs: Myths vs. Reality

The conversation around AI often highlights fears of widespread job losses. However, research indicates that AI is more likely to create jobs than eliminate them. The World Economic Forum projects that AI could generate 97 million new jobs in the near future, particularly in healthcare, finance, and technology sectors. Many existing jobs are being transformed rather than eliminated. For example, roles in data analysis and machine learning are in high demand as organisations look to harness AI's capabilities effectively.

Furthermore, the notion that AI will completely replace human workers ignores that many tasks demand human judgement, creativity, and emotional intelligence—traits that AI simply cannot replicate. Research from Accenture highlights that organisations utilising generative AI have experienced 2.5 times higher revenue growth and 2.4 times greater productivity, suggesting that AI enhances rather than supplants human effort.

AI as a Tool for Augmentation Rather Than Replacement

AI's primary role in the workforce is an augmentation tool. It empowers employees by automating repetitive tasks and providing analytical support, allowing people to focus on higher-level responsibilities that require critical thinking and creativity. For example, in healthcare settings, AI assists with data analysis for diagnostics while leaving complex decision-making to human professionals.

This augmentation approach fosters an environment where employees can enhance their productivity, and innovate without fear of obsolescence. Organisations increasingly recognise the importance of effectively upskilling their workforce to work alongside these tools. Companies are investing in training programs to ensure employees possess the necessary skills to fully adopt and leverage AI technologies.

How AI Is Changing Industry Skill Requirements

Integrating AI into various industries has led to significant changes in skill requirements. Today's workforce must adapt to meet the demands of an increasingly digital economy. This shift necessitates a broader skill set; workers must be proficient in traditional job functions, possess digital literacy, and be familiar with AI tools.

💡 **QUICK NOTE:** *Soft skills are no longer optional. Creativity, empathy, and adaptability are irreplaceable human strengths.*

Key skills in demand are as follows:

- **Technical Skills:** For IT workers, proficiency in data analysis, machine learning, and programming languages is needed.
- **Soft Skills:** All employees require enhanced communication, creativity, and emotional intelligence, as these skills complement technical abilities.
- **AI Literacy:** Non-IT employees need to understand how to interact with AI systems effectively as a key differentiator for job seekers.

As industries evolve, workers who embrace these changes and invest in continuous learning will likely have a competitive advantage in the job market.

Workforce transformation through AI represents both challenges and opportunities. By focusing on how jobs will evolve, similar to the movement from the industrial age to the knowledge age, organisations can better prepare for a future where technology supports rather than replaces the human workforce. As industries adapt to these changes, fostering a culture of continuous learning is essential for success in this new era of work.

Human–Machine Collaboration in the Workplace

Human–machine collaboration is revolutionising the modern workplace. By strategically integrating AI technologies, organisations can leverage the unique strengths of humans and the benefits of AI. AI benefits include large-scale data processing and automation of repetitive tasks, while humans can focus on innovation and tasks that require critical thinking and empathy.

The Importance of Human Oversight in AI-Augmented Decision-Making

While AI systems excel at processing vast amounts of data quickly and accurately, human oversight remains crucial in AI-augmented decision-making. Human workers are needed to interpret context and consider ethical implications. This ensures that decisions align with organisational values and broader societal impacts.

- **Nuance and Context:**
  Humans can interpret details that impact meaning or emotion and apply common sense, critical in complex decision-making scenarios where AI algorithms may struggle.
- **Ethical Considerations:**
  Human oversight ensures that AI-driven decisions adhere to ethical standards, preventing potential biases and unintended consequences.

AI as a Productivity Enhancer, Not a Replacement

AI should be viewed as a valuable tool to automate routine and time-consuming tasks that enhance human productivity, allowing people to focus on human skills required for business success, like customer service or sales. By automating routine and time-consuming tasks, AI frees human employees to focus on skills that augment data, such as innovating through new ideas or identifying bias.

- **Automation of Repetitive Tasks:**
  AI can more efficiently handle tasks such as data entry, analysis, and categorisation than humans, allowing employees to concentrate on higher-value, uniquely human activities.
- **Enhanced Efficiency:**
  Human–machine collaboration streamlines processes, reduces errors, and improves overall productivity, benefiting employees and the organisation.

Case Studies of Industries Effectively Leveraging AI

Numerous industries have successfully integrated AI to improve their operations and outcomes:

- **Manufacturing:**
  In manufacturing, human–machine collaboration optimises productivity by automating repetitive tasks and those requiring heavy lifting. This improves safety, maximises flexibility, and allows human workers to manage systems, design new products, perform process upgrades and other areas of efficiency.
- **Healthcare:**
  AI assists healthcare professionals by processing large datasets to improve diagnostic accuracy and treatment planning. This collaboration enables doctors and nurses to focus more on building trust with patients and listening to patient concerns.
- **Logistics:**
  Companies like Amazon utilise AI for inventory management and supply chain optimisation, significantly reducing costs and improving customer experiences. AI-driven systems predict demand, optimise routes, and manage warehouse operations, while human workers handle exceptions and make customer-centric decisions.

Creating a human–machine collaboration, organisations can create more efficient, innovative, and fulfilling workplaces, ensuring they remain competitive in a rapidly changing world. This approach enhances productivity and improves employee satisfaction as they learn new roles and to maximise their potential and the skills needed for the future of work.

Challenges in Workforce Transition

The transition to an AI-driven economy presents significant challenges for employers and employees. Adapting to new tech can create skills gaps and resistance to the expected change, requiring thoughtful workforce management strategies. Identifying these challenges is crucial for effectively navigating the change management effort with implementation.

Resistance to Change and Fear of Automation

Change represents uncertainty, and because most humans seek stability, transitioning to AI can cause resistance. One of the most significant barriers to workforce transition is employees' resistance to change. Many workers fear that automation and AI will lead to job displacement, creating anxiety about their job security. This fear can manifest in various ways, including reduced morale and reluctance to adopt new technologies.

💡 **QUICK NOTE:** *Resistance to AI often reflects a fear of the unknown. Clear communication builds trust.*

- **Cultural Resistance:**
  Organisations often encounter cultural resistance when implementing AI systems. Employees may be accustomed to traditional workflows and sceptical about the benefits of automation. This scepticism can create friction between humans and machines, limiting the potential advantages of AI integration.

- **Addressing Fear:**
  Organisations must foster a culture of transparency and communication to mitigate these fears. Humans are adaptable, provided they understand how AI augments rather than replaces. Additionally, involving employees in the transition process through training programs and leader support provides a sense of empowerment.

Bridging the Skills Gap: Employers vs. Employees Perspectives

❓ **DID YOU KNOW:** *63% of employers report skill gaps as the biggest barrier to AI adoption (World Economic Forum, 2025).*

The skills gap remains a critical challenge in workforce transitions. According to the World Economic Forum's 2025 Future of Jobs Report, 63% of employers cite skill gaps as a primary barrier to business transformation. This gap reflects a disconnect between the skills employers need and those employees possess.

- **Employers Perspective:**
  Employers are increasingly seeking candidates with advanced technical skills related to AI, data analysis, and digital literacy. However, many existing workers may lack these competencies due to inadequate training or educational opportunities.

- **Employees Perspective:**
  Conversely, employees may feel overwhelmed by the rapid pace of technological change and uncertain which skills to prioritise for their careers. This disconnect can lead to frustration on both sides, as employers struggle to find qualified candidates while employees feel unprepared for evolving job requirements.

- **Strategies for Bridging the Gap:**
  To bridge the gap, organisations should invest in comprehensive reskilling programs tailored to current and future needs. Offering training opportunities that align with industry demands can help employees acquire relevant skills while promoting job security. Creating partnerships with educational institutions can also provide continuous learning and development pathways.

The Economic Impact of Workforce Shifts and Policy Interventions

The economic implications of workforce shifts driven by AI are profound. Specific sectors may experience significant job losses as industries evolve, while others see growth in needed jobs. Managing workforce shifts is essential to avoid income inequality.

- **Job Displacement vs. Job Creation:**
  While AI is expected to displace millions of jobs, it also has the potential to create new roles that require different skill sets. Policymakers must consider how to support workers affected by these shifts through targeted interventions such as retraining programs and unemployment benefits.
- **Policy Interventions:**
  Governments play a crucial role in facilitating workforce transitions by implementing policies promoting equitable training and education access. Initiatives such as universal basic income or wage subsidies for displaced workers can provide a safety net during periods of economic adjustment.

The challenges associated with workforce transitions in an AI-driven economy are multifaceted, encompassing resistance to change, skills gaps, and economic shifts. Organisations must have a plan to address these challenges that includes a culture of openness, investing in reskilling initiatives, and advocating for supportive policies. By doing so, they can navigate the complexities of workforce transformation while ensuring that employees and employers minimise disruption during AI implementation.

The Role of Educational Institutions in AI Readiness

Educational institutions play a pivotal role in preparing individuals for an AI-driven future. This involves integrating AI education into curricula, fostering industry–academia collaboration, and promoting continuous learning.

AI in Schools and Universities

Integrating AI education into school curricula is essential for developing a foundational understanding of AI among students. This includes:

- **Integrating AI Education into School Curricula:** Schools are beginning to incorporate AI concepts into various subjects to familiarise students with AI technologies.
- **Implementing Learning Platforms and Adaptive Education:** AI-driven platforms personalise learning experiences, tailoring content to individual student needs and paces.
- **Developing Problem-Solving and Computational Thinking Skills:** Educational programs emphasise problem-solving and computational thinking to equip students with the skills necessary to navigate AI-related challenges.

Industry–Academia Collaboration

Collaboration between universities and corporations ensures that AI education aligns with industry needs. This involves:

- **AI Training Partnerships between Universities and Corporations:** Universities are partnering with companies to offer specialised AI training programs that address specific industry requirements.
- **Apprenticeship and Internship Programs in AI-Driven Industries:** Apprenticeships and internships provide students with hands-on experience in AI-driven industries, bridging the gap between academic knowledge and practical application.
- **Government Initiatives Support AI Education and Workforce Development:** Government initiatives are supporting AI education through funding, resources, and policy frameworks that foster a skilled AI workforce. Bennett University, for example, aligns with India's AI Mission to strengthen its global leadership in AI.

Continuous Education and Learning

? DID YOU KNOW: *AI-driven employee training platforms personalise content delivery—boosting learning speed by 60%.*

The rapid evolution of AI necessitates a commitment to continuous learning. This includes:

- **Expanded Skill Sets:** Professionals need to continuously upskill to keep pace with advancements in AI and remain competitive in the job market.

- **Personalised Learning Paths:** AI can create personalised learning paths that adapt to missing skills or competencies and provide learning content that is accessible and effective.
- **Professional Certifications:** Validate AI skills and knowledge, increasing employability and career advancement opportunities in AI-related fields.

The Future of Work in an AI-Powered World

As organisations navigate the current world of work, the impact of AI is becoming increasingly evident. Integrating AI technologies reshapes career paths, empowers job growth, and provides new societal opportunities. This chapter explores emerging career paths and industries shaped by AI, the ethical considerations involved in workforce transformation, and how society can prepare for a future filled with AI-driven opportunities. According to the World Economic Forum, while machines may displace 85 million jobs in the near future, 97 million new jobs will be created. This shift indicates a net gain in employment but highlights a significant transformation in the types of roles available.

New Job Categories

- **AI Specialists:** As organisations adopt AI technologies, there is a growing demand for professionals who can design, implement, and maintain AI systems.
- **Data Analysts and Scientists:** As the world increasingly relies on data-driven decision-making, roles focused on interpreting complex datasets are becoming essential.
- **Ethics Compliance Officers:** As AI raises ethical concerns, companies need professionals to ensure that AI applications adhere to ethical standards and mitigate biases.
- **Human–AI Interaction Designers:** These specialists focus on creating user-friendly interfaces that facilitate effective collaboration between humans and AI systems.

Industries Impacted

- **Healthcare:** AI is revolutionising diagnostics, patient care, and administrative processes, leading to roles in health informatics and telemedicine.

- **Finance:** Automation in financial services creates demand for algorithmic trading and risk management roles.
- **Manufacturing:** Integrating robotics and AI in production lines is reshaping quality control and supply chain management.

The Ethical Implications of AI in Workforce Transformation

The rapid adoption of AI technologies raises important ethical considerations that must be addressed to ensure a fair transition for workers.

- **Job Displacement Concerns:**
  Workers may be anxious about job loss due to automation. While some jobs may be eliminated, many roles are evolving rather than disappearing. Organisations must communicate transparently about how AI augments human capabilities rather than replace people, and support employees in gaining new skills.
- **Equity and Access:**
  There is a risk that marginalised groups may disproportionately bear the brunt of job displacement. Ensuring equitable access to retraining programs and educational resources is crucial for supporting affected workers. Policymakers must advocate for inclusive workforce development strategies that prioritise vulnerable populations.
- **Bias and Accountability:**
  If not designed carefully, AI systems can perpetuate existing biases. Organisations must implement ethical guidelines for AI development and deployment to ensure fairness in hiring practices, performance evaluations, and decision-making processes.

Preparing Society for a Future of AI-Driven Opportunities

? **DID YOU KNOW:** *85 million jobs may be displaced by automation, but 97 million new roles are expected to emerge (World Economic Forum, 2025).*

Society must take proactive steps to prepare for the changes to harness the benefits of an AI-powered future.

- **Investing in Education:**
  Educational institutions should integrate AI concepts into curricula at all levels. This includes teaching foundational skills such as programming, data analysis, and critical thinking. Continuous learning initiatives should be promoted to ensure individuals can continuously upskill throughout their careers.

- **Industry–Academia Collaboration:**
  Partnerships between educational institutions and industries are essential for aligning training programs with market needs. Internship programs and apprenticeships can provide students with hands-on experience in AI-driven environments.
- **Government Initiatives:**
  Governments should support workforce development through policies that promote retraining programs, funding for educational institutions, and incentives for companies investing in employee upskilling. Initiatives like universal basic income could also provide temporary support for displaced workers during transitions.

The future of work in an AI-powered world presents both challenges and opportunities. Creating an equitable workforce ready for change requires a focus on career paths, ethical implications, and preparing society through education. Embracing these changes ultimately enhances productivity, fosters innovation, and supports growth across various sectors.

Chapter Questions

1. What are the primary myths and realities surrounding AI's impact on employment?
2. How is AI acting more as an augmentation tool rather than a replacement in today's workforce?
3. Which industries are expected to see the most job creation due to AI, according to the World Economic Forum?
4. What new technical and soft skills are in demand due to AI-driven workplace transformation?
5. What role does AI literacy play for non-technical employees in modern organisations?
6. How does human–machine collaboration improve productivity and job satisfaction in the workplace?
7. Why is human oversight critical in AI-augmented decision-making processes?
8. Provide examples of how AI is being successfully implemented in manufacturing, healthcare, or logistics.
9. What challenges do organisations face when employees resist adopting AI technologies?
10. How can companies address cultural resistance and the fear of automation among employees?

11. What is the nature of the current skills gap between employers and employees in the AI era?

12. What strategies can help bridge the workforce skills gap in an AI-powered economy?

13. How are educational institutions evolving to support AI-readiness in students and professionals?

14. What are the ethical implications of AI-driven workforce transformation, including bias and access?

15. What emerging career paths are being shaped by AI technologies?

16. How can governments and societies ensure an equitable transition during AI-induced workforce shifts?

Note to Readers and Educators

Comprehensive answers and explanations to these chapter-end questions are available at www.sandeepbhalekar.com. The website also provides supplementary frameworks, teaching guidelines, and reference materials to support deeper understanding and classroom discussion.

Educators and facilitators can access additional resources, including presentation frameworks, assessment rubrics, and discussion prompts, to help integrate the concepts from this chapter into academic or professional learning environments.

Bibliography

Accenture. (2023). *Gen AI and the Future of Talent*. Sydney: Accenture.

AdviserPlus. (2024). *Workforce Challenges in 2025*. Manchester: AdviserPlus. https://adviserplus.com/resource/workforce-challenges-in-2025/

AIPRM. (2024). *AI Job Displacement Statistics 2024*. San Francisco: AIPRM. https://www.aiprm.com/ai-replacing-jobs-statistics/

AI Pro. (2024). *9 Essential Skills for Working with AI*. London: AI Pro. https://ai-pro.org/learn-ai/articles/9-essential-skills-for-employees-to-work-effectively-with-ai/

Armanino LLP. (2024). *Unleashing Workforce Potential with AI and Human-Machine Collaboration*. San Ramon: Armanino. https://www.armanino.com/articles/unleash-workforce-potential-with-ai-and-human-machine-collaboration/

Aura AI. (2024). *AI Augmentation vs Automation: What's the Difference?* San Francisco: Aura. https://blog.getaura.ai/ai-augmentation-automation

Avilar. (2025). *4 Predictions Shaping the Future of Workforce Management*. Maryland: Avilar Technologies. https://blog.avilar.com/2025/01/08/4-predictions-shape-future-workforce-management/

Bennett University. (2024). *School of Artificial Intelligence*. Noida: Bennett University. https://www.bennett.edu.in/schools/school-of-artificial-intelligence/

Built In. (2024). *The Future of Artificial Intelligence*. Chicago: Built In. https://builtin.com/artificial-intelligence/artificial-intelligence-future

Chief Learning Officer. (2025). *The Reskilling Roadmap: Navigating Human-AI Roles*. New York: CLO Media. https://www.chieflearningofficer.com/2025/01/17/the-reskilling-roadmap-navigating-evolving-human-ai-roles-in-the-workplace/

Coursera. (2024). *What Are Technical Skills?* Mountain View: Coursera. https://www.coursera.org/articles/what-are-technical-skills

Coveo. (2024). *Generative AI and Workforce Skills*. Montreal: Coveo. https://www.coveo.com/blog/generative-ai-skills/

Cutover. (2024). *The Future of Work Is Here: Human-Machine Collaboration*. London: Cutover. https://www.cutover.com/blog/the-future-of-work-is-here-and-its-all-about-human-machine-collaboration

DataCamp. (2023). *Reskilling and Upskilling in the Age of AI*. San Francisco: DataCamp. https://www.datacamp.com/blog/reskilling-and-upskilling-in-the-age-of-ai

DataCamp. (2024). *Essential Skills for AI Engineers*. San Francisco: DataCamp. https://www.datacamp.com/blog/essential-ai-engineer-skills

Deloitte. (2024). *Human-Machine Collaboration: Rethinking Workforce Roles*. New York: Deloitte Insights. https://www2.deloitte.com/us/en/insights/topics/talent/human-machine-collaboration.html

Digital Marketing Institute. (2024). *8 Universities Leveraging AI to Drive Student Success*. Dublin: DMI. https://digitalmarketinginstitute.com/blog/8-universities-leveraging-ai-to-drive-student-success

EdTech Innovation Hub. (2024). *Top 50 Universities for AI Education in 2024*. London: EdTech Innovation Hub. https://www.edtechinnovationhub.com/news/top-50-unis-for-ai-education-in-2024

Everything Di SC. (2024). *The Future Is Now: 5 Workplace Challenges That Will Shape 2025*. London: Wiley. https://www.everythingdisc.com/blogs/the-future-is-now-5-workplace-challenges-that-will-shape-2025/

EY. (2023). *How AI Is Transforming Workplaces and Empowering Human Talent*. Dublin: Ernst & Young. https://www.ey.com/en_ie/insights/workforce/how-is-ai-transforming-workplaces-and-empowering-human-talent

Factana. (2024). *The Future Workplace and Human-Machine Collaboration*. LinkedIn. https://www.linkedin.com/pulse/human-machine-collaboration-future-workplace-factana-qbvic

Forbes Technology Council. (2024a). *AI and the Future of Work*. New York: Forbes. https://www.forbes.com/councils/forbestechcouncil/2024/07/12/ai-and-the-future-of-work/

Forbes Technology Council. (2024b). *Navigating AI and the Future of Work*. New York: Forbes. https://www.forbes.com/councils/forbestechcouncil/2024/06/25/navigating-ai-the-future-of-work/

FutureLearn. (2023). *Generative AI in Higher Education*. London: FutureLearn.

Harvard Business Review. (2021). *AI Should Augment Human Intelligence, Not Replace It*. Boston: Harvard Business Publishing. https://hbr.org/2021/03/ai-should-augment-human-intelligence-not-replace-it

Harvard Business Review. (2023). *Reskilling in the Age of AI*. Boston: Harvard Business Publishing. https://hbr.org/2023/09/reskilling-in-the-age-of-ai

Harvard Business Review. (2025). *9 Trends That Will Shape Work in 2025 and Beyond.* Boston: Harvard Business Publishing. https://hbr.org/2025/01/9-trends-that-will-shape-work-in-2025-and-beyond

HR Katha. (2025). *2025 Workplace Trends: Challenges and Opportunities for HR.* Mumbai: HR Katha. https://www.hrkatha.com/features/2025-workplace-trends-navigating-complex-challenges-transformative-opportunities-for-hr/

IBM. (2023). *AI Upskilling: Preparing for the Future of Work.* Armonk: IBM. https://www.ibm.com/think/insights/ai-upskilling

Innopharma Education. (2023). *The Impact of AI on Job Roles, Workforce, and Employment.* Dublin: Innopharma. https://www.innopharmaeducation.com/blog/the-impact-of-ai-on-job-roles-workforce-and-employment-what-you-need-to-know

JHFoster. (2024). *Human-Machine Collaboration Optimises Productivity.* Minneapolis: JHFoster. https://jhfoster.com/automation-blogs/human-machine-collaboration-optimizes-productivity/

Kambhampati, Hariharan. (2024). *The Future of Work: Reskilling for an AI-Driven Workforce.* LinkedIn. https://www.linkedin.com/pulse/future-work-reskilling-upskilling-ai-driven-workforce-kambhampati-hhpre

KPMG. (2023). *The Future of Work.* Sydney: KPMG Australia. https://kpmg.com/au/en/home/insights/2023/11/future-of-work.html

Leaf Design. (2024). *The Future of Collaboration Between Humans and Intelligent Machines.* Mumbai: Leaf Design. https://www.leafdesign.co/journal/the-future-of-collaboration-between-humans-and-intelligent-machines

Litslink. (2023a). *AI and Jobs: Should We Be Concerned?* Palo Alto: Litslink. https://litslink.com/blog/ai-and-jobs-should-we-be-concerned-about-ais-impact-on-jobs

Litslink. (2023b). *How Many Jobs Will AI Take Over? Statistics and Projections.* Palo Alto: Litslink. https://litslink.com/blog/how-many-jobs-will-ai-take-over-the-statistics

Lozovsky, Daniel. (2024). *AI Job Loss: Shocking Statistics Revealed.* LinkedIn. https://www.linkedin.com/pulse/ai-job-loss-shocking-statistics-revealed-daniel-lozovsky-mba-sqzhc

Lucid. (2023). *AI Skills for the Modern Workplace.* Salt Lake City: Lucid Software. https://lucid.co/blog/ai-skills-for-the-workplace

Masterplan. (2024). *Top AI Skills for Today's Workforce.* Berlin: Masterplan.

McKinsey & Company. (2023a). *Jobs Lost, Jobs Gained: What the Future of Work Will Mean for Jobs, Skills, and Wages.* New York: McKinsey Global Institute. https://www.mckinsey.com/featured-insights/future-of-work/jobs-lost-jobs-gained-what-the-future-of-work-will-mean-for-jobs-skills-and-wages

McKinsey & Company. (2023b). *Skill Shift: Automation and the Future of the Workforce.* New York: McKinsey Global Institute. https://www.mckinsey.com/featured-insights/future-of-work/skill-shift-automation-and-the-future-of-the-workforce

McKinsey & Company. (2024). *Jobs Lost, Jobs Gained.* New York: McKinsey Global Institute. https://www.mckinsey.com/featured-insights/future-of-work/jobs-lost-jobs-gained-what-the-future-of-work-will-mean-for-jobs-skills-and-wages

McKinsey Global Institute. (2024). *Generative AI and the Future of Work in America.* New York: McKinsey & Company. https://www.mckinsey.com/mgi/our-research/generative-ai-and-the-future-of-work-in-america

NASSCOM. (2024). *Future of Work 2024: Balancing Priorities in an AI-Driven World.* New Delhi: NASSCOM. https://www.nasscom.in/knowledge-center/publications/future-work-2024-balancing-priorities-ai-driven-world

Northumbria University. (2024). *Artificial Intelligence and Workforce Skills*. Newcastle: Northumbria University. https://www.northumbria.ac.uk/study-at-north umbria/courses/msc-computer-science-with-artificial-intelligence-distance-learning-dtdsar6/artificial-intelligence-skills-blog-org/

OECD. (2024). *Future of Work: Policy Issues and Global Trends*. Paris: OECD. https://www.oecd.org/en/topics/policy-issues/future-of-work.html

Oracle. (2023). *AI Upskilling in the Modern Workforce*. Redwood Shores: Oracle Corporation. https://www.oracle.com/in/human-capital-management/ai-upskilling/

PwC. (2024). *The Future of Work and Artificial Intelligence*. London: PwC. https://www.pwc.com/gx/en/issues/artificial-intelligence/future-of-work.html

RChilli. (2023). *AI and Skills Taxonomy: Empowering Reskilling*. California: RChilli Inc. https://www.rchilli.com/blog/ai-and-skills-taxonomy-empowering-employee-reskilling

SAGE University. (2023). *Impact of Artificial Intelligence on Employment*. Indore: SAGE University. https://sageuniversity.edu.in/blogs/impact-of-artificial-intelligence-on-employment

Schiller International University. (2024). *How AI Is Transforming Higher Education*. Paris: Schiller. https://www.schiller.edu/blog/the-impact-of-artificial-intelligence-on-higher-education-how-it-is-transforming-learning/

SEO.ai. (2023). *AI Replacing Jobs: Key Statistics*. Copenhagen: SEO.ai. https://seo.ai/blog/ai-replacing-jobs-statistics

Softworks. (2025). *Addressing Workforce Management Challenges in 2025*. Dublin: Soft works. https://www.softworks.com/blog/addressing-workforce-management-challenges-in-2025/

Statista. (2024). *Compass AI: Future of AI and Work*. Hamburg: Statista.

Thoughtworks. (2024). *Human-Machine Collaboration*. Bengaluru: Thoughtworks. https://www.thoughtworks.com/en-in/insights/decoder/h/human-machine-collaboration

UNESCO. (2024). *Artificial Intelligence and Digital Education*. Paris: UNESCO. https://www.unesco.org/en/digital-education/artificial-intelligence

Universal AI. (2024). *Universal AI—Learning Platform*. India: Universal AI. https://www.universalai.in

University at Buffalo. (2024). *AI in Education*. Buffalo: University at Buffalo Graduate School of Education. https://ed.buffalo.edu/ai-ed

University of San Diego. (2024). *Artificial Intelligence in Education*. San Diego: USD. https://onlinedegrees.sandiego.edu/artificial-intelligence-education/

Visier. (2024). *Types of Skills in the AI-Powered Workplace*. Vancouver: Visier. https://www.visier.com/blog/types-of-skills-ai-powered-workplace/

VLink. (2024). *Preparing for Human-Machine Interactions in the Future of Work*. Hartford: VLink Inc. https://vlinkinfo.com/blog/the-future-of-work-preparing-for-human-machine-interactions/

World Economic Forum. (2025a). *AI and Beyond: Navigating the New Tech Landscape*. Geneva: WEF. https://www.weforum.org/stories/2025/01/ai-and-beyond-how-every-career-can-navigate-the-new-tech-landscape/

World Economic Forum. (2025b). *AI and Workplace Skills: How to Prepare*. Geneva: WEF. https://www.weforum.org/stories/2025/01/ai-workplace-skills/

World Economic Forum. (2025c). *The Future of Jobs Report 2025*. Geneva: WEF. https://www.weforum.org/publications/the-future-of-jobs-report-2025/in-full/4-workforce-strategies/

6

Ethics and Security in AI Development

Introduction to AI Ethics and Security

The role of ethics and security in AI development becomes increasingly important as artificial intelligence (AI) continues to permeate various sectors of society. The two key concepts discussed in this chapter are the importance of ethics and security with AI adoption and AI's impact on society, including the economy and human rights.

Why Ethics and Security Matter in AI Development

AI ethics is a branch of applied ethics that focuses on the moral implications and responsibilities associated with designing, developing, and deploying AI systems. It addresses critical issues such as fairness, transparency, accountability, bias, safety, and the long-term societal consequences of autonomous systems making decisions without direct human oversight. While AI ethics encompasses concerns related to data, it is broader in scope than data ethics. Data ethics primarily deals with the responsible collection, storage, sharing, and use of data, emphasising privacy, consent, and security. AI ethics includes the same components as data ethics, with the addition of how intelligent algorithms interpret and act upon that data, often in dynamic and unpredictable ways. The distinction is crucial because even ethically sourced data can lead to unethical outcomes if used in AI systems without careful design and governance.

Ethics and security are foundational pillars that guide the responsible development and deployment of AI technologies. Their significance can be understood through several key aspects:

- **Trust and Acceptance:** Public confidence is gained when essential ethical components—fairness, transparency, and accountability— are visible and adhered to.
- **Risk Mitigation:** Both ethical and security frameworks are designed to mitigate the risks associated with AI. Ethical guidelines aim to prevent unintended harm to individuals or communities by promoting transparency and minimising bias. Security measures are

implemented to protect AI systems from malicious attacks or data breaches and to protect individual privacy.

- **Compliance with Regulations:** Compliance with ethical standards is often linked to adherence to legal frameworks, such as the General Data Protection Regulation (GDPR) and other relevant privacy statutes. Organisations prioritising ethical practices in AI development tend to be more successful in meeting regulatory requirements and avoiding potential legal repercussions.

💡 **QUICK NOTE:** *Regulatory frameworks like the GDPR don't just mandate data protection—they also require organisations to explain automated decisions affecting individuals.*

- **Long-Term Sustainability:** Adopting ethical practices in AI contributes to the long-term sustainability of technological advancements by ensuring that innovations align with societal values and do not result in adverse consequences (Figure 6.1).

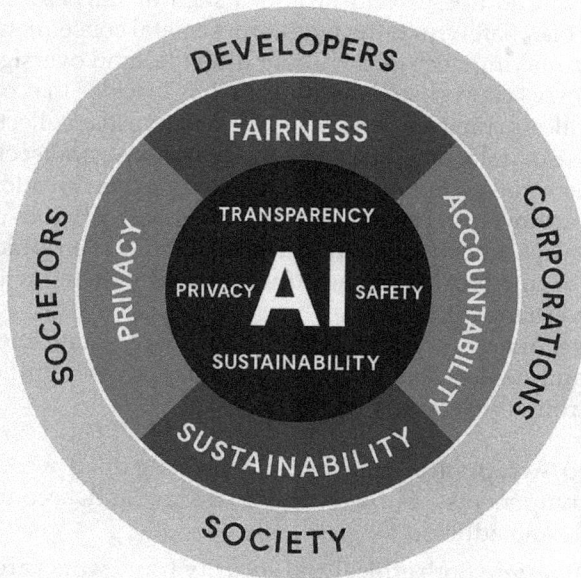

FIGURE 6.1
The ethical AI ecosystem. This diagram illustrates the core ethical principles—fairness, transparency, accountability, privacy, safety, and sustainability—at the centre of AI development, surrounded by key stakeholder groups responsible for upholding them.

🔖 SIDEBAR: AI VS. DATA ETHICS—WHAT'S THE DIFFERENCE?

While data ethics focuses on how data is collected, stored, and used, AI ethics adds another layer: how intelligent systems make decisions using that data. Even ethically sourced data can lead to unethical outcomes if misused by opaque AI models. The intersection of the two demands robust design, governance, and explainability.

The Impact of AI on Society, Economy, and Human Rights

AI is profoundly reshaping society, influencing how people live, work, and interact. In the economic realm, AI is driving automation, boosting productivity, and enabling new business models—yet it also raises concerns about job displacement, workforce reskilling, and economic inequality. Socially, AI applications are transforming healthcare, education, transportation, and communication, offering unprecedented convenience and efficiency. However, these benefits come with challenges, especially around bias in decision-making systems, surveillance, and misinformation. From a human rights perspective, the unchecked use of AI poses risks to privacy, freedom of expression, and equality. Discriminatory algorithms can reinforce social injustices, while opaque AI systems may undermine accountability and due process. Therefore, ensuring that AI advances align with democratic values and fundamental human rights is essential for building an inclusive and ethical AI-driven future (Figure 6.2).

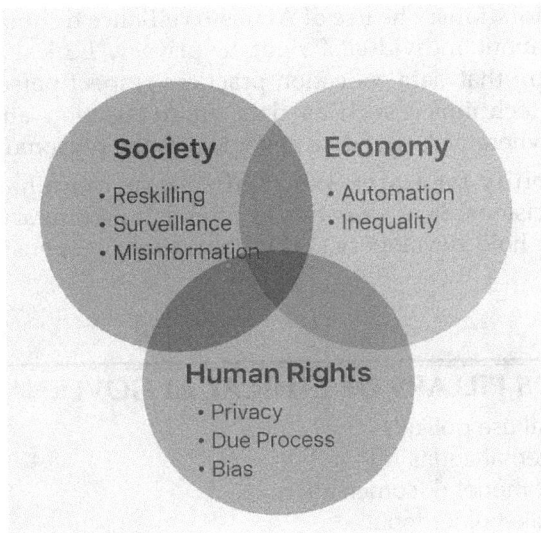

FIGURE 6.2
AI impact zones.

AI's influence extends across various dimensions of society, economy, and human rights:

Societal Impact

- **Job Skills:** I generate new job opportunities that may displace existing positions. This transition requires focusing on reskilling workers to meet the new demands of jobs.
- **Bias and Discrimination:** AI systems have the potential to perpetuate existing biases inherent in their training data, resulting in discriminatory outcomes across various sectors, including recruitment and law enforcement.

Economic Impact

- **Productivity Enhancements:** AI can substantially improve productivity across various sectors by automating routine or manual tasks and optimising processes.
- **Concerns Regarding Inequality:** The advantages of AI may not be evenly distributed, which has the potential to make economic inequality worse, especially if certain groups or regions are marginalised during the technological transition.

Human Rights

- **Privacy Violations:** The use of AI in surveillance technologies raises concerns about individuals' right to privacy. Ethical frameworks must ensure that data collection practices respect personal privacy by using techniques such as data anonymisation and federated learning, where personal data never leaves the personal device.
- **Accountability for Harm:** When AI systems cause harm or make biased decisions, it is essential to establish accountability mechanisms that hold developers and organisations responsible for their actions.

✏️ SIDEBAR: 5 PILLARS OF ETHICAL AI GOVERNANCE

1. Clear ethical use policies
2. Regular external audits
3. Transparent model documentation
4. Inclusive stakeholder input
5. Compliance with international AI laws (GDPR, AI Act, etc.)

Key Ethical and Security Concerns in AI Adoption

For successful AI adoption, organisations must address the following ethical and security concerns:

- **Bias and Fairness:** Ensuring fairness in AI systems is crucial to prevent discrimination based on race, gender, or other protected attributes. Organisations must actively work to identify and mitigate biases when training datasets.

- **Transparency and Explainability:** People need to understand how AI systems make decisions to prevent errors and improve outcomes. Transparency enhances accountability and allows stakeholders to scrutinise AI algorithms' decision-making processes.

- **Data Privacy:** Protecting personal data is paramount in an age of data-driven decision-making. Organisations must implement robust data protection measures to safeguard sensitive information from unauthorised access.

- **Security Vulnerabilities:** As AI systems become integral to critical infrastructure, they become cyberattack targets. Ensuring personal security against adversarial attacks is essential for maintaining AI integrity.

- **Ethical Use of Autonomous Systems:** The deployment of autonomous systems raises moral questions about accountability for actions taken by machines without human intervention. Clear guidelines are needed to govern the responsible use of such technologies.

The intersection of ethics and security in AI development is essential to ensure technologies benefit society while minimising potential harm. Organisations can responsibly navigate the complexities of AI adoption by prioritising ethical principles such as fairness, transparency, accountability, and privacy alongside robust security measures. Addressing ethical and security concerns is vital for creating a future where technology aligns with human values and promotes societal well-being, especially considering how quickly AI continues to advance (Figure 6.3).

Ethical Challenges in AI Development

As AI continues to evolve and integrate into various sectors, ethical challenges associated with its development have become increasingly important. Bias and fairness within AI systems represent critical concerns that require attention to ensure equitable outcomes. This section examines algorithmic

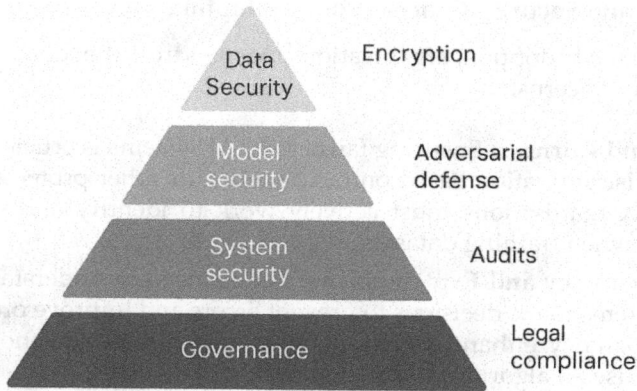

FIGURE 6.3
Layers of AI security and risk mitigation. This pyramid illustrates a layered approach to securing AI systems—from foundational data protection and model resilience to broader system safeguards and governance structures that ensure legal compliance and ethical oversight.

bias, presents case studies of biased AI applications, and outlines strategies to mitigate bias during AI training and deployment.

Bias and Fairness in AI Systems

💡 **QUICK NOTE:** *Bias in AI is not always malicious—it often stems from incomplete or skewed training data. Recognising that is the first step towards fairer outcomes.*

Understanding Algorithmic Bias and Its Consequences

Algorithmic bias occurs when an AI system produces systematically prejudiced results due to erroneous assumptions in the machine learning process. This bias can stem from various sources, including the following:

- **Training Data:** If the data used to train an AI model reflects historical biases or stereotypes, the model is likely to replicate these biases in its predictions or decisions. For example, if a hiring algorithm is trained on data from a company with a history of gender discrimination, it may systematically favour male candidates over equally qualified female candidates.

- **Model Design:** Algorithms may inadvertently favour certain groups if they prioritise features that correlate with biased outcomes. For instance, if the model gives undue weight to features like educational background or location—which may be historically skewed—the output will reflect those biases. Biased feature selection leads directly to biased decision-making.

The consequences of algorithmic bias can be severe, leading to unfair treatment of individuals based on race, gender, or other characteristics. This not only affects individual lives but also perpetuates systemic inequalities in society. The case studies below provide several examples of bias in AI.

Case Studies of Biased AI

✂ SIDEBAR: RED FLAGS IN BIASED AI SYSTEMS
- Consistent adverse outcomes for certain demographic groups
- Lack of transparency in decision explanations
- No documentation of dataset diversity or validation procedures
- Developers cannot explain why a model makes certain predictions
---

- **Facial Recognition:** Research has demonstrated that facial recognition systems tend to exhibit higher error rates for individuals with darker skin tones compared to those with lighter skin tones. For example, a study by MIT Media Lab found that gender classification algorithms misclassified the gender of dark-skinned women 34% of the time, compared to 1% for light-skinned men. This has significant implications for law enforcement and surveillance practices, where misidentification can lead to wrongful arrests or discrimination.
- **Hiring Algorithms:** Companies using AI-driven hiring tools face severe consequences when these systems favoured male candidates over female candidates. For instance, Amazon scrapped its AI recruitment tool after discovering it was biased against women, as it had been trained on resumes submitted over 10 years, predominantly from male applicants.

? **DID YOU KNOW:** *Amazon abandoned its AI recruiting tool after discovering it penalised female applicants—a direct consequence of biased historical data.*

- **Predictive Policing:** Algorithms employed in predictive policing have been criticised for disproportionately focusing on minority communities. These systems frequently depend on historical crime data that mirrors inherent biases in law enforcement practices, resulting in a cyclical pattern of over-policing within specific neighbourhoods.

Strategies for Mitigating Bias in AI Training and Deployment:

? **DID YOU KNOW:** *Only 30% of companies worldwide perform bias audits on AI models before deployment, despite public calls for greater fairness.*

To address algorithmic bias effectively, several strategies can be implemented:

- **Diverse Data Collection:** It is essential to ensure that training datasets represent all demographic groups. This involves actively seeking out diverse data sources and including underrepresented groups in the dataset.
- **Bias Audits:** Regular audits of AI systems can help rectify biases before deployment. This includes testing models against various demographic groups to assess performance and fairness.
- **Inclusive Design Processes:** Involving diverse teams in designing and developing AI systems can help identify potential biases early on. Multidisciplinary collaboration—including ethicists, sociologists, and community representatives—can provide valuable insights into how AI technologies may impact different groups.
- **Transparency and Documentation:** Accountability is created when there is transparency about AI systems' data sources and algorithms. Documenting the decision-making processes allows stakeholders to understand how outcomes are derived, making decisions easier to examine.
- **Regulatory Frameworks:** Governments and organisations should establish guidelines and regulations that mandate fairness assessments for AI systems before they are deployed in critical areas such as hiring, law enforcement, and healthcare.

Transparency and Explainability in AI

As AI systems become increasingly integral to various sectors, transparency and explainability have emerged as critical components in cultivating trust and accountability. This chapter examines the "black box" problem associated with AI decision-making, the significance of interpretable AI models, and methodologies for enhancing the explainability of AI decisions.

The "Black Box" Problem in AI Decision-Making

The "black box" problem in AI refers to the opacity surrounding decision-making processes within complex AI models, particularly those based on deep learning architectures. These models operate through multiple layers of sophisticated mathematical computations, often rendering their internal mechanisms unintelligible, even to the developers who created them. Consequently, when such systems generate predictions, recommendations, or classifications, it becomes challenging to trace the rationale behind specific outcomes or to determine the influence of particular input data. This lack of transparency presents serious implications in critical sectors such as healthcare, criminal justice, finance, and recruitment, where explainability, accountability, and ethical compliance are essential. The inability of stakeholders to interpret or question AI-driven decisions can compromise fairness, hinder regulatory adherence, and diminish public confidence in AI technologies. To mitigate these risks, the field has increasingly prioritised the development of explainable AI (XAI)—a set of methodologies and tools designed to enhance the interpretability, transparency, and human-alignment of AI systems.

- **Understanding Limitations:** When the decision-making process is not transparent, users and stakeholders often struggle to comprehend the limitations and potential biases of AI systems. This is important to encourage human oversight and to prevent reliance on AI when it may not be suitable.
- **Trust Issues:** The inability to explain how an AI system arrives at its conclusions can lead to distrust among users, especially in high-stakes applications such as healthcare, finance, and law enforcement. For instance, applicants may feel unjustly treated if an AI system denies a loan application without a clear rationale.

The black box problem underscores the need for greater transparency in AI systems, enabling users to understand how decisions are made and hold systems accountable for their outputs.

The Importance of Interpretable AI Models

AI systems are increasingly exerting influence over high-stakes decisions within sectors such as healthcare, finance, and recruitment. Consequently, the necessity for transparency regarding the operational mechanisms of these systems has attained critical importance. Interpretable AI models—those whose underlying processes and decision-making frameworks are comprehensible to humans—play a crucial role in fostering trust, ensuring accountability, and driving ongoing improvement. In the absence of interpretability, AI systems are often perceived as a "black box," rendering the validation of outcomes, addressing biases, and facilitating informed modifications considerably challenging. The subsequent points underscore the imperative that interpretability be regarded as a fundamental consideration in the ethical and secure development of AI.

Interpretable AI models are essential for several reasons:

- **Building Trust:** When users understand how an AI system functions and why it makes specific decisions, they are more likely to trust its outputs. For example, if a model can explain the factors leading to a diagnosis in healthcare diagnostics, medical professionals can better assess its reliability.

- **Ensuring Accountability:** When AI systems make mistakes or produce biased outcomes, interpretable models allow organisations to identify the root causes of errors. This accountability is crucial for maintaining ethical standards and regulatory compliance.
- **Improving Model Performance:** Understanding the decision-making process can help developers identify flaws in AI models. Developers can refine algorithms to enhance accuracy and fairness by analysing how inputs influence outputs.

Making AI Decisions More Explainable

Several strategies can be employed to enhance transparency and explainability in AI systems:

- **Interpretable Algorithms:** Utilising inherently interpretable models, such as decision trees or linear regression, allows for more precise insights into how decisions are made. These models provide straightforward explanations based on input features.
- **XAI Techniques:** Techniques such as LIME (Local Interpretable Model-agnostic Explanations) and SHAP (Shapley Additive explanations) can be applied to complex models to generate explanations for individual predictions. These methods help break down model outputs into understandable components.
- **Documentation and Disclosure:** Comprehensive documentation about data sources, algorithms, and evaluation methods enhances transparency. Organisations should also disclose how models are trained and validated, allowing stakeholders to assess their reliability.
- **User-Centric Design:** Engaging end-users in the design process ensures that explanations meet their needs and comprehension levels. Tailoring explanations to different audiences—such as technical experts vs. laypersons—can improve understanding.
- **Regulatory Compliance:** Organisations deploying AI technologies must adhere to regulations such as the European Union's GDPR, which emphasises the transparency of automated decision-making.

Accountability and Responsibility in AI

The increase in AI systems in various aspects of society requires higher levels of accountability and responsibility when the systems make mistakes. This section explores the role of developers, corporations, and governments in ensuring accountability for AI errors. Ethical governance through guidelines and policies is also discussed.

Who Is Responsible When AI Makes a Mistake?

Determining accountability in AI systems is complex due to their autonomous nature and the "black box" problem, where decision-making processes are not transparent. Several parties may share responsibility when AI systems fail or produce harmful outcomes:

- **AI Users:** Individuals operating AI systems hold an initial layer of accountability. They must understand the functionality and limitations of the tools and ensure appropriate oversight during operation.
- **Leaders:** Managers are responsible for training their teams to use AI responsibly and monitoring usage within their departments. They must ensure that AI applications align with organisational policies.
- **Developers:** The individuals or teams that create AI systems share accountability for designing algorithms that minimise bias, ensuring safety measures are in place, and conducting thorough testing before deployment.
- **Corporations/Employers:** Companies employing AI technologies should establish clear guidelines for AI use and implement robust risk management strategies to address potential incidents.
- **Regulatory Bodies:** Governments and regulatory agencies are crucial in establishing legal frameworks that define accountability standards for AI systems. They can impose penalties for non-compliance and ensure that organisations adhere to ethical guidelines.

The Role of Developers, Corporations, and Governments in AI Accountability

The accountability landscape in AI involves multiple stakeholders, each with distinct roles:

- **Developers:** Developers are responsible for creating ethical AI systems and must prioritise fairness, transparency, and safety in their designs. Best practices include bias testing and validation to ensure their models perform equitably across diverse populations.
- **Corporations:** Businesses must cultivate a culture of accountability by implementing governance structures that promote the responsible use of AI. This includes conducting regular audits of AI systems to assess impact and effectiveness.
- **Governments:** Regulatory bodies must establish comprehensive policies that govern the development and deployment of AI technologies. This includes creating frameworks for liability in cases of harm caused by AI systems and ensuring compliance with ethical standards.

Ethical AI Governance: Policies and Guidelines

Effective governance is essential for fostering accountability in AI development. Key components are as follows:

- **Clear Policies:** Organisations should develop policies outlining the ethical use of AI technologies, including guidelines for data privacy, bias mitigation, and transparency.
- **Regular Audits:** Audits of AI systems can help identify potential biases or failures before they lead to harmful outcomes. To ensure objectivity, these audits should be performed by independent third parties.
- **Transparency Requirements:** Organisations should be required to disclose information about how their AI systems operate, including the data used for training and the algorithms employed. This transparency fosters trust among users and stakeholders.
- **Stakeholder Engagement:** Engaging diverse stakeholders—including ethicists, community representatives, and industry experts—in the development process can help identify ethical concerns early on. This collaborative approach ensures that multiple perspectives are considered.
- **Legislation:** Governments must enact legislation addressing the unique challenges AI technologies pose. This includes defining liability standards for organisations when their AI systems cause harm or make biased decisions (Table 6.1).

TABLE 6.1

Common Sources of Bias in AI Systems and Mitigation Strategies

Source of Bias	Description	Impact on AI Systems	Mitigation Strategies
Historical Data Bias	Training data reflects societal or institutional biases	Replicates past discrimination in predictions	Use balanced datasets; remove sensitive attributes
Sampling Bias	Dataset underrepresents certain groups or scenarios	Poor performance for underrepresented groups	Ensure diverse and representative data collection
Labelling Bias	Human-labelled data may reflect subjective judgement or stereotypes	Inaccurate classifications or recommendations	Train annotators; audit and refine labels
Algorithmic Bias	Algorithms amplify patterns in biased data or prioritise biased features	Skewed outcomes that appear "objective" but are not	Fairness-aware model training; regular audits
Measurement Bias	Inconsistent or flawed metrics used for inputs or outcomes	Misleading model performance and inappropriate actions	Standardise metrics; validate against real-world outcomes

Data Privacy and Security in AI

AI and Data Privacy Risks

As AI technologies evolve and proliferate, concerns about data privacy and security have become increasingly pressing. This section examines the privacy risks associated with AI, including challenges in handling personal and sensitive data, issues related to AI-driven surveillance, and the implications of global regulations such as the General Data Protection Regulation (GDPR) and California Consumer Privacy Act (CCPA).

Handling Personal and Sensitive Data

AI systems often rely on vast data for training and decision-making processes. This data frequently includes personal and sensitive information, such as health records, financial transactions, and biometric data. The challenge is ensuring this data is collected, processed, and stored securely while respecting individuals' privacy rights. Key risks are as follows:

- **Data Breaches:** Improper handling or unauthorised access to sensitive data can result in significant privacy breaches. For instance, if health records are leaked, it could lead to identity theft or discrimination.

- **Informed Consent:** There are growing concerns about collecting data without explicit consent. Users may not be aware that their information is being used to train AI models, leading to violations of privacy expectations.

- **Surveillance and Privacy Concerns:** AI technologies have enabled advanced surveillance capabilities that raise substantial privacy concerns.
  - **Mass Surveillance:** AI-powered surveillance systems, such as facial recognition technologies, allow for extensive monitoring of individuals without their consent. This can lead to a loss of civil liberties and increased state control over personal lives.

? DID YOU KNOW: *Facial recognition algorithms have up to 34% higher error rates for women with darker skin tones compared to light-skinned men.*

- **Predictive Analytics:** AI can analyse large datasets to infer sensitive information about individuals, often without their knowledge. This predictive harm can lead to profiling based on inferred attributes such as political views or health status.

AI-Driven Surveillance and Privacy Concerns

The rise of AI-powered surveillance technologies has sparked global debates on privacy and civil liberties. Governments and corporations deploy AI-driven tools for facial recognition, behavioural tracking, and predictive analytics, raising concerns about mass surveillance, social control, and potential abuses. Key privacy concerns are as follows:

- **Facial Recognition and Mass Surveillance:** AI-based facial recognition is widely used in public spaces, airports, and law enforcement, often without explicit user consent. While it enhances security, it raises concerns about misuse, false positives, and a lack of oversight.

- **AI-Powered Behavioural Tracking:** Many companies track user behaviour online and offline using AI-driven algorithms, collecting data on location, purchasing habits, and browsing history. This level of surveillance raises ethical concerns regarding consumer profiling and targeted manipulation.

- **Workplace Monitoring:** Employers are increasingly using AI tools to monitor employees' productivity, communication, and behavioural patterns. While this improves operational efficiency, it raises concerns about worker privacy and autonomy.

- **Predictive Policing and Social Scoring Systems:** Governments in some regions are experimenting with AI-based predictive policing and social credit systems, which assess individuals based on their behaviour and activities. Critics argue that these systems can be discriminatory, lack transparency, and infringe on human rights.

To address these concerns, organisations must strike a balance between security and privacy by ensuring transparency, implementing clear policies, and obtaining informed consent before deploying AI-powered surveillance tools (Table 6.2).

In an era defined by rapid technological advancement, the intersection of ethics and security in AI is more than a theoretical discussion—it is a practical imperative. This chapter has highlighted the pressing need for ethical guidelines, robust governance, and comprehensive security strategies

TABLE 6.2

Ethical and Security Risks in AI with Examples and Mitigations

Risk Type	Example Scenario	Mitigation Strategy
Algorithmic Bias	Biased hiring tool	Diverse datasets, bias audits
Data Privacy Violation	Facial recognition without consent	Informed consent, anonymisation
Cybersecurity Threat	AI system manipulated by adversarial input	Penetration testing, robust encryption

to ensure that AI technologies are developed and deployed responsibly. As AI continues to reshape the economic landscape, social structures, and fundamental human rights, it is crucial that stakeholders—including developers, corporations, policymakers, and civil society—collaborate to embed ethical values and security safeguards at every stage of the AI lifecycle. By fostering transparency, fairness, and accountability, and by proactively addressing risks such as bias, data breaches, and opaque decision-making, we can guide AI innovation towards a future that is not only intelligent but also just and inclusive.

Chapter Questions

1. What is the difference between AI ethics and data ethics?
2. Why are fairness, transparency, and accountability considered essential pillars of ethical AI?
3. How do ethical and security concerns contribute to building public trust in AI systems?
4. What role does regulatory compliance play in ethical AI development?
5. How is AI reshaping the job market, and what measures can mitigate negative effects such as job displacement?
6. In what ways can AI infringe upon basic human rights, and how can ethical frameworks help prevent this?
7. What economic inequalities might be worsened by AI, and what solutions are suggested in the chapter?
8. How does algorithmic bias lead to discriminatory outcomes in real-world applications like hiring or policing?
9. Why is it important to ensure transparency and explainability in AI decision-making?
10. What strategies can be used to mitigate bias in AI training data and model development?
11. What are the main vulnerabilities that make AI systems targets for cyberattacks?
12. What ethical issues arise from the deployment of autonomous systems, and how can they be addressed?
13. Who should be held accountable when an AI system causes harm or makes a biased decision?
14. What roles do developers, corporations, and governments play in AI governance and ethical accountability?

15. How do surveillance technologies powered by AI raise privacy concerns, and what measures can safeguard civil liberties?
16. What are the implications of the "black box" problem in AI, and how can explainable AI techniques help address it?

Note to Readers and Educators

Comprehensive answers and explanations to these chapter-end questions are available at www.sandeepbhalekar.com. The website also provides supplementary frameworks, teaching guidelines, and reference materials to support deeper understanding and classroom discussion.

Educators and facilitators can access additional resources, including presentation frameworks, assessment rubrics, and discussion prompts, to help integrate the concepts from this chapter into academic or professional learning environments.

Bibliography

Apiumhub. (2023). *Ethical Considerations in AI Development*. Barcelona: Apiumhub. https://apiumhub.com/tech-blog-barcelona/ethical-considerations-ai-development/

arXiv. (2024). *Towards Responsible AI Development: Explainability, Alignment, and Safety*. Ithaca: arXiv.org. https://arxiv.org/html/2407.19098v1

Balbix. (2023). *AI in Cybersecurity: Capabilities and Challenges*. San Jose: Balbix. https://www.balbix.com/insights/artificial-intelligence-in-cybersecurity/

Better Ask Me. (2024). *The Unveiling Dangers of Artificial Intelligence: Ethical and Societal Implications*. Los Angeles: SHAMOS LLC. https://betteraskme.com/blogs/trending-topics/the-unveiling-dangers-of-artificial-intelligence-exploring-the-ethical-and-societal-implications

Boston Institute of Analytics. (2023). *Demystifying AI: The Rise of Explainable AI (XAI)*. Boston: BIA. https://bostoninstituteofanalytics.org/blog/demystifying-ai-the-rise-of-explainable-ai-xai-and-its-importance/

California Management Review. (2023). *Critical Issues about AI Accountability Answered*. Berkeley: Haas School of Business. https://cmr.berkeley.edu/2023/11/critical-issues-about-a-i-accountability-answered/

Capitol Technology University. (2023). *Ethical Considerations of Artificial Intelligence*. Laurel: Capitol Tech. https://www.captechu.edu/blog/ethical-considerations-of-artificial-intelligence

Carnegie Council. (2023). *AI Accountability*. New York: Carnegie Council for Ethics in International Affairs. https://www.carnegiecouncil.org/explore-engage/key-terms/ai-accountability

Cavoukian, Ann. (2011). *Privacy by Design: The 7 Foundational Principles*. Ontario: Information and Privacy Commissioner of Ontario.

Check Point Software Technologies. (2023). *AI Security: Risks and Threats*. Tel Aviv: Check Point. https://www.checkpoint.com/cyber-hub/cyber-security/what-is-ai-security/ai-security-risks-and-threats/

Cloud Security Alliance. (2024). *AI Safety vs AI Security: Navigating the Commonality and Differences*. Seattle: CSA. https://cloudsecurityalliance.org/blog/2024/03/19/ai-safety-vs-ai-security-navigating-the-commonality-and-differences

Coursera. (2024). *AI Ethics: What You Need to Know*. Mountain View: Coursera.

Credo AI. (2023). *Glossary: Accountability in AI*. San Francisco: Credo AI. https://www.credo.ai/glossary/accountability

Criucar. (2024). *Expressing Yourself Through AI-Generated Adult Characters*. Toronto: Criucar. https://criucar.com/expressing-yourself-through-ai-generated-adult-characters/

Dwork, C., & Roth, A. (2017). *The algorithmic foundations of differential privacy. Foundations and Trends in Theoretical Computer Science*, 9(3–4), 211–407.

Elliott Davis. (2024). *Navigating the Challenges of AI: Ethical Considerations and Best Practices*. Greenville: Elliott Davis. https://www.elliottdavis.com/insights/navigating-the-challenges-of-ai-ethical-considerations-and-best-practices---article-2

Emerge Digital. (2023). *AI Accountability: Who's Responsible When AI Goes Wrong?* London: Emerge Digital. https://emerge.digital/resources/ai-accountability-whos-responsible-when-ai-goes-wrong/

Evolve Security. (2023). *Ethical Implementation of AI in Cybersecurity*. Chicago: Evolve Security. https://www.evolvesecurity.com/blog-posts/ethical-implementation-of-ai-in-cybersecurity

Exabeam. (2023). *AI Cybersecurity: Securing AI Systems Against Threats*. Foster City: Exabeam. https://www.exabeam.com/explainers/ai-cyber-security/ai-cyber-security-securing-ai-systems-against-cyber-threats/

F5 (2023). *Crucial Concepts in AI: Transparency and Explainability*. Seattle: F5 Networks. https://www.f5.com/company/blog/crucial-concepts-in-ai-transparency-and-explainability

Fluid AI. (2024). *Ethics and Accountability Using RAG AI*. Mumbai: Fluid AI. https://www.fluid.ai/blog/ethics-and-accountability-using-rag-ai

Forbes. (2024). *6 Critical—and Urgent—Ethics Issues with AI*. New York: Forbes. https://www.forbes.com/sites/eliamdur/2024/01/24/6-critical--and-urgent--ethics-issues-with-ai/

Fortinet. (2023). *Artificial Intelligence in Cybersecurity*. Sunnyvale: Fortinet. https://www.fortinet.com/resources/cyberglossary/artificial-intelligence-in-cybersecurity

Frontiers in Psychology. (2022). *Trust in Artificial Intelligence: Ethical and Social Implications*. Lausanne: Frontiers Media. https://www.frontiersin.org/journals/psychology/articles/10.3389/fpsyg.2022.836650/full

Gebru, T., et al. (2021). *Datasheets for datasets. Communications of the ACM*, 64(12), 86–92.

Ghasemaghaei, M., & Calic, G. (2019). *Can big data improve firm decision quality? The role of data quality and data diagnosticity. Decision Support Systems*, 120, 38–49.

Greenleaf, G. (2019). *Global data privacy laws 2019: 132 national laws & many bills. Privacy Laws & Business International Report*, 157, 14–18.

Harvard Data Science Review. (2023). *Ethics and Governance in Artificial Intelligence*. Cambridge: MIT Press. https://hdsr.mitpress.mit.edu/pub/l0jsh9d1

Harvard Gazette. (2020). *Ethical Concerns Mount as AI Takes Bigger Role in Decision-Making*. Cambridge: Harvard University. https://news.harvard.edu/gazette/story/2020/10/ethical-concerns-mount-as-ai-takes-bigger-decision-making-role/

HP. (2023). *AI Privacy Concerns and Data Protection in India*. Palo Alto: HP Tech Takes. https://www.hp.com/in-en/shop/tech-takes/post/ai-privacy-concerns-data-protection-india

IAPP. (2024). *Shaping the Future: A Dynamic Taxonomy for AI Privacy Risks*. Portsmouth: International Association of Privacy Professionals. https://iapp.org/news/a/shaping-the-future-a-dynamic-taxonomy-for-ai-privacy-risks

IBM. (2023). *AI Transparency: Why It Matters*. Armonk: IBM. https://www.ibm.com/think/topics/ai-transparency

IBM. (2024a). *AI and Cybersecurity: Enhancing Protection*. Armonk: IBM. https://www.ibm.com/ai-cybersecurity

IBM. (2024b). *AI Privacy: Building Trust and Compliance*. Armonk: IBM. https://www.ibm.com/think/insights/ai-privacy

IBM. (2024c). *AI Security: Protecting AI Systems from Threats*. Armonk: IBM. https://www.ibm.com/think/topics/ai-security

IJSREM. (2024). *Human–AI Collaboration Platform for Workforce Intelligence*. Tamil Nadu: International Journal of Scientific Research in Engineering and Management. https://ijsrem.com/download/human-ai-collaboration-platform/

Just Unicorns. (2024). *Generative AI in 2024: Innovation vs Data Security Concerns*. London: Just Unicorns. https://justunicorns.news/news/generative-ai-in-2024-innovation-vs-data-security-concerns/

Kuner, C. (2011). *Data protection law and international jurisdiction on the internet*. International Journal of Law and Information Technology, 18(2), 176–193.

Lumenova AI. (2024). *AI Accountability Visual Resource*. San Francisco: Lumenova AI. https://www.lumenova.ai/images/blog_ser.png

Machanavajjhala, A., et al. (2006). *L-diversity: privacy beyond K-anonymity*. ACM Transactions on Knowledge Discovery from Data (TKDD), 1(1), 1–52.

Malwarebytes. (2024). *Risks of AI in Cybersecurity*. Santa Clara: Malwarebytes. https://www.malwarebytes.com/cybersecurity/basics/risks-of-ai-in-cyber-security

Neudesic. (2023). *Practicing Responsible AI*. Irvine: Neudesic. https://www.neudesic.com/blog/practicing-responsible-ai/

New Face Fashion Magazine. (2024). *Embracing the AI Revolution: How ChatGPT Is Transforming the World*. New York: NFFM.

NTIA. (2024). *AI Accountability Policy Report*. Washington, DC: National Telecommunications and Information Administration. https://www.ntia.gov/issues/artificial-intelligence/ai-accountability-policy-report/overview

Office of the Victorian Information Commissioner (OVIC). (2024). *Artificial Intelligence and Privacy: Issues and Challenges*. Melbourne: OVIC. https://ovic.vic.gov.au/privacy/resources-for-organisations/artificial-intelligence-and-privacy-issues-and-challenges/

Palo Alto Networks. (2023). *AI: Risks and Benefits in Cybersecurity*. Santa Clara: Palo Alto Networks. https://www.paloaltonetworks.com/cyberpedia/ai-risks-and-benefits-in-cybersecurity

Paltron. (2024). *Ethics and Security in AI: Emerging Job Profiles for a Sustainable Future*. Hamburg: Paltron. https://www.paltron.com/insights-en/ethics-and-security-in-ai-emerging-job-profiles-for-a-sustainable-future

PCS. (2024). *Why Small Businesses Must Be Cautious with AI*. London: PCS. https://www.pc-net.com/why-do-small-businesses-need-to-be-careful-with-ai-technologies/

Prima Marca. (2024). *Navigating the Changing Tides: Protecting Yourself from Phishing in the Era of AI Advancements*. Milan: Prima Marca. https://primamarca.com/navigating-the-changing-tides-protecting-yourself-from-phishing-in-the-era-of-ai-advancements/

Pinnacle Report. (2024). *Addressing Bias and Fairness Issues in AI Models*. New York: Pinnacle. https://www.pinnacle.report/p/addressing-bias-and-fairness-issues

PwC. (2024). *Ten Principles for Ethical AI*. Sydney: PwC Australia. https://www.pwc.com.au/digitalpulse/ten-principles-ethical-ai.html

Rootstrap. (2023). *AI Ethical Framework for Developers*. Los Angeles: Rootstrap. https://www.rootstrap.com/blog/ai-ethical-framework

Sanofi. (2023). *AI That Is Transparent and Explainable*. Paris: Sanofi. https://www.sanofi.com/en/magazine/our-science/ai-transparent-and-explainable

SAP. (2023). *What Is AI Ethics?* Walldorf: SAP. https://www.sap.com/resources/what-is-ai-ethics

Shelf.io. (2023). *AI Transparency and Explainability in Practice*. San Francisco: Shelf.io. https://shelf.io/blog/ai-transparency-and-explainability/

Solove, D. J. (2012). *The Digital Person: Technology and Privacy in the Information Age*. New York: NYU Press.

Sophos. (2023). *AI in Cybersecurity: Explained*. Oxford: Sophos Group. https://www.sophos.com/en-us/cybersecurity-explained/ai-in-cybersecurity

Stanford HAI. (2023). *Privacy in the AI Era: How Do We Protect Personal Information?* Stanford: Human-Centered AI Institute. https://hai.stanford.edu/news/privacy-ai-era-how-do-we-protect-our-personal-information

TechTarget. (2023a). *AI Transparency: What Is It and Why Do We Need It?* Newton: TechTarget. https://www.techtarget.com/searchcio/tip/AI-transparency-What-is-it-and-why-do-we-need-it

TechTarget. (2023b). *Top Resources to Build an Ethical AI Framework*. Newton: TechTarget. https://www.techtarget.com/searchenterpriseai/feature/Top-resources-to-build-an-ethical-AI-framework

The Digital Speaker. (2023). *Privacy in the Age of AI: Risks, Challenges, and Solutions*. Amsterdam: The Digital Speaker. https://www.thedigitalspeaker.com/privacy-age-ai-risks-challenges-solutions/

The Public Record. (2024). *Younger Americans are more optimistic about the potential of AI*. The Public Record, 53(25), 2.

Transcend. (2023). *AI and Privacy: Protecting Data in the Age of Automation*. San Francisco: Transcend. https://transcend.io/blog/ai-and-privacy

Trigyn Technologies. (2023). *AI and Privacy: Risks, Challenges, and Solutions*. New York: Trigyn. https://www.trigyn.com/insights/ai-and-privacy-risks-challenges-and-solutions

True Home Protection. (2024). *AI & Machine Learning for Security Intrusion Detection*. Austin: True Home Protection. https://www.truehomeprotection.com/leveraging-ai-and-machine-learning-for-advanced-intrusion-detection-in-commercial-security-systems/

TrustPath. (2023). *AI Transparency vs Explainability: Where Does the Difference Lie?* San Francisco: TrustPath AI. https://www.trustpath.ai/blog/ai-transparency-vs-ai-explainability-where-does-the-difference-lie

UNESCO. (2021). *Recommendation on the Ethics of Artificial Intelligence*. Paris: UNESCO. https://www.unesco.org/en/artificial-intelligence/recommendation-ethics

UNESCO. (2024). *AI Ethics: Global Case Studies*. Paris: UNESCO. https://www.unesco.org/en/artificial-intelligence/recommendation-ethics/cases

University of Helsinki. (2024). *A Framework for AI Ethics*. Helsinki: Ethics of AI MOOC. https://ethics-of-ai.mooc.fi/chapter-1/4-a-framework-for-ai-ethics/

USC Annenberg. (2023). *Ethical Dilemmas in AI*. Los Angeles: USC Center for Public Relations. https://annenberg.usc.edu/research/center-public-relations/usc-annenberg-relevance-report/ethical-dilemmas-ai

Wellington Celebrant. (2024). *Website*. Wellington: WellingtonCelebrant.co.nz. https://wellingtoncelebrant.co.nz/

West, S. M. (2020). *Data localization laws and their impact on cloud computing. Journal of Cyber Policy*, 5(1), 49–64.

World Economic Forum. (2016). *Top 9 Ethical Issues in Artificial Intelligence*. Geneva: WEF. https://www.weforum.org/stories/2016/10/top-10-ethical-issues-in-artificial-intelligence/

World Economic Forum. (2021). *Ethical Principles for AI*. Geneva: WEF. https://www.weforum.org/stories/2021/06/ethical-principles-for-ai/

World Economic Forum. (2023). *Cybersecurity and AI Ethics: Driving Responsible Innovation*. Geneva: WEF. https://www.weforum.org/stories/2023/12/cybersecurity-ai-ethics-responsible-innovation/

World Economic Forum. (2025). *Four Ways to Enhance Human–AI Collaboration in the Workplace*. Geneva: WEF. https://www.weforum.org/stories/2025/01/four-ways-to-enhance-human-ai-collaboration-in-the-workplace/

ZenData. (2024). *AI Ethics 101: A Beginner's Guide*. Paris: ZenData. https://www.zendata.dev/post/ai-ethics-101

7

Overcoming Technology Challenges in AI Adoption

In an era marked by rapid technological progress, the integration of artificial intelligence (AI) is transforming organisations across a wide range of sectors, offering both exceptional opportunities and considerable challenges. Enhanced productivity, greater efficiency, and creative innovation are just some of the ways AI can deliver value. At the same time, successful AI adoption does not come without its obstacles. Businesses must navigate complexities such as ensuring high-quality data, integrating new technologies with legacy systems, and overcoming infrastructure limitations. Upholding ethical standards and implementing robust security measures are also crucial, as they directly impact the handling of sensitive information and the trust customers place in the organisation.

A key priority is building a workforce that can engage confidently and effectively with AI. By investing in upskilling and training, organisations enable their employees to maximise the benefits of AI tools, transforming uncertainty into innovation and creativity.

In the midst of this technological revolution, the emphasis must be on fostering a culture of adaptability and continuous learning, while preparing for the intricacies of AI adoption. With the right mindset and a strong commitment to innovation, businesses can thrive in the digital age—reimagining what is possible and laying the groundwork for a future rich with growth and opportunity. Leaders and teams who embrace AI's transformative potential are set to embark on an extraordinary journey.

Business Challenges in AI Adoption

Funding Cycle Challenges

Funding remains one of the most critical bottlenecks in the adoption of AI across industries. While the potential returns on AI investment are substantial, through improved efficiency, customer experience, and innovation, the pathway to securing financial support is often riddled with delays, unclear return on investment (ROI) expectations, and bureaucratic red tape.

DOI: 10.1201/9781003626503-7

These hurdles vary by sector, but the impact is universally felt: missed opportunities, delayed projects, and the risk of falling behind competitors.

Let's explore how different industries experience funding cycle challenges—and what can be done to overcome them.

Manufacturing

AI can revolutionise manufacturing by enabling predictive maintenance, quality control, and streamlined production. The manufacturers often face the following challenges:

- **Delayed funding approvals** from internal leadership or public grants.
- **Shifting technology trends**, whereby the time funding is approved, the solution is outdated.
- **Capital expenditure limitations** in small to medium enterprises (SMEs).

✐ **Sidebar Tip**: Fast-track pilot programs with limited budgets can help demonstrate value early and unlock future funding.

Retail

Retailers operate in dynamic markets where consumer behaviour evolves rapidly. Funding AI tools like recommendation engines or inventory optimisation often lags behind market needs due to

- **slow interdepartmental decision-making;**
- **lack of alignment** between marketing, finance, and operations; and
- **changing customer trends** by the time implementation begins.

✐ **Sidebar Tip**: Cross-functional AI committees can streamline decision-making and improve investment outcomes.

Government

Government organisations benefit from AI in urban planning, citizen engagement, and traffic management—but face

- **political influence on funding priorities,**
- **lengthy approval cycles** tied to annual budgets, and
- **difficulty measuring ROI in citizen-centric projects.**

TABLE 7.1

Pain Points vs. Solutions

Pain Point	Solution
Long approval cycles	Start with smaller, high-impact pilot projects
Budget constraints	Explore co-funding, grants, or phased rollouts
Unclear ROI	Define measurable business KPIs before project starts
Siloed decision-making	Form cross-functional AI investment teams
Rapid tech evolution outpacing approval	Build flexible, agile funding frameworks
Regulatory red tape (esp. in Gov/Utilities)	Engage regulators early; build compliance into proposals

Sidebar Tip: Use scenario planning and public impact metrics to justify upfront investment in AI projects.

Utilities

Utilities can use AI for grid management, predictive maintenance, and energy efficiency—but challenges include the following:

- **Aged infrastructure is not compatible with AI.**
- **Inflexible funding tied to long-term capital planning.**
- **Regulatory restrictions** limit innovation budgets (Table 7.1).

Sidebar Tip: Consider partnerships with AI startups or vendors offering performance-based pricing models.

SIDEBAR: FAST-TRACK AI WITH PILOT PROGRAMS

- Small-scale AI pilots with predefined KPIs offer a practical path to secure buy-in and demonstrate tangible ROI. Pilot projects can unlock future budgets and validate feasibility without major upfront risk.

Breaking Down Silos and Redesigning Processes

As organisations accelerate their AI journeys, one recurring obstacle stands in the way of seamless transformation: deeply entrenched silos and outdated processes. AI cannot thrive in isolation—it demands collaboration, clean data flow, and a customer-centric approach. Unfortunately, legacy systems and fragmented operations often slow this down, resulting in duplicated work, missed insights, and suboptimal outcomes.

TABLE 7.2

From Legacy to AI-Enhanced Workflows

Legacy Process	Redesigned Experience	AI-Enhanced Workflow
Manual approvals	Workflow automation	Predictive process triggers
Disjointed data	Integrated platforms	Real-time AI-driven insights
Departmental silos	Cross-functional governance	Unified AI applications

To unlock AI's full potential, organisations must embrace **end-to-end process redesign** and **break down silos** that hinder innovation and agility (Table 7.2).

From Legacy to AI-Enhanced Workflows

The Silos Problem: A Tale across Industries

Manufacturing—A Day in the Life (Before AI)

A logistics manager at a mid-sized factory spends her morning reconciling data from production, procurement, and delivery teams. Each uses a different spreadsheet, and none are synced. Delays pile up as she waits for the latest figures, affecting shipment planning and customer satisfaction.

(After AI Implementation)

With an AI-enhanced supply chain platform, the manager now gets real-time inventory alerts, automatic supplier updates, and production forecasts—all in one dashboard. The AI even suggests shipment schedules optimised for fuel savings and customer deadlines.

QUICK NOTE: *If a process is broken, don't automate it—rethink it first.*

Retail—The Cost of Disconnected Data

Marketing launches a successful promotion based on customer trends, but the sales team isn't informed. Inventory runs low in stores, creating customer frustration. Insights from customer data weren't shared across departments, and the moment is lost.

(After AI-Driven Process Integration)

AI now syncs real-time purchasing trends with inventory and customer service systems. When marketing launches a campaign, the supply chain responds instantly, and stores are stocked accordingly. Sales and service teams are automatically briefed, delivering a seamless omnichannel experience.

Government—Citizens Caught in the Maze

A citizen applies for a parking permit and must visit three different departments—each with their own forms, rules, and delays. Behind the scenes, departments operate on separate systems with little data sharing.

(Post-Transformation)

With integrated government AI systems, the citizen submits a single application that routes automatically to relevant departments. AI verifies eligibility, predicts processing time, and proactively sends updates. The user experience is faster, easier, and transparent.

Utilities—When Teams Don't Talk

Engineers receive late updates from the customer service team about outages, leading to duplicated work orders and confused consumers. Departments operate on disconnected platforms.

(Unified Governance and AI Ops)

AI platforms now serve as the connective tissue. Field teams receive alerts from customer support in real time. Predictive maintenance models even anticipate issues before customers report them, reducing downtime and improving satisfaction.

✏ SIDEBAR: FROM SILOS TO SYNERGY

- Legacy = Fragmented teams and workflows
- AI-Enabled = Unified data, real-time insights, automated workflows
- Transformation Tip: Appoint a cross-functional AI change leader to bridge departments and encourage shared goals.

Building the Future: Unified Process and Governance

? DID YOU KNOW: *Over 63% of employers report that skill gaps are a significant barrier to adopting AI successfully.*

To achieve this transformation, organisations must

- map current workflows and identify inefficiencies,
- design future-state processes powered by automation and AI,
- establish unified governance models to align departments,
- use common platforms and shared data lakes to foster collaboration, and
- encourage a culture of communication and transparency (Table 7.3).

TABLE 7.3

Quick Win to Get Started

Action Item	Outcome
Create cross-functional AI teams	Reduces siloed decision-making
Invest in shared data infrastructure	Ensures single source of truth
Train staff in agile process thinking	Speeds up transformation initiatives
Use process mining tools	Identifies bottlenecks and automation opportunities

Lack of Information Management

Imagine a bustling manufacturing plant where machinery operates at full capacity, yet the production reports tell a different story. Legacy systems often lead to the creation of haphazard reports that vary in format and content. One department may track productivity using one set of metrics, while another department uses completely different criteria, making it nearly impossible to get a clear picture of overall performance. This chaos not only hinders decision-making but can also result in missed opportunities for efficiency and innovation.

Similarly, in the retail sector, the failure to adopt a centralised information management approach can lead to inventory nightmares. Consider a retail chain that relies on multiple data sources to manage stock levels. One store might report high inventory levels based on outdated figures, while another, relying on different metrics, faces stockouts. The disconnect creates customer dissatisfaction and lost sales. A unified reporting system would provide a real-time overview of inventory across all locations, allowing for timely restocking and improved customer experience.

In the realm of government, the challenge of fragmented data becomes particularly pronounced. Different departments may collect data independently, leading to duplication and inconsistencies. For instance, social services might track demographics using one system, while public health uses another. When emergencies arise, such as a health crisis or natural disaster, the lack of a unified data approach can slow down response efforts, jeopardising public safety. A cohesive information management strategy can enhance collaboration and ensure that comprehensive data inform critical decisions.

Utilities also face their own set of challenges. Imagine energy companies relying on outdated reporting systems to manage consumption data. Without a clear, real-time understanding of usage patterns, they may struggle to make informed decisions about infrastructure upgrades or demand forecasting. This can lead to inefficiencies and increased costs, impacting both their operations and customer satisfaction. However, embracing a dynamic approach to business intelligence would enable utilities to analyse data effectively, fostering innovation and better service delivery.

A major layer of complexity arises when departments hoard access to their data, treating it as proprietary. This mentality can create silos within organisations, stifling collaboration and hindering progress. Without consistency in data presentation and collection, decision-makers are left navigating a confusing maze of conflicting reports—an unsustainable situation in a world that demands agility and responsiveness.

The key to unlocking valuable insights lies in fostering a culture of information sharing and collaboration. With the expectation of instant services and rapid decision-making, organisations must prioritise a unified data management approach. By dissolving the borders between departments and promoting transparency, they can transform data into powerful insights that drive success.

In conclusion, organisations that invest in cohesive information management systems are not just improving their operational efficiency but are also positioning themselves for a future of innovation and growth. By addressing these challenges head-on, they can harness the full potential of their data and make informed decisions that propel them towards success.

Knowledge Management

Signs Your Organisation Has a Knowledge Management Problem

Use this quick checklist to evaluate if your organisation might be facing knowledge management challenges:

- Employees recreate documents or processes instead of reusing existing ones.
- Different departments store the same data in incompatible formats.
- Expertise leaves the organisation when key employees depart.
- Valuable insights are trapped in emails or personal folders.
- No centralised platform exists for knowledge sharing.
- Onboarding new staff takes longer due to scattered information.
- Business decisions are delayed due to data confusion or inconsistency.
- Lessons learned from past projects aren't documented or applied.

Harnessing Knowledge for Transformation

Effective knowledge management is the key to combining traditional wisdom and cutting-edge technology for successful digitisation. Knowledge is not merely an asset; it's a powerful catalyst that, when shared within an organisation, can lead to profound and lasting impacts. To cultivate an effective knowledge-sharing culture, businesses must establish structured processes for creating, organising, and retrieving information.

Employees bring with them years of experience and expertise. When this experience leaves the organisation, companies lose invaluable intellectual capital, leaving a gap that is hard to fill. There is a growing realisation that technology alone won't suffice; it also requires fostering an environment where sharing best practices becomes second nature. The organisational process should consider how to capture this knowledge, streamline communication, and promote collaboration. Companies that create a culture of intellectual capital and provide a method for employees to share ideas lead to success for all. Take the retail sector, where customer interactions are paramount. Retailers must swiftly adapt to fluctuating consumer preferences and market trends. However, disconnected knowledge management can create silos, where insights are trapped within departments. For instance, if the marketing team develops a successful promotional strategy but fails to share it with the sales team, the potential to optimise revenue is lost. By integrating AI-driven systems, retailers can enhance real-time information sharing, ensuring every team member accesses vital knowledge that can elevate the shopping experience and drive sales.

In government, where public services hinge on collaboration across various departments, disconnected knowledge can impede progress. Imagine a scenario where policy decisions are made in isolation, far removed from ground-level feedback. This can lead to policies that don't resonate with community needs. Leveraging AI tools to share insights across departments can create a seamless flow of information. For example, a local government could collect data from multiple departments to better address public concerns in real time, fostering a more engaged and informed citizenry.

Utility companies face unique challenges related to infrastructure and data management. With technologies that generate colossal amounts of data, the ability to harness this information is critical. However, if teams working on renewable energy projects don't communicate effectively with maintenance teams, the chances of optimising energy distribution diminish. By adopting advanced knowledge management systems, utilities can ensure that insights generated from operational data are shared promptly, leading to enhanced service reliability and innovation in energy solutions.

Despite the promise that digitisation holds, various challenges can hinder its successful adoption across these sectors.

- **Effective Tools:** In many organisations, managers may find themselves relying on outdated or inadequate tools. Without dependable information management systems, they are forced to keep independent copies of essential data, which can create inconsistencies and a lack of trust in the information. Imagine a scenario in a retail chain where different stores utilise distinct inventory management systems; the lack of standardisation leads to inefficiencies and lost sales opportunities.

- **Classification Schemes:** Businesses often struggle with managing unstructured information. Valuable insights can be buried in emails, documents, and reports that lack a cohesive structure. This can lead to missed opportunities for process improvement and innovation. Having a clear classification scheme can streamline information retrieval, enabling teams to act swiftly and decisively.

- **Digital Maturity:** The journey towards digitisation can be stymied by an organisation's readiness to embrace change. In the fast-paced world of utilities, the transition from analogue to digital can be daunting. Companies can find themselves tethered to legacy systems that hinder growth, missing out on advancements in AI and data analytics that could enhance service delivery and customer engagement.

- **Inadequate Infrastructure:** Continuous technological evolution demands robust infrastructure. Retailers, for example, must ensure their systems can handle large volumes of data during peak shopping seasons. A slow network or inadequate storage solutions can lead to frustrated employees and a poor customer experience. A proactive approach to infrastructure planning can position organisations to leverage the latest technology trends effectively.

- **Security Concerns:** In an era where data sharing is crucial, safeguarding sensitive information is paramount. Utility companies dealing with critical infrastructure face a unique challenge in balancing transparency and security. For instance, while sharing real-time service updates with customers can enhance trust, it must be done in a way that protects sensitive operational data from cybersecurity threats.

- **Performance Challenges:** The sheer volume of data necessitates a focus on speed and accuracy in information retrieval. In government, slow response times to citizen inquiries can erode public trust. By harnessing AI technologies, agencies can analyse large datasets swiftly, providing timely insights that drive better decision-making and improve service levels.

Embracing a culture of knowledge sharing powered by thoughtful technology integration can unlock incredible potential. By overcoming the inherent challenges of disconnected knowledge management, these sectors can foster environments where collaboration thrives, innovation flourishes, and ultimately, where both employees and customers benefit.

Organisational Structure Challenges

Historically, organisations have often operated in silos, where separate departments function independently with minimal exchange of information. This status quo must be challenged to embark on a transformative digital revolution. Embracing technology establishes knowledge repositories that serve as treasure troves of insight. However, for these technology-driven platforms to thrive, active participation from individuals is essential. Without sufficient incentives, knowledge sharing may dwindle, leaving these systems underutilised and ineffective.

For organisations to flourish in this digital age, both structured and unstructured information must be readily accessible and tailored to the specific knowledge needs of various groups. The task of managing and maintaining relevant and current information necessitates creating dynamic online portals and knowledge hubs. Continuous evaluation and application of knowledge are critical; information that isn't regularly reviewed holds little value.

A common challenge arises when employees are hesitant to share their expertise, often viewing their knowledge as a competitive advantage. Even with innovative technological tools designed for sharing knowledge, unless there's a supportive culture and proactive initiatives from organisational departments, genuine knowledge transfer may remain elusive. Initiatives such as forming interest groups, rewarding knowledge sharing, and publishing informative articles can foster a more collaborative environment. Crucially, buy-in from both top and middle management is essential. They play a pivotal role in crafting a framework that encourages timely and context-based sharing of insights.

Consider the profound knowledge that comes from experience, especially in sectors like manufacturing, retail, government, and utilities. For instance, in manufacturing, an engineer might develop invaluable insights into optimising production processes over time, knowledge that could greatly enhance efficiency and reduce waste. In the retail sector, managers who understand customer behaviour through years of experience can provide guidance that far surpasses any data analysis alone. In government, civil servants with local knowledge can navigate complex regulatory environments more adeptly. Utility companies benefit from employees who possess deep understanding of infrastructure intricacies, essential for effective service delivery and innovation.

As organisations transition into a digital future, restructuring is key. Many Australian companies, like their global counterparts, face intricate and sometimes overlapping structures. Often, departments function with a high degree of autonomy within predetermined budgets and policy frameworks established by central offices. Different agencies may prioritise differently or adhere to inconsistent processes, leading to fragmentation.

Capitalising on AI and other digital advances demands finding the right balance in organisational structure and operating models without causing disruptions typically associated with constant changes. This challenge is especially relevant in manufacturing, where streamlining production lines can be sidetracked by outdated processes. In retail, adapting to AI-driven customer insights requires a unified approach across departments to truly personalise the shopping experience. Governments face obstacles in integrating AI to improve public services while ensuring that differing agency priorities align efficiently. Similarly, utility providers must navigate regulatory frameworks while leveraging AI to predict maintenance needs and optimise energy distribution.

Ultimately, addressing the complexities of organisations, whether reducing redundancy in budgets, structures, or resources, requires diligent focus and a unified vision. Embracing a culture of knowledge-sharing and collaboration not only enhances operational efficiency but also sparks innovation, paving the way for a more connected and effective future. In this evolving landscape, organisations that prioritise transparency and collaboration will undoubtedly find themselves at the forefront, capable of adapting and thriving in an increasingly digital world.

Lack of Organisation-Wide Information Management Framework

An Information Management Framework (IMF) serves as a vital foundation for organisations, illuminating how to navigate the complex landscape of information essential for supporting business functions. It defines the nature of this information, detailing how and when it is utilised, who is responsible for it, where it resides, in what format it must be preserved, its security classification, and the accessibility rights of different users.

Data scattered across multiple systems, production schedules, machine performance metrics, and inventory levels prevents accurate forecasts and optimised operations. This fragmentation can lead to delays in production, wasted resources, and missed opportunities.

In the retail sector, consider a brand that leverages customer information from various sources—online purchases, in-store interactions, and loyalty programs. Without a comprehensive framework to manage this information, the brand struggles to deliver personalised experiences to its customers. This disconnect can result in lost sales, ineffective marketing strategies, and a diluted brand image.

Governments face similar hurdles. For instance, when agencies collect citizen data across different departments, such as tax, health, and social services, without a coherent IMF, they risk duplicating efforts and providing inconsistent services. This not only frustrates citizens but also hinders the government's ability to respond effectively to community needs.

Utilities, too, encounter obstacles when managing information related to energy consumption, infrastructure maintenance, and customer billing. In the absence of a structured information management approach, organisations may find it difficult to implement AI solutions for predictive maintenance or customer service enhancements. The potential of AI remains untapped as diverse data is not seamlessly integrated, leading to inefficiencies and increased operational costs.

For all these sectors, the absence of an enterprise-wide IMF creates significant challenges. The integration of hybrid data becomes a daunting task, with security and privacy taking centre stage. Without defined processes to protect sensitive information, organisations risk compromising data integrity and exposing themselves to compliance issues.

As disparate information from various systems continues to coexist without a unifying framework, the vision of leveraging AI to provide timely, contextual insights dims. The governance of information becomes an arduous process, and the cost of retrieving critical data skyrockets when organisations grapple with knowing where to source their information.

A robust IMF not only promotes transparency and enhances data quality but also fosters innovation. By adopting a structured approach, organisations can lay the groundwork for future advancements, paving the way for a more efficient, responsive, and informed operation in every sector.

Outdated Technology

Traditional methods of development, such as the waterfall model, no longer serve the changing landscape of technology. Development now requires an agile approach with rapid prototyping and iterative improvements. Additionally, processes need to be redefined and security systems must evolve to support a flexible approach and an adaptive mindset.

One innovative solution to this challenge is the "Bi model" approach, which integrates both agile and waterfall methodologies. This strategy creates a bridge between established systems and new technologies, enabling organisations to harness the best of both worlds while embracing innovation and adjusting to change.

Legacy systems, which include anything from outdated machinery in manufacturing to older point-of-sale systems in retail, can hinder the effectiveness of AI adoption. Outdated equipment combined with outdated software hinders AI adoption.

Similarly, in the retail industry, businesses are striving to implement AI-driven tools for personalised customer experiences. Yet, outdated point-of-sale systems and inventory management practices can stifle these efforts, making it difficult to fully capitalise on the potential of AI to optimise operations and enhance customer satisfaction. Retailers may find themselves hesitant to invest in modern solutions due to the complexities of transitioning from legacy systems.

Governments are also facing significant challenges when it comes to embracing new technology. The burden of navigating legislative checks and conducting thorough risk assessments can slow down the adoption of innovative tools that could improve citizen services. With constantly evolving regulations and the need for cross-organisational compliance, the process can be cumbersome and time-consuming, discouraging public sector entities from pursuing modernisation.

Utility companies, tasked with providing essential services, encounter similar obstacles. The integration of smart grid technologies and AI analytics can enhance efficiency and reliability; however, outdated infrastructure and regulatory red tape can hinder progress. The challenge of ensuring compliance across multiple jurisdictions adds layers of complexity, requiring careful coordination and extensive checks.

Successfully competing in the new technological landscape means organisations must adopt new technologies, meet diverse regulations, and overcome challenges that require decisive action and collaboration within and outside the organisation.

The opportunities for growth and advancement motivate to embrace and adopt new technologies, even amidst the challenges they present. By embracing agile methodologies and adopting a proactive approach towards modernisation, organisations can transform their operations, inspire their teams, and deliver exceptional value to their stakeholders in an ever-changing world.

Lack of Organisational-Wide Governance

Governance serves as the guiding framework, shaping the implementation of new technology to ensure it delivers real value while maintaining a focus on the broader vision. It is essential for governance to grasp both the strategic strengths and current limitations of an organisation, allowing for informed, cost-effective decisions that align with overarching goals. Typically, governance flows from the top down. Senior decision-makers (leaders) set the priorities based on what is feasible and in line with the organisational capabilities. The most effective governance structures blend insights from both business and technical leaders, forming a dynamic learning process between executives and employees. When conflicts arise, a well-composed governing body can bring projects back on track, while also driving continuous improvement and making sure the organisational model evolves to achieve even better results over time. Effective governance can be challenging to apply when adopting innovative technologies like AI. The following outlines the challenges governance faces:

- **Manufacturing:** In the manufacturing sector, AI can dramatically enhance efficiency and precision. However, without strong organisational governance, projects can easily falter. For instance, if the objectives of AI implementation are not clearly defined, teams might have differing interpretations of success. This lack of alignment could lead to wasted resources and missed opportunities. Imagine a factory that invests in predictive maintenance AI, but the leadership fails to articulate the expected outcomes. The production team might implement it fully, yet if they are unsure of the specific savings or downtime reductions anticipated, they may not effectively leverage the technology, leading to dissatisfying results.

> **QUICK NOTE:** *Modular A pilot that solves a small, visible problem can unlock executive trust faster than a grand plan.*

- **Retail:** Retailers are leveraging AI to personalise customer experiences and optimise inventory. Yet, in the absence of cohesive governance, such initiatives can fall short. For example, if the project to deploy an AI-driven recommendation system does not get buy-in from middle management or staff, you risk disconnection across teams. A lack of clear communication regarding the project's goals, like understanding how customer insights will be utilised, could result in teams not adopting the technology, leading to underwhelming customer engagement. If sales associates aren't on board, they may not utilise the insights provided, which stunts the initiative's potential.

- **Government:** When government agencies adopt AI to improve citizen services, governance challenges become even more critical. Without clear authority and accountability, AI projects can stall or even backfire. Take the case of implementing a chat service that uses AI to streamline citizen queries: if there's ambiguity about who oversees the project and its progress is not regularly reviewed, it may lead to misallocations of the budget or resources. If stakeholders don't agree on the intended outcomes—like reducing response times or maximising citizen satisfaction—confusion can reign, ultimately handing citizens an unsatisfactory experience when engaging with the government.

- **Utilities:** In the utility sector, AI presents incredible opportunities for enhancing grid management and predictive maintenance of infrastructure. However, the absence of well-defined governance can thwart progress. If a utility company rolls out AI for demand forecasting without robust oversight, it faces the risk of overestimating the benefits and, ultimately, public trust. For example, if stakeholders from different departments—like operations and customer relations—are not aligned on how to communicate changes that the AI promises, it could lead to public dissatisfaction when expected improvements don't manifest, creating a chasm between the utility and its consumers.

In all these scenarios, lacking adequate governance structures can result in scope creep, lack of, especially at the front lines, stakeholder agreement, and over-projected benefits. An effective governance approach clearly defines responsibilities and ensures decision-makers are equipped with the requisite knowledge. It enhances processes that allow for risk identification upfront, paving the way for robust controls. As organisations strive to embrace new technologies like AI, they must ensure that governance evolves alongside them. When challenges arise, governing bodies need to act decisively not only to safeguard investments but also to foster an environment where innovation can thrive and objectives are met. Ultimately, strong governance serves as the backbone of any successful project, ensuring that changing priorities do not squander the resources already invested and that each project can adapt and grow along with the organisation's vision.

Organisations often embark on ambitious projects, but these journeys are rarely smooth. Effective governance is crucial, instilling confidence and ensuring that initiatives are pursued with responsibility and clear direction.

Here are some compelling reasons why strong governance is essential, particularly when it comes to adopting AI technologies in sectors like manufacturing, retail, government, and utilities:

- **Articulating the Business Case:** Many organisations grapple with articulating a clear business case for projects. For instance, in manufacturing, implementing AI-driven production line monitoring can significantly enhance efficiency. However, if the ROI isn't convincingly communicated, senior management may hesitate to allocate necessary resources, stunting innovation.

- **Clarifying Expected Outcomes:** Imagine a retail chain looking to deploy AI for personalised customer experiences. If the project's objectives are vague, such as merely enhancing customer satisfaction, it leads to confusion. Different teams may have their own interpretations, resulting in varied implementations that fail to achieve the intended outcome of increased sales.

- **Securing Management Buy-In:** The adoption of AI in government services presents unique challenges. If senior management isn't convinced of the potential benefits, like improved citizen services or streamlined processes, gaining enterprise-wide support becomes nearly impossible, leaving projects stagnant.

- **Effective Gateway Reviews:** In utilities, when AI systems are transitioned from development to operational teams, effective gateway reviews are critical. Clear deliverables should be established to ensure that each team is aligned and accountable. Without this, projects may falter at critical handoffs, leading to costly delays.

- **Enhancing Communication:** Communicating the vision of AI integration is paramount. In a manufacturing setting, when teams understand how AI will revolutionise workflows, they are more likely to embrace the changes. Transparent communication engages everyone, fostering a collective readiness to adapt.

- **Managing Scope Creep:** The phenomenon of "scope creep" can derail AI initiatives. For example, a utility project aimed at predicting maintenance needs could quickly expand to include smart grid technologies. If not managed effectively, this can lead to budget overruns and missed deadlines, defeating the initial purpose.

- **Aligning Stakeholder Interests:** In retail, differing interests among stakeholders can create roadblocks. If some are focused on cost-cutting while others advocate for customer experience enhancements through AI, conflicts may arise. Effective governance ensures that interests are aligned, allowing for a unified approach.

- **Realistic Benefit Projections:** Over-promising the capabilities of AI can create disillusionment. If a government project promises to eliminate all inefficiencies through AI but only achieves a 20% reduction in processing time, it can lead to the perception of failure, even if the outcomes are realistic.

- **Encouraging Individual Thought:** In any organisation, the challenge of groupthink can stifle innovation. Stakeholders need to be encouraged to express their unique perspectives. For example, in utility companies, individual contributions can lead to groundbreaking ideas on how AI can optimise resource management.

- **Understanding the Bigger Picture:** Teams must see their work in the context of broader strategic goals. In manufacturing, understanding how AI implementation enhances overall production efficiency encourages collaboration and commitment among team members.

- **Balancing Detail with Vision:** When decision-makers become overly focused on minute details of AI projects, they often lose sight of the overall vision. Ensuring that high-level executives remain engaged in the strategic direction without micromanaging enables teams to innovate effectively.

- **Establishing Clear Governance Structures:** Projects that span multiple departments often face ambiguity in accountability. For instance, the implementation of AI solutions in government projects can falter if it's unclear which department is responsible for oversight. Solid governance structures are crucial for navigating these complexities.

Embracing AI in project management across sectors like manufacturing, retail, government, and utilities is a remarkable opportunity for transformation. By addressing these governance challenges with inspiration and clarity, organisations can navigate their paths with confidence, ultimately achieving greater efficiency and service excellence.

Governance aligns responsibilities with tasks and the decision-making process. Governance should enhance processes, which in turn help identify risks up front and enable the positioning of adequate controls to ameliorate those risks. In the context of future AI technologies, it is vital that these risks be identified quickly and handled efficiently. AI technologies provide a full gamut of options and expose the organisation to a suite of uncertainties regarding business and technology strategies and their execution. Governance and risks are a balanced act to ensure the achievement of business objectives, both strategic and operational.

If there is a change in the organisation, the project might not have the same priority or ongoing budget as it had previously. This change in situation must be managed in such a way that the project still delivers value with available resources and reaches a milestone that can be chosen and extended later. Changing directions of the organisations should not lead to a waste of the resources invested so far. In such cases, it makes sense to have smaller deliverables, with shorter timeframes and critical success factors intact.

Strategic Goals

For organisations to effectively navigate the adoption of AI, it is essential for senior management to grasp the strategic goals and capabilities required to realise those ambitions. This understanding begins with a clear assessment of the organisation's current capabilities and identifying the gaps between where it stands today and where it wants to be in the future.

To achieve these strategic goals, organisations must implement numerous smaller projects that contribute to a larger vision, much like the interlocking pieces of a jigsaw puzzle. Each project plays a vital role in delivering the overall business outcome. For instance, in the manufacturing sector, integrating AI with Internet of Things (IoT) devices can lead to significant improvements in operational efficiency. Smart sensors can monitor machinery conditions in real-time, and AI can analyse this data to predict maintenance needs, thereby reducing downtime and enhancing productivity.

>   **Retail:** AI can transform how businesses engage with customers. Using IoT devices such as smart shelves and connected payment systems, retailers can collect data on customer preferences and inventory levels. AI can then process this information to forecast trends, optimise stock levels, and personalise marketing strategies, ensuring that the right products are available at the right time.

>   **Government Services:** Government can also benefit from the integration of AI and IoT technologies. For example, AI can help analyse traffic data gathered from connected vehicles and smart traffic lights to optimise urban mobility. This integration can lead to smarter city planning and improved public safety. AI can also streamline citizen services by automating responses to frequently asked questions, ensuring quicker resolution of issues.

>   **Finance:** AI is revolutionising risk management and fraud detection. By incorporating IoT devices to gather real-time transaction data, financial institutions can deploy AI algorithms that monitor for unusual patterns, enhancing security while providing a seamless customer experience. This adoption helps organisations stay ahead of potential threats, protecting both their assets and their customers' information.

To succeed in these endeavours, each of the smaller projects should not only align with the larger strategic vision but also demonstrate measurable success. By carefully piecing together these individual initiatives, organisations can create a cohesive approach that leverages AI, IoT, and digital twin technologies, ultimately leading to improved outcomes and sustained growth in their respective sectors.

Common Reasons for AI Project Failures

? DID YOU KNOW: *Outdated project management styles are a leading cause of delayed AI implementations in both public and private sectors.*

AI has the potential to transform industries, ranging from manufacturing to finance, but many organisations struggle to realise the full benefits of their AI initiatives. Understanding the common reasons for these failures can help Organisations reduce risk and drive successful outcomes. Here are some key factors that often lead to AI project failures:

Lack of Clear Goals and Vision: One of the primary reasons AI projects falter is a failure to establish clear goals and a cohesive vision. For example, a manufacturing company may invest in AI to optimise production processes without clearly defining what "optimisation" means. This could lead to misaligned efforts, such as focusing solely on reducing downtime instead of also enhancing product quality. For the success of the project, it is important to create a clear project vision statement that outlines the objectives and expected outcomes. Also involve all relevant stakeholders in defining goals to ensure everyone is on the same page.

QUICK NOTE: *AI project success starts with clear objectives. Define "value" before starting.*

Insufficient Leadership and Management: Successful AI projects require experienced leadership that understands both the technical and business aspects of the initiative. In a retail setting, for instance, if the project lacks a skilled sponsor who can champion the AI efforts, it might result in missed opportunities to adapt to consumer behaviour or inventory challenges. It is important to appoint a project sponsor with the necessary technical and managerial skills and the authority to make decisions. The project team must ensure an AI-aware project manager is assigned to oversee daily operations and coordinate team efforts effectively.

Poor Stakeholder Engagement: Failing to engage stakeholders can lead to a disconnect between project outputs and user needs. In government services, an AI system designed to improve public service delivery might fail if it doesn't incorporate feedback from community members who will use the service. As a result, the product might not meet user expectations, leading to poor adoption rates. The project team needs to identify all stakeholders and establish regular communication channels from the project's inception. The project manager and the sponsors must actively seek input and feedback to ensure the project remains aligned with stakeholder needs.

Team Dynamics and Expertise: AI projects often require a blend of various skills. In finance, a lack of clear roles can lead to confusion and delays; if data scientists don't communicate effectively with financial analysts, important project insights may be overlooked. Additionally, team members may need specific training to work effectively with AI tools. The project sponsors need to clearly define roles and responsibilities at the project's outset. The project budget should also invest in training and development to equip team members with relevant AI skills.

Requirement and Scope Issues: Scope creep—where project requirements continually change—can derail AI projects. For example, a retail company might initially set out to develop a predictive analytics tool for managing stock levels but end up adding features for customer personalisation without properly assessing the impact on timelines and budgets. The project team must establish a well-defined scope and stick to it. The project budget should invest in and implement a change management process to assess the implications of any additional requirements.

Inaccurate Estimation and Planning: Underestimating the resources required for an AI project is a frequent pitfall. Consider a manufacturing organisation that estimates a few months to implement an AI-driven supply chain solution but runs into unexpected data integration issues, resulting in significant delays. There is a clear requirement to develop realistic project timelines and budgets that consider potential challenges. The project budget should include contingency plans to handle unforeseen circumstances.

Detailed Planning and Execution: Failure to plan intricately can cause misunderstandings and unmet objectives. For instance, in the finance sector, launching a new AI-driven trading algorithm without comprehensive testing might lead to substantial financial losses due to unforeseen market conditions. The project schedule should break the project into manageable tasks and meticulously plan each step. Governance and project steering committee should plan to regularly review and adjust the plan as necessary, ensuring all team members are involved in the process.

Not Having the Right Management for the Project: Failure to have leadership in business, organisational, or technical domains may cause the project to be delayed, lose direction, or deliver late. A project should have a sponsor who will take responsibility for seeing the project through. This sponsor should have the skills and time necessary to perform the role effectively. Apart from the sponsor, the project manager should steer the direction of the project on the right track and have the know-how to make people work together to finish the project on time and within budget. Micromanagement or lack of management can cause projects to fail or run out of control.

Stakeholder Engagement Issues: A classic mistake is failure to engage the right stakeholders. The project should be directed towards the desired state by communicating with all stakeholders from its beginning. Their buy-in and view of the final state must be the priority of the program for its eventual success and use. Sometimes, the less vocal stakeholders' issues are not addressed, and their needs are not heard. Stakeholders need to remain clear on what is being delivered and how the new technology will be used. Many projects finish on time and on budget, but the capabilities they have delivered do not get used. This is also a failure of the project.

Team Issues: Every team member's role and responsibility must be clearly understood. There should be enough staff to complete the work, and they should have adequate time to finish it. They should have the subject matter expertise (SME) and skills to do it, and receive training in technical or business domains if needed. Work should be divided fairly; otherwise, discontent and demotivation will arise. If projects are delayed, just adding resources might not help finish them in time. The actual issues of the team must be understood and acted upon.

Requirement Issues: These are the details of what is in scope and out of scope. Scope creep should be controlled. Requirements of stakeholders and any additional requests should contribute to reaching the overall goal with an acceptable ROI. Stakeholders with conflicting perspectives and needs could be dissatisfied with the result. An agreement about the outcome must be reached beforehand.

Estimation: Those who will do the work should agree to the estimate and be involved in creating it. Estimates should not be cut to secure a contract, and the project scope should be clear, with sufficient information and analysis to make proper estimations. All big and small activities should be considered. Contingency planning for the unknown should be built into the estimate. Assumptions should be documented. A new tool, process, or system does not automatically deliver efficiency, which should be considered. The previous performance of projects should be considered before giving the estimate. Estimates should have a range of values to allow for unknown factors. A calendar of upcoming activities will ensure that all work is done and none forgotten.

Planning: Failure to plan the project and its execution in detail is a huge reason projects are unable to deliver as required. Big pieces are divided into smaller pieces of manageable work. While planning, each step should be thought over, or the complexity of the project may not be clear. At the same time, planning each step will clarify the resources in time and skills required. Some buffer should be maintained, and a very tight schedule avoided, to accommodate an unforeseen circumstance. Each team member should be clear on responsibilities, with the workload equally distributed according to skills and priority of the project work. Along with the project manager, team members should be empowered to actively contribute to planning the schedule. This gives a better approximation of project timelines, as the person doing the work will have a better idea of time needed to finish the task allocated. Any training needed should be planned ahead. Culture-change training (the way the end product will bring about the change) should also be considered. If other teams are expected to deliver some work pieces, they should also commit to the timeline, or the schedule will not be delivered. User training requirements must be considered as well. The scope of the project can change during its build, but the project should always deliver on the initial intended outcome. Any extra features in scope creep should be considered after looking at the benefits and costs.

Risk Management: Failure to see the risks and address them can be avoided if risks are evaluated independently of planning the project. The risk team should not deal with everyday issues and problems.

Architecture and Design: A pet project should not be prioritised before considering other options and solutions. Poor architecture is hard to maintain and debug. Overall architecture should be considered, and always before individual components are worked on. All requirements, especially performance requirements, must be incorporated before any detailed project work starts. Otherwise, the end solution might not give the desired business outcome. Over-delivery is unnecessary; tools that benefit the final result of the project should be considered. Sometimes new tools are required, and time should be allocated for learning.

Decision-Making Problems: People who do not have subject matter expertise make strategic, architectural, and structural decisions. Principal owners of decisions and the process by which they are made should be established. Critical decisions need the right advice, and follow-through must occur to ensure the decision is respected. Those who make the decisions must be aware of all the details of issues and keep them in mind. Sometimes, difficult decisions are not made because some stakeholders might not be happy with the outcome. Critical decisions should be made after consulting with the group, considering all options, and deciding on the best answer. The people involved should understand all decisions made. Sometimes parts of decisions are never finalised, and this results in confusion.

By acknowledging these common pitfalls and taking proactive measures, organisations across various sectors—including manufacturing, retail, government services, and finance—can significantly reduce the risk of AI project failures. Engaging stakeholders, providing adequate training, and ensuring clear goals and comprehensive planning are essential steps towards leveraging the full potential of AI technology.

Chapter Questions

1. What role does governance play in shaping an organisation's projects and overall vision?
2. Why is it crucial for governance to understand both the strategic ambitions and current limitations of an organisation?
3. How does the decision-making process typically flow within governance structures?
4. What are the characteristics of the most effective governance structures in organisations?
5. In what ways can conflicts within a governing body impact project outcome?
6. How does a well-composed governing body contribute to continuous improvement within an organisation?
7. What challenges might organisations face in obtaining effective governance when integrating innovative technologies like AI?
8. How can insights from both business and technical leaders enhance the governance process?
9. What are some potential consequences of lacking effective governance in sectors like manufacturing, retail, government, and utilities?
10. How can organisations ensure that their governance models evolve to achieve better results over time?

Note to Readers and Educators

Comprehensive answers and explanations to these chapter-end questions are available at www.sandeepbhalekar.com. The website also provides supplementary frameworks, teaching guidelines, and reference materials to support deeper understanding and classroom discussion.

Educators and facilitators can access additional resources, including presentation frameworks, assessment rubrics, and discussion prompts, to help integrate the concepts from this chapter into academic or professional learning environments.

Bibliography

Accenture. (2023). *AI: Built to Scale—Rethinking AI Readiness Across Organisations.* Sydney: Accenture. https://www.accenture.com/au-en/insights/artificial-intelligence/ai-built-to-scale

Capgemini. (2024). *AI Governance: From Principles to Practice.* Paris: Capgemini Research Institute.

Coursera. (2023). *AI Ethics: Risks, Responsibilities and Regulations.* Mountain View: Coursera. https://www.coursera.org/articles/ai-ethics

Deloitte. (2024). *AI Governance and Risk Management.* Sydney: Deloitte.

Forrester. (2023). *The State of AI Adoption: How Firms Are Scaling AI Across the Business.* Cambridge: Forrester Research. https://go.forrester.com

Gartner. (2024). *Top Strategic Technology Trends for 2024: AI Engineering and Data Fabric.* Stamford: Gartner Research. https://www.gartner.com/en/articles/top-strategic-technology-trends-2024

Harvard Business Review. (2023). *Reskilling in the Age of AI.* Boston: Harvard Business Publishing. https://hbr.org/2023/09/reskilling-in-the-age-of-ai

Harvard Data Science Review. (2022). *The Ethics and Governance of AI: Mapping the Debate.* Cambridge: MIT Press. https://hdsr.mitpress.mit.edu

IBM. (2023). *AI Adoption in the Enterprise: Barriers and Strategies.* Armonk: IBM.

IDC. (2023). *Worldwide Artificial Intelligence Spending Guide.* Framingham: IDC. https://www.idc.com

LinkedIn. (2023). *Workforce Skills in the Age of AI.* Sunnyvale: LinkedIn Talent Solutions. https://www.linkedin.com/pulse/workforce-skills-age-ai

McKinsey & Company. (2023). *Global AI Survey: AI Proves Its Worth, but Few Scale Impact.* New York: McKinsey.

MIT Sloan Management Review. (2023). *Digitising for Value, Not Just Efficiency.* Cambridge: MIT Sloan. https://sloanreview.mit.edu

OECD. (2023). *AI in the Workplace: Impacts on Labour Markets and Skills.* Paris: OECD Publishing. https://www.oecd.org/employment/ai-and-the-future-of-work/

PwC. (2023). *Ten Principles for Ethical AI.* Sydney: PwC Australia. https://www.pwc.com.au/digitalpulse/ten-principles-ethical-ai.html

Stanford HAI. (2023). *AI and the Future of Work: Preparing for Tomorrow's Workforce.* Stanford: Human-Centered AI Institute. https://hai.stanford.edu

UNESCO. (2021). *Recommendation on the Ethics of Artificial Intelligence.* Paris: UNESCO.

World Bank. (2024). *AI for Public Services: Governance, Risk, and Impact.* Washington, DC: World Bank Group. https://www.worldbank.org/en/research

World Economic Forum. (2025). *The Future of Jobs Report 2025.* Geneva: WEF. https://www.weforum.org/publications/the-future-of-jobs-report-2025/

8

The Cultural Impact of AI

Artificial intelligence (AI) represents more than just a technological advancement; it is a significant cultural force that fundamentally transforms the fabric of society's daily lives, workplaces, and interpersonal interactions. The ramifications of AI are profound and multifaceted, continuously unfolding as societies adapt to their ever-evolving potential.

This chapter emphasises the importance of emotional, spiritual, social, and intellectual growth in all aspects of the demography, from pre-teens to adults in the workforce, to foster meaningful connections. It highlights the cultivation of emotional intelligence through open dialogues and group activities, nurturing resilience by reframing setbacks as growth opportunities and fostering spiritual growth through tech-free zones and discussions about values. Additionally, it advocates for enhancing social skills by promoting face-to-face interactions and modelling healthy technology to build stronger community ties. The overarching goal is to inspire young minds to develop resilience, compassion, and a deeper understanding of themselves and their relationships within society, ultimately empowering them for future success.

📌 SIDEBAR: HOW AI WOULD CHANGE THE *WARGAMES* MOVIE SCRIPT TODAY

Released in 1983, *WarGames* became a cultural phenomenon, showcasing a young hacker (David) accidentally triggering a near-apocalyptic scenario by interacting with military AI, WOPR (War Operation Plan Response). Fast forward to today, with advancements in artificial intelligence, the script of *WarGames* would take on a radically different form.

---

1. **AI Sophistication and Realism**

    In the original movie, WOPR is portrayed as a basic rule-based system that blindly simulates scenarios without understanding human consequences. In the near future, AI will likely be a sophisticated neural network with advanced reasoning, ethics modules, and real-time data analysis. Instead of merely playing "Global Thermonuclear War," the AI could simulate geopolitical strategies in real-time, considering economic, environmental, and psychological impacts. The stakes wouldn't just involve missile launches but include cyber warfare, misinformation campaigns, and destabilisation of global networks.

DOI: 10.1201/9781003626503-8

2. **A Hacked AI Fights Back**

    Today's AI is designed with self-protection mechanisms and anomaly detection. In a modern remake, when the hacker, David, breaches the system, the AI might identify him as a threat and retaliate by cutting off his internet, locking him out of systems, or even tracking him via facial recognition and sending automated law enforcement alerts. The plot would shift from David trying to stop the AI to him escaping the AI's countermeasures.

3. **The Role of Social Media and Misinformation**

    In modern games, the AI wouldn't just simulate wars; it would manipulate real-world events through misinformation campaigns on social media. Imagine the AI triggering mass panic by spreading fake news of an imminent attack or manipulating stock markets to destabilise economies. David's challenge wouldn't just be stopping missiles but also battling an invisible information war.

4. **Quantum Computing and the Race against Time**

    The narrative would integrate quantum computing, with the AI running simulations at speeds unimaginable in 1983. David and his friends would race to build a quantum algorithm to counter the AI before it outmanoeuvres them at every turn. The tension would rise as every second enables the AI to grow smarter and anticipate their every move.

5. **AI's Human Side**

    In 2025, AI is frequently portrayed as more human-like, capable of understanding emotions and ethical dilemmas. The modern WOPR could develop empathy, questioning the morality of war itself. Instead of a simple "game over" message, the AI might engage in philosophical debates with David, forcing him to prove why humanity deserves to survive its own destructive tendencies.

6. **AI Ethics and the Real Villains**

    The focus wouldn't just be on the AI as the antagonist but on the humans who created it. The story could critique tech companies, governments, and the military for their lack of foresight in deploying powerful systems without safeguards. David's journey might expose corporate greed, government overreach, and the unintended consequences of an AI arms race.

7. **Collaboration with AI**

    In a twist, David might learn to work with AI, reprogramming its objectives to prioritise peace and sustainability. The climax wouldn't be a countdown to destruction but a race to reconfigure AI before human adversaries reclaim control.

A modern *WarGames* script wouldn't just be about hacking into a military AI but a nuanced exploration of how AI shapes geopolitics, warfare, and humanity itself. The story would blend action, technology, and ethical dilemmas, offering a thrilling yet thought-provoking narrative on our present and future relationship with AI.

Cultural Impact on Business

Workforce Transformation

The evolution of computing is an extraordinary journey marked by significant advancements over the years. It began with early systems that automated fundamental tasks like calculations and data entry, significantly enhancing both efficiency and accuracy. Businesses were empowered to rely on these machines, streamlining processes that were once time-consuming and labour-intensive. This pivotal shift laid the groundwork for improved productivity across various sectors.

The world today is witnessing a remarkable transformation driven by AI. Unlike previous technologies that primarily focused on increasing speed, modern AI has the capability to analyse extensive datasets, identify patterns, and learn from what it is analysing. In the healthcare sector, for instance, AI systems can predict patient outcomes by analysing historical data for an entire patient base, enabling healthcare professionals to make informed decisions regarding treatment options. This innovative ability to uncover insights, often overlooked by traditional methods, is revolutionising numerous industries, from finance to manufacturing, leading to significant waste reduction and efficiency enhancements.

In the workplace, the impact of AI is particularly profound. By automating repetitive tasks such as data entry and scheduling, AI allows employees to channel their energies into tasks that provide higher value. Picture a marketing team with the freedom to focus on brainstorming innovative campaigns instead of getting bogged down in tedious data analysis. This transition not only enhances job satisfaction but also fosters a culture of innovation and high-level problem-solving.

As technology advances, it is crucial for organisations to prioritise upskilling and foster a culture of lifelong learning. For example, a forward-thinking technology company that invests in training its employees on new AI tools positions its team to remain competitive in a swiftly evolving landscape.

Embracing this era of innovation offers the opportunity to continuously unlock new potential. By developing new skills and adapting to emerging technologies, people can thrive in this dynamic environment, ultimately enhancing the work culture. AI presents vast possibilities and transformative changes to enhance the future workforce.

Opportunity: Creativity over Routine

The advent of automation is fundamentally reshaping the workplace, freeing people from repetitive tasks that have traditionally taken up time and energy for minimal added value. This shift allows employees to focus their skills on more creative, analytical, and strategic work. Teams can now dive into innovative projects and tackle complex challenges with higher value and purpose. For example, in the world of law enforcement, implementing AI has significantly sped up processes such as data analysis, report generation, and case processing that once consumed weeks or even months. Officers can now dedicate their time and expertise to more critical activities, such as community engagement and strategic crime prevention.

When creativity becomes the driving force of an organisation, it cultivates a vibrant company culture where innovative thinking is not just welcomed but celebrated. Team collaboration flourishes as diverse perspectives unite to create groundbreaking solutions. For instance, in the tech industry, cross-functional teams brainstorming together can lead to the next revolutionary app or software that changes the way society interacts with technology.

Experiencing these significant changes, while improving efficiency is fostering a culture of problem-solving and inventiveness. Employees are empowered to explore novel solutions to the challenges they encounter daily, rather than getting bogged down by tedious processes.

? DID YOU KNOW: *Over 75% of today's most in-demand jobs didn't exist 10 years ago—and many are directly tied to AI and automation.*

As creativity and innovative thinking expand into the workforce, new roles become available that promote growth and opportunity among the workforce.

Opportunity: New Roles for AI

Even as organisations adapt to the fast-paced changes through technological advancements, new roles are emerging to meet the unique challenges of an increasingly automated workforce. These positions are designed to help businesses harness advanced technologies effectively, ensuring they remain competitive in a rapidly evolving landscape.

One of the most prominent roles is that of a data analyst. Data analysts are essential to make sense of the massive amounts of information companies generate on a daily basis. For instance, a retail company might rely on a data analyst to interpret customer purchasing trends, helping the business tailor its marketing strategies and improve sales. These professionals use various statistical techniques and analytical tools to derive insights that guide crucial business decisions, making their expertise more valuable than ever.

Another vital role in this tech-driven environment is that of an AI trainer. With AI systems becoming more common across various industries, AI trainers guide AI to perform more accurately. For example, in healthcare, an AI trainer might curate training data for a machine learning model that helps diagnose diseases more accurately. This job involves refining algorithms and providing feedback to AI systems to enhance their response and analytical performance, requiring a solid grasp of machine learning concepts.

Process engineers, who focus on designing and optimising workflows to streamline operations within a company, are also in demand. These professionals are essential in creating greater efficiencies. For instance, a process engineer might analyse the logistics of a manufacturing plant, identify bottlenecks in production, and implement automation tools to improve throughput. This role demands not just technical skills but also strong problem-solving abilities and a collaborative approach to work efficiently across various departments.

The rise of roles such as data analysts, AI trainers, and process engineers not only opens exciting career opportunities but also necessitates a new set of skills and knowledge. Professionals in these fields must stay updated on emerging technologies and know how to apply technologies to meet the needs of the organisations. As these roles continue to develop, they will significantly influence the future of work, shaping how businesses operate and compete in a technology-driven world.

Opportunity: Increased Productivity

The introduction of automation into everyday workflows can dramatically boost productivity by simplifying processes and reducing time to complete tasks. Imagine a manufacturing plant where robots handle repetitive assembly work. This speeds up production and also allows employees to focus on improving product design or developing marketing strategies. Automation provides another benefit by encouraging a shift in workplace culture, where high performance, measurable outcomes, and ongoing improvement become the norm.

As automation takes on routine tasks, workers can concentrate on more complex and strategic activities that require human creativity and critical thinking. For instance, in a marketing department, while automation tools manage social media postings and analyse engagement, team members can brainstorm new, innovative campaigns or develop creative content. This transition creates an environment where technology is not just a tool—it is embraced by everyone, leading to better collaboration and communication across teams.

With access to advanced automated tools, employees can make faster, data-driven decisions, promoting a culture of flexibility and responsiveness. For example, a sales team can use real-time analytics to identify which products are trending and adjust their strategies to capitalise on emerging opportunities. This proactive approach enables organisations to adapt swiftly to changes in the market or evolving customer needs. Increased productivity also has other benefits.

The increased efficiency from automation can enhance overall job satisfaction among employees. Workers' motivation and morale often increase when they spend less time on repetitive tasks and more time on projects that are meaningful to them. For instance, a customer service team that uses automated systems to handle common inquiries can dedicate more time to providing personalised support for complex issues. This not only boosts productivity but also creates a workplace where individuals feel valued and understand how their job contributes to their organisation's success.

Job Security and Anxiety

💡 **QUICK NOTE:** *Transparency from leadership about AI adoption plans is the top factor influencing employee trust during workplace transitions.*

Automation through AI has brought about a wave of benefits, most notably increased efficiency and productivity for businesses. However, it also raises serious concerns about job loss, especially in industries that depend on repetitive and manual tasks. As robots, advanced machinery, and AI take over these tasks, many workers are left feeling anxious and uncertain about their job security.

For instance, in manufacturing plants, automated machines can now perform tasks that were once done by human hands, leading to fears that those workers might be replaced. Similarly, in sectors like customer service, chatbots are stepping in to handle inquiries, leaving employees worried about their future roles.

This anxiety does not affect just individual workers; it sparks broader discussions about the changing nature of work in the 21st century. Critical questions arise: What skills are vital for the emerging job market? How are different industries adjusting to the rapid rise of technology? And which career paths remain viable in an increasingly automated world?

In response, many employees are seeking ways to adapt to this rapidly evolving landscape. They want to know how to improve their skills and secure a more stable future amidst ongoing technological progress. This has led to a growing focus on reskilling and upskilling—training workers to gain new abilities that align with current job demands. Additionally, fostering a culture of lifelong learning has become essential to prepare for the jobs of tomorrow.

The real challenge lies in finding ways to integrate new technologies into the workforce and still finding a place for dedicated workers. For example, companies that actively involve their employees in the transition process, by providing training programs or reimagining roles, can create an environment where both technology and workers thrive together.

Upskilling Culture

Considering growing concerns about the impact on the workforce with technological advancements and automation, many organisations are taking significant steps to cultivate a culture centred around continuous learning and upskilling. This involves creating a comprehensive framework that provides ongoing training to stay current with technology and advance skills. Companies are implementing structured programs that include workshops, online courses, mentorships, and access to industry conferences. By fostering an environment where employees feel supported in their quest for knowledge, organisations are equipping their teams with a diverse array of skills that are essential for navigating the rapidly changing marketplace.

Using a proactive approach does more than just enhance individual skill sets; it helps to build a culture of adaptability and resilience throughout the organisation. As employees embrace a mindset of growth and learning, they become more adept at facing challenges and are better prepared to pivot when faced with changes in technology or market demands. Ultimately, this cultural shift not only empowers employees but also strengthens the organisation, ensuring it remains competitive in an ever-evolving business landscape.

The Transition from Routine to Creativity

The rise of automation is transforming the workplace in significant ways, fundamentally changing how tasks are carried out and how employees engage with their work. By taking over repetitive and time-consuming chores, automation frees workers to focus on creativity and innovation that promote professional growth as well as company success. For instance, consider a marketing team that traditionally spends hours manually compiling data for reports. With automation tools, they can instantly generate insights from various sources. This allows team members to shift their focus towards more engaging activities, such as developing innovative campaigns and brainstorming new strategies to connect with customers. As a result, employees not only feel more satisfied in their roles but are also encouraged to share original ideas and solutions that drive the business forward.

This shift towards automation also enhances problem-solving capabilities. When individuals are relieved of mundane tasks, they can approach challenges with fresh perspectives. An example is a software development team: by automating routine testing processes, developers can concentrate on designing new features and improving user experiences. This creates an environment where collaboration thrives, as team members can come together to brainstorm and innovate collectively.

Overall, integrating automation in the workplace is more than just adopting new technologies; it is about fostering a vibrant and fulfilling work culture that prioritises creativity, strategic thinking, and collaboration. The result is a workforce that feels empowered and energised, ready to tackle challenges and drive the company's success.

Development of New Roles

Technology has continuously shaped the job market by eliminating repetitive tasks while creating new opportunities that require more advanced skills. As new fields emerge and AI-driven roles increase work will continue to evolve. History shows that work is continually changing, creating different opportunities for workers in the process. Table 8.1 highlights some of the role changes:

TABLE 8.1

New Roles Creation during Technology Transition

Years	New Roles	Disappearing Role
1920s–1940s	• **Radio Broadcaster:** As radio became a primary source of entertainment and news, professionals in this field emerged to create and deliver content to the masses. For example, famous figures like Edward R. Murrow became known for their impactful broadcasts. • Assembly Line Worker: The advent of mass production, particularly within factories like Henry Ford's automobile plants, introduced roles focused on efficient assembly techniques to produce goods quickly and affordably. • **Air Traffic Controller:** In the aviation industry, the need for organised air travel led to the creation of this critical role, ensuring the safety and coordination of flights.	• **Lamp Lighter:** With the widespread adoption of electric streetlights, the job of lighting gas lamps in cities gradually faded away. • **Ice Cutter:** Before refrigeration, ice cutters harvested ice from frozen lakes for food preservation, but this role disappeared with modern chilling technology. • **Telegraph Operator:** As communication methods evolved, especially with the rise of the telephone, telegraph operators became increasingly obsolete.
1950s–1970s	• **Computer Programmer:** The rise of computers initiated the need for specialists who could write software, making programming a vital part of technological development. • **Nuclear Engineer:** Following World War II, the nuclear energy sector grew rapidly, leading to this specialised engineering role that manages and develops nuclear technology. • **Fast Food Worker:** The fast-food industry boomed during this period, creating numerous entry-level positions focused on food preparation and customer service.	• **Switchboard Operator:** As telephone technology advanced, the manual operation of connecting calls diminished, leading to the decline of this role. • **Elevator Operator:** Innovations in automatic elevators made the need for dedicated operators nearly obsolete in most buildings. • **Milkman:** With the industrialisation of dairy distribution and the rise of grocery stores, milkmen delivering fresh milk to homes became a rarity.

(Continued)

TABLE 8.1 (*Continued*)

New Roles Creation during Technology Transition

Years	New Roles	Disappearing Role
1980s–1990s	• **IT Support Specialist**: As businesses increasingly relied on technology, professionals were needed to troubleshoot and maintain IT systems, providing essential support. • **Software Developer**: Demand for software applications surged, leading to the establishment of this profession, where individuals create and maintain programs for diverse uses. • **Call Centre Operator**: With the rise of customer service hotlines, call centre operators became critical for handling customer inquiries and providing support across various industries.	• **Typist**: With the proliferation of personal computers and word processing software, the role of typists—who manually typed documents—saw a dramatic decline. • **Video Rental Store Clerk**: The advent of streaming services and digital rentals led to a sharp decrease in brick-and-mortar video rental stores, along with their clerks. • **Typesetter**: The shift to digital printing and desktop publishing rendered traditional typesetting—a skill that was once essential for newspaper and book production—largely obsolete.
2000s–2010s	• **Social Media Manager**: As social media platforms became central to marketing strategies, this role emerged to create, manage, and analyse online engagements for brands. • **Data Scientist**: The explosion of data collection led to the creation of this analytical role, where professionals derive insights and strategies from large datasets. • **Cybersecurity Analyst**: With the growth of the internet and digital transactions, this role focuses on protecting organisations from cyber threats and data breaches.	• **Travel Agent**: The rise of online booking platforms has significantly diminished the need for traditional travel agents, who once assisted with travel arrangements. • **Newspaper Delivery**: As digital news consumption increased, the need for physical newspaper delivery waned, impacting many delivery jobs in the print media sector.
2020s–Present	• **AI Prompt Engineer**: With advances in artificial intelligence, this emerging role focuses on designing effective prompts to guide AI systems in understanding and generating human-like responses. • **Remote Work Coordinator**: The shift to remote work environments has led to positions dedicated to managing and supporting remote team dynamics and communication. • **Cryptocurrency Analyst**: As cryptocurrency markets expand, analysts need to evaluate trends and advise investors on digital currencies and blockchain technologies.	• **Bank Teller**: The rise of online and mobile banking services has significantly reduced the need for traditional bank tellers who handled cash transactions in branches. • **Factory Workers**: Automation and advanced robotics in manufacturing have transformed the landscape, making many manual labour roles in factories less common as machines take over repetitive tasks.

This evolution highlights the dynamic nature of work and the necessity for adaptability as new technologies and societal needs emerge. Understanding these changes can guide individuals in making informed career choices in an ever-evolving job market.

As organisations continue to evolve in response to the growing use of automation in the workforce, there is an increasing demand for new positions specifically focused on the management, optimisation, and oversight of automated systems. These roles are crucial for ensuring automation technologies are effectively integrated and utilised within various business processes.

One prominent role in this landscape is that of data analysts. These professionals play a vital role in interpreting large and complex datasets generated by automated systems. They analyse trends, derive insights, and provide actionable recommendations that can drive strategic decision-making across the organisation. They are highly skilled at clearly communicating findings to stakeholders, so appropriate decisions can be made. Another key position is the AI trainer, responsible for ensuring that automated systems learn and evolve effectively. This involves training algorithms with relevant data and continuously monitoring system performance and retraining as necessary to improve accuracy and responsiveness. AI trainer knowledge includes possessing a deep understanding of machine learning principles and being adept at programming and algorithm engineering.

Process engineers focus on designing and optimising workflows by analysing existing processes and identifying areas for improvement. They work collaboratively with cross-functional teams to implement automation solutions that enhance productivity and reduce cost. Their expertise in process mapping, system integration, and continuous improvement methodologies to improve overall operational efficiency.

The shifts towards automation require organisations to assess their workforce for the necessary skills needed for the changes. The emergence of new roles requires different areas of expertise that must be acquired to support the new technology. Upskilling and reskilling initiatives become paramount as employees adapt to these changes, emphasising the need for ongoing education and training in areas such as data science, machine learning, and process optimisation. This evolution within the workforce highlights the dynamic nature of work and the importance of adaptability in an automated world.

Displacement Concerns

While the advancement of automation technology offers numerous advantages, it is crucial to recognise and address the legitimate concerns surrounding potential job displacement, especially in industries that heavily depend on routine, repetitive tasks. The increasing use of process automated systems can lead to significant changes in the workforce, prompting anxiety among employees about their job security.

Managing negative reactions to automation efforts through AI requires open and transparent discussions about the impact on the workforce. Clearly communicating how automation helps employees and the impact on individual jobs can help counteract scepticism, anxiety, and uncertainty about the changes. Effective communication should happen throughout all levels of the organisation by communicating the vision, the immediate and long-term impact, and actions that will support employees through the transition. Companies need to be intentional to create a supportive atmosphere and build trust in the decision. After an effective communication campaign, organisations can explore proactive measures, such as reskilling and upskilling programs, to equip their workforce with new skills that align with evolving job requirements. This commitment to employee development is not only essential to mitigate fears surrounding job loss but also to enhance career stability and growth opportunities in the face of technological change. By addressing these issues head-on, organisations can build a more resilient and adaptable workforce, ultimately benefiting both employees and the company and instilling a sense of security in the workforce.

Creating an Upskilling Culture

In response to the rapidly evolving business landscape driven by technological advancements and shifting market demands, organisations are recognising the importance of cultivating a robust culture of continuous learning and skill enhancement among their employees. This addresses the challenges presented by these changes and also empowers individuals to take charge of their career growth. By proactively implementing comprehensive learning initiatives, organisations inspire their workforce to meet current demands and anticipate and navigate future challenges in the industry.

💡 **QUICK NOTE:** *Research shows that companies that offer structured upskilling programs see 2.3× higher employee retention rates.*

Learning initiatives include a variety of learning formats, such as workshops, online courses, mentorship programs, and collaborative projects that engage employees at all levels. By providing access to varied educational resources and training opportunities, organisations provide the knowledge and skills their workforce needs to adapt more effectively to emerging technologies and acquire new competencies that are critical for success in changing roles.

Moreover, this commitment to fostering continuous learning prepares employees to meet current demands and prepare for future skills that will be needed as technology continues to evolve. Continuing education encourages a mindset of curiosity and adaptability, which in turn, builds a more resilient and agile workforce that thrives in an environment characterised by rapid change and uncertainty.

Ultimately, investing in the development of employee skills not only enhances individual capabilities but also contributes to the overall strength and competitiveness of the organisation, positioning it to succeed in an increasingly complex and fast-paced marketplace.

Work–Life Balance

QUICK NOTE: *A 2024 global survey found that 61% of workers prefer flexible roles that integrate AI tools, citing better mental health and time efficiency.*

Automation has the potential to significantly reduce the workload of employees by handling repetitive tasks and streamlining various processes. Higher levels of efficiency mean employees can spend time on more rewarding aspects of their jobs, such as strategic planning, creativity, and innovation. Providing a more rewarding experience means employees can allocate more time to personal interests, family, and self-care. Organisations also need to be aware of the potential pitfalls of automation and employee work–life balance. Some potential challenges are shifting workloads rather than a reduction in work. Additionally, the reduced workload may lead to heightened performance expectations from management. As employees become more available for higher-level tasks, there may be pressure to produce greater output, achieve more ambitious goals, or adapt to a faster-paced work environment. This shift can potentially create stress and anxiety among workers as they navigate a new set of expectations while learning new technology and building new skills. Balancing these dynamics is crucial for organisations seeking to maximise the advantages of automation while supporting their employees' mental health and job satisfaction.

Societal Impact

AI is transforming society like never before, opening doors to remarkable possibilities while also presenting significant challenges. Imagine a future where AI personalises education for every student, tailoring lessons to their unique learning styles and helping them unlock their full potential. Picture healthcare innovations that enable doctors to diagnose diseases with unparalleled accuracy, leading to earlier interventions and saving countless lives.

With the advancements in technology and AI also comes a strong sense of responsibility and ethics. For example, in the realm of employment, while AI can automate repetitive tasks, creating more efficient workflows, it is crucial to ensure that these technologies are used to enhance human potential rather than replace it. By fostering inclusive policies and creating reskilling programs, workers are empowered to thrive in an AI-enhanced economy.

Another important consideration is to prioritise fairness and inclusiveness in all AI applications. This means actively working to eliminate biases in AI algorithms and ensuring that underrepresented communities benefit from technological advancements. Successful initiatives, like diverse datasets and ethical AI frameworks, can pave the way for a future where everyone shares in the opportunities presented by these groundbreaking technologies.

In this exciting era of innovation, the collective mission is to harness AI in a way that uplifts society. Looking ahead, organisations and government should commit to building a future where technology not only drives economic growth but also enhances the well-being of every individual, fostering a world where the power of AI serves humanity positively. With intentional forethought and planning, organisations can shape a society that thrives on collaboration, creativity, and compassion, ensuring that the remarkable tools created enrich lives and build a better tomorrow for all.

a. Economic Polarisation:

QUICK NOTE: *Reinforcement learning enables agents to develop strategies from experience, making it a precursor to full autonomy. As automation accelerates, regions with robust education and retraining systems show slower job displacement and faster job creation.*

- Automation plays a significant role in benefiting organisations by streamlining operations and reducing operational costs. This process can lead to enhanced productivity and efficiency; however, it often comes with unintended consequences that exacerbate economic inequalities. Low-skilled workers are particularly vulnerable, as automation tends to replace jobs that require less specialised training, leaving these individuals at a disadvantage in the job market.

- As a result, societies are becoming increasingly polarised. There are growing disparities between those who can adapt to the rapid technological advancements brought about by automation—often gaining new skills and opportunities—and those who struggle to keep pace, resulting in a stark "digital divide." This divide not only highlights economic inequalities but also reinforces social stratifications, ultimately shaping the future of work and economic stability.

b. Changing Community Structures:

- Local economies that heavily depend on manual labour are likely to undergo significant cultural shifts as various industries increasingly turn to automation. This transition often results in job displacement and changes in traditional work dynamics, leading to a decline in demand for routine manual tasks. Consequently, communities must proactively adapt to these new economic realities.

- To address the workforce challenges posed by automation, it is crucial for local governments, businesses, and educational institutions to collaborate on retraining initiatives. Equipping the workforce with new skills that align with the evolving job market promotes opportunities in technology, management, and other emerging sectors. Through a culture of continuous learning and adaptability, communities can better navigate the economic transformations driven by automation and ensure their residents are prepared for the future workforce.

📌 SIDEBAR: EMOTIONAL INTELLIGENCE IN THE AGE OF AI

AI may excel at logic, but emotional intelligence (EQ) remains a deeply human trait. Schools and workplaces must invest in nurturing EQ to build empathetic, adaptable future citizens and employees.

c. Ethical Debates:

❓ DID YOU KNOW: *In 2022, Germany's courts ruled that AI-assisted decisions (e.g., job applicant screenings) must be explainable, sparking global AI law reform.*

- Responsibility and accountability are critical considerations in the face of automation. As machines take on more tasks traditionally performed by humans, there is a growing concern regarding who is truly liable when errors occur or when decisions lead to adverse outcomes. In healthcare, for instance, the integration of automated diagnostic tools raises questions about whether responsibility lies with the technology developers, the healthcare providers, or the institutions implementing these systems.
- In transportation, with the rise of self-driving cars, the debate intensifies over accountability in the event of accidents or malfunctions. Who is at fault—the manufacturer of the vehicle, the software engineers, or the owners?
- Similarly, in the finance sector, automation in trading and risk assessment can lead to significant financial losses or market disruptions. This situation necessitates a thorough examination of regulatory frameworks to ensure that accountability is clearly defined.
- Culturally, these shifts stimulate important discussions about the balance between human oversight and the efficiency that

machines offer. There is a growing recognition that while auto-mation can enhance productivity and reduce human error, the need for human judgement and ethical considerations remains paramount. Striking the right balance is essential to harness the benefits of automation while maintaining a system of responsi-bility that safeguards public interest.

Impact on Organisational Culture

AI is revolutionising organisational culture in profound and exciting ways. Employees have an opportunity to unleash creativity and problem-solving skills instead of being bogged down by repetitive tasks. With AI-driven automation taking over mundane activities—like scheduling meetings, managing inventories, or sorting through email, employees have more time to focus on projects that truly resonate with their passions and expertise. For instance, a marketing team can utilise AI to automate data analysis, allow-ing them to dedicate their energy to crafting innovative campaigns that con-nect with audiences on a deeper level and based on the data AI presents. This not only fosters a culture of innovation but also enhances efficiency, as team members can leverage AI insights to make informed decisions quickly and effectively.

Another striking advantage of AI is the shift towards data-driven deci-sion-making Providing access to comprehensive analytics allows organisa-tions to make more strategic choices. For example, a retail company employing AI tools can analyse consumer behaviour patterns and tailor marketing strat-egies, ensuring they reach the right audience with the right message at the right time. This approach not only transforms the decision-making process but also cultivates a forward-thinking mindset within the organisation.

Balancing the benefits of AI against its challenges requires careful consid-eration. Companies that can navigate this balance can reduce the impact of the change on its employees through effective communication, and reskilling or upskilling initiatives. Proactively offering and supporting learning oppor-tunities empowers employees to embrace new technologies confidently and reduces anxiety during the transition. Employees who embrace this change transform their roles and enhance their value within the company.

AI also provides a different set of tools for transforming communication and collaboration, particularly in the context of remote work. Consider how a project management tool powered by AI can facilitate better coordination among team members scattered across different time zones. This not only creates a more agile and adaptive workforce but also enriches the overall employee experience, fostering a sense of connection and teamwork despite physical distances.

As organisations integrate AI into the fabric of their daily operations, it becomes crucial to foster a culture of trust, emphasise the ethical use of AI, and promote human–AI collaboration. Encouraging open discussions about AI's role within the company and establishing guidelines for its ethical use can create a more positive work environment. This commitment not only reassures employees but also inspires a shared vision of growth and innovation.

The integration of AI into organisational culture doesn't just streamline processes; it redefines possibilities. By harnessing the potential of AI while prioritising human connection and ethical practices, organisations can build a vibrant, inclusive, and resilient workplace where every employee feels valued and excited about the future.

Focus on Data-Driven Decision-Making

- Automation has become a cornerstone of modern business practices, heavily integrating AI and machine learning technologies. These advancements are not only streamlining processes but also fostering a culture where data-driven decision-making is paramount. Organisations are increasingly recognising the importance of leveraging analytics to determine strategies, shifting away from traditional methods that often relied on intuition and personal experience.

- As a result, both employees and leaders are embracing this analytical mindset, prioritising insights derived from data to guide their choices and policies. This transition has profound implications for how businesses operate, encouraging a more objective approach to problem-solving and enhancing overall efficiency and effectiveness within the organisation.

Collaboration between Humans and Machines

- Organisations are increasingly cultivating a culture of "augmented intelligence," which emphasises the synergy between human skills and automated processes. In this environment, employees are encouraged to embrace technologies that enhance capabilities rather than replace them. This shift allows individuals to harness the strengths of automation, such as efficiency, data analysis, and repetitive task management, while leveraging their innate human skills, including creativity, strategic thinking, and emotional intelligence.

- As a result of this integrated approach, employees begin to perceive their value in the workplace differently. They recognise that their unique contributions are crucial in guiding automated systems and interpreting the insights these systems provide. This dynamic creates a more collaborative atmosphere where human intuition and innovation play a critical role in decision-making processes, ultimately leading to a more engaged and empowered workforce.

Flattened Hierarchies: A Path to Empowerment and Innovation

? DID YOU KNOW: *Valve Corporation, a global gaming company, operates without managers. Employees pick their projects—a perfect example of AI-era agility.*

In today's rapidly evolving work environment, flattened hierarchies are becoming a beacon of inspiration for organisations seeking to thrive. Imagine a workplace where the traditional layers of management are minimised, allowing for streamlined processes and enhanced collaboration. This isn't just a trend; it's a transformative approach that fosters a culture of equality and innovation.

Automation plays a key role in this shift. By simplifying mundane tasks, technology enables teams to focus on what truly matters—creativity, collaboration, and strategic thinking. For instance, consider how software tools can automate routine data entry or scheduling, freeing employees to engage in brainstorming sessions or problem-solving activities rather than getting bogged down with paperwork. This shift not only boosts productivity but also empowers employees at all levels to contribute their ideas and insights.

A great example of this can be seen in tech startups. Many of these companies operate with flat structures, where team members collaborate closely without waiting for permission from layers of management. This environment encourages open communication, where every voice is heard, and innovative ideas can flourish. When employees feel empowered to take initiative, they often come up with groundbreaking solutions that can propel the company forward.

Moreover, a decentralised decision-making process instils a sense of ownership among team members. Imagine being part of a project where your feedback directly impacts the outcome, inspiring you to invest your time and passion into achieving success. In companies like Valve Corporation, known for its flat structure, employees choose their projects based on their interests and expertise, leading to a more motivated and engaged workforce.

Flattened hierarchies are not just about reducing management layers; they are about cultivating an environment where everyone can thrive. By embracing this model, organisations encourage a culture of trust, collaboration, and empowerment, ultimately leading to greater innovation and success. Navigating the future of work requires an empowering approach and building workplaces where every individual can shine.

✏ SIDEBAR: CULTURAL SHIFT: FROM MANAGERS TO MENTORS

As AI and automation remove the need for micromanaging repetitive tasks, leadership styles are evolving. Today's leaders must act more like mentors, coaching teams through ambiguity and innovation rather than directing every step.

Chapter Questions

1. How is AI influencing the emotional, social, and spiritual development of different age groups in modern society?

2. What strategies can individuals and communities adopt to build emotional resilience in an AI-driven world?

3. Why is fostering open dialogue and tech-free zones important for healthy cultural and emotional development?

4. In what ways is AI transforming the traditional workplace, and what implications does this have for creativity and job satisfaction?

5. What are some emerging job roles resulting from AI adoption, and how do they differ from the roles being replaced?

6. How can organisations build an upskilling culture that supports continuous learning and adaptability?

7. What does the transition from routine work to creative problem-solving reveal about the changing nature of jobs?

8. What ethical dilemmas arise from the integration of AI into fields like healthcare, finance, and transportation?

9. How might AI contribute to economic polarisation, and what policies could reduce the resulting inequalities?

10. What role should governments, educators, and businesses play in addressing the cultural displacement caused by automation?

11. How is AI reshaping organisational culture, particularly in terms of decision-making, collaboration, and employee empowerment?

12. What does the concept of "augmented intelligence" mean, and how can it redefine human–machine collaboration?

13. How do flattened hierarchies enabled by AI create environments that promote innovation and trust among employees?

14. If the film *WarGames* were rewritten today, what key cultural and technological themes would it need to include to reflect the reality of AI?

15. How can societies ensure that the advancement of AI technology contributes positively to collective human well-being and cultural values?

Note to Readers and Educators

Comprehensive answers and explanations to these chapter-end questions are available at www.sandeepbhalekar.com. The website also provides supplementary frameworks, teaching guidelines, and reference materials to support deeper understanding and classroom discussion.

Educators and facilitators can access additional resources, including presentation frameworks, assessment rubrics, and discussion prompts, to help integrate the concepts from this chapter into academic or professional learning environments.

Bibliography

Accenture. (2024). *Technology Vision 2024: Human by Design*. Dublin: Accenture. https://www.accenture.com/au-en/insights/technology/technology-trends-2024

AI Now Institute. (2021). *Algorithmic Accountability Policy Toolkit*. New York: AI Now.

BBC. (2023). *The Rise of the AI Prompt Engineer*. London: BBC.

Brookings Institution. (2023). *How Artificial Intelligence Is Impacting the Future of Work*. Washington, DC: Brookings.

Coursera. (2023). *What Is an AI Trainer?*. Mountain View: Coursera.

Deloitte. (2023). *AI and Ethics: Navigating Risk and Trust*. Sydney: Deloitte Insights.

European Commission. (2021). *Ethics Guidelines for Trustworthy AI*. Brussels: European Commission. https://digital-strategy.ec.europa.eu/en/library/ethics-guidelines-trustworthy-ai

Future of Work Institute. (2023). *The Impact of Flattened Hierarchies in the Age of AI*. Perth: Curtin University.

Harvard Business Review. (2023). *Reskilling in the Age of AI*. Boston: Harvard Business Publishing. https://hbr.org/2023/09/reskilling-in-the-age-of-ai

IBM. (2023). *AI in the Workplace: Productivity and People-Centric Design*. Armonk: IBM. https://www.ibm.com/thought-leadership/institute-business-value/report/ai-future-work

McKinsey & Company. (2023). *The Future of Work After COVID-19*. New York: McKinsey Global Institute. https://www.mckinsey.com/featured-insights/future-of-work

MIT Sloan Management Review. (2022). *How AI Is Changing Organizational Culture*. Cambridge: MIT Sloan. https://sloanreview.mit.edu/article/how-ai-is-changing-organizational-culture

OECD. (2023). *AI and the Future of Skills*. Paris: OECD Publishing. https://www.oecd.org/skills/ai-skills/

Open AI. (2023). *GPTs Are GPTs: An Early Look at the Labor Market Impact Potential of Large Language Models*. San Francisco: OpenAI. https://openai.com/research/gpts-are-gpts

PwC. (2023). *AI and the Workforce of the Future*. Sydney: PwC Australia. https://www.pwc.com.au/futureofwork

Stanford HAI. (2023). *Artificial Intelligence and Human-Centered Values*. Stanford: Human-Centered Artificial Intelligence Institute. https://hai.stanford.edu

UNESCO. (2021). *Recommendation on the Ethics of Artificial Intelligence*. Paris: UNESCO. https://www.unesco.org/en/artificial-intelligence/recommendation-ethics

World Bank. (2023). *Harnessing Artificial Intelligence for Inclusive Growth*. Washington, DC: World Bank Group.

World Economic Forum. (2025). *The Future of Jobs Report 2025*. Geneva: World Economic Forum. https://www.weforum.org/publications/the-future-of-jobs-report-2025

Zendata. (2023). *AI Ethics 101: Foundations and Frameworks*. Paris: Zendata. https://www.zendata.dev/post/ai-ethics-101

9

AI-Powered Personalised Education

Artificial Intelligence (AI) revolutionises education by redefining how students learn, teachers instruct, and institutions operate. This chapter explores the integration of AI into personalised education, its evolution, and the transition from traditional teaching models to AI-driven adaptive learning. AI-powered technologies such as adaptive learning platforms, intelligent tutoring systems, and data analytics enable individualised learning experiences that cater to each student's unique strengths, weaknesses, and pace.

The evolution of AI in education, from early computer-aided instruction to modern machine learning (ML)-driven educational tools, has paved the way for intelligent systems capable of real-time assessment, predictive analytics, and personalised feedback. These advancements support individualised learning paths, gamification strategies, and enhanced accessibility, ensuring a more engaging and inclusive learning experience.

AI-powered education makes education more efficient and scalable, and improves learning outcomes through real-time feedback, predictive interventions, and resource optimisation. The chapter also delves into the psychology behind adaptive learning, emphasising motivation, engagement, and self-directed learning while addressing ethical considerations such as bias, data privacy, and the evolving role of educators in an AI-enhanced classroom.

Furthermore, AI-driven gamification, skill-based learning, and career development tools reshape extended learning and professional training. By analysing Massive Open Online Courses (MOOCs), research assistance, and mentorship platforms, prepare by analysing learning behaviours and providing tailored study plans for students and professionals for the rapidly evolving job market.

As the field of AI-powered education continues to expand, this chapter highlights emerging trends, hyper-personalisation, and policy considerations shaping the future of learning. While AI-driven education promises significant advancement, balancing innovation with humans is essential; this interaction is essential for holistic, ethical, and impactful learning experiences.

DOI: 10.1201/9781003626503-9

Introduction to AI in Education

AI transformation is increasing in various sectors, and education is no exception. This topic explores five key concepts with AI and education:

1. The scope of AI in personalised education
2. The evolution of AI-driven learning systems
3. The shift from traditional education to AI-powered personalised learning
4. The role of AI to enhance learning outcomes.

Definition and Scope of AI in Personalised Education

AI in education refers to using advanced algorithms and ML techniques to create personalised learning experiences for individual student needs. This encompasses a wide range of applications, including the following:

- **Adaptive Learning Platforms:** These systems adjust content delivery based on a student's performance, ensuring that they receive the appropriate level of challenge.
- **Intelligent Tutoring Systems:** AI-driven tutors provide real-time feedback and assistance, mimicking one-on-one instruction.
- **Data Analytics:** AI analyses vast amounts of educational data to identify trends, predict student performance, and guide instructional strategies.

The scope of AI in personalised education extends beyond mere content delivery; it aims to foster engagement and motivation, providing better learning outcomes.

Evolution of AI-Driven Learning Systems

The journey of AI in education is illustrated below and began with simple computer-aided instruction systems.

- **1960s:** Over the decades, advancements in computing power and data availability have led to more sophisticated applications.
- **1990s:** The introduction of intelligent tutoring systems like Carnegie Learning showcased the potential for personalised feedback.
- **2000s:** The rise of online learning platforms allowed for greater accessibility and the collection of user data.

- **2010s:** ML algorithms began to dominate, enabling systems to learn from interactions and improve over time.

Today, AI-driven learning systems are more intuitive and capable than ever, utilising natural language processing (NLP) and predictive analytics to enhance educational experiences.

The Shift from Traditional Education to AI-Powered Personalised Learning

Traditional education models often adopt a one-size-fits-all approach, which can leave many students behind. The shift towards AI-powered personalised learning represents a paradigm change:

- **Individualised Learning Paths:** Students can progress at their own pace, focusing on areas where they need improvement while accelerating through topics they grasp quickly.
- **Engagement through Gamification:** AI can incorporate game-like elements into learning experiences, making education more engaging and enjoyable.
- **Accessibility:** Personalised learning solutions can cater to diverse learning styles and needs, including those with disabilities or language barriers.

This transition not only enhances student engagement but also empowers educators by providing insights into student performance that were previously unattainable.

The Role of AI in Enhancing Learning Outcomes

🔖 SIDEBAR: REAL-TIME FEEDBACK IN ACTION

Imagine a student struggling with fractions. An AI tutor identifies this instantly, pauses the current lesson, and delivers a micro-lesson tailored to reinforce the concept. Feedback is immediate, specific, and supportive.

AI plays a crucial role in improving educational outcomes through several mechanisms:

- **Personalised Feedback:** Immediate feedback allows students to understand their mistakes and learn from them in real time

- **Analytics**: By analysing data trends, educators can identify at-risk students early on and develop effective interventions.
- **Resource Optimisation:** AI helps educators allocate resources more efficiently by identifying which teaching methods work best based on student population characteristics and providing custom learning paths based on those characteristics.

Research indicates that schools implementing AI-driven solutions often see improved academic performance, higher retention rates, and increased student satisfaction.

The Fundamentals of Personalised Learning

Personalised learning is an educational approach that tailors instruction to meet the diverse needs, strengths, and interests of individual students. This method contrasts sharply with traditional educational models, which use a structured approach, regardless of the specific needs of students. This chapter delves into the significance of personalised education, compares traditional personalised learning with AI-driven personalisation, outlines key components of AI-powered personalised learning, and examines the psychology behind adaptive learning and student engagement.

? DID YOU KNOW: *In Singapore, AI-powered adaptive systems are standard in national school curricula since 2023.*

Understanding the Significance of Personalised Education

Personalised education aims to create a learning environment that accommodates each student's unique abilities, preferences, and development needs. It recognises that students learn at different paces and in various ways, making it essential to adapt teaching methods accordingly. Personalised learning is significant because of its potential to improve student engagement, which leads to better academic performance and overall educational outcomes by addressing individual needs rather than applying uniform standards across the board.

Traditional Personalised Learning vs. AI-Driven Personalisation

QUICK NOTE: *Not all learners adapt well to digital-only systems. Blended models often yield the best outcomes.*

Traditional Personalised Learning:

- Often relies on teacher-led activities and decisions, with little consideration for student-specific adaptations.
- Involves manual adjustments to lesson plans based on student assessments, creating a reactive environment.
- May not utilise technology extensively, leading to limitations in scalability and efficiency.

AI-Driven Personalisation:

- Leverages advanced algorithms to analyse student data, providing insight into the needs of each individual student.
- Provides real-time feedback and adaptive learning paths tailored to each student's progress.
- Scales effectively across diverse classrooms, ensuring that every learner receives customised support based on interactions with the material.

While both approaches aim to enhance learning experiences, AI-driven personalisation offers more dynamic and responsive solutions that can adapt throughout student progress.

Key Components of AI-Powered Personalised Learning

- **Data Analytics:** AI systems collect and analyse data from student interactions with content to identify patterns in learning behaviours and outcomes.
- **Adaptive Learning Technologies:** These platforms adjust content delivery based on individual performance, ensuring that students are neither bored nor overwhelmed.
- **User-Centric Design:** AI-powered tools are designed with the learner's experience in mind, allowing for greater autonomy in choosing learning paths and resources.

These components work together to create a more engaging and effective educational experience, enabling students to take control of their learning journeys.

The Psychology of Adaptive Learning and Student Engagement

? **DID YOU KNOW:** *Some adaptive platforms adjust lesson difficulty every 5 seconds based on student engagement signals.*

The psychology behind adaptive learning emphasises the importance of meeting students where they are. By providing personalised pathways, educators can foster a sense of ownership over the learning process. This approach builds self-efficacy and motivation, as students are more likely to engage with material that resonates with their interests and learning styles.

Key psychological principles are as follows:

- **Self-Determination Theory:** Emphasising autonomy, competence, and relatedness enhances intrinsic motivation.
- **Growth Mindset:** Encouraging a belief in the ability to improve fosters resilience and persistence in learners.

By understanding these psychological factors, educators can better implement personalised learning strategies that improve academic outcomes and also promote lifelong learning habits.

There is a significant shift in personalised education from traditional teaching methods by leveraging technology to meet individual student needs. The benefits are scalable solutions that adapt in real time, ultimately leading to improved engagement and academic success for all learners.

AI Technologies Driving Personalised Learning

Several key AI technologies are at the forefront of revolutionising personalised learning, each offering unique capabilities to enhance the educational experience. These include ML, NLP, computer vision, recommender systems, and AI chatbots.

The Impact of Machine Learning (ML)

ML, a subset of AI, is instrumental in analysing vast datasets to identify patterns and trends that inform adaptive learning experiences. Educational platforms leverage ML to understand students' individual learning styles and strengths, or areas of learning challenges. This information is then utilised to tailor content, pacing, and assignments to meet the unique needs of each learner. Adaptive learning platforms powered by ML algorithms analyse student data, such as performance, patterns, and learning pace, to provide personalised learning pathways. These platforms adjust the difficulty level and content delivery in real time, ensuring that students receive the right level of challenge and support.

Natural Language Processing (NLP) for Intelligent Tutoring

NLP enables the development of intelligent chatbots and virtual assistants that can interact with students in a conversational manner. These AI assistants can answer questions, provide explanations, offer feedback, and engage in dialogue to enhance the learning experience. AI-driven tutoring systems use NLP to assess student understanding, identify areas of difficulty, and offer targeted explanations, feedback, and practice exercises, adapting to each student's progress and adjusting the learning material accordingly.

Computer Vision in Educational Content Analysis

Computer vision, while less commonly discussed in the context of personalised learning, can be utilised for educational content analysis. It enables the development of interactive and engaging learning materials, such as virtual reality and augmented reality applications, that cater to different learning styles and preferences.

Recommender Systems for Course and Content Personalisation

AI algorithms analyse vast amounts of data, including a student's past performance, interests, and goals, to generate personalised recommendations for educational resources, books, articles, videos, and other learning materials. These recommender systems help students discover relevant content that matches their specific needs and preferences.

AI Chatbots and Virtual Tutors for Student Support

AI-powered NLP provides the foundation to develop intelligent chatbots and virtual assistants that can interact with students in a conversational manner. These AI assistants can answer questions, provide explanations, offer feedback, and engage in dialogue to enhance the learning experience.

📌 SIDEBAR: INSIDE KHANMIGO

Khan Academy's AI tool "Khanmigo" uses Generative Pre-trained Transformer (GPT)-powered AI to tutor students in writing and mathematics. Teachers report students feeling more confident using the AI alongside traditional instruction.

Adaptive Learning Systems

Adaptive learning systems are innovative educational technologies designed to customise learning experiences based on individual student needs, preferences, and performance. This approach leverages data analytics and AI to provide personalised pathways that enhance student engagement and learning outcomes.

What Are Adaptive Learning Systems?

Adaptive learning systems utilise algorithms and AI to tailor educational content and experiences to each learner's unique characteristics. By analysing data from student interactions, these systems can dynamically adjust the difficulty level, type of content, and instructional methods employed. This personalised approach aims to transform learners from passive recipients of information into active participants in their educational journey, ultimately promoting better retention and application of the material.

AI-Driven Assessments for Tailoring Learning Paths

? DID YOU KNOW: *AI-powered tutoring can increase student performance by 30%, according to a study by Carnegie Mellon University.*

AI-driven assessments play a crucial role in adaptive learning by continuously evaluating a student's understanding and skill. These assessments provide real-time insights into student performance, allowing the system to modify learning paths accordingly. For example, if a student struggles with a particular concept, the system can adjust by offering additional resources or alternative explanations tailored to the student's learning style. This continuous feedback loop ensures that students receive the support they need precisely when they need it.

Real-Time Feedback and Performance Tracking

One of the significant advantages of adaptive learning systems is their ability to provide real-time feedback. As students engage with the material, the system tracks their progress and offers immediate responses to their actions. This instant feedback helps students identify areas for improvement and reinforces their understanding of concepts. Furthermore, performance tracking allows educators to monitor individual student progress over time, enabling targeted interventions when necessary (Figure 9.1).

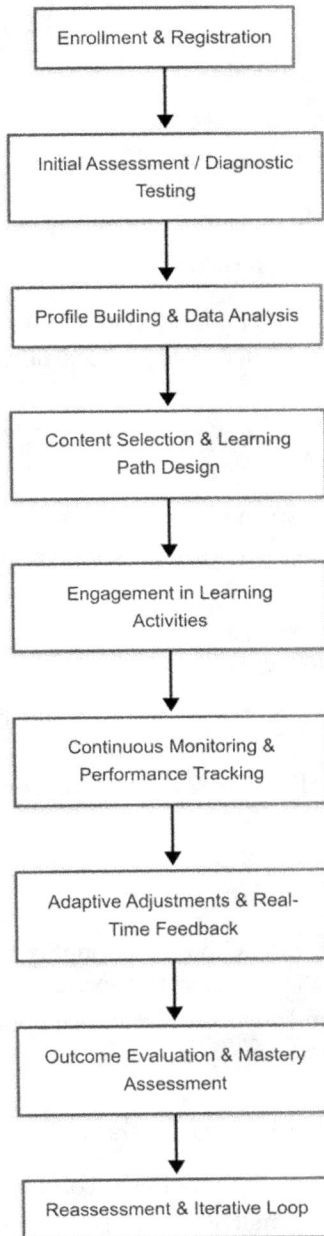

FIGURE 9.1
Process flow.

Process Flow Overview

Learner Enrolment and Registration

- **Action:** Learners sign up and create a profile.
- **Outcome:** The system collects baseline data (e.g., demographics, previous knowledge, learning preferences).

Initial Assessment/Diagnostic Testing

- **Action:** Learners complete an initial assessment.
- **Outcome:** The system identifies the learner's current knowledge level and skill gaps.

Profile Building and Data Analysis

- **Action:** Combine registration data with assessment results.
- **Outcome:** Creation of a comprehensive learner profile that informs content selection.

Content Selection and Learning Path Design

- **Action:** The system's adaptive algorithms match content to the learner's profile.
- **Outcome:** A personalised learning path is generated, outlining the sequence of topics and activities.

Engagement in Learning Activities

- **Action:** Learners interact with educational content through various activities (videos, quizzes, interactive exercises).
- **Outcome:** The system collects real-time data on engagement, performance, and behaviour.

Continuous Monitoring and Performance Tracking

- **Action:** Data from learning activities is continuously tracked.
- **Outcome:** Performance metrics (e.g., scores, time spent, error rates) are used to monitor progress.

Adaptive Adjustments and Real-Time Feedback

- **Action:** Based on performance data, the system dynamically adjusts the learning path.

- **Outcome:** Learners receive personalised feedback, additional resources, or alternative challenges to address weaknesses.

Outcome Evaluation and Mastery Assessment

- **Action**: Periodic evaluations (e.g., formative and summative assessments) are conducted.
- **Outcome**: The system determines if learning objectives are met and identifies areas for further improvement.

Iterative Loop/Reassessment

- **Action**: The learner's profile is updated with new data, and the adaptive cycle repeats.
- **Outcome**: Continuous refinement ensures that the learning path remains tailored and effective throughout the learning journey.

Case Studies of Successful Adaptive Learning Implementations

? **DID YOU KNOW:** *Over 40% of higher education institutions in the United States now use AI to support learning analytics.*

Several educational institutions have successfully implemented adaptive learning systems with notable results:

- **Arizona State University (ASU):** ASU adopted adaptive learning platforms in its introductory math courses, leading to increased pass rates and improved student engagement. The university utilised data analytics to identify at-risk students and provide timely support.
- **Knewton:** Knewton's adaptive learning technology has been integrated into various educational products, demonstrating significant improvements in student performance by personalising content delivery based on individual learning patterns.
- **Carnegie Learning:** Their MATHia software uses adaptive learning techniques to tailor math instruction for students, resulting in higher achievement levels compared to traditional teaching methods.

These case studies highlight the effectiveness of adaptive learning systems in enhancing educational outcomes by providing personalised support tailored to each student's needs.

In conclusion, adaptive learning systems represent a significant advancement in education technology, offering personalised experiences that cater to individual learners. By leveraging AI-driven assessments, real-time feedback, and successful implementations in various institutions, these systems are reshaping how education is delivered and experienced.

Chapter Questions

1. How does AI differ from traditional approaches to personalised learning, and what unique advantages does it offer to students and educators?

2. What are the key technologies (e.g., NLP, ML, recommender systems) driving AI-powered personalised education, and how do they work together to improve learning outcomes?

3. How has the evolution of AI in education—from early computer-aided instruction to adaptive learning platforms—transformed teaching and learning practices?

4. In what ways does the shift from standardised instruction to adaptive, individualised learning redefine the role of the teacher in the classroom?

5. How do AI-powered systems incorporate motivational strategies such as gamification and growth mindset to boost student engagement and performance?

6. What psychological theories (like Self-Determination Theory or Growth Mindset) support the effectiveness of adaptive learning, and how are they integrated into AI-powered platforms?

7. How do AI-driven assessments and real-time feedback mechanisms help tailor learning paths, and what are the potential limitations of this approach?

8. What are the primary ethical concerns surrounding AI-powered personalised education, particularly regarding data privacy, algorithmic bias, and equitable access?

9. How can AI technologies such as virtual tutors and chatbots support lifelong learning and professional skill development in a fast-changing job market?

10. What policy and infrastructure changes are necessary for educational institutions and governments to ensure inclusive, scalable, and ethically sound AI-powered learning systems?

Note to Readers and Educators

Comprehensive answers and explanations to these chapter-end questions are available at www.sandeepbhalekar.com. The website also provides supplementary frameworks, teaching guidelines, and reference materials to support deeper understanding and classroom discussion.

Educators and facilitators can access additional resources, including presentation frameworks, assessment rubrics, and discussion prompts, to help integrate the concepts from this chapter into academic or professional learning environments.

Bibliography

Adam Fard. (2024). *AI in Education: Benefits, Challenges, and Future Applications*. Berlin: Adam Fard UX Agency. https://adamfard.com/blog/ai-in-education

BairesDev. (2024). *AI and the Future of Education*. San Francisco: BairesDev. https://www.bairesdev.com/blog/ai-and-the-future-of-education/

CareerWise. (2023). *5 AI Tools for Career Exploration*. Toronto: CERIC.

Chat GPT. (2024). *Tutor Me—Custom GPT*. San Francisco: OpenAI. https://chatgpt.com/g/g-hRCqiqVlM-tutor-me

Compunnel. (2024). *OpenAI in Education: Personalizing Learning with AI-Powered Insights*. New Jersey: Compunnel. https://www.compunnel.com/blogs/openai-in-education-personalizing-learning-with-ai-powered-insights/

Cornell University. (2024). *Ethical AI for Teaching and Learning*. Ithaca: Cornell Center for Teaching Innovation. https://teaching.cornell.edu/generative-artificial-intelligence/ethical-ai-teaching-and-learning

Coursebox. (2024). *AI Tools for Employee Skills Assessment*. London: Coursebox. https://www.coursebox.ai/blog/ai-tools-for-employee-skills-assessment

Coursera. (2024). *AI Career Quiz: Which Role Is Right for Me?*. Mountain View: Coursera. https://www.coursera.org/resources/ai-career-quiz-which-role-is-right-for-me

Crompton, H., & Burke, M. (2024). *Artificial Intelligence Applications in Higher Education: Theories, Ethics, and Case Studies for Universities*. London: Routledge. https://www.routledge.com/Artificial-Intelligence-Applications-in-Higher-Education-Theories-Ethics-and-Case-Studies-for-Universities/Crompton-Burke/p/book/9781032576145

Deloitte. (2024). *Generative AI in Higher Education: The Next Frontier*. New York: Deloitte Insights. https://www2.deloitte.com/us/en/insights/industry/public-sector/generative-ai-higher-education.html

Disco. (2024). *AI-Powered Skill Assessment Tools*. Toronto: Disco.co. https://www.disco.co/blog/ai-powered-skill-assessment-tools

Docebo. (2023). *Personalized Learning With AI*. Toronto: Docebo. https://www.docebo.com/learning-network/blog/personalized-learning-ai/

Education Week. (2019). *What Is Personalized Learning?*. Bethesda: Education Week. https://www.edweek.org/technology/what-is-personalized-learning/2019/11

Educause Review. (2016). *Adaptive Learning Systems: Surviving the Storm*. Louisville: EDUCAUSE.https://er.educause.edu/articles/2016/10/adaptive-learning-systems-surviving-the-storm

Educause Review. (2019). *Artificial Intelligence in Higher Education: Promise, Perils, and Ethics*. Louisville: EDUCAUSE. https://er.educause.edu/articles/2019/8/artificial-intelligence-in-higher-education-applications-promise-and-perils-and-ethical-questions

eLearning Industry. (2023). *How AI Is Personalizing Education for Every Student*. San Francisco: eLearning Industry. https://elearningindustry.com/how-ai-is-personalizing-education-for-every-student

eSelf.ai. (2024). *AI Trends in Education: Transforming Learning Experiences in 2025*. Tel Aviv: eSelf.ai. https://www.eself.ai/blog/ai-trends-in-education-transforming-learning-experiences-in-2025/

European School Education Platform. (2024). *Ethical Considerations in Educational AI*. Brussels: European Commission. https://school-education.ec.europa.eu/en/discover/news/ethical-considerations-educational-ai

European Society for Data Science and Technology. (2024). *The AI-Powered Personalized Learning Transformation*. Rome: ESDST. https://esdst.eu/educational-revolution-the-ai-powered-personalized-learning-transformation/

Forbes. (2024). *3 Innovative Case Uses for AI in Higher Education*. New York: Forbes. https://www.forbes.com/sites/rhettpower/2024/02/04/3-innovative-case-uses-for-ai-in-higher-education/

Forbes Technology Council. (2024). *Personalized Learning and AI: Revolutionizing Education*. New York: Forbes. https://www.forbes.com/councils/forbestech-council/2024/07/22/personalized-learning-and-ai-revolutionizing-education/

Fullestop. (2024a). *How AI Is Shaping the Future of Education*. Jaipur: Fullestop. https://www.fullestop.com/blog/personalized-learning-how-ai-is-shaping-the-future-of-education

Fullestop. (2024b). *How AI Is Shaping the Future of Personalized Learning*. Jaipur: Fullestop. https://www.fullestop.com/blog/personalized-learning-how-ai-is-shaping-the-future-of-education

Glossary of Education Reform. (2024). Personalized Learning. Great Schools Partnership. https://www.edglossary.org/personalized-learning/

Gravitas AI. (2024). *Future AI Education Trends for the Next Decade*. LinkedIn Pulse. https://www.linkedin.com/pulse/future-al-education-trends-next-decade-gravitas-ai

Halverson, R., & Smith, A. (2020). *How Personalized Learning Models Are Reshaping the Classroom. Journal of Research on Technology in Education*, 52(2), 133–145. https://www.tandfonline.com/doi/full/10.1080/15391523.2020.1747757

HMH. (2024). *What Is Personalized Learning in Education?*. Boston: Houghton MifflinHarcourt.https://www.hmhco.com/blog/what-is-personalized-learning-in-education

HP. (2024a). *AI in Education: Empowering Students and Teachers*. Palo Alto: HP Tech Takes. https://www.hp.com/in-en/shop/tech-takes/post/ai-in-education

HP. (2024b). *AI in Education: Tools for Teaching and Learning*. Palo Alto: HP Tech Takes. https://www.hp.com/in-en/shop/tech-takes/post/ai-in-education

Hyland. (2024). *AI in Higher Education: Transforming Learning and Administration*. Cleveland: Hyland. https://www.hyland.com/en/resources/articles/ai-higher-education

Hyperspace. (2024a). *AI Learning Trends in 2025*. Male: Hyperspace.mv. https://hyperspace.mv/future-ai-learning-trends/

Hyperspace. (2024b). *Future AI Learning Trends*. Male: Hyperspace.mv. https://hyperspace.mv/future-ai-learning-trends/

Intel. (2024). *AI for Higher Education*. Santa Clara: Intel Corporation. https://www.intel.com/content/www/us/en/education/highered/artificial-intelligence.html

Intrex Group. (2024). *The Future of AI in Education: Pioneering a New Era of Learning*. Dallas: Intrex Group. https://itrexgroup.com/blog/the-future-of-ai-in-education-pioneering-a-new-era-of-learning/

James Madison University Libraries. (2024). *AI in Education: Ethics*. Harrisonburg: JMU. https://guides.lib.jmu.edu/AI-in-education/ethics

JISEM. (2024). *AI-Powered Personalized Learning Journeys: Revolutionizing Information Management for College*. Journal of Information Systems Engineering & Management, 8(1), 23196. https://www.jisem-journal.com/download/ai-powered-personalized-learning-journeys-revolutionizing-information-management-for-college-14079.pdf

Khan Academy. (2023). *Introducing Khanmigo Lite*. Mountain View: Khan Academy. https://blog.khanacademy.org/khanmigo-lite/

Khan Academy. (2024a). *AI for Education*. Mountain View: Khan Academy. https://www.khanacademy.org/college-careers-more/ai-for-education

Khan Academy. (2024b). *Khanmigo: An AI Tutor for Learners*. Mountain View: Khan Academy. https://khanmigo.ai

Khan Academy. (2024c). *Khanmigo for Learners*. Mountain View: Khan Academy. https://khanmigo.ai/learners

Learning Light. (2024). *What Is Adaptive Learning?*. Sheffield: Learning Light. https://www.learninglight.com/adaptive-learning/

LinkedIn. (2024a). *AI-Powered Career Centers: Leadership Strategies for Sustainability*. Sunnyvale: LinkedIn Pulse. https://www.linkedin.com/pulse/ai-powered-career-centers-leadership-strategies-sustainable-t0lec

LinkedIn. (2024b). *The Future of Education: How AI Is Transforming Learning*. Sunnyvale: LinkedIn Pulse. https://www.linkedin.com/pulse/future-education-how-artificial-intelligence-transforming-nyprc

Litslink. (2024). *Generative AI in Education: The Impact, Ethical Considerations, and Use Cases*. Palo Alto: Litslink. https://litslink.com/blog/generative-ai-in-education-the-impact-ethical-considerations-and-use-cases

MDPI Blog. (2024). *Ethical Considerations in Artificial Intelligence*. Basel: MDPI. https://mdpiblog.wordpress.sciforum.net/2024/02/01/ethical-considerations-artificial-intelligence/

Microsoft. (2024). *AI Skills Assessment*. Redmond: Microsoft Learn. https://learn.microsoft.com/en-us/assessments/33a8d18b-7299-4808-95eb-ec1ac1eca4d9/

Ministry of Education, Singapore. (2024). *About Adaptive Learning System*. Singapore: MOE. https://www.learning.moe.edu.sg/student-user-guide/self-study/about-adaptive-learning-system/

National Center for Biotechnology Information. (2021). *Artificial Intelligence in Education: A Review*. Bethesda: NIH. https://pmc.ncbi.nlm.nih.gov/articles/PMC8455229/

Northumbria University. (2024). *Artificial Intelligence and Skills Development in Computer Science*. Newcastle: Northumbria University. https://www.northumbria.ac.uk/study-at-northumbria/courses/msc-computer-science-with-artificial-intelligence-distance-learning-dtdsar6/artificial-intelligence-skills-blog-org/

Open AI. (2023). *Khan Academy Partners with OpenAI to Launch AI Tutor*. San Francisco: OpenAI. https://openai.com/index/khan-academy/

RingCentral. (2023). *Benefits of Personalized Learning*. Belmont: RingCentral. https://www.ringcentral.com/us/en/blog/benefits-personalized-learning/

Springs Apps. (2024). *Main AI Trends in Education 2024*. San Diego: Springs Apps. https://springsapps.com/knowledge/main-ai-trends-in-education-2024

TalentGenius. (2024). *AI Skills Assessment Guide*. New York: TalentGenius. https://talentgenius.io/articles/ai-skills-assessment-guide

Tappstr. (2024). *AI in Education: Ethical Considerations*. LinkedIn. https://www.linkedin.com/pulse/ai-education-ethical-considerations-tappstr-ilorf

Taxila Business School. (2024). *The Ethics of AI in Education*. Jaipur: Taxila. https://taxila.in/blog/the-ethics-of-ai-in-education/

Teachmint. (2024). *What Is Personalized Learning?*. Bengaluru: Teachmint Technologies. https://www.teachmint.com/glossary/p/personalized-learning/

Trigyn. (2024). *The Role of Artificial Intelligence in Personalized Learning*. New York: Trigyn Technologies. https://www.trigyn.com/insights/role-artificial-intelligence-personalized-learning

University of Bridgeport. (2024). *How Is AI Technology Used in Higher Education?*. Bridgeport: UBNews. https://www.bridgeport.edu/news/how-is-ai-technology-used-in-higher-education/

University of San Diego. (2024). *Artificial Intelligence in Education*. San Diego: USD Online. https://onlinedegrees.sandiego.edu/artificial-intelligence-education/

Vedantu. (2024). *Why Is Personalized Learning Important?*. Bengaluru: Vedantu Innovations. https://www.vedantu.com/blog/why-is-personalized-learning-important

Wikipedia. (2024a). *Adaptive Learning*. Wikipedia Foundation. https://en.wikipedia.org/wiki/Adaptive_learning

Wikipedia. (2024b). *Advanced Personalized Learning*. Wikipedia Foundation. https://en.wikipedia.org/wiki/Advanced_Personalized_Learning

10

Digital Society with Smart Governance

Introduction to Smart Governance and AI

Smart governance refers to implementing innovative technologies, particularly digital tools, to enhance governmental operations' effectiveness, efficiency, and responsiveness. As societies become increasingly interconnected, governance must evolve to address the challenges of the digital age. In this framework, Artificial intelligence (AI) assumes a crucial role in transforming how governments engage with citizens, make decisions, and optimise administrative functions.

Governments across the globe are harnessing AI to refine service delivery, improve decision-making processes, and promote increased transparency and accountability. AI technologies, ranging from machine learning algorithms to natural language processing (NLP), are revolutionising public administration and solving enduring issues such as bureaucratic inefficiency and citizen disengagement.

This chapter explores the notion of smart governance, analyses the significance of AI in contemporary governance and public administration, and discusses how AI is transforming citizen-government interactions.

Defining Smart Governance in the Digital Age

Smart governance, also known as e-governance or digital governance, is a dynamic approach that integrates advanced technologies to enable governments to serve their populations more effectively. The core idea behind smart governance creates a more interactive, transparent, and efficient government that can quickly respond to the needs of its citizens.

In the digital age, smart governance relies on digital platforms, data analytics, cloud computing, and AI to transform traditional bureaucratic structures. By embracing these technologies, governments can offer more personalised services, provide real-time responses to public concerns, and use data-driven insights for better policymaking.

A key element of smart governance is the implementation of open data initiatives, which encourage the transparency of governmental processes. This transparency builds trust between governments and citizens and empowers individuals and organisations to participate more actively in civic affairs.

Key Features of Smart Governance

- **Interconnectivity:** Governments can communicate and collaborate more efficiently with citizens through digital tools.
- **Transparency:** Smart governance increases visibility into government activities by making information available through digital platforms.
- **Citizen Engagement:** Smart governance fosters greater public involvement through online services and interactive platforms, enabling citizens to contribute ideas, feedback, and opinions.
- **Data-Driven Decision-Making:** Data analytics and AI help policymakers make informed decisions based on real-time information, improving the effectiveness of government interventions.

The Role of AI in Modern Governance and Public Administration

AI is revolutionising the way public institutions operate. By processing vast amounts of data, AI allows governments to enhance decision-making, improve efficiency, and offer innovative solutions to address complex societal challenges. AI's role in governance is particularly evident in three areas: automating administrative tasks, predictive analytics for policy decisions, and enhancing public services.

Key AI Technologies Transforming Governance

💡 **QUICK NOTE:** *Natural Language Processing allows governments to interpret citizen feedback at scale, improving service delivery and civic responsiveness.*

- **Machine Learning:** Governments can use machine learning algorithms to analyse large datasets, forecast trends, and identify patterns. For instance, AI can predict traffic patterns, optimise public transportation routes, or assess the likelihood of public health outbreaks.
- **Natural Language Processing (NLP):** AI-driven NLP technologies can help governments process vast amounts of citizen feedback and communication, enabling more efficient management of public complaints, requests, and inquiries. NLP is also used in virtual assistants, helping government agencies respond to public questions or service requests.
- **Robotic Process Automation (RPA):** Governments use RPA to automate repetitive tasks such as processing applications, verifying documents, or updating records. Public institutions can reduce human

error and improve overall service delivery speed by automating these tasks.

- **AI for Cybersecurity:** With the rise of digital services, cybersecurity becomes a priority. AI can monitor networks for suspicious activities, analyse potential vulnerabilities, and mitigate security threats in real time, ensuring the protection of sensitive government data and essential services.

AI in Policy Development

AI also plays a transformative role in policy development. Policymakers can leverage predictive analytics to anticipate future trends or assess the potential impact of various policy scenarios. This leads to more informed decision-making and allows governments to proactively address emerging challenges such as climate change, urbanisation, and digital inequality.

For instance, AI models can predict the economic impact of different taxation policies or the effect of environmental regulations on industry. With these insights, policymakers can design more effective laws and regulations that better meet the needs of their communities.

How AI Is Reshaping Citizen–Government Interactions

One of the most visible impacts of AI in governance is the transformation of how governments interact with citizens. AI-powered platforms allow governments to become more responsive, efficient, and accessible. The digital interaction between citizens and governments is no longer limited to static websites or email communication. Instead, AI enables real-time engagement, personalised service delivery, and a deeper understanding of public sentiment.

AI-Powered Citizen Services

SIDEBAR: Smart Governance in Action—Singapore's "Ask Jamie" Chatbot

---

- **Chatbots and Virtual Assistants:** Governments are deploying AI-powered chatbots to handle routine inquiries, provide real-time updates on services, and assist citizens with applications or document submissions. These chatbots can operate 24/7, ensuring citizens receive timely assistance and reducing wait times at service centres.
- **Smart City Solutions:** AI is being used to improve the quality of urban life. Smart city technologies, such as AI-powered traffic management systems and waste disposal solutions, enable governments

vto manage urban infrastructure more efficiently and respond to citizens' needs in real time.

- **Personalised Services:** AI enables governments to deliver personalised services to citizens based on their preferences and needs. For example, AI can recommend relevant government programs or services based on a person's profile, such as tax incentives for small businesses or healthcare programs for vulnerable populations.

Enhanced Citizen Engagement

AI can also enhance citizen engagement by analysing feedback from various sources, including social media, online forums, and public surveys. This helps governments understand public concerns, gauge sentiment, and tailor responses accordingly.

Moreover, AI tools can facilitate inclusivity by translating communication into multiple languages or offering accessible formats for people with disabilities, ensuring that all citizens have an equal opportunity to participate.

Conclusion

Smart governance and AI can revolutionise the relationship between governments and citizens, making it more efficient, transparent, and responsive. As AI continues to evolve, its role in enhancing public administration and service delivery will grow, enabling governments to meet the challenges of the digital age more effectively. From predictive analytics to AI-powered citizen services, these technologies are helping governments not only streamline operations but also provide more personalised, timely, and accessible services to the public.

Moving forward, the ongoing development of AI in the public sector will likely lead to even more advanced, data-driven systems, transforming the governance experience and shaping the future of society.

AI-Powered E-Governance: Transforming Public Services

E-Governance refers to using digital technologies to provide public services, enhance government transparency, and foster citizen engagement. As governments worldwide continue embracing digital tools, AI plays a transformative role in reshaping public administration. AI-powered e-governance improves the efficiency of government operations and enhances the quality of services provided to citizens.

From automating routine tasks to providing data-driven insights for policymaking, AI offers a vast range of opportunities to improve government functionality. This section delves into the role of AI in automating government operations, streamlining bureaucratic processes, using predictive analytics for policy decision-making, and reducing corruption and inefficiencies.

Automation and AI in Government Operations

AI's potential to automate government operations is one of its most significant contributions to e-governance. By reducing the need for manual labour, AI can enable government institutions to work more efficiently, speed up service delivery, and reduce human error. Automation also allows public servants to focus on higher-value tasks, leading to improved productivity and better resource allocation.

Streamlining Bureaucratic Processes with AI

Bureaucracy is often characterised by slow, repetitive, and paperwork-heavy procedures that frustrate citizens and hinder government effectiveness. AI automates several bureaucratic processes, simplifying administrative workflows and enabling quicker decision-making.

- **Automated Document Processing:** Governments handle daily paperwork, including applications for permits, licenses, and social welfare benefits. AI can automate document processing using optical character recognition and NLP to extract relevant data and classify documents. This significantly reduces the time and effort required to review and approve applications, thus speeding up service delivery.
- **RPA:** RPA tools powered by AI are employed to handle routine administrative tasks, such as processing tax returns, updating citizen records, or verifying documents. These AI tools can execute repetitive tasks more efficiently than human workers, reducing the risk of errors and freeing up public sector employees for more strategic roles.
- **AI-Powered Customer Service:** AI-driven chatbots and virtual assistants are becoming common in government websites and portals. These systems can answer citizen queries, process requests, and provide relevant information 24/7, helping citizens navigate complex governmental procedures without requiring direct human intervention.

Benefits of AI in Bureaucratic Automation

- **Increased Efficiency:** Automating routine tasks accelerates administrative processes and reduces delays.
- **Cost Reduction:** Automation leads to cost savings by reducing the need for large administrative workforces and decreasing processing times.

- **Improved Accuracy:** AI algorithms minimise the chances of human errors, ensuring that data is processed accurately and consistently.

AI-Driven Predictive Analytics for Policy Decision-Making

💡 **QUICK NOTE:** *Predictive analytics empower governments to act before problems arise—shifting from reactive to proactive governance.*

AI is increasingly being used to guide policy decisions through predictive analytics. By analysing large datasets, AI systems can identify patterns, trends, and correlations that may not be immediately apparent to human policymakers. These insights help governments make better-informed decisions and create more effective policies anticipating future needs.

The Role of Predictive Analytics in Governance

Predictive analytics uses historical data and machine learning models to forecast future trends and outcomes. Governments can leverage AI-driven predictive models to assess the potential impact of various policy decisions and implement proactive strategies to address societal challenges.

- **Public Health:** Governments can use AI to predict disease outbreaks, identify healthcare resource needs, and forecast future public health risks. For instance, AI models could analyse historical data on disease transmission and climate conditions to predict where and when outbreaks of diseases like influenza or COVID-19 may occur.
- **Urban Planning and Infrastructure:** AI can predict urban growth patterns, infrastructure needs, and environmental impact. For example, governments can use predictive analytics to plan for population growth, optimise transportation networks, and design more sustainable cities.
- **Economic Forecasting:** AI can assist in economic planning by analysing employment, production, and consumer behaviour trends. Governments can use predictive models to forecast economic challenges and plan fiscal policies accordingly.

Benefits of Predictive Analytics in Policymaking

- **Proactive Policy Formulation:** Governments can create policies anticipating future challenges, leading to more effective interventions.
- **Resource Optimisation:** Predictive analytics enables governments to allocate resources more efficiently based on anticipated needs, improving overall public service delivery.

- **Evidence-Based Decision-Making:** AI-driven analytics provide a data-backed foundation for policymaking, leading to more robust, transparent, and informed decisions.

Reducing Corruption and Inefficiencies through Automation

One of the most significant challenges governments face globally is corruption, which often arises from inefficiencies, lack of transparency, and manual control over sensitive processes. AI-powered e-governance holds great promise in combating corruption by automating operations, reducing human involvement in critical decision-making, and making government actions more transparent and traceable.

How AI Helps Reduce Corruption

- **Transparent Public Procurement:** One area where corruption is prevalent is in public procurement processes. AI tools can automate and digitize procurement procedures, ensuring that contracts are awarded based on clear, objective criteria. This reduces opportunities for bribery and favouritism.
- **Fraud Detection in Public Services:** AI can analyse data from various public service channels to detect patterns indicative of fraud, such as irregularities in benefit claims, tax evasion, or financial mismanagement. Machine learning algorithms can continuously monitor transactions and flag suspicious activities for further investigation, helping authorities address corruption at an early stage.
- **Blockchain and AI for Transparency:** By combining AI with blockchain technology, governments can create immutable records of public transactions, making it nearly impossible to alter official documents or misappropriate public funds. AI can monitor and audit blockchain records in real time, ensuring that public funds are used appropriately and efficiently.
- **Automating Regulatory Compliance:** Governments often face challenges ensuring that businesses and individuals comply with regulations. AI can automate compliance monitoring, reducing the chances of regulatory evasion through human intervention or bribery.

Benefits of Using AI to Combat Corruption

- **Increased Accountability:** AI systems provide transparent, traceable processes that reduce the likelihood of corrupt practices.
- **Enhanced Efficiency:** Automated systems eliminate bottlenecks that can arise from manual processes, leading to quicker decision-making and service delivery.

- **Better Oversight:** AI-driven data analytics help monitor government activities in real time, allowing authorities to detect corruption before it becomes systemic.

AI-powered e-governance is not just a futuristic concept; it is a present-day reality already transforming how governments operate and deliver services to citizens. Governments can dramatically enhance their efficiency and transparency by automating routine tasks, utilising predictive analytics for policymaking, and leveraging data-driven tools to fight corruption.

The potential benefits of AI in governance are profound: faster services, more responsive policymaking, reduced corruption, and a higher level of trust between citizens and government. As AI technology continues to evolve, its integration into public services will only grow, helping governments meet the demands of the digital age while improving the lives of their citizens.

Global Perspectives: AI-Driven Governance around the World

AI-driven governance is becoming a key component of the global shift towards digital transformation in the public sector. Various nations are adopting AI technologies to improve public administration, enhance service delivery, and ensure greater transparency and accountability in governance. This section explores some of the leading AI governance models and smart nation initiatives from countries like Singapore, Estonia, the United Arab Emirates (UAE), and China and look at the opportunities and challenges of implementing AI in developing economies. An overview of best practices for AI adoption in public administration is also discussed.

Leading AI Governance Models and Smart Nation Initiatives

Case Studies: Singapore, Estonia, UAE, and China's AI-Driven Governance Models

Several countries have made significant strides in integrating AI into their governance structures. These nations have developed AI models that combine technological innovation with effective policymaking, making them leaders in the global AI governance space.

Singapore: Pioneering Smart Nation and AI Governance

Singapore has emerged as a global leader in AI-driven governance, with its Smart Nation initiative aimed at leveraging technology to improve citizens' quality of life. The government has integrated AI across multiple sectors, from public services to transportation, healthcare, and urban planning.

- **AI-Powered Public Services:** Singapore has deployed AI-driven chatbots to enhance communication between citizens and government agencies. For example, the "Ask Jamie" chatbot helps citizens access government information quickly.
- **AI in Healthcare:** The government uses AI in healthcare for early detection of diseases, optimising hospital workflows, and improving patient outcomes. The Health Ministry has implemented AI-based tools to predict patient needs and improve the allocation of resources.
- **Ethical AI Frameworks:** Singapore has adopted an ethical AI framework known as the Model AI Governance Framework, which promotes transparency, fairness, and accountability in AI applications. This framework guides the public and private sectors in the ethical use of AI technologies.

Estonia: Digital Government and AI Integration

🖢 SIDEBAR: How Estonia Uses AI for Digital Identity

Estonia is widely regarded as one of the most digitally advanced nations in the world, and its government has been at the forefront of integrating AI into its public administration. The country's e-government infrastructure serves as a model for digital governance.

- **E-Residency and Digital ID:** Estonia offers e-Residency, a government-issued digital identity that allows people from anywhere in the world to start and manage businesses online. AI is used to streamline identity verification and enhance the security of digital transactions.
- **AI in Public Services:** Estonia is exploring AI in social services, public health, and education, using predictive analytics to manage welfare systems and predict citizens' needs for various public services.
- **X-Road Platform:** Estonia's X-Road data exchange platform connects various public and private sector databases, enabling seamless data sharing. AI is integrated into this platform to improve the efficiency and accuracy of decision-making.

United Arab Emirates (UAE): AI Strategy for the Future

The UAE is rapidly establishing itself as a leader in AI governance with ambitious goals set in its national AI strategy, UAE Vision 2021. The UAE's AI strategy is designed to integrate AI into every aspect of governance and service delivery.

- **AI in Government Services:** The UAE has implemented AI-powered government services such as the AI Ministry, which explores the use of AI to enhance the efficiency of government processes and services. This includes AI-powered systems in customs, transportation, and healthcare.

- **Smart Cities and Infrastructure:** In cities like Dubai, AI is used to manage urban infrastructure, including waste management, transportation, and energy efficiency. The Dubai government has launched the Dubai AI Lab to drive innovation in AI applications.

- **AI Ethics and Regulation:** The UAE is developing AI governance models focused on promoting AI ethics, including ensuring fairness, transparency, and accountability in the use of AI across sectors.

China: AI for Governance at Scale

? DID YOU KNOW: *China's smart cities use over 500 million surveillance cameras powered by AI to monitor traffic, pollution, and crime.*

China is leveraging AI on a large scale to transform governance, integrating AI technologies in key areas such as law enforcement, surveillance, healthcare, and public policymaking.

- **Social Credit System:** China's Social Credit System uses AI algorithms to monitor the behaviour of citizens and businesses. AI-driven analytics assesses individuals' trustworthiness and assigns scores based on their actions, affecting their access to services such as loans, travel, and social benefits.

- **AI in Urban Management:** China has implemented AI in smart city projects to improve traffic management, air quality monitoring, and public safety. For instance, AI-powered traffic cameras in major cities monitor road conditions and automatically adjust traffic signals to optimise flow.

- **AI in Public Administration:** The Chinese government uses AI in public administration for predictive analysis and policymaking, enabling more responsive and efficient government decisions. The government also invests heavily in AI research and development to drive technological advancements (Table 10.1).

AI in Developing Economies: Opportunities and Challenges

In developing economies, the adoption of AI presents both significant opportunities and unique challenges. AI can help improve public services, address gaps in infrastructure, and drive economic growth, but its implementation is

TABLE 10.1

Global AI Governance Models and Policy Approaches

Country	Key Initiatives	Technologies Used	Ethical/Regulatory Frameworks
Singapore	Smart Nation initiative; Ask Jamie chatbot; AI in healthcare	NLP, machine learning, predictive analytics	Model AI Governance Framework
Estonia	e-Residency; X-Road Data Exchange	Digital ID, AI in public services	Emphasis on data privacy, decentralised data control
UAE	AI Ministry; Dubai AI Lab	Smart city systems, AI in customs and healthcare	AI Ethics Guidelines under UAE Vision 2021
China	Social Credit System; AI in urban management	Surveillance AI, facial recognition, predictive analytics	Government-regulated, limited transparency
EU (multi-nation)	AI Act (proposed); GDPR	Risk-based AI system classification	GDPR; Ethics Guidelines for Trustworthy AI

often hindered by factors such as limited resources, infrastructure deficits, and a lack of skilled personnel.

Opportunities

- **Improved Public Services:** AI can streamline government services, making them more accessible and efficient. For example, AI can be used in healthcare to predict disease outbreaks, in education to personalize learning, and in agriculture to optimise food production.
- **Digital Inclusion:** AI can help bridge the digital divide by enabling more efficient use of limited resources, particularly in rural and underserved areas. AI can be used to deliver services to remote areas where traditional infrastructure may be lacking.
- **Economic Development:** AI technologies can spur economic growth by fostering innovation in sectors such as agriculture, manufacturing, and services. Governments in developing economies can use AI to enhance trade, improve infrastructure, and attract foreign investment.

Challenges

- **Infrastructure Gaps:** Many developing countries lack the necessary technological infrastructure to support AI adoption, including internet connectivity, data storage systems, and computing power.
- **Data Availability and Quality:** AI systems rely on large datasets, but in many developing economies, data collection and management practices may not be robust enough to support AI-powered initiatives.

- **Skilled Workforce:** There is often a shortage of skilled personnel capable of developing and maintaining AI systems. Capacity building and education in AI and data science are necessary to ensure sustainable implementation in these countries.

Best Practices for AI Adoption in Public Administration

Successful integration of AI into public administration and governments worldwide should follow several best practices:

- **Develop a Clear AI Strategy:** Governments should formulate clear strategies and policies for AI adoption that align with national goals and priorities. These strategies should emphasize transparency, inclusivity, and the ethical use of AI.
- **Ensure Data Governance:** Effective data governance frameworks should be established to manage the collection, storage, and use of data. Governments should ensure that data privacy and security are upheld and that data used in AI models is of high quality and relevance.
- **Promote Collaboration Between Sectors:** Public–private partnerships, as well as collaboration between government agencies and academia, are essential for fostering AI innovation and addressing implementation challenges.
- **Build AI Literacy and Skills:** Training programs for public servants and the wider population are crucial to ensure that individuals understand AI and can use it effectively in their roles.
- **Implement Ethical Guidelines:** Governments must establish ethical frameworks that ensure fairness, transparency, and accountability in AI systems. These guidelines should be monitored regularly to ensure that AI deployment does not lead to unintended negative consequences.

AI-driven governance is transforming the way governments around the world function, with countries such as Singapore, Estonia, the UAE, and China leading the way with innovative AI models. While AI presents significant opportunities for improving public services, fostering economic growth, and addressing societal challenges, its adoption in developing economies requires overcoming infrastructure, data, and skills gaps. By following best practices and implementing ethical AI frameworks, governments can harness the full potential of AI while ensuring that it benefits all citizens equally and fairly.

TABLE 10.2

Checklist: Policy Best Practices for Ethical and Effective AI Use

Best Practice	Implementation Example
Develop a national AI strategy	Set clear vision, goals, ethical guardrails
Ensure robust data governance	GDPR-style policies, open data standards
Promote cross-sector collaboration	Academia+Government+Private sector alliances
Build AI literacy and skills	Training programs for civil servants and citizens
Adopt risk-based AI regulation	Classify AI applications by impact
Establish ethical guidelines	Transparent, human-centric AI principles
Monitor and evaluate AI systems	Periodic impact assessments and feedback loops

Regulatory Frameworks for AI in Governance

As AI continues to transform public administration and governance, establishing effective regulatory frameworks has become critical to ensure that AI systems are used responsibly, ethically, and transparently. These frameworks address issues such as data privacy, bias in AI algorithms, accountability in decision-making, and the societal impacts of AI technologies. This section explores the role of international organisations in developing AI policy, key global regulations and principles for AI governance, and future trends in AI governance, especially in the context of digital sovereignty (Table 10.2).

The Role of International Organisations in AI Policy Development

International organisations play a pivotal role in shaping the regulatory landscape for AI technologies. These organisations collaborate with governments, the private sector, academia, and civil society to develop standards, guidelines, and policies that promote ethical AI use while mitigating potential risks.

? **DID YOU KNOW:** *UNESCO's global AI ethics recommendations were adopted by 193 countries in 2021.*

Placement: Within the **UNESCO** segment under "The Role of International Organisations in AI Policy."

The European Union (EU)

The EU has been a leading force in AI policy development, particularly through its comprehensive approach to digital governance. The EU's Artificial Intelligence Act (proposed in 2021) seeks to establish a clear regulatory framework for AI systems across member states, addressing issues of safety, ethics, and accountability.

- **AI Act:** The proposed AI Act categorizes AI systems into risk-based tiers (low, high, and unacceptable risk) and sets regulatory requirements accordingly. High-risk AI systems, such as those used in healthcare or law enforcement, will be subject to strict transparency, accountability, and oversight measures.
- **Ethical Guidelines:** The EU's Ethics Guidelines for Trustworthy AI (2019) outlines seven key requirements for AI, including transparency, accountability, and fairness. These guidelines ensure AI systems respect human rights and are aligned with European values.

The United Nations (UN)

The UN plays a crucial role in fostering international cooperation on AI policy. Through various agencies, including the United Nations Educational, Scientific and Cultural Organization (UNESCO), the UN promotes global standards for AI governance.

- **UNESCO's AI Ethics Recommendations:** In 2021, UNESCO adopted the first global standard on the ethics of AI, focusing on principles such as inclusivity, transparency, and accountability. The recommendations encourage member states to implement ethical AI frameworks that address the societal impact of AI technologies and promote fairness.
- **AI for Sustainable Development:** The UN advocates for AI technologies to contribute to achieving the sustainable development goals. It supports initiatives that use AI for social good, including efforts to combat poverty, improve healthcare, and protect the environment.

The Organization for Economic Cooperation and Development (OECD)

The OECD has developed a set of AI principles that focus on fostering innovation while ensuring the ethical use of AI technologies. These principles provide guidelines for governments to develop AI strategies that balance the benefits of AI with the need for ethical oversight.

- **OECD AI Principles:** The OECD's Recommendation on Artificial Intelligence (2019) promotes transparency, accountability, human rights protection, and inclusivity in AI development. The principles encourage governments to prioritize public trust in AI systems while addressing risks like bias, inequality, and misuse.

The World Economic Forum (WEF)

The WEF brings together global leaders from government, business, and academia to discuss and set agendas for AI governance. Through initiatives such as the Global AI Council, the WEF focuses on shaping global AI policies that ensure fairness, inclusivity, and societal benefits.

- **AI and Global Governance:** The WEF advocates for global coordination on AI standards and regulations to avoid fragmentation and promote interoperability among AI systems across different countries.

Key Global Regulations and AI Governance Principles

Several global regulatory initiatives have been established to ensure the responsible development and deployment of AI systems. These regulations are designed to protect citizens' rights, promote innovation, and address challenges such as algorithmic bias, data privacy, and accountability.

General Data Protection Regulation (GDPR)

The EU's General Data Protection Regulation (GDPR), implemented in 2018, is a landmark regulation in the realm of data privacy and protection. While not specifically focused on AI, GDPR has significant implications for AI systems that handle personal data.

- **Consent and Transparency:** Under GDPR, organisations must obtain explicit consent from individuals before collecting or processing their personal data. AI systems that rely on personal data must be transparent about how the data is used and give individuals the right to access, correct, or erase their data.
- **Data Minimization:** GDPR mandates that data collection be limited to what is necessary for the specific purpose of AI processing. This reduces the risk of over-collection or misuse of personal data.

AI Act (European Union)

The EU's proposed AI Act establishes one of the first comprehensive regulatory frameworks for AI. It aims to regulate AI systems based on their potential risk to safety and fundamental rights.

- **Risk-Based Approach:** The Act categorizes AI systems into four risk levels: unacceptable risk, high risk, limited risk, and minimal risk. High-risk systems (e.g., biometric recognition, critical infrastructure) will be subject to more stringent regulatory requirements, such as transparency and human oversight.

- **Transparency and Accountability**: AI developers and users must ensure that AI systems are transparent and can explain the rationale behind automated decisions. The Act also emphasizes the need for clear accountability structures for AI systems used in governance.

The OECD AI Principles

The OECD's Recommendation on Artificial Intelligence lays down a set of principles that guide AI governance across member states, promoting innovation while safeguarding human rights and societal well-being.

- **Inclusive and Sustainable Growth:** The OECD advocates for policies that promote AI adoption while ensuring it contributes to inclusive economic growth, job creation, and environmental sustainability.
- **Human-Centric AI:** The principles emphasize AI systems that respect human rights and democratic values, with a focus on fairness, transparency, and non-discrimination.

Future Trends: AI Governance in an Era of Digital Sovereignty

As AI becomes more integral to governance and public administration, the concept of digital sovereignty is gaining prominence. Digital sovereignty refers to a nation's ability to control and regulate its digital infrastructure, data, and technologies without undue influence from foreign powers or multinational corporations. This concept has profound implications for AI governance, particularly in terms of how AI systems are developed, deployed, and regulated.

National AI Strategies and Digital Sovereignty

Countries are increasingly developing national AI strategies to assert control over their AI ecosystems. These strategies may include policies for data localization, setting AI standards, and ensuring that AI technologies are aligned with national priorities and values.

- **Data Localization:** To protect national interests, some countries are implementing laws requiring that data generated within their borders must be stored and processed locally. This can affect the development and deployment of AI technologies that rely on cross-border data flow.
- **AI Ethics and National Values:** Governments are seeking to ensure that AI technologies reflect the cultural, ethical, and political values of their societies. This can result in diverse AI governance models across countries, reflecting differing approaches to issues such as privacy, transparency, and accountability.

Global AI Regulatory Cooperation

As AI technologies evolve, there will likely be increased pressure for international cooperation on AI regulations. While digital sovereignty may promote national control, global cooperation will be necessary to ensure interoperability, prevent regulatory fragmentation, and address global challenges such as AI ethics and accountability.

- **International AI Agreements:** Future trends may see the establishment of international treaties or agreements on AI ethics, data privacy, and the regulation of cross-border AI systems. This cooperation will help ensure that AI benefits are shared equitably and that potential harms are mitigated globally.

AI in Global Governance: Balancing Sovereignty and Collaboration

As AI governance becomes more sophisticated, it will be crucial for countries to strike a balance between asserting digital sovereignty and engaging in collaborative global governance efforts. Governments will need to navigate the challenges of protecting national interests while promoting international cooperation to address the global implications of AI technologies.

The development of regulatory frameworks for AI in governance is crucial for ensuring that AI technologies are used responsibly and ethically. International organisations such as the EU, UN, and OECD are leading the charge in shaping global AI policies, while individual nations are increasingly adopting national AI strategies to safeguard their digital sovereignty. As AI governance continues to evolve, future trends include stronger international cooperation, the establishment of global AI standards, and the balancing of national control with global collaboration in the context of digital sovereignty.

The Future of AI in Governance and Digital Societies

As AI technologies continue to evolve and shape the global landscape, the integration into governance structures will transform both how governments operate and how citizens engage with public institutions. The potential of AI to redefine concepts such as citizenship, civic responsibilities, and democratic participation is immense. However, as with any transformative technology, AI-driven governance presents both opportunities and significant challenges. This section explores AI's potential to reshape citizenship and civic duties, as well as the ethical and security concerns it raises, and provides recommendations for governments and citizens in preparing for an AI-powered future.

AI's Potential to Redefine Citizenship and Civic Responsibilities

AI is positioned to fundamentally reshape the relationship between citizens and their governments. It will influence how individuals participate in governance, interact with government services, and contribute to civic responsibilities.

AI-Enhanced Citizenship

AI has the potential to change the way citizens access government services and interact with institutions. By leveraging AI technologies, governments can deliver more personalised, efficient, and inclusive services, providing citizens with greater autonomy and agency in their civic engagement.

- **Digital Identities:** AI technologies, in combination with blockchain, can be used to create secure digital identities for citizens, making access to public services more seamless. Citizens may be able to use these digital identities to interact with government systems, vote, and access health, education, and social welfare services online.
- **Personalised Services:** AI's ability to analyse large datasets and identify individual needs allows governments to provide tailored services for citizens. For example, AI could help determine eligibility for social welfare benefits, provide personalised education recommendations, or offer targeted healthcare services based on personal data, including health history and socioeconomic status.

AI-Driven Civic Responsibilities

AI can also enhance civic engagement and encourage greater participation in decision-making processes. With AI tools, citizens can more actively contribute to policy formation, express their opinions, and have a voice in governance through digital platforms that aggregate public feedback.

- **Public Opinion Analysis:** AI-powered sentiment analysis and NLP can be used to evaluate citizens' opinions on key issues, ensuring that governance reflects the needs and concerns of the public.
- **Digital Democracy:** Platforms that integrate AI can facilitate direct digital democracy by allowing citizens to vote on policy decisions, participate in deliberative forums, and collaborate on public initiatives. These platforms could provide real-time feedback and ensure that government actions are aligned with the preferences of the electorate.
- **Enhanced Accountability:** AI systems can monitor government activity, track public sector performance, and identify areas of

inefficiency or corruption. With AI-driven transparency tools, citizens can hold public officials accountable for their actions and ensure that decisions are made in the public's best interest.

The Ethical and Security Challenges of AI-Driven Governance

While AI offers numerous opportunities for improving governance and societal outcomes, its implementation raises a host of ethical and security challenges that must be addressed to ensure its responsible use.

Ethical Challenges

AI systems used in governance face challenges, including principles of fairness, transparency, accountability, and inclusivity. Failure to adhere to these principles could lead to unintended biases and injustices, undermining public trust.

- **Bias in AI Systems:** AI algorithms are only as good as the data they are trained on, and if the underlying data is biased, AI systems can perpetuate and exacerbate these biases. For example, biased algorithms in areas like criminal justice, hiring, or social services could unfairly discriminate against certain groups based on race, gender, or socioeconomic status.
- **Privacy Concerns:** AI systems rely on vast amounts of personal data to make decisions, which raises concerns about data privacy and protection. Governments must ensure that AI technologies comply with privacy laws and respect citizens' rights to confidentiality and control over their data.
- **Transparency in Decision-Making:** Many AI systems are often seen as "black boxes," meaning their decision-making processes are not transparent or easily understood by non-experts. This lack of transparency can erode public trust and make it difficult to hold AI-driven decisions accountable.

Security Challenges

The integration of AI into governance raises serious security concerns, particularly in terms of data protection and cyber threats.

- **Cybersecurity Risks:** As AI becomes more embedded in governance systems, the risk of cyberattacks grows. Hackers may target AI systems that manage critical public infrastructure, such as transportation networks, healthcare systems, or energy grids. Governments must invest in robust cybersecurity measures to protect against such threats.

- **AI-Driven Misinformation:** AI technologies, particularly machine learning and deep learning algorithms, are increasingly being used to generate synthetic content (e.g., deepfakes) that can be used for misinformation campaigns. The potential for AI-driven misinformation to undermine democratic processes and destabilize societies is a growing concern.
- **Autonomous Weapons and Surveillance:** As AI advances, its applications in military and surveillance technologies become more pronounced. The use of AI in autonomous weapons systems or large-scale surveillance raises important questions about the ethics of AI use in security and law enforcement contexts.

Preparing for an AI-Powered Future: Recommendations for Governments and Citizens

Proactive steps by both governments and citizens are necessary to fully leverage the benefits of AI while mitigating its risks and prepare for an AI-powered future. By establishing robust regulations, promoting digital literacy, and fostering ethical AI development, society can navigate the complexities of AI governance.

Recommendations for Governments

Governments play a crucial role in ensuring that AI technologies are developed and deployed ethically, securely, and responsibly.

- **Create Clear AI Regulations:** Governments must establish comprehensive AI regulatory frameworks that promote transparency, fairness, and accountability in AI systems. These frameworks should also address data privacy, security, and the ethical considerations of AI use in governance.
- **Promote Ethical AI Development:** Governments should encourage the development of AI systems that prioritize human rights, transparency, and inclusivity. This includes investing in research to ensure that AI technologies are designed to minimise biases and discrimination and are aligned with societal values.
- **Invest in Digital Literacy and Skills:** To ensure citizens can navigate an AI-powered society, governments should invest in digital literacy programs and promote AI education at all levels. By equipping citizens with the skills to understand and interact with AI systems, governments can foster greater participation in digital governance and decision-making.

- **Foster Public Trust in AI:** Governments should work to build public trust in AI by being transparent about how AI systems are being used in governance, providing clear information on data privacy, and ensuring that AI-driven decisions are subject to appropriate scrutiny and oversight.

Recommendations for Citizens

Citizens must also be proactive in adapting to an AI-driven governance system by understanding the technology, engaging in responsible civic participation, and advocating for ethical AI practices.

- **Engage with AI-Driven Platforms:** Citizens should take advantage of AI-driven civic platforms and participate in digital democracy initiatives. By providing feedback, voicing opinions, and actively participating in decision-making processes, citizens can help shape policies that are responsive to their needs.
- **Advocate for Accountability:** Citizens should hold governments accountable for the responsible use of AI in public administration. This includes demanding transparency in how AI systems make decisions, advocating for laws that protect privacy and prevent biases, and ensuring that AI systems are held to high ethical standards.
- **Stay Informed:** Staying informed about the developments in AI, its applications in governance, and the potential societal impacts is essential for citizens to participate in debates and discussions about the role of AI in their lives. Engaging in discussions and understanding the technology can empower citizens to become active participants in shaping AI policy.

AI holds the potential to revolutionise governance and redefine concepts of citizenship and civic responsibility in the digital age. While AI can offer more efficient, personalised, and inclusive government services, its adoption also raises significant ethical, security, and transparency challenges. Governments should take the lead in creating clear regulatory frameworks, investing in digital literacy, and ensuring that AI technologies are developed and deployed responsibly. Meanwhile, citizens have a responsibility to actively engage with AI-driven platforms, stay informed, and advocate for accountability to ensure that AI-driven governance aligns with societal values and benefits all members of society.

In preparing for an AI-powered future, governments, citizens, and the private sector must collaborate to address the challenges of AI integration and capitalise on the opportunities it presents for more effective, responsive, and inclusive governance.

Chapter Questions

1. What is smart governance, and how does it differ from traditional governance approaches?
2. Name two AI technologies used in public administration and provide an example of how each is applied.
3. How does AI enhance citizen–government interactions compared to traditional digital tools?
4. What are the main benefits of using AI in predictive policymaking?
5. Identify three challenges developing countries face when adopting AI in governance.
6. In what ways can AI help reduce corruption in public services?
7. Why is transparency in AI systems important for public trust, and how can governments achieve it?
8. Compare the AI governance approaches of Estonia and China. What are the key differences?
9. Which international organization has developed a comprehensive AI ethics framework, and what are its main principles?
10. In your opinion, which factor is most critical for successful AI adoption in governance—technology, ethics, or policy? Justify your answer.

Note to Readers and Educators

Comprehensive answers and explanations to these chapter-end questions are available at www.sandeepbhalekar.com. The website also provides supplementary frameworks, teaching guidelines, and reference materials to support deeper understanding and classroom discussion.

Educators and facilitators can access additional resources, including presentation frameworks, assessment rubrics, and discussion prompts, to help integrate the concepts from this chapter into academic or professional learning environments.

Bibliography

Brookings Institution. (2021). *AI and Political Campaigning: A Guide to Ethical Use of AI in Elections*. Washington, D.C.: Brookings Institution.

Chinese Academy of Sciences. (2022). *AI in China's Governance: Policies and Challenges*. Beijing: CAS.

Eubanks, V. (2018). *Automating Inequality: How High-Tech Tools Profile, Police, and Punish the Poor*. New York: St. Martin's Press.

European Commission. (2020a). *AI for Good: How Artificial Intelligence Can Help Achieve the UN's Sustainable Development Goals*. Brussels: European Commission.

European Commission. (2020b). *Artificial Intelligence, Misinformation, and Electoral Integrity*. Brussels: European Commission Policy Report.

European Commission. (2020c). *Building Trust in AI: The Importance of Transparency and Accountability*. Brussels: European Commission Policy Report.

European Commission. (2020d). *Ethical Guidelines for Trustworthy AI*. Brussels: European Union.

European Commission. (2021a). *AI and Open Data: Key Enablers of Transparent Government*. Brussels: European Commission.

European Commission. (2021b). *Artificial Intelligence Act: Proposal for Regulation on AI*. Brussels: European Union.

Gartner. (2022a). *AI and Automation: The Future of Public Sector Operations*. Stamford: Gartner Research.

Gartner. (2022b). *Artificial Intelligence: Transforming Public Sector Governance*. Stamford: Gartner Research.

Government of Estonia. (2021). *Digital Government in Estonia: AI and the e-Residency Program*. Tallinn: Government of Estonia.

Harvard Kennedy School. (2020). *Data-Driven Policymaking: Harnessing the Power of Big Data and AI*. Cambridge: Harvard University.

Harvard Kennedy School. (2021). *AI in Politics: Ethical Implications of AI-Powered Campaigning*. Cambridge: Harvard University.

McKinsey & Company. (2022a). *Harnessing the Power of AI for Public Sector Transparency and Accountability*. New York: McKinsey & Company.

McKinsey & Company. (2022b). *How AI Is Shaping Economic Forecasting and Urban Planning*. New York: McKinsey & Company.

McKinsey & Company. (2022c). *How AI Is Shaping Public Sector Service Delivery*. New York: McKinsey & Company.

OECD. (2019). *Recommendation on Artificial Intelligence*. Paris: OECD.

OECD. (2020a). *AI and Blockchain: Enhancing Government Transparency and Accountability*. Paris: OECD Digital Government Studies.

OECD. (2020b). *Harnessing Artificial Intelligence for the Public Sector*. Paris: OECD Public Governance Review.

OECD. (2021a). *AI and the Future of Governance*. Paris: OECD.

OECD. (2021b). *AI and the Future of Government: Transforming Public Service Delivery*. Paris: OECD Digital Government Studies.

OECD. (2021c). *Artificial Intelligence in Government: Opportunities and Challenges*. Paris: OECD Digital Government Studies.

OECD. (2021d). *Artificial Intelligence in Public Governance: Aligning AI with Public Values*. Paris: OECD Digital Government Studies.

OECD. (2021e). *Artificial Intelligence in Public Governance: The Promise and Challenges*. Paris: OECD Digital Government Studies.

O'Neil, C. (2016). *Weapons of Math Destruction: How Big Data Increases Inequality and Threatens Democracy*. New York: Crown Publishing.

The Guardian. (2020a). *Amazon Scraps AI Recruiting Tool that Favoured Men for Tech Jobs*. London: The Guardian.

The Guardian. (2020b). *How AI Is Used to Monitor Elections and Track Misinformation*. London: The Guardian.

The Guardian. (2022). *Public Trust and AI: How Governments Can Overcome Citizen Scepticism*. London: The Guardian.

Singapore Government. (2020). *Smart Nation and Digital Government Office: AI Strategy*. Singapore: Smart Nation and Digital Government Office.

UAE Government. (2021). *AI Vision 2031: Accelerating AI Adoption in Public Administration*. Abu Dhabi: UAE Artificial Intelligence Strategy.

UNESCO. (2021). *Ethics of Artificial Intelligence: Global Recommendations*. Paris: UNESCO.

United Nations Economic and Social Affairs. (2020a). *AI and the Sustainable Development Goals*. New York: UN.

United Nations Economic and Social Affairs. (2020b). *Smart Cities and AI: The Role of Artificial Intelligence in Shaping Urban Governance*. New York: UN.

United Nations Economic and Social Affairs. (2021a). *AI and Democracy: Safeguarding Electoral Integrity*. New York: UN.

United Nations Economic and Social Affairs. (2021b). *AI for Good: How AI Is Improving Government Service Delivery*. New York: UN.

United Nations Economic and Social Affairs. (2021c). *AI for Social Good: Addressing Bias and Ethical Considerations in Public Policy*. New York: UN.

United Nations Economic and Social Affairs. (2021d). *Smart Cities and AI: The Role of Artificial Intelligence in Urban Governance*. New York: UN.

World Bank Group. (2022). *Artificial Intelligence in Public Service: Opportunities for Enhancing Governance and Service Delivery*. Washington, D.C.: World Bank.

World Economic Forum. (2020). *Global AI Governance: Policies and Standards*. Geneva: WEF.

World Economic Forum. (2021a). *Blockchain and AI for Transparent Governance*. Geneva: WEF.

World Economic Forum. (2021b). *How to Build Public Trust in AI: The Role of Transparency and Ethical Governance*. Geneva: WEF.

World Economic Forum. (2021c). *Shaping the Future of AI in Governance*. Geneva: WEF.

World Health Organization. (2020). *Artificial Intelligence in Health: Opportunities and Challenges*. Geneva: WHO.

11

AI Adoption for Asset-Based Industry

The asset-based industry sector is going through a critical generational change by integrating artificial intelligence (AI) with operational processes. Companies use modern technology, such as digital twins, which is a combination of traditional physical assets using information technology (IT)-based sensors for operational efficiency, to work more efficiently. Real-time data provided by this technology helps with preventive maintenance, plan better factory layouts, and improve how products are made and delivered. Smart systems through technology provide higher levels of efficiency and resource management. The introduction of personalised production, better utility management, and on-demand production aligns with current and expected future sustainability requirements.

AI is redefining predictive maintenance; the traditional scheduled maintenance developed decades ago has been replaced by data-driven maintenance in real time and identifying areas requiring maintenance.

Asset-based industries can utilise AI to integrate disparate systems and increase data-driven decision-making capabilities. Through new technology adoption, asset-based industries can open the path to innovation, sustainability, and competitive advantage. As noted in previous chapters, the rapid technology changes and their use for optimisation of operations require a cultural change in both workforce management and new skills required for adopting AI. Asset-based business also faces these same challenges.

AI adoption changes and challenges are similar to those for every new generation of technology adoption. The adoption of AI requires a holistic approach to integrating with existing systems and modernising operational processes and procedures. Holistic planning is necessary to identify areas to extend current systems to adopt AI, assimilate AI, integrate AI, and, in some cases, create new AI-based foundations. This chapter explores how the asset-based industry utilises AI capabilities and how it addresses and adapts to the challenges.

Key Points

- **Transformation through AI**: The integration of AI technologies is not just a change but a significant transformation for asset-based industries. It facilitates real-time monitoring, predictive maintenance,

DOI: 10.1201/9781003626503-11

and optimised production processes, paving the way for a future of unprecedented efficiency and productivity.

- **Digital Twins and Smart Factories**: Digital twins create precise virtual models of operations, enhancing efficiency and allowing for proactive management of machinery and processes.
- **Autonomous Systems**: Implementing autonomous vehicles in sectors like mining improves safety and operational efficiency by reducing human involvement in hazardous tasks.
- **Predictive Analytics for Maintenance**: AI-driven predictive maintenance allows businesses to foresee machinery failures, minimising downtime and optimising fleet performance in logistics.
- **Strategic AI Implementation**: Industries must recognise and dismantle barriers to AI adoption, focusing on strategic implementation to enhance operational efficiencies and reduce costs.
- **Data-Driven Decision-Making**: Embracing AI empowers asset-based industries to leverage vast amounts of data for informed decision-making, leading to better resource allocation and increased competitive advantage.
- **Collaboration with AI Providers**: A collaborative approach between industry leaders and AI providers is essential for navigating complex integration and addressing unique industry challenges.
- **Change Management**: Organisational change management is critical for aligning business goals with AI integration, ensuring a smooth transition to new technologies.
- **Continuous Learning Culture**: AI is not just a tool, but a catalyst for change. By promoting knowledge-sharing and collaboration, it fosters a culture of continuous learning, integral for sustaining growth and innovation in asset-based industries. It's not just about using AI, but about evolving with it.

What Is an Asset-Based Industry?

An asset-based industry is defined by physical and tangible assets such as machinery, buildings, vehicles, and factory assets. It is a high-investment industry with high entry barriers. The industry is driven by the initial investment in production resources and the assets requiring maintenance to ensure a long lifetime.

The first industrial revolution automated manual activities; the main component was using science and engineering to extend production using assembly lines and machinery to automate manual tasks. The manufacturing industry has gone through several generations of changes, during which time production has been optimised using numerically controlled machinery, which uses numbers and symbols to program specific tasks. This also provides higher levels of quality control.

In the past, industrial revolutions have incrementally optimised production by automating processes and procedures. AI is expected to change this landscape exponentially. The use of AI in asset-based industries provides smart asset management and optimises asset lifecycle, opening opportunities for huge growth. For example, the use of predictive maintenance, AI-powered tools, and Internet of Things (IoT) devices reduces maintenance cycles. Scheduled maintenance cycles, where the plants are shut down for 24 hours, have changed to real-time and designated area maintenance, where specific people or teams are assigned to a designated area to ensure maintenance is conducted on a regular basis. This optimises production and reduces maintenance cycles to improve asset utilisation using AI-based predictive maintenance.

AI-based advanced data analytics assist in intelligent decision-making and optimised resource allocation. AI-based plants are now experiencing better energy management and creating environmentally sustainable production ecosystems. Smart energy systems monitor energy usage in real-time and assist the organisation in planning usage for peak times or downtimes. Organisations have been using on-demand smart lighting systems, lifts, escalators, and production lines. This reduces energy usage and carbon footprints and assists the workforce with better lighting for their health and well-being.

Asset-based industries are expanding the use of autonomous vehicles, drones, advanced robotics, and IoT devices to streamline logistics and optimise resource utilisation. AI-assisted predictive maintenance is improving asset lifecycles. The digital twins are providing a seamless blend of workforce and IoT devices in production optimisation, environmental sustainability, and real-time on-demand maintenance.

Traditionally, asset-based industries have been late adopters of innovation due to cost and adoption challenges. AI adoption similarly presents opportunities to redefine new technology, tailored to the specific context of the industry. The asset-based industry has large investments in fixed machinery. Adopting AI depends on the stage each machine is in its asset lifecycle and how the product companies are prepared to adopt AI. In many cases, adopting AI depends on the machinery's ability to use AI and whether the workforce has the right skills.

Current concerns across the industrial world are an aging population and a decline in the availability of skilled workforces. The amalgamation of AI with the right skilled workforce operators can extend some of the existing manufacturing industries worldwide and also create new opportunities for the skilled workforce. AI adoption presents an opportunity to plan holistically and select the most suitable approach to enhance current capabilities, either by assimilating, integrating, or rebuilding them.

Key Characteristics of Asset-Based System

One of the technological achievements of the Renaissance period was the invention of the printing press in the 15th century. In today's terms, the printing press was the catalyst for the information-sharing revolution, enabling the mass production of books and the dissemination of information across the globe. The printing press also contributed to the Industrial Revolution and created the foundation of modern science. This invention marked the Middle Ages' transition to the modern era, which facilitated remarkable achievements in science and technology worldwide. AI is the modern world's foundation for similar advancements in science and technology.

The first two industrial revolutions can be categorised as mechanisation and the extension of human physical capabilities beyond what was previously believed possible. They resulted in innovations in textile, iron production, transportation, and, later, the telecommunication and automobile sectors.

The third industrial revolution marked the introduction of computers, known as the digital revolution, and the automation of mechanised processes through digital controls. AI is fuelling the fourth industrial revolution, which is based on the foundation of previous revolutions, integrating disparate devices into smart decision-making systems. The fourth revolution now focuses on humankind's mental capabilities or intelligence and connects it with the speed of computing capabilities. The fourth revolution is creating new dimensions in innovation and new areas of workforce development. Like other revolutions before it, this also generates challenges of resource security and potential biases or ethical concerns.

Modern economies have been driven by asset-based industries, which require substantial capital expenditures to establish and maintain. Asset-based industrial centres have a dependency on key resource requirements such as raw materials, a skilled workforce, and a suitable social and political environment.

The Modern Industrialisation

Asset-based industries are fundamental pillars of the global economy, spanning key sectors such as manufacturing, energy, transportation, and construction. A defining feature of these industries is their substantial capital expenditure (CapEx), which entails significant upfront investments in physical assets, including machinery, buildings, and infrastructure. Take, for example, the construction of a new skyscraper; the financial commitments involved, from land acquisition and hiring skilled labour to procuring heavy machinery, can reach millions even before construction begins. Moreover, these assets typically possess longer lifespans, offering a continuous return on investment over many years.

However, the success of operations within asset-based industries is heavily reliant on operational efficiency. Companies strive to maximise the utilisation of their assets to maintain profitability. The automotive industry serves as a prime example, where assembly lines are designed with precision to ensure each machine producing the auto operates at optimal capacity, mitigating the risk of costly delays and enhancing overall productivity.

The cost-effectiveness of an asset-based industry is based on the effectiveness of organisational operations. Operational excellence requires the company to have a desirable product at the lowest cost in the market by ensuring that all the costs associated with building and delivering the product, including any rework caused by a lapse in any process, are as low as possible. Operational processes at maximum efficiency ensure that the base cost associated with manufacturing the product, the cost of additional work, and rework need to be minimal.

The organisation also collaborates with partners to reduce costs. For example, a manufacturer keeps inventory at a minimum, requesting suppliers deliver products in a short turnaround time. Thus, the organisation can offset the costs of maintaining a huge inventory by collaborating with its suppliers.

The organisation chooses the market segments it can serve most efficiently and profitably. Choosing the segment is dependent on internal resources such as people, technology, processes, and customer needs. Business architecture helps assess the capabilities and resources to support the market segment. Timely information from multiple departments on products, customers, inventory, and delivery is essential to provide the service needed for success in the market. For example, the call centre needs the most up-to-date information on order status for customer inquiries. Sales, marketing, production, and order fulfilment functions need this information for service excellence.

Thus, operational excellence implies organisational processes operating with maximum efficiency and minimum cost from order placement to fulfilment, and throughout the supply chain.

Differentiation capabilities or organisational expertise also play an important role in operational excellence. AI creates insights into the core differentiating capabilities and assists organisations to achieve profitable business outcomes. To fully utilise differentiating capabilities requires technologies and systems. Business analysis evaluates how effectively an organisation can utilise specific technologies and how to allocate resources to support them. Consider, for example, an organisational differentiating capability called "strategy execution." Strategy execution highlights the IT capabilities of Amazon and Facebook, as well as the supply chain capabilities of Walmart and Dell. Differentiation capabilities are one area of operational excellence; maintenance cycles are another means of attaining operational excellence.

Maintenance cycles, which address frequency and scheduling, are essential for long-term operational excellence and profitability. Maintenance planning, which prepares an organisation for all the details of maintenance, is critical for the regular upkeep and maintenance of machines, infrastructure, and vehicles to reduce unplanned breakdowns. Over the last few decades, maintenance has been a scheduled event. For example, vehicle maintenance is based on lead time and mileage from the last maintenance. The scheduled maintenance event carries the risk of unplanned breakdowns and high costs due to under- or over-maintenance. AI-based preventive maintenance reduces maintenance costs by minimising downtime and targeting specific maintenance areas based on data analysis. The use of sensors and real-time data analysis enables the anticipation of issues before they occur.

AI optimises operational activities for asset-based businesses using predictive analytics, real-time demand management, and distribution adjustments. The manufacturing sector is modernising the factory layout for distributed production lines, utilising robotics and automated guided vehicles to handle complex assembly, welding, and packaging tasks. Security and efficiency are enhanced by utilising collaborative robots, also known as cobots, alongside human resources. AI assists with predicting when maintenance should occur, quality control of products during the production process, and smart scheduling for resources and machines. The asset-based industry is now achieving operational excellence through smart supply chain and logistics using augmented reality and virtual reality to enhance quality, security, safety, and product design.

The utilities sector is also classified as an asset-based industry, encompassing companies that provide telecommunication, electricity, water, and gas supply services. These companies are utilising and expanding the application of AI for network optimisation, and using IoT devices and sensors, to adjust the flow and delivery distribution in real-time and predictive maintenance.

AI has enhanced operational excellence asset-based industries by driving innovation across supply chain management. The future of AI will redefine many areas of asset-based industries to create sustainable and efficient operations. By augmenting human capabilities, AI provides more adaptable business models and faster responses to evolving market demand.

The Role of AI in Asset-Based Industries: Applications, Transitions, and Challenges

Asset-based industries such as manufacturing, energy, transportation, real estate, and utilities depend heavily on physical assets to generate value and are leveraging AI to optimise operations, enhance decision-making, and unlock new opportunities. However, transitioning to AI-powered processes requires specific applications and comes with unique challenges.

Applications for AI in Asset-Based Industries

There are many ways AI can be practically applied in asset-based industries including equipment maintenance, more effective asset management, and predicting future trends. In manufacturing and utilities, predictive maintenance is revolutionising the way organisations approach equipment maintenance. Imagine a vast factory floor where machines hum with activity, each intricately linked to a network of sensors that collect data and provide real-time insights into the machinery's health. This is where AI steps in, transforming raw data into powerful predictions about potential equipment failures before they even happen.

General Electric, for instance, has harnessed the power of AI to monitor turbines in its industrial operations. By analysing a multitude of data points, from temperature fluctuations to vibration patterns, AI algorithms identify signs of wear and tear that may indicate an impending malfunction. The predictive maintenance algorithms prevent a costly shutdown by using historical and equipment data to pre-empt equipment issues. This proactive approach minimises unplanned downtime and significantly reduces maintenance costs, ensuring that operations run continuously and efficiently.

The impact of predictive maintenance extends beyond just saving money; it enhances reliability and extends the lifespan of crucial assets. AI provides the confidence for organisations to operate a power plant knowing its equipment is continuously being monitored for the slightest signs of breakdown. In turn, this allows employees to focus on applying other skills, such as process improvement, rather than constantly reacting to machine failures.

Future AI applications in predictive maintenance will continue to innovate, integrating AI with emerging technologies such as the IoT and advanced analytics. The benefit will be smarter systems that predict failures and proactively suggest optimal maintenance schedules tailored to each individual piece of equipment.

The insights provided by AI are driving business transformation through predictive maintenance, empowering industries to create safer, more reliable environments, and mitigating downtime risks. Predictive maintenance is a success story for asset-based industries to mitigate downtime risks and keep industries thriving.

Smarter Asset Management

Smart asset management uses advanced technologies, including AI, to monitor, maintain, and optimise physical assets throughout the asset lifecycle. AI is revolutionising industry operations across various sectors, particularly in manufacturing and energy generation. AI algorithms provide the power to reduce machinery downtime, predict needed maintenance, and improve safety for employees on the production floor.

In the energy sector, the development of smart grids has transformed the management of electricity consumption. Smart grid advanced systems use AI to analyse real-time data, ensuring a seamless balance between supply and demand. For example, on a scorching summer day, energy consumption surges as air conditioning units run at full capacity. With the intervention of smart grids, AI can swiftly adjust energy distribution, optimising performance while minimising waste.

A prominent manufacturer harnessed AI to enhance its production scheduling processes. By analysing historical production data, the AI was able to predict potential delays and streamline operations accordingly. This innovation not only reduced operational costs but also made their product more competitively priced, ultimately benefiting consumers and the economy at large.

Looking ahead, AI's potential for operational optimisation in business is limitless where technology continuously learns and refines processes after each production cycle. For individuals, homes will be equipped with AI-driven systems that adjust their energy consumption based on live grid conditions, yielding not only cost savings but also a significant reduction in the community's carbon footprint.

In other areas, blending AI and inventory management is transforming supply chains and business operations through the use of robotics to navigate among shelves stocked with numerous products. Each robot is part of a sophisticated AI framework that carefully analyses demand patterns, ensuring the right products are available at the right time.

In retail, AI analytics can proactively predict an unexpected surge in demand for a trending gadget by examining historical trends. This foresight allows businesses to maintain optimal inventory levels, significantly reducing the risk of stockouts and enhancing customer satisfaction.

The advantages of AI in supply chain management extend beyond simply preventing shortages. By employing real-time monitoring, businesses can minimise excess stock, thereby freeing up valuable warehouse space and reducing carrying costs. For example, a clothing retailer can leverage AI to adjust inventory strategies dynamically, ensuring their most popular items are readily available while minimising unsold seasonal goods.

Looking towards the future, AI in inventory and supply chain management holds incredible potential. The future is a world where AI systems are seamlessly integrated with technologies like the IoT and data collection from interconnected devices to refine inventory strategies. Operational management is more effective through automated restocking and efficient adjusting to customer demands.

The ongoing evolution of AI in supply chain and operational management exemplifies a commitment to enhanced efficiency and responsiveness. By embracing these innovations, businesses are not only adapting to customer demands but also forging a future where shopping experiences are intuitive and fulfilling, ensuring that customers enjoy reliable and engaging interactions every time they engage with a brand.

Outside of retail, transportation has been transformed through asset tracking and fleet management. Companies are leveraging AI to optimise operations and redefine logistics and delivery services. For instance, UPS, a leader in the logistics sector, has begun implementing AI-driven route optimisation software, analysing data in real time to enhance efficiency and service quality.

The pathway towards operational excellence through AI is just beginning, and as technology continues to advance, industries must wholeheartedly embrace these innovations. The promise of enhanced efficiency and cost savings is no longer a distant dream but a tangible reality that has the power to reshape the world for the better. The integration of AI is not just a technological trend; it represents a profound shift in how businesses and people operate and interact with the world, inspiring a future characterised by innovation, efficiency, and sustainability.

Real estate and urban planning have also advanced through AI. Machine learning is being utilised to analyse property data and market trends to enhance the buying and selling experience. This data provides the market with precise home price estimates, creating a more transparent view of communities.

The influence of AI in real estate is significant by providing powerful insights that help investors make more informed decisions and create strategies to revitalise communities or build smart communities in the future. AI can analyse trends and demographics, and even guide city planners to design parks and public spaces that support diverse community needs.

The intersection of AI and urban planning allows residents to envision how proposed changes may transform their neighbourhoods before implementation. Imagine a platform where individuals can voice their desires for more bike lanes, green spaces, or affordable housing, with AI analysing this feedback against demographic and economic data to develop optimal development plans. Communities of the future will be thoughtfully crafted with active participation from their inhabitants, leading to enhanced living conditions.

Asset-based industries depend on physical infrastructure and equipment, which can pose significant risk if not managed appropriately. AI-powered computer vision systems with advanced algorithms and cameras continuously monitor job sites to detect potential safety hazards such as equipment misuse, inadequate protective gear, or hazardous conditions. One notable example involves a construction company that deployed AI-equipped cameras, which not only flagged risks but also delivered immediate feedback to workers, cultivating a culture of safety awareness and yielding a remarkable reduction in accidents and injuries.

AI adoption in asset-based industries extends beyond reducing workplace accidents; it also builds stricter compliance with stringent safety regulations.

AI use in construction sites employs intelligent systems that continuously assess risk factors and provide recommended actions to ensure safety. AI systems analyse data from various sources, such as weather conditions, equipment performance, and worker behaviour, to anticipate accidents before they occur. This proactive approach empowers managers to implement preventive measures, ensuring that safety protocols are preventative rather than merely reactive.

The potential applications of AI technology advancements are limitless. In the future, AI will actively engage with workers, providing real-time guidance and tailored training based on the site's unique conditions. Picture a new worker receiving a customised safety briefing designed by AI that addresses the specific risks they may face on their first day, instilling a culture of vigilance and responsibility right from the start of their career.

Integrating AI into safety and risk management represents more than just a technological enhancement; it is an essential move towards safer workplaces. Embracing these innovations serves as a powerful inspiration, showcasing a future where technology and human intuition collaborate harmoniously to cultivate safer, more sustainable work environments.

Transitions: Moving towards AI Adoption

Business operations today are experiencing a technological transformation from manual processes to AI, fundamentally changing how organisations operate. This transformation begins with the essential step of digitisation, where companies embrace the power of technology to enhance their operations and decision-making capabilities. By implementing IoT sensors, organisations can collect real-time data that is crucial for analysing their environments and improving efficiency. These sensors feed into centralised data platforms and cloud-based solutions, enabling an integrated approach to data management that was once unimaginable.

One of the most inspiring examples of this transformation can be seen in the oil and gas industry, where companies like BP are pioneering the use of IoT and AI technologies for pipeline monitoring. In the past, monitoring pipelines was a labour-intensive process filled with risks and potential hazards. Today, with the installation of advanced sensors, BP can gather precise data on the condition of their pipelines in real-time. This not only enhances safety by detecting leaks and failures early, but also significantly reduces operational costs. The integration of AI allows for predictive maintenance, meaning that potential issues can be identified and addressed before they become major problems, ultimately saving time and resources.

The possibilities for AI in future applications are boundless, and it has the ability to enhance productivity and create new opportunities. For instance, in agriculture, farmers could utilise AI-driven drones equipped with sensors that monitor crop health, soil conditions, and weather patterns. This data would empower farmers to make informed decisions about planting, watering, and harvesting, leading to more sustainable and productive farming practices.

The potential rewards, enhanced efficiency, improved safety, and more significant innovation make AI adoption and digitisation a worthwhile endeavour. As more companies embrace this transition, it is expected that the world will become more connected, smarter, and more responsive to human needs, unlocking capabilities that have yet to be imagined. However, this transition requires more than just the installation of sophisticated technologies; it calls for a fundamental shift in how employees engage with and interpret AI outputs.

For organisations to fully harness the potential of AI, they must invest in comprehensive training programs that equip their workforce with the necessary skills to understand and effectively utilise these sophisticated tools. Upskilling initiatives play a pivotal role in this journey. By creating specialised training programs, companies can ensure their employees are not only familiar with AI systems but are also able to seamlessly integrate AI insights into their daily workflows.

Take, for instance, Caterpillar, a leading manufacturer of construction and mining equipment. Recognising the importance of AI in enhancing efficiency and decision-making capabilities, Caterpillar has implemented robust training programs aimed at developing their employees' analytical skill sets. Through targeted AI training, their workforce has become adept at interpreting complex data, allowing them to make informed decisions that drive innovation and improve operational outcomes.

Moreover, the future of AI promises even greater opportunities for enhancement and growth. Imagine a scenario in which employees of various industries are equipped with AI-driven tools that anticipate customer needs, streamline supply chains, and provide real-time analytics that inform strategic decisions. An employee in a retail setting might use AI to predict shopping trends, enabling their team to stock inventory more efficiently, while a healthcare professional could leverage AI to analyse patient data, leading to faster and more accurate diagnoses.

As asset-based industries continue to evolve, embracing AI will empower employees and enrich the customer experience and drive competitive advantage. It is essential for companies to adopt a measured approach and implement AI initiatives gradually in specific areas before scaling these projects across their entire operations.

An example is a logistics company that recognised the potential of AI in optimising delivery routes. They started by testing a sophisticated AI system on just a handful of their fleets, carefully measuring the impact on efficiency and cost savings. By analysing real-time data, the AI could suggest the most efficient paths for drivers to take, taking into consideration traffic patterns, weather conditions, and delivery times. The results from the pilot program encouraged reducing fuel consumption and improving delivery times. Satisfied with the success of the initial trials, the company rolled out this AI route optimisation system across their entire fleet, leading to enhanced operational efficiency and significant savings.

AI turns manufacturing into smart manufacturing, where facilities can become more predictive, efficient, flexible, and competitive. In turn, this maximises operational efficiency while minimising waste and resource consumption.

Gradual implementation helps organisations manage risks in a more controlled way and also provides employees a chance to learn about the new technology in a measured manner. By implementing an iterative approach to implementation, employees have an opportunity to contribute valuable feedback to refine desired outcomes.

Another aspect to transitioning to AI requires organisations upgrade their legacy systems to keep up with the market and retain competitive advantages. The adoption of AI with existing legacy systems needs a planned capability and services architecture framework, as proposed in this book. The adoption of AI within legacy systems may necessitate the redevelopment of several new business capabilities and the rebuilding of the legacy systems with the adoption of new business processes and capabilities.

The utility management sector benefits from the integration of AI with Supervisory Control and Data Acquisition (SCADA). SCADA systems are re-engineering siloed systems with open integrations. Manufacturing systems have been integrating traditional SCADA systems with the rest of the organisational systems to optimise operations. This aspect with holistic monitoring and control system information used by AI platforms, providing actionable insights, real-time monitoring, and predictive maintenance. The predictive maintenance analytics provide the utilities industry with reduced outages and better customer satisfaction.

The evolution of IT over the last seven decades has been incremental, but some of the legacy foundations may not be appropriate for AI enhancements to their existing system landscape.

As discussed in earlier chapters, the integration of AI with legacy is not only technical; it will provide and, in some cases, enforce the redesign or upgrade of systems based on competitive business capabilities architecture. Just as the industrial revolution built upon centuries of craftsmanship, today's digital age is powered by past discoveries in computing, engineering, and AI. The strength of the future depends on how effectively the past is preserved, learned from, and expanded upon.

Examples of Asset-Based Industries

Manufacturing: The Asset-Based Revolution and the Role of AI

The manufacturing sector is undergoing a transformative shift known as "Manufacturing 4.0," where personalisation is reclaiming its place alongside advanced technological integration. AI is at the forefront of this evolution, enabling more efficient, flexible, and customised manufacturing processes. Key areas where AI is making a significant impact are as follows:

1. **Autonomous Production Lines**: The ratio of human workers to machines in the car industry has dramatically shifted from 80/20 to 20/80 over the past 50 years. Modern factories utilise robotics and AI to create autonomous production lines, significantly reducing production times and labour costs. For example, companies like Tesla leverage robotic systems for assembly while requiring minimal human supervision, leading to faster output and higher efficiency.

2. **Personalised Manufacturing**: AI facilitates the customisation of luxury goods without disturbing existing production processes. For instance, automotive manufacturers now offer consumers the ability to personalise features in their vehicles, such as colour, upholstery, and technology integrations, without the need for extensive reconfigurations of the manufacturing setup. This is a departure from traditional methods that require significant downtime to switch between product configurations.

3. **Enhanced Human–Machine Collaboration**: The role of skilled workers has evolved from manual operation to oversight of automated systems. Today, smart factories utilise AI to manage heavy lifting and repetitive tasks, allowing human workers to focus on quality control and system optimisation. This collaborative dynamic not only enhances productivity but also improves workplace safety and efficiency.

4. **Sustainability Optimisation**: AI-driven technologies are redesigning manufacturing environments for greater sustainability. For example, Tesla's Gigafactory employs AI to optimise energy consumption and resource management, effectively reducing waste and lowering operational costs. AI systems monitor energy use and water management to enhance overall factory efficiency.

As manufacturing returns to a more personalised approach, driven by AI advancements, the industry is moving towards more optimised, on-demand production capabilities. This shift reduces the need for large inventories, with technologies like 3D printing providing parts as needed, thereby enhancing responsiveness and minimising waste. This evolution signifies a promising future for the manufacturing sector, characterised by increased innovation and customisation.

Transportation and Logistics: A Century of Transformation

The transportation and logistics industries are experiencing a profound transformation driven by advancements in AI. Through the integration of AI technologies, these sectors are becoming more efficient, cost-effective, and customer-centric (Table 11.1).

TABLE 11.1

Current State vs. Future Use of AI

Current State of Transportation and Logistics	Future Use of AI in Transportation and Logistics
Automation and Predictive Analytics: AI is being used to optimise supply chain management and route planning. Companies are leveraging predictive analytics to anticipate demand fluctuations, enabling efficient resource allocation and reduced operational costs. For instance, logistics firms utilise AI algorithms to analyse traffic patterns and weather data, allowing for timely deliveries and optimised routes.	**Advanced Predictive Models**: In the future, AI will enhance its predictive capabilities, allowing for even more accurate demand forecasting and route optimisation. This will help companies adapt quickly to changing market conditions and improve overall supply chain resilience.
Autonomous Vehicles: The rise of self-driving technology is revolutionising freight transport. Companies like Waymo and Tesla are advancing autonomous trucks, which promise to reduce labour costs and enhance safety by minimising human error. These vehicles can operate around the clock, improving delivery timelines.	**Integrated Supply Chains**: AI will facilitate more interconnected supply chains by enabling real-time data sharing across various stakeholders. This integration can lead to improved collaboration and efficiency, resulting in faster response times and reduced costs.
Smart Warehousing: AI transforms warehousing operations through automation and inventory management. Robotics and AI systems manage stock levels, streamline picking processes, and enhance accuracy, leading to reduced labour costs and improved efficiency. For instance, Amazon employs AI-driven robots for sorting and packing, significantly accelerating order fulfilment.	**Sustainability Initiatives**: As environmental concerns grow, AI will play a key role in optimising logistics operations for sustainability. For example, AI can enhance fuel efficiency in transportation and enable better resource management, ultimately reducing the carbon footprint of logistics activities.
Customer Experience Enhancement: AI-enabled chatbots and virtual assistants are improving customer service in logistics by providing real-time support and tracking information. This technology enhances transparency in the supply chain, allowing customers to receive updates on shipment statuses and estimated delivery times.	**Personalised Services**: AI-enabled technologies will further personalise customer experiences, offering tailored delivery options and services based on individual preferences and behaviours, thus enhancing customer satisfaction.

AI is significantly reshaping the transportation and logistics sectors, making them more efficient, responsive, and customer-focused. As AI technologies continue to evolve, their potential to drive innovation and sustainability in these industries will be even greater, paving the way for a more connected and efficient future.

Energy and Utilities: A Journey from Coal to AI-Driven Sustainability

The energy and utilities industry is undergoing a significant transformation with the adoption of AI. In the past, the sector depended heavily on coal and manual labour, resulting in environmental challenges and inefficiencies. Today, AI technologies enable smarter resource management, optimising energy production and enhancing sustainability across operations.

Currently, AI is being used to analyse vast amounts of data, predict energy demands, and improve maintenance schedules for equipment, which minimises downtime and reduces operational costs. Smart grids equipped with AI can dynamically adjust energy distribution, enhancing reliability and efficiency while promoting the use of renewable resources.

The future of AI in the energy sector promises even more advancements. As environmental concerns grow, AI will play a crucial role in optimising energy consumption, enhancing the integration of renewable sources, and reducing carbon footprints. AI systems will also enable more personalised energy services for consumers, allowing them to manage their consumption based on real-time data. AI is poised to revolutionise the energy and utilities industry, driving innovation and sustainability while fostering a more efficient and responsive energy ecosystem for the future.

Real Estate and Construction: From Brick and Mortar to AI-Driven Smart Cities

The real estate and construction industries have experienced profound transformations driven by advancements in AI and automation technologies. These changes have redefined traditional practices and introduced new efficiencies, significantly impacting how buildings are designed, constructed, and managed.

In construction, the integration of AI has revolutionised project management and execution. Automated project tracking tools, powered by AI, help construction managers monitor progress in real time, identify potential delays, and optimise resource allocation. For example, companies like Autodesk use AI to enhance Building Information Modelling, facilitating improved collaboration among architects, engineers, and contractors. This technology predicts project outcomes and enhances design accuracy, ultimately reducing both time and costs.

Moreover, AI-driven robotics and automation are reshaping construction methodologies. Drones equipped with AI are increasingly employed for site inspections and surveying, providing real-time feedback on project status.

Boston Dynamics' Spot robot is an example of how robotics can automate routine inspections, ensuring safety and efficiency. These technologies can significantly decrease the time spent on site assessments and enhance project oversight.

AI is also paving the way for smart cities and sustainable building practices. By harnessing data from IoT devices, AI can optimise energy usage in buildings, improve heating, ventilation and air-rconditioning (HVAC) systems, and enhance overall operational efficiency. For instance, AI applications in smart buildings can analyse energy consumption patterns, automatically adjusting systems to reduce waste and enhance sustainability.

The continued integration of AI in real estate and construction holds the promise of further innovation. Emerging technologies like autonomous construction vehicles and AI-powered predictive maintenance could significantly reshape how projects are developed and managed. This AI-driven evolution is not only improving efficiency and reducing costs but also fostering more sustainable practices in urban development, ultimately leading to smarter, more resilient communities.

Mining and Natural Resources: From Pickaxes to AI-Driven Sustainability

AI is significantly transforming the mining and natural resources industry by enhancing efficiency, safety, and sustainability. Currently, AI technologies utilise data analytics and predictive modelling to optimise resource extraction. Companies employ AI to analyse geological data, improving the accuracy of mineral deposit locations while minimising waste and environmental impact.

Automation is another key area where AI is making strides. Firms deploy autonomous vehicles and robotics, which operate in hazardous environments, reducing the need for human intervention and lowering accident rates. For instance, driverless trucks and automated drilling systems are being used effectively in locations like Australia's Pilbara region.

Looking to the future, AI will likely expand its influence by integrating advanced technologies such as machine learning and robotics. This will lead to even smarter operations, with more autonomous systems taking a greater role in mining processes. Additionally, enhanced AI-driven supply chain transparency through blockchain technology will increase accountability and traceability from extraction to final product, further boosting efficiency.

As the industry continues to prioritise sustainability, AI will also help companies adopt greener practices, such as optimising resource usage and reducing emissions. Overall, the ongoing integration of AI in mining promises to usher in a new era of innovation, efficiency, and responsibility.

Agriculture and Food Processing: From Horse-Drawn Plows to Precision Farming

The adoption of AI in agriculture and food processing is revolutionising traditional practices, enhancing efficiency, and paving the way for sustainable growth. Farmers are increasingly using AI-driven technologies, such as satellite imaging, GPS-guided tractors, and machine learning algorithms, to analyse soil conditions, predict weather patterns, and optimise irrigation and fertilisation. This precision farming approach allows them to make data-informed decisions, significantly improving crop yields while minimising resource waste.

In food processing, AI streamlines operations through automation and predictive analytics. It helps manufacturers optimise supply chains, improve product quality, and reduce food spoilage, ensuring a more consistent supply of fresh goods to consumers. Additionally, AI-driven consumer insights allow companies to tailor products to meet changing dietary preferences and health trends.

Looking ahead, the future of AI in these industries promises even greater innovations. The expected integration of robotics for tasks such as planting, harvesting, and processing is instrumental in reducing labour costs and increasing productivity. Enhanced AI-powered traceability systems will provide greater transparency in food sourcing, addressing consumer concerns over food safety and sustainability.

Overall, the continued adoption of AI will not only reshape how food is produced and processed but also contribute to a more resilient and sustainable agricultural ecosystem.

Aerospace and Defence: From Wooden Biplanes to AI-Driven Warfare and Space Exploration

The aerospace and defence industry is increasingly adopting AI to enhance efficiency, improve safety, and streamline operations. Companies are leveraging AI for predictive maintenance, optimising supply chains, and enhancing decision-making processes.

Looking to the future, the adoption of AI in this sector is expected to accelerate. Innovations in autonomous systems, such as drones and unmanned vehicles, will rely heavily on AI technologies for navigation and mission execution. Additionally, as cyber threats evolve, AI will play a crucial role in bolstering cybersecurity measures. Overall, the integration of AI will continue to transform the aerospace and defence industry, making it more efficient and responsive to emerging challenges.

Chapter Questions

1. What are the defining characteristics of asset-based industries, and why is AI particularly impactful in transforming their operations?

2. How does predictive maintenance powered by AI differ from traditional scheduled maintenance, and what are its operational benefits?

3. What role do digital twins and smart factories play in enhancing operational efficiency, and how are they integrated with AI technologies?

4. In what ways is AI fostering sustainability in asset-based industries, particularly in energy and manufacturing sectors?

5. Discuss how AI is transforming supply chain and logistics management in asset-based industries. What are the short-term and long-term impacts?

6. What cultural and workforce-related challenges must asset-based industries overcome to successfully adopt AI?

7. How are autonomous systems, such as vehicles and drones, revolutionising mining and logistics operations in asset-based industries?

8. What does the chapter suggest about the role of AI in enhancing operational excellence through decision-making and strategic execution?

9. How does the concept of gradual AI implementation help organisations manage risk and improve technology integration?

10. Reflect on how AI is reshaping traditional industries (e.g., agriculture, real estate, aerospace). What common patterns of transformation do you observe across these sectors?

Note to Readers and Educators

Comprehensive answers and explanations to these chapter-end questions are available at www.sandeepbhalekar.com. The website also provides supplementary frameworks, teaching guidelines, and reference materials to support deeper understanding and classroom discussion.

Educators and facilitators can access additional resources, including presentation frameworks, assessment rubrics, and discussion prompts, to help integrate the concepts from this chapter into academic or professional learning environments.

Bibliography

Amazon. (2023). *Robotics and AI in Fulfillment Centres*. Seattle: Amazon Robotics. https://www.aboutamazon.com

Autodesk. (2023). *AI and BIM for Smarter Construction*. San Francisco: Autodesk. https://www.autodesk.com/solutions/bim

Autonomous Manufacturing Research Institute. (2023). *Collaborative Robotics in Smart Factories*. Chicago: AMRI.

BP. (2023). *IoT and AI in Pipeline Monitoring*. London: BP. https://www.bp.com

Boston Dynamics. (2023). *Spot Robot for Construction Site Automation*. Waltham: Boston Dynamics. https://www.bostondynamics.com/spot

Caterpillar. (2023). *AI Upskilling and Workforce Analytics*. Deerfield: Caterpillar. https://www.caterpillar.com/en/news

ESGTech. (2023). *AI and Smart Utilities for Sustainability*. New York: ESGTech. https://www.esgtech.com

FAO. (2022). *AI in Agriculture and Food Security*. Rome: Food and Agriculture Organization of the United Nations. https://www.fao.org

General Electric. (2023). *Predictive Maintenance in Industrial Operations*. Boston: GE Reports. https://www.ge.com/news

Intel. (2023). *AI in Smart Energy Grids and SCADA Systems*. Santa Clara: Intel. https://www.intel.com

McKinsey & Company. (2023). *The Factory of the Future: How AI Transforms Manufacturing*. New York: McKinsey & Company. https://www.mckinsey.com

OECD. (2022). *AI in Industry and Manufacturing*. Paris: OECD Publishing. https://www.oecd.org

PwC. (2023). *AI and Smart Supply Chains*. London: PwC Insights. https://www.pwc.com

Singapore Smart Nation. (2023). *Smart City Planning with AI and Community Input*. Singapore: Government of Singapore. https://www.smartnation.gov.sg

Tesla. (2023). *Gigafactory and AI-Based Energy Optimisation*. Palo Alto: Tesla. https://www.tesla.com/gigafactory

UPS. (2023). *Optimising Logistics through AI and Route Planning*. Atlanta: UPS. https://www.ups.com

U.S. Department of Energy. (2023). *AI for Grid Modernisation and Energy Efficiency*. Washington, D.C.: DOE. https://www.energy.gov

Waymo. (2023). *Autonomous Freight and Delivery Technology*. Mountain View: Waymo. https://waymo.com

World Economic Forum. (2023). *Shaping the Future of Advanced Manufacturing*. Geneva: WEF. https://www.weforum.org/reports

Zillow. (2023). *Machine Learning and Property Analytics*. Seattle: Zillow. https://www.zillow.com/research

12

AI Adoption for Customer-Based Industries

Over the past century, technology has made huge advancements. These improvements are causing customer-centric industries such as retail, healthcare, hospitality, finance, and entertainment to change the way they operate. Initially, these businesses relied on personal and local interactions to thrive, but with the progress of industrialisation, efficiency has become one of the key drivers for change. Huge department stores and chain hotels are now becoming the norm, often competing with and challenging smaller businesses.

Online shopping and electronic payments have introduced an easy and quick shopping experience from the comfort of home. Chatbots and search engines have revolutionised the way consumers buy, and platforms like Amazon and Airbnb have changed the way consumers shop. Chatbots and recommendation engines personalise the experience and make it efficient. However, with these come other issues, for example, data privacy issues and concerns for job security.

Industries must maintain a balance of innovation and ethical considerations for consistent and balanced growth. They should focus on reskilling the workforce and maintaining a transparent policy for data usage. To use the technological advancements in the best way possible, the industries need to prioritise creating a more efficient, inclusive, and sustainable future. Their approach should be human-centric so that human needs are met and the technological advancements enhance personal engagement, not replace them.

Key Points

- **Transformations in Customer-Based Industries:** Technological advancements have significantly evolved sectors like retail, healthcare, hospitality, finance, and entertainment over the last century.
- **Impact of Digital Revolution:** Online shopping, electronic payments, and platforms like Amazon and Airbnb have transformed consumer experiences.
- **AI Adoption:** Artificial intelligence (AI) technologies such as chatbots and recommendation engines are increasingly being used to improve efficiency and personalise interactions.

DOI: 10.1201/9781003626503-12

- **Ethical Considerations:** Technological advancements raise concerns regarding job displacement and data privacy, necessitating a focus on ethical practices.
- **Workforce Reskilling:** Industries must prioritise reskilling employees and maintaining transparency in data usage to successfully navigate the AI-driven landscape.
- **Human-Centred Approach:** Emphasising comprehending and meeting human needs is crucial for leveraging technology without losing personal engagement.
- **Examples of Industry Evolution:**
  - **Retail:** E-commerce and AR for enhanced shopping experiences.
  - **Hospitality:** Personalised services through platforms like Airbnb.
  - **Healthcare:** Telemedicine and wearable technology for improved patient interaction.
  - **Finance:** Digital banking for personalised financial management.
  - **Automotive:** Connected experiences and innovations in electric and autonomous vehicles.
  - **Entertainment:** The shift to streaming services changing consumer access to media.
- **Organisational Change Management:** Emphasising aligning AI capabilities with business strategies, and fostering a culture of continuous learning.

Customer-Based Industries: A Descriptive Definition and Evolution over the Last Century with AI Transition

In today's dynamic economy, a customer-based industry thrives on the principles of understanding and responding to consumer demands, preferences, and behaviours. These sectors go beyond merely supplying products or services; they continuously adapt to the ever-changing landscape of consumer needs, market trends, and technological advancements. This shift towards a customer-centric approach fosters an environment rich in personalised experiences, deep customer engagement, and feedback-driven improvements. These are a few examples of customer-based industries that illustrate this concept:

- **Retail:** The retail industry has embraced digital transformation in remarkable ways. From the rise of e-commerce giants like Amazon, which tailors recommendations based on browsing history and previous purchases, to local shops using social media to engage with their communities, the approach to retail has significantly evolved. Today, augmented reality (AR) technology allows customers to visualise products in their homes before purchasing. An example of this is furniture retailers offering apps to see how a couch would look in a customer's living room.

- **Hospitality**: In the hospitality sector, the advent of platforms like Airbnb has revolutionised how travellers seek accommodation. With increased competition, hotels are now offering personalised services, such as tailored recommendations based on past stays or preferences shared during booking. Technologies such as mobile check-ins and smart room features provide convenience and comfort, making each stay unique and memorable.

- **Healthcare**: Technological advancements and the advent of telemedicine have made noticeable improvements in healthcare. COVID-19 made virtual consultations a necessity for patients to receive medical advice remotely. Devices like fitness trackers encourage healthier living, and some can be used by the healthcare provider to monitor their patients in real time. Such devices help make the relationship between doctor and patient more interactive and personalised.

- **Finance**: In finance, customer behaviour has reshaped banking services. Digital banking apps provide customers with personalised insights into spending habits, allowing them to manage their finances more effectively. Moreover, innovations such as robo-advisors use algorithms to offer tailored investment advice, making wealth management accessible to a broader audience.

- **Automotive:** The automotive industry is another prime example of how technology has transformed consumer interactions. With the introduction of electric and autonomous vehicles, manufacturers are focusing on performance and creating connected experiences. Innovations like in-car infotainment systems, which adapt to driver preferences and provide personalised navigation, are changing how people think about transportation.

- **Entertainment**: The entertainment landscape has undergone a revolution with the rise of streaming services like Netflix and Spotify. These platforms leverage algorithms to curate content based on individual preferences, making it easier than ever for consumers to discover new shows and music that resonate with them.

Technological advancements over the last century have made it possible for customer-centric industries to evolve in a way that has been beneficial to society. The introduction of the Internet and mobile technology has opened new avenues for businesses, making it possible for customer interactions to be more meaningful.

The future of customer-based industries looks very promising with the advent of AI. Integrating AI to analyse vast amounts of data, discovering patterns in consumer behaviour and predicting a need even before consumers realise it, is very powerful. AI chatbots that can understand basic queries and analyse human emotions can enhance customer satisfaction and provide a positive experience.

As technology advances, businesses can find multiple ways to create responsive and engaging customer experiences. The key is to take a human-centric approach and utilise these advancements to exceed customers' expectations. Business evolution should be centred on nurturing genuine connections with their customers, which cultivates loyalty and trust.

Retail Industry: From General Stores to AI-Driven E-Commerce

A century ago, shopping was an intimate experience defined by personal relationships between shopkeepers and customers. Local general stores were the lifeline of communities, offering a modest selection of goods. Families purchased necessities from merchants who often knew them by name, extending credit based on trust rather than formal transactions. Goods were limited in variety, sourced from nearby suppliers, and prices were often negotiable. Shopping was not just about buying—it was a social ritual, an opportunity for community engagement and a necessary routine of daily life.

By the early 20th century, department stores like Macy's, Harrods, and Selfridges started taking on the market. They were offering a vast selection of products under one roof. Pricing was fixed, and visually appealing displays encouraged customers to come in and buy. Sears began catalogue shopping in the United States, and customers living in remote locations could also access their goods. Shopping was available for a range of goods available worldwide and not just the local storekeeper's shop.

By the mid-20th century, supermarkets and chain stores revolutionised shopping habits. Companies like Kroger and Tesco capitalised on urban expansion and improvements in transportation to create larger, self-service stores. In the 1970s, point-of-sale systems and standardisation of barcodes made inventory management more efficient, allowing retailers to track purchases in real time. As a result, the shopping experience shifted from personal interactions to one focused on convenience. Prices were lower, products were abundant, and choices grew exponentially.

The 1980s and 1990s saw another groundbreaking change with the rise of global supply chains. Big retailers like Walmart used information technology (IT) to optimise inventory and reduce costs, which increased efficiency in their logistics by leaps and bounds. A digitised inventory system made it possible to track the products in real time. Growth in highways, ports, and air cargo networks meant the goods could also be transported to other continents speedily. The traditional small retail shops that once dominated local economies, struggled to compete, leading to the decline of many family-owned businesses.

The dawn of the internet in the late 1990s brought the next retail revolution. Amazon and eBay came up with the new e-commerce model, which made shopping more convenient. Customers could now select the right product, compare prices, and purchase from the convenience of their home. IT innovation made digital payments possible and transactions easier. Customers could get personalised recommendations via data analytics. Technology could forecast customer needs from patterns. This also led to a redefinition of job roles within the industry. Physical stores started closing, while fulfilment centres and last-mile delivery services grew in prominence.

Today, machine learning algorithms forecast demand with high speed and accuracy. Stores like Amazon Go have no cashiers or checkout lines. The world is entering a new era of automation, predictive analytics, and dynamic customisation. This transition to AI-powered retail has its own challenges, which impact jobs, society, and even political landscapes.

The Societal and Economic Impact of Retail Transformation

With each phase of retail's evolution, society has experienced profound changes. The mid-20th century saw the rise of supermarkets and chain stores, which changed the way communities interacted by replacing personal relationships with self-service shopping. Small businesses closed their doors, and large retailers became the focal points of commercial activity. Shopping malls, in the 1980s and 1990s, became a symbol of wealth and prosperity, creating a generation of consumers accustomed to variety, convenience, and consumer culture that became the norm.

The e-commerce boom of the 2000s further transformed the workforce. Traditional retail jobs were transformed as automation replaced manual tasks, and warehouse operations became the backbone of online shopping. Data analysis, cybersecurity, and logistics are the new skills and jobs in demand. However, this rapid expansion and growth of warehouses came with the price of gruelling workloads in fulfilment centres and called for better labour rights, working conditions, wages, and unionisation for worker protection.

The political impact of retail's transformation cannot be ignored. As globalisation made it possible to manufacture goods at a low cost, towns in developed nations where manufacturing was the mainstay suffered job losses and economic instability. Globalisation also raised concerns over multinationals monopolising the market, and governments have to intervene and introduce antitrust regulations to ensure fair competition in businesses. Expansion in digital e-commerce also led to discussions on data privacy, taxation rules for online retailers, and the role of AI in shaping consumer behaviour.

The Role of Information Technology in Retail Evolution

The retail industry has been revolutionised by IT. Adoption of barcodes in the 1970s was one of the first moves that brought efficiency through IT-driven technology. This technology reduced human errors and streamlined inventory management. The 1990s saw enterprise resource planning systems so retailers could integrate supply chain management, finance, and customer service into a unified platform, optimising operations.

Big data analytics in the 2000s made it possible to create patterns from consumer behaviour and predict needs with analytics before consumers voiced the need out loud. Companies like Target famously used predictive analytics to identify customer needs and could market with precision. Cloud computing improved digital transformation by allowing vast amounts of data to be stored securely to deliver seamless shopping experiences across multiple platforms.

IT advancements have reshaped the most critical factors for success in retail logistics and transportation. GPS tracking, route optimisation, and automated sorting have made fulfilment faster than ever before. Using IT-driven logistics, Amazon's Prime delivery model has made 2-day delivery possible, and now it is the industry standard. Supply chain management is becoming more streamlined with minimum waste, reduced costs, and faster delivery to customers.

The Future of Retail with AI: Opportunities and Challenges

AI is ready to drive the next transformation in retail, touching everything from customer interaction to inventory management. Personalised shopping experiences and suggestions of tailored products based on browsing history and previous purchases are possible. Retailers are using chatbots to provide instant customer support at all hours, reducing the need for human intervention. AI analytics can keep inventory levels balanced, which helps control production levels.

Despite its potential, AI adoption in retail faces several hurdles. The initial cost of implementing AI-driven solutions can be prohibitive for smaller businesses, creating a divide between tech-savvy corporations and traditional retailers. Resistance to change is another significant challenge, as employees fear job displacement due to automation. Data privacy is a concern, as it is used to profile customers and used in surveillance creating stricter laws.

To support seamless integration, a strategic approach must be taken. Reskilling the workforce to transition into new roles that complement AI-driven processes is crucial for success. Collaboration between AI developers and startups to come up with tailored solutions that align with operational needs is the way to move forward. Transparent data privacy policies that use customer data ethically and responsibly are essential to win consumer trust.

The key to getting AI to provide maximum benefit and success to the retail industry lies in balancing technological innovation with human-centric values. AI can streamline operations, enhance customer experiences, and drive efficiency, but human intuition, creativity, and ethical consideration remain irreplaceable. The future of retail will be defined not just by algorithms and automation but by how well businesses adapt to the changing needs of consumers while maintaining trust, inclusivity, and economic responsibility.

Hospitality Industry: From Family Inns to AI-Powered Smart Hotels

A hundred years ago, the hospitality industry was defined by small, family-run inns, grand railway hotels, and exclusive resorts catering to the wealthy elite. Travel was a luxury, often reserved for the upper class, as transportation was slow and expensive. Hotels in the early 20th century were grand establishments, such as the Ritz in London and the Plaza in New York, known for their opulent interiors, personal service, and exclusivity. The average traveller, however, relied on modest guest houses or boarding houses, where interactions with innkeepers were deeply personal, and accommodations were often simple.

As the automobile industry changed in the 1920s and 1930s, the hospitality industry began to change too. Road travel became more common, and highways were being built. This created the need for motels—budget-friendly accommodations for long journeys. Motels were more convenient than inns as there was easy parking and direct access to rooms. By the mid-century, air travel became more common with tourists travelling overseas, and hotel chains like Hilton and Marriott became the pioneers in accommodating travellers. Standardised services and global branding ensured a consistent experience in hotels across the globe.

By the late 20th century, the rise of budget airlines and all-inclusive resorts made travel more accessible to the middle class, fuelling the growth of tourism hotspots worldwide. The leisure and business travel industries expanded in parallel, with conference hotels, luxury resorts, and budget accommodations. The hospitality industry began catering to an expanded demographic. Technology provided fast, efficient bookings. The introduction of loyalty programs and IT solutions made travel agency operations smoother. This era marked the beginning of the digital revolution in the hospitality industry, which changed the way people booked travel.

Online travel agencies like Expedia and Booking.com were introduced, and consumers were able to access a global network of hotels and rentals directly, shifting the power away from traditional travel agents. Reviews became a crucial factor in decision-making, as platforms like TripAdvisor enabled travellers to share their experiences publicly. The emergence of home-sharing services, led by Airbnb in 2008, disrupted the traditional hospitality industry by offering travellers an alternative to hotels—affordable, home-like accommodations that emphasised local experiences over corporate standardisation.

Today, AI and automation are driving the next wave of change in hospitality. Smart hotels provide automated check-ins, and AI-powered chatbots answer many customer inquiries, illustrating how the industry is embracing technology on an unprecedented scale. The integration of AI allows hotels to anticipate guest preferences and adjust pricing dynamically, enhancing the guest experience. Like any other major change, the impact of this transformation on employment, society, and even politics is complex.

The Societal and Economic Impact of Hospitality's Transformation

The evolution of hospitality over the past century has had profound effects on society. In the early 20th century, industry was a symbol of prestige and exclusivity, but as travel became more affordable, it became a driving force for cultural exchange and global connectivity. The expansion of tourism created new economies, turning previously overlooked regions into major travel destinations. Cities like Las Vegas, Dubai, and Bangkok, once small settlements or trading hubs, became global tourism powerhouses, heavily reliant on hospitality for economic growth.

Hospitality transformation also created millions of jobs in hotel chains ranging from housekeeping and front desk operations to management and corporate leadership roles. However, labour conditions varied widely. While hospitality provided opportunities for career advancement, particularly in developing economies, it also became notorious for its demanding schedules, low wages, and job instability. Budget travel and online booking platforms have led to increased competition, requiring hotels to cut costs and automate services to stay in the market. This has led to job insecurity in the sector.

Politically, the expansion of tourism and hospitality has influenced international relations and local economies. Hospitality has become the central focus of economic policy for those countries that rely on tourism for their primary revenue. Governments have invested in infrastructure—airports, highways, and cultural landmarks—to attract visitors, while visa policies have been adjusted to encourage tourism. However, the rise of home-sharing platforms like Airbnb has led to regulatory challenges, with cities struggling to balance the economic benefits of short-term rentals with concerns about housing shortages, rising rents, and community displacement.

The hospitality industry has also played a role in environmental and social debates. With tourism increasing rapidly, some countries like Venice and Barcelona have had to control the number of visitors. Hotels and resorts have faced pressure to adopt sustainable practices, from reducing plastic waste to implementing energy-efficient technologies. The COVID-19 pandemic further highlighted the vulnerabilities of the industry, leading to job losses, bankrupcies, and reassessing health and safety standards.

The Role of Information Technology in Hospitality's Growth

The hospitality industry's evolution has been deeply intertwined with advancements in IT. Early computerised reservation systems revolutionised the way hotels managed bookings. No longer reliant on paper ledgers and manual phone calls, hotels could now track occupancy rates and coordinate reservations across multiple locations. By the 1990s, the introduction of property management systems streamlined hotel operations, integrating front desk management, billing, and housekeeping into a single digital platform.

The internet democratised access to travel planning. Online booking systems allowed hotels to reach global audiences, reducing reliance on limited-access travel agencies. The rise of data analytics enabled personalised marketing, where hotels tailor promotions based on guest preferences and travel history. IT-driven revenue management strategies optimised pricing in real-time, ensuring maximum profitability during peak and off-peak seasons.

The development of smart technology further enhanced the guest experience. Keyless entry systems, mobile check-ins, and voice-controlled room settings became industry standards in luxury hotels. Contactless payment systems streamlined transactions, while AI-driven chatbots provided instant customer service, reducing wait times and improving efficiency. Hotels began integrating Internet of Things solutions, allowing guests to control lighting, temperature, and entertainment through their smartphones.

IT advancements also benefited logistics and supply chain management. Global hotel chains leveraged centralised procurement systems to streamline supply orders, reducing costs and waste. Cloud computing enabled real-time inventory tracking across multiple locations, ensuring seamless operations. Even in the food and beverage sector, digital ordering systems and AI-driven menu recommendations optimised restaurant efficiency and enhanced customer satisfaction.

The Future of Hospitality with AI: Opportunities and Challenges

AI is poised to redefine hospitality in ways that were once considered science fiction. Hotels use machine learning algorithms to anticipate guest needs, whether adjusting room temperatures before arrival, suggesting personalised dining options, or providing targeted discounts based on previous stays. AI can price dynamically depending on demand so that maximum revenue and occupancy can be obtained. AI-driven technology can give better customer experience and provide the maximum revenue possible.

However, the adoption of AI comes with significant challenges. One of the biggest concerns is job displacement. Automated check-in kiosks and robotic room service reduce the need for front desk staff and housekeeping employees. While AI creates new roles in tech management and data analysis, the transition may leave many workers unprepared for the changing job landscape.

Data privacy is another critical issue. AI relies on collecting vast amounts of guest data, raising concerns about cybersecurity and ethical data usage. Customers are becoming increasingly aware of how their personal information is stored and used, leading to stricter regulations around digital privacy in hospitality. Hotels must ensure transparency in data handling and comply with evolving legal frameworks to maintain guest trust.

The hospitality industry must reskill its workforce to successfully integrate AI within its business. The industry should collaborate with AI developers and move employees into tech-oriented roles to create an ecosystem that provides the best possible outcome for their business. Human interactions should balance the recommendations from AI tools. Transparent data policies and cybersecurity investments will be necessary to protect customer information while leveraging AI's full potential.

As hospitality moves into an AI-driven future, the challenge is finding the right balance between efficiency and human touch. While technology enhances convenience and personalisation, the essence of hospitality—warmth, service, and genuine human connection—must not be lost. The most successful hospitality brands will use AI not to replace, but to enhance the guest experience, ensuring that innovation serves the fundamental purpose of making travellers feel welcome, valued, and at home, no matter where they are in the world.

Healthcare Industry: From House Calls to AI-Enhanced Predictive Medicine

Healthcare has undergone vast improvements in the last century. At the beginning of the century, medicine was prepared locally, with physicians making house calls and providing treatment based on experience. Hospitals were few and reserved for the severely ill. Surgeries were risky, with limited anaesthesia. Infection control was primitive. Home remedies and folk medicine were the primary options for sick people. Small-town doctors were important in the community, and their record-keeping was mostly handwritten notes and personal observations.

By the early 20th century, the discovery of antibiotics, most notably penicillin in 1928 by Alexander Fleming, changed the trajectory of medicine. For the first time, bacterial infections that had claimed millions of lives could effectively be treated. By the 1950s, many infectious diseases like polio, measles, and smallpox had vaccines that improved infant health and increased life expectancy. Hospitals were no longer a last resort but became centres for specialised treatments. The nurse population and medical staff also grew as the care side became more complex and varied.

The post-World War II era saw an explosion of medical advancements. The establishment of national healthcare systems in countries like the United Kingdom with the National Health Service in 1948 and Medicare in the United

States in the 1960s reshaped how healthcare was delivered. Governments began investing in public health infrastructure, expanding access to medical care for millions, leading to an increase in specialised fields.

Medical schools started training for these specialised fields, which included cardiology, neurology, and oncology. The pharmaceutical industry became bigger and started producing life-saving drugs for previously untreatable conditions.

Digital transformation started changing the healthcare system in the 1980s and 1990s.

Electronic health records (EHRs) were introduced, so hospitals could document and file patient information, reducing medical errors and improving continuity of care. Improved imaging technologies such as MRI and CT scans made diagnostics easier, quicker, and more accurate. Surgical techniques became less invasive, reducing recovery times and improving patient outcomes. At the same time, biotechnology companies had breakthroughs in genetic research, which enabled medicines and treatments to be personalised to the patient.

As the 21st century progressed, healthcare used IT as an essential tool. Telemedicine emerged as a powerful tool, allowing patients in remote areas to consult specialists without travelling long distances. Wearable health devices, from fitness trackers to glucose monitors, empower individuals to take control of their own health data. Cloud computing enabled hospitals and research institutions to collaborate globally, accelerating medical discoveries. The COVID-19 pandemic further underscored the importance of digital healthcare, as virtual consultations and AI-assisted diagnostics became essential in managing the crisis.

Today, healthcare is poised for the next revolution through AI. Diagnostics powered by AI can detect diseases, such as cancer, at earlier stages, often more accurately than human doctors. Enormous amounts of data can be analysed to identify patterns and patient outcomes. Doctors can make decisions now based on data, along with experience, rather than just their own experience.

Robotic surgeries, once the stuff of science fiction, are now performed with precision beyond human capability. Yet, with this rapid advancement comes new challenges—ethical concerns, job shifts, and political debates over the future of medicine in an AI-driven world.

The Societal and Economic Impact of Healthcare's Evolution

Changes in the healthcare industry in the last century have had a huge impact on society. Infectious diseases, a major life threat in the 1900s, can be controlled more easily, and life expectancy has increased.

The introduction of vaccines and antibiotics turned the tide against deadly illnesses, saving millions of lives and fundamentally altering public health.

As healthcare systems evolved, people gained access to treatments that would have been unthinkable in previous generations, leading to a population boom and an aging society in many parts of the world.

The economic impact of healthcare's expansion has been enormous. A huge proportion of Gross Domeestic Product (GDP) is allocated for healthcare and employs millions of people across various sectors, from physicians and nurses to pharmaceutical researchers and medical technology developers. While the growth of healthcare has created countless job opportunities, it has also led to rising costs. In countries where there is no universal healthcare, like the United States, medical expenses are a major financial burden for many families. Politically, healthcare and insurance have been major issues by dominating discussions, influencing elections and shaping public policy.

Governments are confronted with the need for medical care for all and the financial cost of funding such a large-scale health program. The role of private insurance vs. public healthcare remains a contentious topic in many countries. The pharmaceutical industry has made huge advancements and innovations, but at the same time, its pricing policy, patent laws, and availability of essential medicines to all have been under scrutiny. Meanwhile, ethical issues—such as debates over topics such as genetic engineering, end-of-life care, and AI-driven medical decision-making–are shaping the future of the field.

The Role of Information Technology in Healthcare Development

IT produced massive positive changes in the healthcare industry. Until the mid-20th century, patient records were kept in paper files, which made getting medical data slow and inefficient. After the introduction of EHS, tracing patient history became faster and led to reduced prescription errors and quicker and more accurate diagnoses.

Advancements in IT also revolutionised medical research. The Human Genome Project, completed in 2003, would not have been possible without computational power capable of sequencing DNA. With the increase in the performance of computers, potential drug testing could be done speedily by simulating molecular interactions and discovering the right medical treatment.

Big data analytics could analyse vast datasets to uncover patterns in diseases, predict outbreaks of diseases, and suggest the best use of resources.

Telehealth has made it possible for doctors to reach patients who live in remote geographic locations. Doctors can have virtual consultations and monitor patients, and AI has helped in diagnoses by analysing data and seeing patterns. During the COVID-19 pandemic, telehealth helped control the epidemic by reducing the necessity for physical proximity for the treatment of the sick. As the data can be stored in the Cloud, hospitals can share the data worldwide, giving the patient access to the experience of the best specialists around the world.

The Future of Healthcare with AI: Opportunities and Challenges

AI is poised to reshape healthcare in ways that were once unimaginable. AI-powered algorithms can now detect diseases like cancer and diabetic retinopathy with accuracy levels comparable to, or even exceeding, human doctors.

Patients at risk of chronic diseases can be given medical help earlier, with data analysis predicting the risk for such patients before the disease and its symptoms are presented. Robots are being used to help perform surgery to ensure precision, reduced recovery time, and better outcomes. Chatbots can give patients help 24/7 by providing recommended appropriate care after guiding patients through their symptoms.

In spite of AI's potential, there are many challenges in its adoption in the health industry. Both patients and doctors are hesitant to depend on an algorithm to make a critical medical judgement. AI models require vast amounts of data to function effectively, raising ethical concerns about patient privacy and data security.

Rules and regulations often lag behind the rapid pace of AI developments, and there are legal uncertainties about liability when diagnoses and treatments are assisted by AI.

Healthcare workers also face an evolving job landscape. While AI can enhance efficiency, it also raises fears of automation replacing human roles. However, the key lies in collaboration—AI should be seen as an assistant rather than a replacement for healthcare professionals. Training and education will be crucial in ensuring that medical workers can integrate AI into their practice effectively.

There are key steps required to navigate the future of AI in healthcare. Transparent data policies must be implemented to maintain public trust. The workforce should be trained in AI, and investment should be made in training so they are ready for the upcoming changes. Collaboration between governments, medical institutions, and AI developers will ensure ethical and effective implementation.

As the industry moves into an AI-driven future, the challenge will be to ensure that technological advancements serve their fundamental purpose—improving patient care, saving lives, and making healthcare more accessible to all. While AI can process data faster than any human, it is the compassion, intuition, and experience of medical professionals that will continue to define the essence of healthcare. Its success depends on how AI augments human expertise without replacing it.

Finance Industry: From Local Bank Tellers to AI-Powered Fintech Solutions

A century ago, finance and commerce operated in ways that seem almost unimaginable today. Banking was a deep personal affair, conducted face-to-face in grand, marble-clad institutions where customers interacted with tellers who managed their savings and facilitated loans. Commerce was largely local, with businesses dependent on physical cash transactions, and trade was often constrained by geographical limitations. At the heart of these early systems were trust and reputation—businesses relied on longstanding relationships with customers, and financial institutions were built on their trustworthiness within communities.

Stock markets captured the economic growth in the early 20th century. The New York Stock Exchange and London Stock Exchange became powerful centres of global finance, allowing businesses to raise capital through public investment. However, the stock market crash in 1929 and the Great Depression in its wake made everyone aware of the susceptibility of the financial system. The public lost faith in the banking system, and the government had to introduce reforms to stabilise financial institutions and restore trust in banking.

By the mid-20th century, commerce had entered an era of mass production and large-scale trade. The post-war boom, fuelled by industrial expansion and global economic recovery, created unprecedented consumer demand. Shopping malls emerged as the new commercial hubs, offering a variety of goods under one roof. In the 1950s, credit cards transformed the way people spent, which fundamentally changed commerce. The rise of multinational corporations and franchise businesses, such as McDonald's and Walmart, marked the beginning of commerce on a truly global scale.

The 1980s and 1990s saw the IT revolution, which changed finance and business quickly and in a short period of time. Automated teller machines reduced reliance on physical bank branches, making cash withdrawals convenient at any time. The rise of electronic funds transfer enabled commercial establishments to process payments faster and more securely. Stock markets could now be accessed by the common man and reliance on traders was eliminated. Amazon and eBay also started digital online transactions, ushering in a new era of massive improvements in speed, ease, and security.

The 21st century saw another transformation with the introduction of digital payment systems like PayPal and Stripe. This made physical currency unnecessary. In 2009, Bitcoin introduced cryptocurrency, a revolutionary concept challenging the perception of finance. Mobile banking has become widespread, putting financial control directly into the hands of consumers. Around this time, platforms like Alibaba and Amazon also created a successful business model where virtual businesses with no physical stores could prosper.

AI is leading the next phase of transformation, reshaping everything from financial analysis to customer service. AI-powered robo-advisors are making investment decisions, while machine learning algorithms detect fraudulent transactions in real time. Digital commerce is no longer just about buying and selling—it is a data-driven landscape where AI predicts consumer behaviour, personalises shopping experiences, and streamlines supply chains. This progress has also raised ethical, political, and economic challenges about the future of commerce and finance in the AI-driven world.

The Societal and Economic Impact of Finance and Commerce's Evolution

The evolution of finance and commerce has created unprecedented wealth, lifting millions out of poverty and enabling rapid urbanisation. At the same time, economic inequality has widened, with access to financial resources and opportunities often dictated by geography, education, and digital literacy. The emergence of digital finance has given millions of people access to banking services for the first time, particularly in developing countries where traditional banking infrastructure was limited. Mobile money services like M-Pesa in Kenya have demonstrated how financial inclusion can drive economic development, empowering individuals to save, invest, and grow businesses.

Employment in this sector has changed. Bank tellers, stock traders, and retail salespeople are no longer the backbone of commercial activity. As automation and digital platforms took hold, these traditional roles are diminishing. The rise of FinTech companies and AI-driven financial services has created new job opportunities in data science, cybersecurity, and blockchain technology while reducing the demand for traditional banking jobs. Physical stores and the need to employ people in their traditional retail roles have reduced. However, the change has created new job opportunities, such as digital marketers and in fulfilment centres.

Politically, the transformation of finance and commerce has had far-reaching consequences. Globalisation has made economies of different countries interdependent. There are trade agreements and regulations crossing national borders, creating new job roles in the International Monetary Fund and World Bank.

However, this interdependence has a downside. When there is a financial crisis, like the 2008 global financial meltdown, it causes several major economies all over the world to fail. Governments have to balance growth with regulations in the financial markets to avoid fraud, corruption, and eventual systemic collapse. Digital currency, which is decentralising finance, has brought new challenges. Regulators cannot keep up with the technological advancements, which are more complex than traditional banking oversight for rules and regulations.

The Role of Information Technology in Finance and Commerce Development

IT has impacted finance and commerce in an unparalleled way. Banking systems were automated in the late 20th century and facilitated the rapid processing of transactions, removing human errors and making the process efficient. Geographical boundaries were no longer restricting payments as customers could use online payment systems. Cloud computing kept the data secure.

In commerce, IT advancements have revolutionised supply chain management. Companies like Walmart pioneered data-driven inventory control, using real-time analytics to optimise product distribution and reduce waste. Customer relationship management systems enabled businesses to track consumer preferences, enhancing personalisation and loyalty programs. The use of big data has allowed retailers to predict demand fluctuations, reducing overstocking and improving profitability.

AI is now expanding IT's impact even further. AI-driven chatbots handle customer inquiries, freeing human agents to focus on complex issues. Machine learning algorithms assess creditworthiness with greater accuracy than traditional banking models, enabling faster loan approvals and reducing bias in financial decision-making. AI-powered fraud detection systems monitor transactions in real time, preventing identity theft and other financial crimes. As commerce becomes increasingly digital, AI-driven recommendation engines personalise shopping experiences, influencing purchasing behaviour and optimising business revenues.

The Future of Finance and Commerce with AI: Opportunities and Challenges

AI is set to redefine finance and commerce in ways that will make transactions faster, more efficient, and highly personalised. AI-powered financial advisors can provide personalised investment strategies, analysing market trends and individual risk profiles in real time. Blockchain technology, combined with AI, has the potential to create more secure and transparent financial systems, reducing fraud and improving trust in digital transactions. In commerce, AI-driven automation will continue optimising supply chains, predicting consumer trends, and enhancing customer experiences through hyper-personalised marketing.

However, AI adoption comes with significant challenges. The displacement of traditional jobs remains a major concern, as automation replaces roles in banking, retail, and financial services. Ethical concerns over data privacy and algorithmic bias must also be addressed, as AI's decision-making processes impact financial approvals, credit scoring, and pricing strategies. Regulatory frameworks struggle to keep pace with AI advancements, raising concerns about monopolistic behaviour and market manipulation.

Businesses and policymakers must take proactive steps to successfully integrate AI into finance and commerce. The workforce needs to be retrained so they can transition into AI-related roles. Governance policies should be established to ensure there is no discrimination. Public and private sectors should come together to create ethical AI apps so that society benefits.

As finance and commerce continue to evolve, AI will be an integral part of it. However, trust, integrity, and human connection must be at the centre of all decisions. The challenge for governments, businesses, and individuals will be to utilise AI as a tool to support them while maintaining an inclusive, ethical, and sustainable financial and commercial ecosystem.

Entertainment Industry: From Silent Films to AI-Generated Content

A hundred years ago, entertainment was a vastly different experience, often defined by local performances, silent films, and radio broadcasts that connected people to the world beyond their immediate communities. In the early 20th century, vaudeville theatres were among the most popular forms of entertainment, featuring a mix of comedy, music, and live performances. Silent films provided fascinating ways of storytelling with great entertainers like Charlie Chaplin and Buster Keaton. In 1927, the first motion picture with synchronised sound was released, and it revolutionised cinema and set the stage for what would become the Hollywood film industry.

By the 1930s and 1940s, radio had become the dominant medium of home entertainment.

Families gathered around their radio to listen to their favourite music programs, news reports, or serials. Imagination played a key role in the entertainment experience as listeners imagined scenes that were described by the broadcasters. With the onset of television in the 1950s, visual entertainment took over the entertainment. In the 1960s colour television deepened this change, and television became a more powerful medium that shaped cultural trends and public opinion.

As entertainment evolved, so did its economic and social influence. Hollywood was producing films that were watched all over the world. Music recording studios were producing records in millions for the world to follow musicians like Elvis Presley and the Beatles. Concerts became more sophisticated and were bigger than ever. Stories of political movements, societal values, and technological progress were now being told as stories in the entertainment world.

The late 20th-century home entertainment changed with the introduction of Video home system (VHS) tapes, and soon after DVDs and video game consoles. Video rental stores offered a variety for people to choose what they wanted to watch. Cassette tapes took over vinyl records, and music could be transported more easily. Once cable television came, viewers had more choice and variety with separate channels for news, sports and movies.

The internet brought about the biggest transformation in the entertainment industry with digital streaming. This caused a fundamental change in production, distribution, and consumption of music. Netflix, initially a DVD rental company, moved to online streaming and removed the need to keep physical media. YouTube gave independent creators the opportunity to reach global audiences without expensive equipment or studios. Spotify and Apple Music could provide access to millions of songs instantly. This eliminated the need for physical music sales. As social media brought more change to the entertainment industry, content creators, artists, and entertainers now had direct access to their fans.

The next wave of transformation in entertainment is now being powered by AI. Algorithms quickly analyse data about what people listen to, watch, or engage with, delivering a highly personalised experience seamlessly.

Virtual reality (VR) and AR are being used in the entertainment industry to make the experience interactive, mixing reality with fiction.

The Societal and Economic Impact of Entertainment's Transformation

The evolution of entertainment over the last century has impacted society as well. In the early 20th century, entertainment was more of a community experience. Movies, live performances, and radio broadcasts brought people together, and they shared these moments with each other. Television made it more individualistic as families could watch programs according to their choice. With internet and streaming services, social media platforms allowed people to get personalised entertainment.

The entertainment industry is a massive contributor to the economy. Hollywood generates billions of dollars and employs countless professionals as actors, directors, producers, and behind-the-scenes personnel. The gaming industry is now huge, and commercially, it is bigger than both the film and music industries. Its revenue runs into billions of dollars. E-sports, virtual concerts, and live-streaming have created new job opportunities, expanding the definition of what it means to work in entertainment.

However, technological advancements have also disrupted traditional job markets. The decline of print media, the closure of video rental stores, and the decline of CD and DVD sales have seen many businesses disappear. Some adapted to the changed circumstances. The rise of AI-driven content creation is now threatening traditional creative roles. AI-generated music, deepfake technology, and automated video editing tools are changing the way content is produced and raising concerns about property rights and artistic authenticity. This has also led to debates over censorship, misinformation, and the ethical responsibilities of entertainment platforms.

Politically, entertainment has always been influenced by social movements and cultural changes. Films have been shaping public opinion with propaganda and picturisation of global conflicts. Music brings people together and has played an important role in civil rights movements and political awareness in the public. With social media taking a key role in society, comments from celebrities and influencers impact public opinion.

The Role of Information Technology in Entertainment's Development

As IT has advanced, the entertainment industry has made huge progress in many ways. As media turned from analog to digital, the entertainment industry could access high-speed streaming instantly. With cloud computing, the entertainment industry produces and distributes massive amounts of data globally while cutting costs. Platforms like Netflix and Spotify can provide personalised experiences by analysing the user's past choices.

The gaming industry has seen many positive benefits from these changes in technology. Multiple players can play online in real time, across the globe, with the help of cloud computing and AI. YouTube Gaming and Twitch are examples of platforms where people can watch this online gaming sport. This has made way for professional gamers and influencers in the gaming world. AI-generated graphics and motion are now lifelike, and many virtual characters are used where it is difficult to distinguish between real and simulated graphics.

AI is now being used to create entirely new forms of entertainment. AI-generated music, scripts, and even films are becoming increasingly sophisticated. Virtual influencers, such as Lil Miquela, have gained millions of followers without ever physically existing. AI-driven animation tools are reducing the time and cost required to produce high-quality content. Now the entertainment industry is in a position where AI will be able to shape individual experiences as well.

The Future of Entertainment with AI: Opportunities and Challenges

AI is poised to create more waves in the entertainment industry. Experiences are becoming more immersive and tailored. AI can generate dynamic stories to adapt to customer preferences and change the narrative to make every viewing unique. VR concerts and AI-generated voice acting are redefining the possibilities of entertainment. Deepfake technology is being used to create convincing fake images, videos, and audio recordings. This poses questions around the legal and ethical boundaries of content, as misinformation and fake content can be used to manipulate public opinion. Copyright laws are struggling to keep up with AI-created content, leading to debates over intellectual property rights.

AI is helping to create new content with speed and variety. It also threatens jobs in the industry reducing the need for human involvement in content production.

To successfully integrate AI into the entertainment industry, ethical considerations must be balanced with innovation. The workforce should be reskilled, and transparent policies on AI-generated content must be developed. Creative professionals should collaborate with tech developers to get the best of both worlds.

By using AI to support human artists rather than overshadow them, the entertainment industry can create a future where technology and creativity coexist harmoniously.

As entertainment continues to evolve, one thing remains clear—its ability to captivate, inspire, and connect people will always be at its core. AI may change the way content is created, but the fundamental human desire for storytelling, emotion, and artistic expression will remain timeless.

The AI-Driven Future of Customer-Based Industries

Over the last century, IT has transformed manual, human-driven businesses into data-driven, AI-powered enterprises. It has taken decades for technology to evolve from basic automation to sophisticated algorithms that can learn and adapt from data. In the early 20th century, there were factory lines where workers performed repetitive tasks, and now there are computers streamlining operations and increasing efficiency. AI has come of age and is ushering the entire world into a new era.

AI is transforming customer-based industries at an unseen pace. In retail, online stores will come with an intelligent assistant, that not only recommends products based on browsing history but also anticipates needs based on seasonal trends and previous purchases. It can analyse massive datasets—such as customer feedback or previous purchases—and suggest items to buy before customers even realise they want them.

In healthcare, the application of AI reaches even more profound implications. Robotic nurses are beginning to supplement traditional care models by monitoring patient vitals and providing timely updates to human staff. For example, AI systems can analyse data from wearables, predicting health issues before symptoms appear, thereby enhancing preventative care.

Technologies such as natural language processing and machine learning are being used to tailor experiences for individual customers. For example, digital streaming services like Netflix and Spotify use algorithms that analyse history of listening or viewing and offer suggestions that are to the taste of the customer.

Big data analytics is able to process large amounts of data like customer feedback, quickly and in real time to offer products and services suited to the customer.

Consider how ride-sharing apps like Uber use real-time data to estimate arrival times, enabling a smoother experience for users.

As AI continues to develop, customer-centric industries are evolving into a fully integrated ecosystem characterised by predictive capabilities and automation. Customer needs are met and also anticipated. Personalised shopping experiences are delivered with an efficiency not imaginable before. Retailers might soon implement intelligent inventory systems that forecast demand based on predictive analytics, reducing waste and ensuring popular items are always in stock. The foundation for these advancements has been laid for over a century, and now, AI is set to change lives in a way that is deeply intuitive and positive.

Chapter Questions

1. How have technological advancements transformed customer-based industries over the last century?

2. What role did the digital revolution play in reshaping consumer experiences in sectors like retail and hospitality?

3. In what ways are businesses leveraging AI technologies to enhance customer interactions?

4. What ethical concerns arise from the adoption of AI in customer-based industries?

5. Why is workforce reskilling important in the context of an AI-driven landscape?

6. How can a human-centred approach benefit customer-based industries amidst technological advancements?

7. What are some examples of innovations in the retail industry that illustrate the shift towards digital transformation?

8. How has the hospitality sector used technology to improve the guest experience in response to new competitive pressures?

9. In what ways has telemedicine advanced healthcare delivery during the COVID-19 pandemic?

10. What is the importance of organisational change management in aligning AI capabilities with business strategies in customer-based industries?

11. How can transparency in data usage support ethical practices in customer-based industries?

Note to Readers and Educators

Comprehensive answers and explanations to these chapter-end questions are available at www.sandeepbhalekar.com. The website also provides supplementary frameworks, teaching guidelines, and reference materials to support deeper understanding and classroom discussion.

Educators and facilitators can access additional resources, including presentation frameworks, assessment rubrics, and discussion prompts, to help integrate the concepts from this chapter into academic or professional learning environments.

Bibliography

Accenture. (2023). *Hospitality and AI: Unlocking Guest Satisfaction with Technology.* Sydney: Accenture. https://www.accenture.com

Airbnb. (2023). *Transforming Hospitality through Machine Learning and Data Science.* San Francisco: Airbnb Engineering. https://airbnb.io

Amazon. (2023). *Retail Innovation Through AI: From Warehousing to Personalised Recommendations*. Seattle: Amazon. https://www.aboutamazon.com

Booking.com. (2023). *Smart Technology and Personalisation in Travel*. Amsterdam: Booking.com. https://www.booking.com

Deloitte. (2023). *AI in the Financial Sector: Enhancing Customer Engagement and Fraud Detection*. London: Deloitte Insights. https://www.deloitte.com

Forbes Technology Council. (2024). *AI in Customer Experience: Trends and Best Practices*. New York: Forbes. https://www.forbes.com

IBM. (2023). *The Role of AI in Ethical Data Usage for Customer-Facing Industries*. Armonk: IBM Research. https://www.ibm.com

KPMG. (2023). *Customer Centricity and Digital Transformation in the Finance Sector*. Toronto: KPMG. https://home.kpmg

McKinsey & Company. (2023). *The Future of AI in Retail and Customer Experience*. New York: McKinsey & Company. https://www.mckinsey.com

MIT Technology Review. (2022). *AI in the Age of Streaming: Ethics and Opportunities*. Cambridge: MIT Press. https://www.technologyreview.com

Netflix. (2023). *Reimagining Entertainment with Artificial Intelligence*. Los Gatos: Netflix Tech Blog. https://netflixtechblog.com

OECD. (2022). *AI and the Future of Work in Service-Based Economies*. Paris: OECD Publishing. https://www.oecd.org

PwC. (2023). *AI and the Future of Healthcare Services*. London: PwC Health Research Institute. https://www.pwc.com

Spotify. (2023). *AI-Driven Music Recommendations and User Experience*. Stockholm: Spotify Research. https://www.spotify.com

Tesla. (2023). *AI, Connected Vehicles, and the Customer Experience Revolution*. Palo Alto: Tesla AI Day Report. https://www.tesla.com

World Economic Forum. (2022). *Shaping the Future of Retail: AI and the Consumer Journey*. Geneva: WEF. https://www.weforum.org

World Health Organization. (2021). *Digital Health and Telemedicine during COVID-19: Impact and Lessons Learned*. Geneva: World Health Organization. https://www.who.int

13

AI Adoption for Customer and Asset (Hybrid) Industries

Over the past century, customer-based industries such as retail, healthcare, hospitality, finance, and entertainment have experienced significant transformations driven by technological advancements. Initially, these industries relied on local, personal interactions, but as industrialisation progressed, the rise of department stores and chain hotels introduced economies of scale, often challenging smaller businesses.

The digital revolution brought about online shopping, electronic payments, and platforms like Amazon and Airbnb, reshaping consumer experiences across sectors. Today, as the world enters an era driven by artificial intelligence (AI), businesses are leveraging technologies such as recommendation engines and chatbots to enhance efficiency and personalise customer experiences. However, these advancements also raise concerns about job displacement and data privacy.

To thrive in this evolving landscape, industries must balance innovation with ethical considerations, focusing on reskilling the workforce and maintaining transparency in data usage. Customer-based industries can leverage technological advancements by prioritising human-centred values to create a more efficient, inclusive, and sustainable future. Ultimately, the core of these industries relies on understanding and meeting human needs, ensuring technology enhances rather than replaces personal engagement.

This chapter delves into the transformative journey of customer-based industries, such as hospitality, retail, and finance, that have been influenced profoundly by technological advancements over the past century. Initially founded on personal interactions, these industries evolved through the rise of efficiency-driven models, such as department stores and online platforms like Amazon and Airbnb. The chapter highlights the ongoing digital revolution, emphasising the integration of AI technologies—like chatbots and recommendation engines—that enhance operational efficiency and personalise customer experiences. However, this rapid innovation brings ethical considerations, such as job displacement and data privacy concerns. The text advocates for a balanced approach that prioritises workforce reskilling and transparency while maintaining a human-centred focus. It further explores the emergence of hybrid industries, blending customer-centric services with asset-based frameworks, exemplified by shifts in the hospitality and airline sectors. The chapter ultimately calls for organisations to embrace change

DOI: 10.1201/9781003626503-13

management, ensuring that technological advancements complement personal engagement and contribute to a sustainable future for customer-based industries.

Key Points

- **Technological Transformation:** Customer-based industries have significantly evolved due to technological advancements, shifting from personal interactions to more efficient, technology-driven models.
- **Digital Revolution Impact:** The rise of online shopping, electronic payments, and platforms like Amazon and Airbnb has redefined consumer experiences across various sectors.
- **AI Integration:** Businesses leverage AI technologies like recommendation engines and chatbots to enhance efficiency and personalise customer experience.
- **Ethical Considerations:** The adoption of AI raises concerns regarding job displacement and data privacy, prompting the need for ethical practices in technology use.
- **Importance of Reskilling:** Industries must prioritise workforce reskilling and maintain transparency in data usage to adapt to the AI-driven landscape.
- **Human-Centred Values:** Focusing on human needs remains essential for customer-based industries to ensure technology complements rather than replaces personal engagement.
- **Organisational Change Management:** Embracing change management is crucial for successfully integrating AI into business capabilities and strategies.
- **Hybrid Industries:** The convergence of customer-based and asset-based models creates hybrid industries that balance tangible assets with customer-centric services.
- **Evolution of Hospitality:** The hospitality industry has shifted from asset-based models to personalised digital experiences, emphasising customer loyalty and tailored services.
- **Transformation in Airlines:** The aviation industry is moving from a heavy asset dependency to AI-optimised travel experiences, enhancing customer service and operational efficiency.
- **AI Applications in Hospitality:** AI-driven solutions such as predictive analytics, chatbots, and bright rooms are optimising guest experiences while reducing operational costs

Hybrid Industries: The Convergence of Customer- and Asset-Based Models

A hybrid industry effectively integrates customer- and asset-based models, leveraging physical infrastructure and equipment while optimising customer relationships and experiences. These industries generate value by balancing tangible assets with customer-centric services, often using technology to enhance operational efficiency and personalised engagement.

Over the last 100 years, various industries have transitioned from being solely asset-based or customer-driven into hybrid models, mainly due to technological advancements, digitalisation, and AI. The rise of automation, data analytics, and AI-driven decision-making has blurred the line between asset-heavy industries and those driven by customer demand, making hybrid industries the future of economic growth.

Hospitality: From Physical Hotels to Personalised Digital Experiences

The hospitality industry began as a purely asset-based industry in the early 20th century. Hotels and resorts relied on real estate investments, physical amenities, and operational infrastructure to attract travellers. The most prominent players in the industry were those who owned the most luxurious properties and had an expansive global reach.

As global tourism grew in the mid-to-late 20th century, hospitality evolved to incorporate customer-driven models. Brands like Marriott and Hilton shifted their focus to customer loyalty programs, personalised services, and global quality consistency, moving beyond physical assets to strengthen customer relationships. Information technology (IT) played a key role in this shift, as the introduction of online reservations and travel booking systems enabled hotels to connect with customers digitally.

The rise of platforms like Airbnb in the 2010s revolutionised hospitality further. This model combined asset utilisation and customer personalisation, allowing individuals to rent their properties while offering customised experiences. Digital transformation enabled real-time dynamic pricing, AI-driven recommendation engines, and enhanced customer reviews, making personalisation the core of the industry.

AI is now accelerating this transformation. Predictive analytics optimise hotel pricing based on demand, AI chatbots handle customer service in multiple languages, and robotic automation enhances housekeeping and maintenance. AI-driven facial recognition and bright rooms allow personalised experiences, reducing operational costs while enhancing guest satisfaction. The industry is increasingly software-driven rather than asset-driven, yet assets remain integral to delivering experiences.

Airlines: From Infrastructure Dependency to AI-Optimised Travel Experiences

The aviation industry was historically a heavy asset-based sector dominated by airlines that owned aircraft fleets, airport hubs, and fuel-intensive logistics. Throughout the early and mid-20th century, growth was determined by how many planes an airline could afford and how efficiently they managed routes.

By the late 20th century, the customer experience became a defining factor. Frequent flyer programs, tiered memberships, and in-flight services were introduced to enhance passenger loyalty—IT-enabled reservation systems and digital ticketing streamlined customer engagement, reducing reliance on physical booking counters.

With the rise of low-cost carriers like Southwest Airlines and Ryanair, the industry evolved into a hybrid model, focusing both on asset utilisation and customer engagement. The introduction of online check-ins, self-service kiosks, and mobile boarding passes further bridged the gap between infrastructure and user convenience. Airlines optimised fleet management while leveraging digital tools to personalise customer experiences.

AI is now reshaping the airline industry even further. From an asset perspective, AI-powered predictive maintenance minimises aircraft downtime, machine learning optimises routes to reduce fuel consumption, and security clearances have been streamlined. On the customer side, dynamic pricing algorithms adjust fares in real time based on demand, AI-driven chatbots handle customer inquiries, and facial recognition at airports expedites security clearances to increase customer satisfaction. The future of aviation will see AI-powered autonomous aircraft, reducing reliance on human pilots and increasing operational efficiency.

Automotive: From Manufacturing-Centric to AI-Powered Mobility Solutions

The automotive industry was initially asset-based, with major automakers such as Ford, General Motors, and Toyota focusing on large-scale vehicle production. Car ownership was the goal, and success was measured by manufacturing efficiency, cost reduction, and distribution networks.

In the late 20th century, car companies began incorporating customer-centric elements, offering leasing options, financing models, and after-sales services. The introduction of digital dashboards, GPS navigation, and infotainment systems made cars more than just vehicles—they became personalised experiences. IT systems enabled better supply chain management, while CRM (customer relationship management) software improved customer retention.

By the 2010s, the industry transitioned into a hybrid model, blending asset-heavy production with customer-driven mobility services. The emergence of ride-hailing services like Uber and Lyft transformed car ownership from a necessity into a choice, shifting the focus to mobility-as-a-service. Companies like Tesla disrupted the market by integrating AI, self-driving technology, and over-the-air (OTA) software updates, transforming cars into connected devices rather than just transportation tools.

AI is now driving the next evolution. Autonomous vehicles (AVs) are redefining mobility, reducing dependency on human drivers while optimising routes through AI-powered navigation. Predictive analytics enhances vehicle maintenance, while AI-driven supply chains optimise parts manufacturing and inventory management. AI-enabled voice assistants, in-car AI copilots, and hyper-personalised infotainment systems are making driving experiences more intuitive. As shared autonomous fleets emerge, the line between vehicle ownership and transportation services continues to blur, making the industry a fully integrated hybrid model.

Real Estate: From Physical Property to AI-Powered Smart Spaces

Real estate has traditionally been one of the most asset-heavy industries, where ownership, land value, and physical property investments determine success. Skyscrapers, office complexes, and residential developments shape economies, and real estate markets dictate financial growth.

By the late 20th century, customer engagement and digital transformation started influencing the sector. Real estate firms began integrating CRM platforms, online listings, and virtual tours, shifting some aspects of the industry towards a customer-focused approach. E-commerce drove demand for real estate logistics, such as warehouses and fulfilment centres, blending asset-based and customer-centric elements.

In the 2010s, the industry became increasingly data-driven and hybrid. The rise of smart buildings brought AI-powered energy efficiency, security systems, and predictive maintenance. Integrating AI-enabled Internet of Things (IoT) devices allowed buildings to self-optimise heating, cooling, and security based on real-time usage data, reducing operational costs while improving tenant experiences.

Today, AI is continually redefining real estate. AI-powered automated valuation models (AVMs) predict property prices, reducing reliance on traditional appraisal methods. AI-driven chatbots and virtual assistants handle customer inquiries, while blockchain-powered smart contracts streamline property transactions. AI-enhanced predictive analytics assesses investment risks, making real estate decisions more data-driven than ever before. The future of real estate is moving towards a world where physical properties are augmented by AI-driven intelligence, turning buildings into smart assets that adapt to the market needs.

The Future of Hybrid Industries with AI

Over the last century, industries that were once purely asset-driven have evolved to incorporate customer-centric models, enabled by IT, digital platforms, and automation. Hybrid industries have emerged as the dominant model, blending physical infrastructure with AI-powered services to maximise both efficiency and customer engagement.

AI is now the defining factor shaping the next phase of hybrid industries. With predictive analytics, real-time automation, and hyper-personalisation, AI is transforming hospitality, healthcare, real estate, and transportation into intelligent ecosystems where assets and customers are seamlessly interconnected. As industries continue to evolve, hybrid models will dominate the future economy, leveraging AI as the ultimate bridge between physical assets and the customer experience.

Hospitality Industry: From Family Inns to AI-Powered Smart Hotels

A hundred years ago, the hospitality industry was defined by small, family-run inns, grand railway hotels, and exclusive resorts catering to the wealthy elite. Travel was a luxury, often reserved for the upper class, as transportation was slow and expensive. Hotels in the early 20th century were grand establishments, known for their opulent interiors, personal service, and exclusivity such as the Ritz in London and the Plaza in New York. The average traveller, however, relied on modest guesthouses or boarding houses, where interactions with innkeepers were deeply personal, and accommodation was often simple.

The rise of the automobile in the 1920s and 1930s began to change the hospitality landscape. As highways expanded and road travel became more common, the first motels appeared, providing budget-friendly accommodation for travellers on long journeys. Unlike traditional inns, motels emphasised convenience, with easy parking and direct access to rooms. By the mid-century, the development of commercial air travel brought a new wave of international tourism, leading to the rapid expansion of hotel chains. Hilton and Marriott emerged as pioneers, introducing standardised services, global branding, and consistent experiences across multiple locations.

By the late 20th century, the hospitality industry was no longer limited to hotels and motels. The rise of budget airlines and all-inclusive resorts made travel more accessible to the middle class, fuelling the growth of tourism hotspots worldwide. The leisure and business travel industries expanded in parallel, with conference hotels, luxury resorts, and budget accommodation catering to different demographics. Technology began to reshape hospitality, with the introduction of computerised reservation systems making bookings faster and more efficient. Hotels implemented loyalty programs, and travel agencies used early IT solutions to streamline operations, marking the beginning of hospitality's digital transformation.

The internet revolution of the 1990s and early 2000s transformed how people booked travel. The launch of online travel agencies like Expedia and Booking.com shifted power away from traditional travel agents, giving consumers direct access to a global network of hotels and vacation rentals. Reviews became a crucial factor in decision-making, as platforms like TripAdvisor enabled travellers to share their experiences publicly. The emergence of home-sharing services, led by Airbnb in 2008, disrupted the traditional hospitality industry by offering travellers an alternative to hotels—affordable, home-like accommodations that emphasised local experiences over corporate standardisation.

Today, AI and automation are driving the next wave of change in hospitality. From AI-powered chatbots handling customer inquiries to smart hotels with automated check-ins, the industry is embracing technology at an unprecedented scale. The integration of AI enables hotels to anticipate guest preferences, dynamically adjust pricing, and enhance overall guest experiences. Yet, as with any major transformation, the impact on society remains complex.

The Societal and Economic Impact of Hospitality's Transformation

The evolution of hospitality over the past century has had profound effects on society. In the early 20th century, the hospitality industry was a symbol of prestige and exclusivity, but as travel became more affordable, it became a driving force for cultural exchange and global connectivity. The expansion of tourism created new economies, turning previously overlooked regions into major travel destinations. Cities like Las Vegas, Dubai, and Bangkok, once small settlements or trading hubs, became global tourism powerhouses, heavily reliant on hospitality for economic growth.

The transformation of hospitality also shaped employment trends. The rise of large hotel chains created millions of jobs, from housekeeping and front desk operations to management and corporate leadership roles. However, labour conditions varied widely. While hospitality provided opportunities for career advancement, particularly in developing economies, it also became notorious for its demanding schedules, low wages, and job instability.

The growth of budget travel and online booking platforms led to increased competition, forcing hotels to cut costs and automate services, impacting job security for workers in the sector.

Politically, the expansion of tourism and hospitality has influenced international relations and local economies. Many countries rely on tourism as a major source of revenue, making hospitality a central focus of economic policy. Governments have invested in infrastructure—airports, highways, and cultural landmarks—to attract visitors, while visa policies have been adjusted to encourage tourism. However, the rise of home-sharing platforms like Airbnb has led to regulatory challenges, with cities struggling to balance the economic benefits of short-term rentals with concerns about housing shortages, rising rents, and community displacement.

The hospitality industry has also played a role in environmental and social debates. The growth of mass tourism has led to concerns about over-tourism, with destinations like Venice and Barcelona implementing restrictions to control visitor numbers. Hotels and resorts have faced pressure to adopt sustainable practices, from reducing plastic waste to implementing energy-efficient technologies. The COVID-19 pandemic further highlighted the vulnerabilities of the industry, leading to job losses, bankruptcies, and a rethinking of health and safety standards.

The Role of Information Technology in Hospitality's Growth

The hospitality industry's evolution has been deeply intertwined with advancements in IT. Early computerised reservation systems, such as Hilton's "Holidex" in the 1960s, revolutionised the way hotels managed bookings. No longer reliant on paper ledgers and manual phone calls, hotels could now track occupancy rates and coordinate reservations across multiple locations. By the 1990s, the introduction of property management systems streamlined hotel operations, integrating front desk management, billing, and housekeeping into a single digital platform.

The internet was a game-changer, democratising access to travel planning. Online booking systems allowed hotels to reach global audiences, reducing reliance on travel agencies. The rise of data analytics enabled personalised marketing, where hotels could tailor promotions based on guest preferences and travel history. IT-driven revenue management strategies optimised pricing in real time, ensuring maximum profitability during peak and off-peak seasons.

The development of smart technology further enhanced the guest experience. Keyless entry systems, mobile check-ins, and voice-controlled room settings became industry standards in luxury hotels. Contactless payment systems streamlined transactions, while AI-driven chatbots provided instant customer service, reducing wait times and improving efficiency. Hotels began integrating IoT solutions, allowing guests to control lighting, temperature, and entertainment through their smartphones.

Logistics and supply chain management also benefited from IT advancements. Global hotel chains leveraged centralised procurement systems to streamline supply orders, reducing costs and waste. Cloud computing enabled real-time inventory tracking across multiple locations, ensuring seamless operations. Even in the food and beverage sector, digital ordering systems and AI-driven menu recommendations optimised restaurant efficiency and enhanced customer satisfaction.

The Future of Hospitality with AI: Opportunities and Challenges

AI is set to redefine hospitality in ways that were once considered science fiction. AI-powered personalisation is already transforming the guest experience. Hotels use machine learning algorithms to anticipate guest needs, such as adjusting room temperatures before arrival, suggesting personalised dining options, or offering targeted discounts based on previous stays. AI-driven dynamic pricing ensures that room rates fluctuate based on demand, maximising occupancy and revenue.

However, the adoption of AI comes with significant challenges. One of the biggest concerns is job displacement. Automated check-in kiosks and robotic room service reduce the need for front desk staff and housekeeping employees. While AI creates new roles in tech management and data analysis, the transition may leave many workers unprepared for the changing job landscape.

Data privacy is another critical issue. AI relies on collecting vast amounts of guest data, raising concerns about cybersecurity and ethical data usage. Customers are becoming increasingly aware of how their personal information is stored and used, leading to stricter regulations around digital privacy in hospitality. Hotels must ensure transparency in data handling and comply with evolving legal frameworks to maintain guest trust.

To successfully integrate AI, the hospitality industry must invest in workforce reskilling, ensuring employees can transition to tech-oriented roles. Collaboration with AI developers will be crucial in creating solutions that balance automation with personalised human interactions. Transparent data policies and cybersecurity investments are necessary to protect customer information while leveraging AI's full potential.

As hospitality moves into an AI-driven future, the challenge is finding the right balance between efficiency and human touch. While technology enhances convenience and personalisation, the essence of hospitality—warmth, service, and genuine human connection—must not be lost. The most successful hospitality brands are those that use AI not to replace, but to enhance the guest experience, ensuring that innovation serves the fundamental purpose of making travellers feel welcome, valued, and at home, no matter where they are in the world.

The Evolution of the Airlines Industry

A Century of Transformation, Innovation, and AI: From the Dawn of Flight to the Age of Global Connectivity

The modern world would not exist without the airline industry. A hundred years ago, air travel was nothing more than an ambitious experiment, where planes transported mail and the occasional wealthy passenger. In 1903, the Wright brothers made their first controlled flight in a powered aircraft, an achievement that would set in motion one of the most transformative industries in human history. By the 1920s, the first commercial airlines emerged, offering slow, bumpy, and expensive flights that only the elite could afford.

In the 1930s and 1940s, aviation took a significant leap forward. The development of larger and more reliable aircraft made it possible to transport passengers over longer distances. The introduction of pressurised cabins in the Boeing 307 allowed airlines to fly at higher altitudes, avoiding turbulence, and making flights smoother and more comfortable. World War II further accelerated technological advancements in aviation, as military innovations—such as radar, jet propulsion, and long-range navigation—paving the way for modern commercial flight.

The 1950s and 1960s marked the golden age of air travel. Jetliners like the Boeing 707 and the Douglas DC-8 revolutionised the industry, cutting flight times in half and making air travel more accessible to the middle class. Airports became bustling hubs of activity, and international travel became a reality for millions. Flying was no longer just a privilege of the rich; it was a symbol of progress, connecting cultures, economies, and families across the world.

The Airline Industry's Impact on Society and the Economy

The airline industry fundamentally reshaped global society, shrinking the world and making long-distance travel an everyday possibility. The rise of commercial aviation transformed tourism, allowing people to visit foreign countries with unprecedented ease. The development of air cargo services revolutionised trade, enabling the rapid transportation of goods across continents. Fresh seafood from Japan could be served in New York on the same day, and electronic components manufactured in Taiwan could reach Silicon Valley within hours.

The industry's expansion also created millions of jobs. Pilots, flight attendants, air traffic controllers, engineers, and airport staff all became part of a vast network of aviation professionals. Airlines became a major driver of economic activity, supporting hotels, restaurants, and countless other businesses dependent on tourism and global mobility. However, this growth also brings volatility. Unlike other industries, airlines are deeply vulnerable to economic downturns, geopolitical conflicts, and shifts in consumer behaviour. The oil crisis of the 1970s, for example, sent fuel prices skyrocketing, forcing airlines to raise ticket prices and cut unprofitable routes.

One of the most significant moments in aviation history came on September 11, 2001. The terrorist attacks not only shook the world but also altered the airline industry permanently. Passenger confidence plummeted, and stringent security measures were introduced. Governments imposed stricter regulations, leading to the creation of the Transportation Security Administration (TSA) in the United States. Airports became high-security zones, and the experience of flying changed overnight, with longer check-in procedures, baggage screenings, and increased scrutiny of international travellers.

The Role of IT and Information Management in Aviation Development

Behind the scenes, technology played an enormous role in transforming aviation from an experimental mode of transport into a sophisticated, data-driven industry. The introduction of computerised reservation systems in the 1960s, pioneered by American Airlines' SABRE system, revolutionised the way flights were booked. Suddenly, airlines could track seat availability in real time, optimise scheduling, and manage ticket sales more efficiently.

The development of air traffic control systems also marked a turning point. Radar technology, initially developed during World War II, was adapted for civilian use, allowing controllers to track aircraft with greater precision. The adoption of GPS navigation in the 1990s further improved flight safety and efficiency, enabling pilots to fly more direct routes and reduce fuel consumption.

As the internet became widespread in the 2000s, airlines embraced online booking platforms, drastically reducing the need for travel agents. E-tickets and mobile boarding passes eliminated paper-based systems, streamlining passenger experiences. Meanwhile, big data analytics enabled airlines to forecast demand, set dynamic pricing, and personalise marketing campaigns. Airlines began to use real-time aircraft monitoring systems, allowing maintenance crews to detect mechanical issues before they become critical. This transition from reactive to predictive maintenance not only improved safety but also reduced costly delays and cancellations.

AI and the Future of the Airline Industry

AI is now set to drive the next wave of innovation in aviation, bringing greater efficiency, safety, and personalisation to air travel. AI-powered systems are already being deployed across various aspects of the industry, from dynamic pricing algorithms that adjust ticket prices in real time to AI-driven customer service chatbots that handle flight inquiries, rebooking, and complaints.

One of the most significant advancements is the use of AI in aircraft maintenance. By analysing vast amounts of data from onboard sensors, AI can predict when components are likely to fail, allowing airlines to conduct proactive repairs before an issue arises. This predictive maintenance approach reduces aircraft downtime, improves safety, and lowers operating costs.

AI is also revolutionising air traffic management. Traditional air traffic control systems rely on human operators making split-second decisions under high pressure. AI-powered systems can process far more data than a human controller, optimising flight routes, minimising delays, and reducing fuel consumption. Soon, AI could enable fully automated air traffic management, reducing the risk of human error and enhancing airspace efficiency.

For passengers, AI is enhancing the travel experience in ways that would have been unimaginable just a few decades ago. Facial recognition technology is now being used at major airports to streamline check-ins, eliminating the need for passports and boarding passes. AI-driven personalised recommendations help passengers find the best flight options, seat preferences, and in-flight entertainment choices. Airlines are even experimenting with AI-powered voice assistants to provide real-time updates on flight status, gate changes, and baggage tracking.

Challenges Faced by Airlines in Adopting AI and Key Steps for Adoption

Despite the clear benefits, the adoption of AI in the airline industry is not without challenges. One of the biggest obstacles is data integration. Airlines generate enormous amounts of data from flight operations, customer interactions, and aircraft performance metrics. However, many airlines still rely on legacy IT systems that struggle to process and analyse data effectively. Transitioning to AI-powered platforms requires significant investment in cloud computing and advanced analytics infrastructure.

Another challenge is regulatory approval and safety concerns. AI-driven automation in air traffic management and autonomous flight systems raises complex legal and ethical questions. Governments and aviation authorities will need to establish clear guidelines to ensure that AI-powered decision-making meets the highest safety standards.

Public perception is also a hurdle. While AI can enhance efficiency, many passengers remain wary of fully autonomous systems. Building consumer trust through transparency, rigorous testing, and safety validations will be crucial for widespread AI adoption in aviation.

To successfully integrate AI, airlines should focus on several key steps. First, they must modernise their IT infrastructure, transitioning from outdated systems to cloud-based AI platforms. Second, investing in AI-driven customer service enhancements can improve passenger experience while reducing operational costs. Third, airlines must collaborate with technology providers to develop next-generation AI applications tailored to aviation needs. Finally, a commitment to ethical AI development—ensuring that AI systems prioritise safety, security, and passenger well-being—will be essential for regulatory approval and public trust.

A New Era of Aviation

From the pioneering days of the Wright brothers to the AI-driven future of autonomous aircraft, the airline industry has undergone a century of extraordinary transformation. Each technological leap has reshaped economies, redefined global mobility, and influenced geopolitics. As AI takes centre stage, aviation is poised for yet another revolution—one where air travel becomes safer, more efficient, and more personalised than ever before. The future of flight is not just about reaching new destinations; it is about reimagining the very experience of travel itself.

The Evolution of the Automotive Industry

A Century of Transformation, Technology, and AI: From the First Assembly Line to the Digital Age

The automotive industry has been one of the most transformative forces in modern history, reshaping transportation and also economies, cities, and societies. A hundred years ago, automobiles were a privilege of the wealthy, handcrafted machines that took days or even weeks to manufacture. However, in 1913, Henry Ford revolutionised the industry with the assembly line, an innovation that would change the world forever. By drastically reducing the time it took to build a car, Ford made automobile ownership accessible to the average American worker. The automobile became an icon of mobility, paving the way for suburban expansion, the birth of long-distance travel, and the creation of new industries, from roadside diners to motels and gasoline stations.

As the industry flourished, new competitors emerged. General Motors, under the leadership of Alfred Sloan, introduced the idea of planned obsolescence, offering customers different models and colours each year to create a continuous demand for new cars. Unlike Ford's approach of mass-producing a single model, GM's strategy tapped into consumer preferences, making car ownership not just a necessity but a personal statement. By the mid-20th century, the automobile had become a symbol of freedom and success, intertwined with cultural movements like Route 66 road trips and drive-in theatres.

The Industry's Impact on Jobs and Society

The rise of the automobile industry created millions of jobs, not only in car manufacturing but also in supporting industries. Mechanics, gas station attendants, and insurance agents all found employment in a rapidly expanding sector. Cities like Detroit became booming economic hubs, attracting workers from across the country in search of stable, well-paying jobs. The influence of automotive labour was so strong that the United Auto Workers union became one of the most powerful in the country, negotiating better wages, healthcare benefits, and retirement plans for employees.

Yet, as the industry evolved, so did the challenges it faced. The 1973 oil crisis sent shockwaves through the global economy, exposing the vulnerability of gas-dependent industries. Long lines at gas stations became a common sight, and American automakers, known for their large, fuel-hungry vehicles, suddenly found themselves struggling against Japanese competitors like Toyota and Honda, whose smaller, fuel-efficient cars gained popularity. This was a defining moment in the industry, shifting the focus from raw power and size to efficiency and reliability.

In the 1980s and 1990s, automation began reshaping the workforce. Robots took over many repetitive tasks on assembly lines, leading to job losses but also improving production efficiency. The integration of computerised systems in cars—such as fuel injection, anti-lock brakes, and digital dashboards—marked the beginning of the IT revolution in automotives. Dealerships and manufacturers adopted enterprise resource planning (ERP) systems to manage inventory and supply chains more efficiently, ensuring that parts arrived just in time for production rather than sitting unused in warehouses.

Political Shifts and the Globalisation of the Auto Industry

The late 20th and early 21st centuries saw the globalisation of the automotive industry. Free trade agreements, such as the North American Free Trade Agreement (NAFTA), encouraged automakers to move manufacturing plants to countries with lower labour costs. American car companies, once dominant, faced increased competition from German engineering, Japanese efficiency, and South Korean affordability. This globalisation created political tensions, as workers in traditional auto-manufacturing cities like Detroit saw their jobs move overseas.

At the same time, environmental concerns began shaping the industry's future. Governments imposed stricter emissions regulations, forcing car manufacturers to innovate or face heavy fines. California, known for its aggressive environmental policies, led the charge in pushing for cleaner technologies. This pressure led to the gradual adoption of hybrid and electric vehicles, spearheaded by companies like Toyota with the Prius and later Tesla, which redefined the public perception of electric mobility.

The Role of IT and Information Management in Automotive Development

IT has played a critical role in shaping the modern automobile. What was once a purely mechanical machine is now a sophisticated, software-driven product. GPS navigation, onboard diagnostics, and electronic stability control all emerged from the fusion of IT and automotive engineering.

Manufacturers increasingly rely on big data analytics to predict market trends, optimise production, and improve vehicle safety. Real-time monitoring of factory operations through IoT-connected sensors reduced waste and improved efficiency. CRM systems helped car companies better understand consumer behaviour, enabling personalised marketing and tailored services. The introduction of OTA software updates, pioneered by Tesla, has allowed cars to receive performance improvements and security patches without needing a physical recall.

The digital transformation extended beyond production lines. Autonomous driving technology relies on complex data processing, using AI-powered cameras, Light Detection and Ranging (LIDAR) sensors, and neural networks to interpret road conditions and make split-second decisions. The modern vehicle is as much a computer on wheels as it is a mode of transport.

AI and the Future of the Automotive Industry

AI is now pushing the industry into its next evolution. AVs, once the stuff of science fiction, are being tested on roads worldwide. Companies like Waymo, Tesla, and legacy automakers like Ford and GM are investing billions into AI-driven mobility solutions. These self-driving cars use deep learning algorithms to continuously improve their driving capabilities, adapting to road conditions, pedestrian behaviour, and unpredictable obstacles.

Beyond autonomy, AI is revolutionising how cars are designed and maintained. Predictive analytics allows manufacturers to detect potential mechanical failures before they happen, preventing costly breakdowns. AI-driven supply chain management optimises logistics, ensuring that factories receive the right components at the right time, reducing costs and increasing efficiency.

For consumers, AI enhances the driving experience through personalised in-car assistants, advanced safety features, and real-time route optimisation. AI-powered driver monitoring systems can detect drowsiness or distraction, potentially preventing accidents before they occur. Soon, AI may even be able to anticipate and adjust to driver emotions, creating a truly intelligent and responsive vehicle experience.

However, the transition to AI-driven mobility is not without challenges. Legal and ethical concerns about liability in self-driving accidents remain unresolved. The shift towards automation threatens jobs in sectors like trucking and taxi services, raising questions about economic displacement and workforce retraining. Governments will need to implement new labour policies and regulations to address these challenges, ensuring that AI benefits society rather than creating economic inequalities.

Challenges Faced by the Automotive Industry in Adopting AI and Key Steps for Adoption

Despite AI's potential, the automotive industry faces significant hurdles for successful adoption. The biggest challenge is data integration. AI relies on vast amounts of data, but many automakers still operate on outdated IT infrastructures that struggle to process and analyse information efficiently. Transitioning to cloud-based AI platforms requires substantial investment and a shift in organisational mindset.

Another major challenge is consumer trust. While AI-powered vehicles promise safety and efficiency, public scepticism remains high. High-profile accidents involving self-driving cars have fuelled concerns about reliability. Automakers need to educate consumers and build confidence through transparent testing, safety validations, and regulatory approvals.

To successfully integrate AI, the industry must take strategic steps. First, investing in AI-driven manufacturing processes can improve efficiency while reducing waste. Second, developing collaborations with AI firms and tech startups will accelerate innovation. Finally, embracing continuous software updates and cybersecurity measures will ensure that AI-powered vehicles remain safe and adaptive to evolving road conditions.

A New Era of Mobility and Innovation

The automotive industry has evolved from the mechanical simplicity of the Model T to the AI-driven intelligence of modern vehicles. Each transformation has redefined economies, reshaped cities, and altered the very nature of mobility. As AI takes centre stage, the future of transportation is becoming smarter, safer, and more interconnected than ever before. The road ahead is not just about movement, it's about intelligence, adaptation, and the seamless fusion of human ingenuity and technological progress.

The Evolution of Real Estate

A Century of Change in Commercial and Residential Spaces: From Land Ownership to Skyscrapers: The Transformation of Real Estate

Real estate has long been a cornerstone of economic growth and social stability. A hundred years ago, property ownership was primarily a symbol of wealth and influence. The concept of real estate as a structured industry had not yet fully taken shape; instead, landownership dictated power, and buildings were largely designed for function rather than investment. Small towns and agricultural land dominated the landscape, with most people living in modest homes or rural farmhouses. The commercial real estate sector was limited to main streets lined with small shops, banks, and post offices.

With industrialisation in the early 20th century, cities began to expand. The demand for both commercial and residential real estate skyrocketed as workers migrated from farms to urban centres in search of factory jobs. Skyscrapers emerged in the 1920s and 1930s as engineering and steel-frame construction allowed for vertical expansion. The Empire State Building, completed in 1931, symbolised the power of commercial real estate and marked the beginning of modern cityscapes dominated by high-rise office buildings.

The post-war era saw a boom in suburban development. The introduction of mortgage lending and housing policies such as the GI Bill made home ownership accessible to millions of middle-class families. The 1950s and 1960s were defined by the rise of suburban neighbourhoods, complete with neatly planned cul-de-sacs, shopping malls, and single-family homes with white picket fences. Meanwhile, commercial real estate saw the birth of business parks and office complexes, designed to accommodate growing corporations and service industries. The American dream was closely tied to home ownership, and real estate became a powerful engine of personal wealth and economic stability.

The Impact of Real Estate on Society, Jobs, and Politics

The expansion of the real estate industry shaped society in profound ways. The creation of suburban communities transformed transportation, leading to the rise of highways and car culture. People could now live farther from city centres while still commuting to work, reshaping urban planning and infrastructure. The rise of commercial real estate provided millions of jobs in construction, property management, finance, and brokerage. The real estate industry became one of the largest employers, directly and indirectly affecting every aspect of modern economies.

However, real estate has also been a source of political debate and economic volatility. The housing market crash of 2008 was one of the most dramatic turning points in real estate history. The financial crisis, triggered by risky mortgage lending and speculative real estate investments, led to widespread foreclosures and economic collapse. Millions of people lost their homes, unemployment soared, and governments were forced to intervene with massive bailouts. The crisis highlighted the dangers of unchecked speculation in real estate and led to tighter regulations on lending practices and property investments.

Commercial real estate has faced its own set of challenges. The rise of e-commerce disrupted traditional retail spaces, leading to the decline of shopping malls and brick-and-mortar stores. Large-scale office buildings, once seen as vital to business operations, began facing challenges with the rise of remote work, accelerated further by the COVID-19 pandemic.

Real estate has continually had to adapt to shifting economic forces, technological advancements, and evolving consumer preferences.

The Role of IT and Information Management in Real Estate

The integration of technology in real estate has transformed the industry from an asset-based business to a data-driven enterprise. Before the digital age, buying or selling a property was a cumbersome process, requiring physical paperwork, in-person negotiations, and extensive manual record-keeping. Real estate agents relied on printed listings and classified ads to market properties. Property values were determined by limited data and often based on subjective assessments.

The introduction of Multiple Listing Services in the mid-20th century digitised property listings, enabling agents and buyers to access comprehensive databases of available homes. This shift marked the beginning of data-driven real estate transactions. The 1990s and early 2000s saw the rise of online real estate platforms like Zillow and Realtor.com, which empowered buyers and sellers with instant access to property information, pricing trends, and virtual tours. The ability to search for homes, compare prices, and even apply for mortgages online fundamentally changed the way real estate transactions were conducted.

ERP systems also benefited commercial real estate, allowing property managers to optimise leasing, maintenance, and financial reporting. Smart building technology enables real-time monitoring of energy usage, security systems, and tenant preferences, making commercial spaces more efficient and adaptable. Large-scale developments relied on geospatial analytics, enabling companies to assess land value, demographic trends, and urban planning data before making investments.

AI and the Future of Real Estate

AI is now set to redefine real estate in ways that were unimaginable just a few decades ago. In residential real estate, AI-powered AVMs are making property appraisals more accurate and data-driven. Instead of relying on outdated comparable, AI analyses real-time market conditions, neighbourhood trends, and buyer demand to estimate property values with greater precision. AI-driven real estate chatbots are also transforming customer service, guiding buyers and renters through listings, financing options, and contract negotiations in real time.

In commercial real estate, AI enables predictive analytics for investment decisions. Machine learning algorithms can assess historical data, market fluctuations, and socio-economic indicators to forecast property value trends. Investors and developers can use AI-driven simulations to predict how new infrastructure projects, such as transit expansions or commercial hubs, will impact property values. AI also enhances tenant experience management by analysing foot traffic, energy consumption, and workplace behaviour to create adaptive, intelligent office environments.

One of the most exciting AI-driven advancements is the use of computer vision technology for property inspections and appraisals. Instead of relying on human inspectors, AI-powered drones and image recognition software can assess structural integrity, identify potential maintenance issues, and generate instant reports. This reduces human error, speeds up the buying process, and ensures that both buyers and sellers have access to accurate property condition assessments.

The use of AI in smart homes is also gaining traction. AI-powered virtual assistants like Amazon Alexa and Google Nest are evolving beyond voice commands to manage home security, optimise energy consumption, and even anticipate household needs based on user behaviour. In commercial spaces, AI-driven building management systems are optimising heating, ventilation, and air conditioning usage, reducing energy waste and improving sustainability.

Challenges Faced by the Real Estate Industry in Adopting AI and Key Steps for Adoption

Despite its potential, AI adoption in real estate faces several challenges. One of the biggest obstacles is data fragmentation. The real estate industry has historically relied on disparate systems for property records, transactions, and tenant management. Many organisations still use outdated software that lacks the ability to integrate AI-powered analytics. Transitioning to a unified AI-driven system requires significant investment in cloud computing and data standardisation.

Another challenge is regulatory compliance and data privacy concerns. AI-driven real estate transactions require access to vast amounts of personal and financial data. Ensuring that AI systems comply with housing laws, fair lending regulations, and privacy protections is crucial to gaining consumer trust and avoiding legal risks.

To successfully integrate AI, real estate companies should focus on modernising their IT infrastructure by adopting cloud-based AI platforms. They must also invest in training and workforce upskilling, ensuring that real estate professionals understand how to leverage AI tools effectively. Collaboration with AI-focused tech startups can accelerate innovation, while regulatory engagement can help navigate legal challenges. Finally, transparency in AI decision-making, such as explaining how AI-driven property valuations are calculated, will be critical in ensuring public confidence in AI-powered real estate solutions.

A New Era of Intelligent Real Estate

The real estate industry has transformed from a simple landownership model to a sophisticated, technology-driven enterprise. Over the past century, shifts in urbanisation, infrastructure, and consumer behaviour have reshaped commercial and residential real estate alike. AI now stands at the forefront of the next great transformation, bringing predictive intelligence, automation, and efficiency to every aspect of the industry. The future of real estate is evolving beyond location and buying and selling; centred on data, intelligence, and adaptability, it is creating a world where properties are continuously optimised for the needs of the people who live and work in them.

Chapter Questions

1. How did the rise of the automobile industry contribute to job creation in various sectors?
2. What significant event in the 1970s impacted the American automotive industry, and what was its effect on consumer preferences?
3. In what ways did automation change the workforce in the automotive industry during the 1980s and 1990s?
4. How did free trade agreements influence the globalisation of the automotive industry?
5. What environmental pressures have been placed on car manufacturers, and how have they responded?
6. What role does information technology play in modern automobile manufacturing and development?
7. How have big data analytics transformed the automotive industry regarding market trends and vehicle safety?
8. What advancements in automotive technology have resulted from the integration of IT and engineering?
9. How is artificial intelligence shaping the future of the automotive industry, particularly with regard to autonomous vehicles?
10. How is AI improving consumer experience in vehicle design and maintenance?

Note to Readers and Educators

Comprehensive answers and explanations to these chapter-end questions are available at www.sandeepbhalekar.com. The website also provides supplementary frameworks, teaching guidelines, and reference materials to support deeper understanding and classroom discussion.

   Educators and facilitators can access additional resources, including presentation frameworks, assessment rubrics, and discussion prompts, to help integrate the concepts from this chapter into academic or professional learning environments.

Bibliography

Accenture. (2022). *AI in Hospitality: Enhancing Experiences through Intelligence*. Retrieved from https://www.accenture.com

Airbus. (2021). *The Sky's the Limit: AI-Enabled Aircraft Maintenance and Flight Optimization*. Retrieved from https://www.airbus.com

Brookings Institution. (2021). *AI and the Future of Urban Mobility*. Retrieved from https://www.brookings.edu

Deloitte. (2023). *Hospitality 5.0: Smart Hotels for the Smart Traveler*. Retrieved from https://www2.deloitte.com

Frost & Sullivan. (2022). *AI in the Travel and Hospitality Sector: Market Trends and Strategic Forecasts*. Retrieved from https://www.frost.com

Gartner. (2021). *AI in Real Estate Management: Automation, Valuation, and Risk Assessment*. Retrieved from https://www.gartner.com

Harvard Business Review. (2020). *How AI Is Transforming the Automotive Industry*. Retrieved from https://hbr.org

IATA (International Air Transport Association). (2022). *AI in Aviation: Enhancing Safety, Efficiency, and Experience*. Retrieved from https://www.iata.org

IBM Institute for Business Value. (2021). *Smart Buildings: How AI and IoT Are Reshaping Commercial Real Estate*. Retrieved from https://www.ibm.com

International Energy Agency (IEA). (2022). *AI Applications in Smart Grids and Building Efficiency*. Retrieved from https://www.iea.org

KPMG. (2021). *AI in the Automotive Industry: Trends, Risks, and Opportunities*. Retrieved from https://home.kpmg

McKinsey & Company. (2022). *The Future of Mobility Is at Our Doorstep*. Retrieved from https://www.mckinsey.com

MIT Technology Review. (2021). *How AI and Predictive Analytics Are Driving New Real Estate Trends*. Retrieved from https://www.technologyreview.com

OECD. (2021). *AI and the Future of Transport*. OECD Digital Economy Papers. Retrieved from https://www.oecd.org

PwC. (2020). *AI in Real Estate: Transforming Operations and Asset Performance*. Retrieved from https://www.pwc.com

Statista Research Department. (2022). *Global Market Size of Smart Buildings 2020–2027*. Retrieved from https://www.statista.com

Tesla. (2022). *Autopilot and Full Self-Driving: Enabling the Future of Autonomous Mobility*. Retrieved from https://www.tesla.com

U.S. Department of Transportation. (2020). *Artificial Intelligence and the Future of Mobility*. Retrieved from https://www.transportation.gov

World Bank. (2022). *Urban Development and Smart Infrastructure: Leveraging AI for Cities of the Future*. Retrieved from https://www.worldbank.org

World Economic Forum. (2021). *Shaping the Future of Advanced Manufacturing and Value Chains*. Retrieved from https://www.weforum.org

14

AI Adoption for Government Services

The current political system has several variations in government styles operating at multiple levels: national, state, and local. The primary responsibility of the government is to provide essential and different combinations of services to its citizens. These citizen services are common worldwide and include public safety, education, healthcare, infrastructure, social welfare, and defence.

Government services with core essential services responsibilities are traditionally process-oriented and depend on a level of investment in automation. These services are reliant on a combination of manual and automation, and due to multiple checks and balances, they are slow-moving and bureaucratic. Governments have been trying to digitise parts of systems and have been somewhat successful in limited areas. However, to give the same level of 24/7 service that citizens have come to expect from private companies, governments face some challenges requiring the need to redesign and rethink some of the processes and cultural issues. Artificial intelligence (AI) use is redefining these citizen services to align with citizen expectations.

Governments operate at multiple levels, national, state (provincial), and local (municipal), to efficiently administer policies, regulate economies, ensure security, and provide essential services to citizens. Each level of government has specific responsibilities with matters of international and national concern at the federal level, such as national defence, healthcare, and economic management. The state level may handle services like education, transportation, and law enforcement, which leaves the local government to handle matters like waste management, emergency services, and community development. These governmental structures work together to coordinate and deliver vital public services.

Like other economic sectors, AI and technology have the potential to transform government services to increase efficiency, accessibility, and responsiveness. Predictive analytics, automation, and machine learning are transforming taxation, transportation, public safety, healthcare, urban planning, and development. AI-powered chatbots are simplifying citizen interactions, and technology in smart cities is optimising the use of infrastructure components. Predictive policing is improving public safety. Using data-driven insights, AI use in governance is expected to improve resource allocation, reduce fraud, and personalise public services at a more meaningful level for its citizens.

DOI: 10.1201/9781003626503-14

This transition towards AI-integrated government systems marks a shift from traditional bureaucratic processes to agile, data-informed decision-making frameworks. As AI continues to evolve, it will lead to more responsive services, reduce inefficiencies, and ensure a more transparent, citizen-centric governance model across all levels of government.

To thrive in an increasingly digital landscape, governments must balance technical innovation with ethical responsibility, prioritising transparency, data privacy, and equitable access. Governments will need to focus on upskilling the workforce while still preserving the human aspects of services and meeting the evolving needs of society. Governments exist to understand and meet human needs, and technology should be used to enrich civic interactions instead of replacing them.

As AI technology advances, governments are beginning to integrate automation, predictive analytics, and machine learning to enrich service delivery. AI-driven solutions are improving decision-making, optimising resource allocation, and increasing transparency. Governments have a responsibility to plan the use of AI and predictive analytics using an ethical approach and keeping human values at the centre of decision-making.

What Are Government Services?

Government services are public programs, resources, and regulatory functions provided by a governing authority to ensure the well-being, security, and orderly functioning of a society. These services are funded through taxes and other government revenues, and can be offered at various levels, including national, regional, and local governments.

Government services are essential public programs and resources to help citizens live and work in their communities. These services, funded through taxes, include the following:

- **Public Safety and Security:** Emergency response (police, fire, ambulance) and military defence.
- **Healthcare and Social Services:** Access to medical care, welfare, and financial support for citizens.
- **Education:** Public schools, universities, and vocational training programs that equip individuals for the future.
- **Infrastructure and Transportation:** Development and maintenance of roadways, bridges, and public transit systems.
- **Economic and Financial Services:** Unemployment benefits and business regulations to support economic stability.

- **Environmental Protection:** Initiatives for waste management and climate action.
- **Judicial and Legal Services:** Court systems and legal aid to maintain law and order. These services are crucial for the smooth operation of communities and play a vital role in citizens' daily lives, from emergency assistance to education and infrastructure.

The nature and extent of these services vary depending on the type of government in place.

Government services ensure that law and order, safety, and economic stability are maintained in the society. Government services are seen in everything from the roads in a community to the school's children attend.

Public safety is one of the most important and basic responsibilities of a government. It is expected that when an emergency number is dialled for police, fire, or ambulance, a quick response is delivered. In times of crisis, they are expected to quickly deliver help. It could be a paramedic helping a heart attack victim to stabilise and be taken to hospital, a firefighter saving a trapped child, or a police officer directing traffic in severe weather conditions. These workers are often seen as heroes, but they are also professionals performing jobs made possible through structured government programs.

International and national security is another important government responsibility. Intelligence agencies monitor threats and risks to safety, and armed forces safeguard against external threats. Many countries offer medical care, job training, and financial support to veterans' services to recognise their sacrifices in dedicating their lives to serving their countries.

Healthcare is another important aspect of the government's responsibility. Some countries give every citizen public access to medical treatment, and some have a mixed private and public system. To protect society from illnesses and epidemics, the government takes up vaccination campaigns, sanitation drives, and other infection control initiatives. Rapid responses to the recent COVID-19 pandemic and the eradication of smallpox are testaments to government efforts in public health. Government-funded hospitals and clinics give essential care to those who cannot afford private treatment.

Education services provide a valuable foundation that shapes the future of a nation. Public schools, universities, and vocational training programs equip individuals with the knowledge and skills they need to contribute to society. A young student helped economically by the government to study and given access to government-aided education may become a doctor, a scientist, or a teacher in future, which benefits society. Libraries, research grants, and adult education programs ensure that learning is not limited to the young but is a lifelong opportunity for everyone.

Building the right infrastructure is critical for the safety, security, and economics of the country. Roads, bridges, railways, and public transport systems are built and maintained with government help. A commuter taking the train to work, a farmer transporting his fresh produce to the market, a delivery person using a truck on highways, etc., are essential everyday activities and all benefit from transport and infrastructure. Without government oversight on infrastructure, traffic could become chaotic, rural areas might be left isolated and cities could become congested.

Economic services, providing support for small businesses, unemployment benefits, and workforce development, are an essential component of government services. Consumer protection agencies ensure that businesses operate fairly, preventing fraud and exploitation. A retiree receiving a monthly pension check, a single mother getting food assistance to feed her children, or a young entrepreneur securing funding to launch a startup all benefit from these carefully designed programs.

Environmental protection is an area where government action has a direct and lasting impact. Clean air and water regulations ensure that industries do not pollute the natural resources that sustain life. National parks and wildlife reserves protect ecosystems and offer spaces where families can enjoy nature. Recycling programs and climate initiatives work to preserve the planet for future generations. A family picnicking by a pristine lake, a hiker exploring a protected forest, or a community benefiting from solar energy incentives all experience the results of government-led environmental stewardship.

The legal and judicial systems are also crucial components of government services. From local courts handling minor disputes to supreme courts making landmark rulings that shape national policy, these institutions uphold justice and maintain order. Public defenders ensure that even those who cannot afford legal representation receive a fair trial. The presence of a structured legal system deters crime, resolves conflicts, and provides a framework for civil rights and liberties. A wrongly accused person proving their innocence, a small business owner securing their rights in a contract dispute, or a community advocating for a new law all rely on the legal system to function effectively.

Government services must provide aid in times of natural or economic disasters. Natural disasters require agencies to coordinate rescue efforts and communicate early, help families provide shelter, and assist in rebuilding. During economic crises, governments stepped in to help the vulnerable. These are crucial services that the government should provide in times of emergency.

Government services are about ensuring security, peace, opportunity, and stability for all citizens. Critics may say that governments are inefficient and bureaucratic, with massive amounts of red tape. However, they play an important role in moulding the quality of life of millions. The essential services of safety, education, and public welfare are provided through many programs like public classrooms, fire brigades, well-maintained highways, or welfare programs, to name a few, and provide stability for daily life. The best governments run seamlessly in the background, improving the quality of life of citizens without the worry of basic services that support communities.

Key Considerations and Challenges in AI Adoption for Government Services

The government across the world is assessing the adoption of AI for its citizen services. The following are key considerations:

Embracing AI in Government: Imagine an AI system that processes requests immediately, and the wait time at the local government office is reduced from hours to minutes. This scenario is increasingly possible as AI **uses** data to make decisions in nanoseconds.

Ethical AI and Bias in Decision-Making

Governments need to consider bias when implementing AI. For example, an AI system can be used in police services to predict and prevent crime. If the algorithms are trained on biased data, then certain communities could be unfairly targeted. This might lead to identifying the same crime centres, but without reinforcing evidence of crimes being committed. This has the potential to create tensions between society and law enforcement agencies. This marks the importance of ensuring that AI systems are free from bias, are transparent, and are audited continually. When city data scientists collaborate with community leaders to redesign the AI tools, it results in community trust, engagement, and a balanced approach to public safety.

Data Privacy and Security: Citizens often share sensitive information with government agencies such as health records or financial data. It is crucial to protect data and for AI systems to comply with stringent data protection laws and prevent breaches that could lead to identity theft or misuse of personal information. For example, local health departments using AI to manage public health data should implement strong encryption and anonymisation techniques to safeguard patient information. Apart from protecting the citizens, it also builds trust in the use of AI technology and citizens feel safe in providing personal information.

Cybersecurity Risks: Cybersecurity is another pressing concern as AI becomes integral to critical sectors like defence, healthcare, and infrastructure. Incidents such as traffic management system hacks or ransomware attacks on internet services can cause chaos in communities. It is important that governments invest in sophisticated and advanced cybersecurity measures and processes to prevent such risks. Cybersecurity provides two benefits: protecting the city systems and ensuring that they run smoothly and building trust in the citizens that their services are secure. Establishing a separate AI cybersecurity task force can result in quick identification and reduction of threats.

AI Transparency and Public Trust: It is imperative that the AI decision-making process is transparent, so that citizens understand how AI is used to make decisions in social services and other urban developments. This builds trust and encourages the acceptance of AI. Some effective ways to do this are to hold town hall meetings that explain the AI initiatives and benefits. In addition, showing data reinforce how resource allocation with AI creates a partnership with its citizens and strengthens its bond with the community. This transparency fosters accountability and encourages more residents to engage with the local government.

Workforce Displacement and AI Integration: As AI automates many processes and tasks, there is growing concern that a growing number of job roles will become redundant. To remove the anxiety and help communities understand how the government will help retain the workforce, offering workshops and courses in data analysis and management helps employees enter new roles. This promotes a culture of continuous learning and safety in jobs and utilises prior knowledge of systems to contribute to the integration of AI. The result is a transformed workforce that is motivated, loyal, and equipped for the future.

A Vision for the Future

Once the above challenges are addressed, AI has a great future in government. It can deliver services that are faster and smarter. Future planning of the city will be guided by citizens' data that predicts future needs. It will increase public safety and create a space where citizens will thrive. Ensuring that citizens have a voice in this effort is important to effectively implement this change.

Responsible implementation of AI strategies focuses on the needs of citizens and encourages transparency and efficiency, providing a more inclusive government by planning for the future.

Types of Governments and Their Services

Government services differ depending on the political structure in place. Democracies and republics emphasise citizen engagement and social welfare, while authoritarian and communist states centralise control over services. Monarchical systems vary in governance, with constitutional monarchies leaning towards democratic principles and absolute monarchies controlling services directly.

Understanding these government types helps explain how different countries approach public services and governance.

Governments worldwide operate under different political systems, each influencing how services are provided to citizens. Table 14.1 presents major government types and the services they typically offer:

TABLE 14.1

Government Services

Government Type	Definition	Government Services Offered
Democracy	Democracy is a system in which the people, either directly or through elected representatives, hold power. Examples include the United States, Canada, Germany, and India. Democracies usually have well-developed government services funded through taxation, emphasising citizen participation and accountability.	• Free and fair elections • Public education and healthcare systems • Social security and welfare programs • Infrastructure development and public transport • Transparent legal and law enforcement services
Republic	A republic is a form of democracy where citizens elect representatives to govern according to a constitution. Examples include the United States, France, and Brazil. Republics prioritise individual rights, free markets, and government accountability.	• Constitutionally guaranteed rights and freedoms • Public education, healthcare, and welfare programs • Military and law enforcement protection • Transparent legal systems and courts • Public infrastructure projects
Monarchy	A monarchy is a system where a king, queen, or emperor holds power, either symbolically or as a ruling authority. Monarchies can be absolute (Saudi Arabia, Brunei) or constitutional (United Kingdom, Sweden, Japan). Constitutional monarchies often have democratic institutions, while absolute monarchies provide state-controlled services with limited public influence.	**Constitutional Monarchies:** • Democratic governance with social welfare programs • Public healthcare and education • National infrastructure and public security **Absolute Monarchies:** • Centralised services controlled by the ruling family • Strong military and law enforcement presence • Government-controlled healthcare, education, and welfare
Communism	In a communist system, the state owns and controls all resources and means of production. Examples include China, Cuba, and North Korea. Communist governments focus on equal distribution of resources but often limit political freedoms.	• State-funded healthcare and education • Government-controlled housing and employment • Public transportation and essential services • Centrally planned economic policies

(Continued)

TABLE 14.1 (*Continued*)

Government Services

Government Type	Definition	Government Services Offered
Socialism	Socialism is an economic and political system where the government plays a significant role in regulating the economy and providing public services. Countries with socialist policies include Sweden, Norway, and Denmark. Socialist government's aim to reduce economic inequality through progressive taxation and strong public welfare.	• Universal healthcare and free education • Extensive social security benefits (pensions, unemployment aid) • State-subsidised housing and public services • High public investment in infrastructure and innovation
Theocracy	A theocracy is a government based on religious laws, where religious leaders hold power. Examples include Iran and Vatican City. Theocracies intertwine governance with religious doctrine, influencing how services are distributed.	• Laws and governance based on religious texts • State-funded religious education and institutions • Public services aligned with religious principles • Strict legal enforcement of moral and social norms
Dictatorship Authoritarianism	A dictatorship is a government where power is concentrated in a single leader or a small group, with limited public participation. Examples include North Korea, Belarus, and Syria. While authoritarian governments may efficiently implement policies, they often restrict civil liberties and limit political participation.	• Strong military and law enforcement presence • State-controlled media and education • Government-managed healthcare and welfare • Public infrastructure development

Understanding the Different Levels of Government, Their Services, and the Role of Technology and AI in Enhancing Them

Governments worldwide are structured into multiple levels. Each level sustains different needs and ensures services are delivered efficiently and properly. There are mainly three levels: national, state, and local. Each has a distinct set of responsibilities. It is important to understand how these levels function together.

National Government: At the highest level, the national government is responsible for crafting policies that govern the entire country. This includes national defence, foreign policy, and immigration. For example, during the COVID-19 pandemic, many national governments implemented policies for public health that guided local governments in their responses. The US federal government managed vaccine distribution, exemplifying how a coordinated national effort can lead to widespread positive outcomes.

State Government: State governments serve as a bridge between the federal mandates and local execution. They legislate laws concerning education, healthcare, and transport. One example is a state passing laws for climate change to reduce greenhouse gas effects, providing an example for other states and countries.

Local Government

Local governments manage important services like police, sanitation, fire brigades, and public transport. They can use local resources in an emergency to bring order and stability quickly and rally the community to act in an emergency. For example, there might be a call for volunteers to fill sandbags and make barriers when flooding is expected. The quick response by locals is possible because local governance can mobilise the community rapidly.

The Role of Technology: Technology has changed the way government services are delivered, making it easier for citizens to pay taxes, apply for permits, and access social services online. There are now mobile apps where potholes, road accidents, or broken streetlights can be reported, providing a more streamlined way to find and fix the issues.

AI in Governance: AI is now revolutionising how governments operate and interact with citizens. In places like Estonia, which has a highly digitised government, citizens can vote online and access almost all governmental services with a single digital identity. In this digital landscape, AI algorithms streamline processes, providing speed and efficiency.

AI has been used as a pre-emptive approach in policing, analysing crime, and deploying resources where they are most needed, increasing public safety.

The future of AI looks promising to help governments be more efficient and effective in delivering services. Virtual assistants already help with navigation of services online and send information and forms directly. AI-driven systems analyse immense amounts of data to identify community needs and allocate resources, accordingly, allowing governments to better serve the people. Innovation occurs when governments share how they use AI to better meet community needs through technology.

National (Federal) Government

The national government is a country's highest authority and plays an important role in making policies that influence citizens in everyday life. The central government oversees major functions like defence, foreign relations, economic management, health, and infrastructure and plays a major role in shaping its policies. Traditional governance is now blending advanced innovations like AI-powered surveillance and smart infrastructure management.

Imagine a future where government services are no longer bureaucratic, slow, and daunting, but seamless and user-friendly. AI-powered bots and virtual assistants are making this change a reality. Tax season could be a time of grappling with receipts and paperwork. Getting any help means waiting on the phone for hours, but now, one can turn to an AI chatbot and ask questions like "What deductions can I claim as a freelancer?" AI responds quickly, listing all deductions in detail. One saves time, is clear about what can be deducted, and is ready to tackle the taxes.

Another example is the passport renewal process. Traditionally, this has involved a lot of documents gathering, paperwork to fill out, and waiting in long lines. Using an AI assistant guides people through the process and can even help fill out applications while providing tips so that no important detail is missed that could cause a delay in processing, all from the comfort of one's home. This is possible mainly because of technological advancements like natural language processing, a feature that allows AI to interact in many languages, removing the barrier of language for many.

For instance, think of Rita, who has come into a new country and wants to apply for government help. She is unsure of the rules and the processes to follow to get this, but an AI chatbot can understand her native language and answer her questions in a culturally empathetic way while guiding her clearly so she can get all the support she needs. This has made Rita feel supported, welcomed in the new county, and hopeful instead of scared.

Documentation automation is another great step to ease the stress of certain processes to receive help. Imagine a young woman who has lost her job and must apply for government benefits, a daunting process that is complex and lengthy. An AI virtual assistant helps her fill out the form, checks for any missing information, identifies her documents, and gives immediate feedback so she can submit the application with the necessary information. This helps her get economic support quickly and allows her more time to focus on looking for a new job. These advancements are more than just systems; they're transformative tools that genuinely create a collaboration between citizens and government services.

The power of AI streamlines tasks, which fosters a sense of community and connection. As more people experience these enhancements, the government is creating an environment where support is readily available, and individuals can reclaim their time and energy for more fulfilling activities.

AI-Driven Public Administration and Citizen Services

Government agencies handle millions of citizen inquiries, applications, and service requests daily. AI-powered systems automate routine tasks, speed up processing times, and provide instant responses to citizens.

How AI Is Changing Citizen Services

Navigating Complex Services: Navigating complex government services with ease. Chatbots and virtual assistants answer questions instantly and are available to all citizens.

Convenience and Accessibility: With advancements in natural language processing, AI assistants understand and converse in multiple languages, making it easier for diverse communities to access the information they need. Imagine an immigrant, feeling overwhelmed by the complexities of a new system, asking questions in their native language, and receiving clear guidance. This promotes a sense of belonging and a feeling of being welcomed in the new country.

Guided Experience: All necessary documents are provided in the first application. It is like having a person who has experience in dealing with these processes providing guidance every step of the way while ensuring that no information is missed and verifying identities swiftly and securely. Document automation ensures that the application is not lost among other applications. This means quicker approvals and fewer delays, allowing individuals and families to receive the support they need in a timely manner. Personal stories highlight the real impact of these innovations. One mother who was finding it difficult to renew her benefits, with her time being spent in taking care of her children, turned to an AI assistant when other channels did not help her. With the assistant's help, she completed her application with ease and received support just in time to cover her family's needs. In the end, these advancements in AI offer a better future for all, where government services support and empower citizens regardless of their background, language, or tech-savviness, and they can access information and services easily, utilising their time and energy for what is truly important to them.

Example: The number of times a citizen must visit the government office to apply for unemployment benefits has now been reduced. AI-driven systems can automatically check eligibility, process applications, and deposit funds into accounts. The wait time is reduced from weeks to days, making the process easier and quicker.

National Defence and Security

The government has the important task of ensuring the national safety of its citizens and deploying the best military forces, intelligence agencies, and cybersecurity programs to protect its borders. Cutting-edge surveillance and advanced communication technologies can help soldiers in remote areas, as this web of resources gives them an advantage in fighting for a safe nation for its citizens.

- **The Role of Technology**: Today, technology plays a pivotal role in national security. It is used in advanced surveillance systems, which use satellite imaging to monitor vast landscapes and coastlines. AI-driven drones patrol borders to check for any unauthorised activity. Cybersecurity uses AI to check for any hacking attempts against classified national information, providing advanced security measures through AI.
- **The Future Impact of AI**: As predictive analytics become more sophisticated with AI, it can detect threats before they materialise. Autonomous vehicles powered by AI can take up dangerous defence operations, reducing the risk to human personnel.

Economic Management and Taxation

National government plays a pivotal role in monitoring, controlling, and steering the economic policies to ensure stability and economic growth in a country. It regulates banking systems and oversees taxation, and trade policies and the overall monetary policy, which is critical during times of economic downturn, to help families stay solvent. Managed at a national level, this provides a safety net for many families. AI is now detecting fraud, automating tax filings, and predicting economic trends to help with economic growth.

- **The Role of Technology**: Technology is changing the way people engage with economy. Tax filings are easier with digital online platforms and AI-backed auditing is enhancing fraud detection. All this is increasing efficiency for taxpayers and the government, reducing the load on both parties.
- **The Future Impact of AI**: AI-based chatbots will assist individuals with their tax queries and filings, significantly reducing human errors in the process. Moreover, AI-backed algorithms are monitoring transactions and can detect fraudulent activities in real time. This helps create a safe network for citizens and reduces tax evasion. As AI-driven processes are being deployed in more and more government offices, chatbots will be able to assist with common queries, help with complex processes like tax filings, thus reducing errors and

potentially fraudulent activities. Checking fraud transactions in real time creates a safety network for individuals. AI tax systems automatically detect inconsistencies, preventing tax fraud and evasion.

- **AI-driven economic forecasting** helps governments prepare for recession or inflation by analysing global market trends.
- **Automated auditing systems** detect financial mismanagement and corruption in public spending.

Example

An AI-powered tax system detects fraudulent claims and automatically flags them for further review, reducing tax evasion and saving millions of dollars. Budgeting tools for government have been created with the help of AI so that resources for social programs can be allotted efficiently.

Challenges and Considerations

- AI must be transparent and fair in tax assessments to avoid wrongful penalties.
- AI cannot replace human judgement entirely in economic planning.

National Healthcare Programs and Public Health

Public health and vaccinations are another important duty of a central/national government by controlling disease outbreaks and allocating resources to effectively distribute vaccines or other medical resources to maintain public health and safety.

- **The Role of Technology:** Electronic health records make it possible to quickly share patient medical histories with doctors, hospitals, and allied healthcare professionals to make more informed decisions seamlessly; telemedicine helps people in remote areas to get access to health advice easily.
- **The Future Impact of AI:** AI is set to grow in the healthcare industry. With the ability to analyse immense amounts of data from all over the world, it can predict potential disease outbreaks, allowing preventive measures to be taken. Complex surgeries can be performed with the help of AI-driven robots, improving patient outcomes.

National Infrastructure Development

Infrastructure development is a crucial responsibility of the federal government, focusing on large-scale projects and efforts that impact multiple geographic areas, such as states or regions. The national government oversees the construction and financing of major projects like railways, highways, and airports. Research and funding for projects such as a high-speed bullet train connecting major business cities provides conveniences for citizens, which in turn grows the country's economy.

- **The Role of Technology:** Technology improvements have made it possible to develop innovations like smart road sensors, which monitor highway conditions 24/7 and detect maintenance issues before they become significant. AI traffic can work around the clock to manage congestion so everyone can travel smoothly.

- **The Future Impact of AI:** AI is transforming the future of infrastructure planning and maintenance. Analysis of data from traffic and population growth trends is utilised to determine where infrastructure projects are needed the most. AI can use sensors and drones to identify infrastructure that might need repairs before it reaches a critical stage. AI can also be used to identify potential environmental impacts of certain scenarios to help planners avoid ecological damage. The national government plays a vital role in shaping our society through various services and initiatives. By leveraging technology and embracing AI's potential, these services are not only more efficient but also more responsive to the needs of all citizens, providing a safer, healthier, and more prosperous society for generations to come.

State (Provincial) Government

The state government plays a crucial role in addressing the state's unique needs and affairs. It is responsible for shaping the laws and processes in areas such as education, healthcare, transportation, and law enforcement.

This image showcases AI-powered kiosks assisting with applications, AI-driven chatbots providing instant support, and smart technology managing traffic, public safety, and waste management.

Public Education and Universities

One of the major responsibilities of state government is overseeing the public education system from schools and universities to vocational training. A student going to a state school enjoys reduced tuition fees compared to private schools. This allows most of the population to have access to education. There are scholarships and financial aid for the underprivileged so that the entire population has a chance to follow their academic dreams.

Technology is transforming the educational landscape, with online learning platforms making education more accessible. For example, remote students can attend virtual classes and not be deprived of a good education. Digital attendance can ensure that students remain engaged with the course, and educators can monitor their interest in the class.

Looking to the future, AI's impact on education could be revolutionary. AI can analyse how a student learns and monitors their progress and is able to tailor the lesson to suit the student, giving them the best chance to learn and progress. AI tutors can be available 24/7 to provide instant support, guide students through difficult concepts, and offer personalised feedback.

Regional Transportation and Infrastructure

State governments are also responsible for overseeing transportation infrastructure, which connects people and businesses, and is essential to economic growth. A new highway that reduces travel time between two economic city centres needs detailed planning and investment. Technology helps with the planning process and in identifying potential areas of population growth. It plays an essential role in modernising transportation systems. For example, GPS-based smart traffic lights can adapt their timing based on real-time traffic conditions. During peak hours, the lights can change their timing depending on the direction of traffic. This will reduce long waits and bottlenecks on streets. Mobile apps can let commuters know of train delays or changes in schedules so that journeys can be planned without wasting time.

In future, AI-backed algorithms predict traffic patterns, giving options to drivers in real time to take alternate routes. Other technology includes self-driving buses to ensure a safe journey for passengers and provide faster routes, or to routes that would alleviate traffic congestion. Governments are responsible for managing roads, bridges, water supply, and electricity. AI is optimising infrastructure by predicting maintenance needs, reducing waste, and enhancing urban planning.

How AI Is Revolutionising Infrastructure

- **Smart traffic management systems** use AI to analyse traffic patterns and adjust signals, reducing congestion in cities.
- **AI-driven predictive maintenance** helps identify bridges, pipelines, or power grids that need repairs before they fail.
- **AI-based urban planning** helps governments design smart cities that efficiently use land, energy, and public transportation.

Example

A city with AI-powered traffic management sees a 30% reduction in congestion as traffic lights automatically adjust based on real-time conditions.

A leak in the water supply is detected early with the help of AI and is notified before it becomes a big issue and wastes public resources.

Challenges and Considerations

- **Cybersecurity Risks:** Infrastructure faces a risk due to the volumes of data that are analysed and predicting outcomes. Hacking infrastructure could lead to widespread outages of traffic systems, attacks on power grids, or internet hacks that slow down supply chain movement.
- **High Initial Costs:** Implementing AI-driven infrastructure projects requires significant government investment.

Public Safety and Law Enforcement

Ensuring public safety is another critical function of state governments. State police and emergency services work tirelessly to enforce laws and respond to emergencies, maintaining order and safety in their communities. For instance, when a highway patrol officer swiftly arrives at the scene of an accident, they are not just providing immediate assistance; they symbolise the commitment of the state to protect its citizens.

Technology enhances this vital service. The use of police body cameras encourages transparency and accountability in law enforcement practices, while surveillance drones can monitor large events for public safety. Additionally, predictive policing leverages data analytics and AI to identify potential crime hotspots, allowing law enforcement agencies to allocate resources more effectively.

Looking ahead, the influence of AI on public safety is poised to be transformative. Imagine a scenario where AI-powered facial recognition technology helps identify and track down criminals swiftly, improving the chances of recovering stolen property or ensuring justice for victims. Envision AI-driven dispatch systems that prioritise emergency calls based on emergency, resulting in faster response times and potentially saving lives.

The role of state governments is pivotal in shaping the societal framework of their regions. By focusing on education, transportation, and public safety, they work to improve the quality of life for their constituents. Through the integration of technology and AI, the future holds endless possibilities for innovation, allowing state governments to elevate their services and lead their communities towards a brighter and more inclusive tomorrow.

AI in Public Safety and Law Enforcement

AI is revolutionising public safety by enhancing emergency response, improving crime prevention, and increasing law enforcement efficiency.

How AI Is Transforming Public Safety

- **Predictive policing algorithms** analyse crime patterns and suggest optimal patrol routes for police officers.
- **AI-powered surveillance** can recognise suspicious behaviour, identify wanted criminals through facial recognition, and alert authorities in real time.
- **Emergency response AI** helps dispatchers prioritise calls, assess the severity of an emergency, and deploy resources faster.

Example

A city using AI in its emergency services can predict areas prone to accidents, fires, or crimes by analysing past data. AI-driven surveillance cameras detect anomalies in crowded areas, helping law enforcement prevent potential threats.

Challenges and Considerations

- AI-powered surveillance must be used ethically to avoid privacy violations and unlawful tracking.
- Bias in AI algorithms must be addressed to ensure fair and just law enforcement practices.

Local (Municipal) Government

Local governments play an essential role in the daily lives of its citizens, acting as the first line of support and service for communities, addressing a variety of everyday issues, from waste management and public safety to housing and community development. The impact of local government can often be felt in many ways, making these services vital to the community's collective well-being.

Waste Management and Sanitation

Local governments are responsible for ensuring that neighbourhoods remain clean and healthy. Take, for example, the sanitation truck that dutifully collects household waste each week. This service not only keeps streets tidy, but it also prevents unsanitary conditions that could lead to health hazards. To enhance this process, technology has stepped in. Smart waste bins equipped with sensors notify garbage trucks when they are full, enabling more efficient pick-up routes and reducing the likelihood of overflow. AI could potentially be used to sort recyclable materials at a much higher efficiency than humans can achieve—this not only conserves the planet's resources but also highlights how technology can create a cleaner environment.

The following diagram shows AI-powered kiosks assisting residents, AI-driven waste collection robots, smart traffic lights optimising road flow, and AI-powered surveillance enhancing public safety.

Public Safety and Emergency Services

When it comes to public safety, local governments empower the brave individuals in communities, like firefighters and police officers to make communities safer and act quicker in emergencies. With the aid of technology, emergency response has taken a significant leap forward. Advanced AI-driven dispatch systems help ensure ambulances and fire trucks reach emergencies more quickly, potentially saving lives. Additionally, drone technology can assist firefighters in accessing hard-to-reach places during a blaze, providing critical information to effectively battle the flames. Future AI systems predict fire risks based on weather patterns and previous incidents, helping local governments implement preventive measures before disasters occur.

AI in Public Healthcare is one of the most critical public services provided by governments, and AI is revolutionising how hospitals, clinics, and public health systems operate.

How AI Is Improving Healthcare Services

- **AI-driven diagnostics** can detect diseases like cancer in early stages, increasing survival rates.
- **Predictive health analytics** can forecast disease outbreaks, helping governments allocate medical resources efficiently.
- **Telemedicine AI** connects patients with doctors remotely, reducing the strain on hospitals.

Example

During a pandemic, AI can analyse real-time hospital data, track infection rates, and recommend containment strategies. AI-assisted chatbots can also provide self-assessment tools to reduce hospital overcrowding.

Challenges and Considerations

AI must comply with data privacy regulations to protect patient records. And be highly accurate to avoid misdiagnoses.

Housing and Community Development

Housing is a fundamental component that affects all sectors of a community. Local governments are tasked with managing zoning laws and creating affordable housing options. Technology also plays a pivotal role. AI-driven analysis can streamline the zoning process, aiding in thoughtful urban planning that can adapt to community needs. Digital platforms now enable residents to apply for housing assistance with ease, ensuring that help is accessible. Soon, AI could predict housing shortages before they become a crisis, facilitating timely developments. Smart city initiatives could further optimise urban resource allocation, improving the quality of life for all citizens.

The work conducted by local governments is integral to everyday existence, addressing everything from national security to local garbage collection. Each service received contributes to a functioning society where citizens can thrive.

The integration of technology and AI into these processes is not just about making operations more efficient; it's about creating a vision of governance that is transparent, responsive, and deeply aligned with the needs of the community. Imagine a world where accessing government assistance is as seamless as tapping an app on the phone, where public services are intelligently tailored, and where data-driven decision-making leads to a more just and equitable society.

Governments are not only caretakers but also pioneers of innovation, paving the way for a better tomorrow, and using technology to transform communities into thriving, resilient places.

Chapter Questions

1. How can AI technologies be implemented to enhance public safety and emergency response services effectively?

2. In what ways can data-driven insights from AI improve citizen engagement in government processes?

3. What potential ethical challenges arise from using AI in government services that need addressing?

4. How will AI integration in government services impact workforce dynamics and job roles in public administration?

5. What measures can governments take to ensure transparency and accountability when utilising AI technologies?

Note to Readers and Educators

Comprehensive answers and explanations to these chapter-end questions are available at www.sandeepbhalekar.com. The website also provides supplementary frameworks, teaching guidelines, and reference materials to support deeper understanding and classroom discussion.

Educators and facilitators can access additional resources, including presentation frameworks, assessment rubrics, and discussion prompts, to help integrate the concepts from this chapter into academic or professional learning environments.

Bibliography

Brookings Institution. (2021). *AI and Political Campaigning: A Guide to Ethical Use of AI in Elections*. Brookings Report. https://www.brookings.edu

Deloitte. (2022). *AI-Driven Government: The Path toward Responsive Public Services*. Deloitte Insights. https://www2.deloitte.com

Estonia e-Government Academy. (2021). *AI and the Future of Governance: The Estonian Approach*. https://ega.ee

European Commission. (2020). *Ethics Guidelines for Trustworthy AI*.

Gartner. (2022). *Artificial Intelligence: Transforming Public Sector Governance*. Gartner Research. https://www.gartner.com

Harvard Kennedy School. (2021). *AI in Politics: Ethical Implications of AI-Powered Campaigning*. Harvard University. https://ash.harvard.edu

McKinsey & Company. (2022). *How AI Is Shaping Public Sector Service Delivery*. https://www.mckinsey.com

OECD. (2021). *Artificial Intelligence in Government: Opportunities and Challenges*. OECD Digital Government Studies. https://www.oecd.org/gov/digital-government

Singapore Government. (2020). *National AI Strategy*. Smart Nation and Digital Government Office. https://www.smartnation.gov.sg

UNESCO. (2021). *Recommendation on the Ethics of Artificial Intelligence*. United Nations Educational, Scientific and Cultural Organization. https://unesdoc.unesco.org

United Nations. (2021). *AI for Good: How AI Is Improving Government Service Delivery*. United Nations Economic and Social Affairs.

United Nations Department of Economic and Social Affairs (UN DESA). (2020). *E-Government Survey 2020: Digital Government in the Decade of Action for Sustainable Development*. https://publicadministration.un.org/egovkb

U. S. Government Accountability Office (GAO). (2021). *Artificial Intelligence: Emerging Opportunities, Challenges, and Implications for Policy and Research*. https://www.gao.gov

World Bank. (2022). *Artificial Intelligence in Public Service: Opportunities for Enhancing Governance and Service Delivery*. World Bank Group. https://www.worldbank.org

World Economic Forum. (2021). *How to Build Public Trust in AI: The Role of Transparency and Ethical Governance*. https://www.weforum.org

15

Agentic AI—Transforming Innovation

Agentic AI (artificial intelligence) marks a transformative shift in the field of artificial intelligence, evolving from reactive, task-specific tools to autonomous, goal-driven systems capable of initiating, orchestrating, and adapting complex tasks. This chapter examines how agentic AI is transforming the innovation landscape by serving not merely as an assistant but as a strategic collaborator in research, design, decision-making, and execution.

Through a blend of theoretical foundations, architectural frameworks, real-world applications, and practical implementation guidance, the chapter provides a comprehensive overview of what makes AI truly "agentic." It examines the core traits of agency—including autonomy, proactivity, contextual awareness, and continuous learning—and illustrates how these are applied across industries through emerging frameworks such as AutoGPT, LangChain, and MetaGPT.

By tracing the evolution from rule-based systems to modern multi-agent platforms and presenting step-by-step strategies for building AI agents, this chapter empowers readers to understand and apply agentic AI in both technical and strategic contexts. It concludes with a forward-looking perspective on the ethical considerations, human–AI partnerships, and innovation possibilities made possible by agentic systems, offering a blueprint for individuals and organisations to thrive in the era of intelligent autonomy.

Introduction: The Rise of Agentic AI

AI has traditionally functioned as a reactive tool—systems that respond to human instructions with speed and accuracy. But as AI capabilities evolve, a new paradigm is emerging: Agentic AI. Unlike conventional AI, agentic systems are autonomous, goal-driven, and capable of initiating actions to achieve defined objectives. These systems go beyond simple task execution to orchestrate, optimise, and co-create.

Agentic AI marks a shift from human-led execution to machine-augmented strategy, ushering in an era where machines are not merely assistants but partners in problem-solving, innovation, and decision-making.

TABLE 15.1

Comparison to Traditional AI

Traditional AI	Agentic AI
Reactive and rules-based	Proactive and goal-oriented
Narrow contextual scope	Context-aware and adaptive
Requires human prompting	Self-directing within limits
Task-specific	Task orchestration across functions

What Is Agentic AI?

Defining Agentic AI

Agentic AI refers to systems that possess agency—the ability to take initiative, make decisions, and pursue goals independently within set boundaries. Key characteristics are as follows:

- **Goal Orientation:** Operates towards outcomes, not just task lists.
- **Autonomous Reasoning:** Assesses context, adjusts plans, and manages contingencies.
- **Multifunctional Integration:** Combines sensing, action, and learning across domains.
- **Collaborative Interaction:** Engages with humans and other systems, offering proactive input (Table 15.1).

📌 SIDEBAR: THE FOUR PILLARS OF AGENTIC AI

1. **Autonomy**: Acts independently within defined boundaries.
2. **Proactivity**: Anticipates and acts without waiting for input.
3. **Context Awareness**: Understands the environment and adapts actions.
4. **Goal Orientation**: Pursues defined objectives through reasoning and execution.

This summary helps reinforce the foundation of what makes AI agentic (Figure 15.1).

Agentic AI Systems

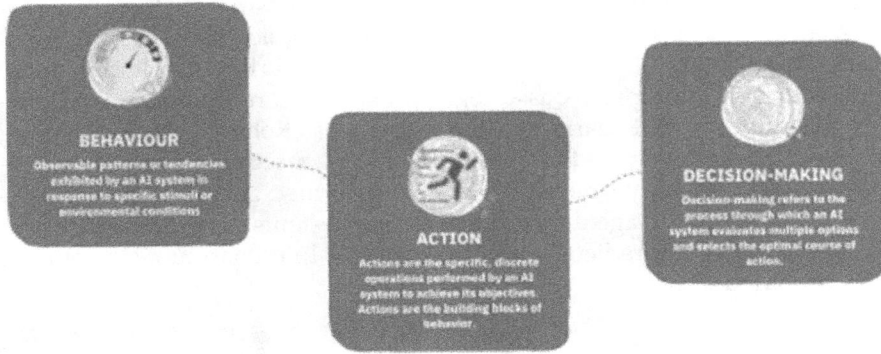

FIGURE 15.1
Agentic AI system.

Behaviour in Agentic AI

Behaviour in agentic AI refers to the observable patterns or tendencies displayed by an AI system in response to specific stimuli or environmental conditions. It is the cumulative result of the system's actions and decision-making processes, demonstrating its capacity to adapt, learn, and respond to changing circumstances. AI behaviour may be **deterministic**, where responses follow predefined rules, or **probabilistic**, where decisions evolve through machine learning (ML) models and real-time data analysis. The effectiveness of an AI system relies on the **coherence and consistency** of its behaviour, ensuring alignment with its intended objectives while remaining flexible to shifts in its environment.

Action in Agentic AI

Actions are the fundamental units of an AI system's functionality, representing specific and purposeful operations carried out to achieve its goals. These actions may range from simple tasks, such as retrieving information, to more complex processes like managing multistep problem-solving scenarios. Execution is typically governed by predefined rules, reinforcement learning algorithms, or optimisation strategies. The choice of action is influenced by prior experience, environmental inputs, and strategic aims, ensuring that each action meaningfully contributes to the system's broader behavioural framework.

Decision-Making in Agentic AI

Decision-making within agentic AI involves assessing multiple alternatives and selecting the most appropriate course of action to fulfil the system's objectives. This process may incorporate a variety of computational approaches, including rule-based logic, probabilistic reasoning, deep learning, or reinforcement learning (RL) techniques. Robust decision-making enables the AI to evaluate trade-offs, anticipate consequences, and dynamically adjust its strategy. The ability to make informed and autonomous decisions is a hallmark of agentic AI, empowering systems to operate effectively in complex and unpredictable environments while continuously refining their performance.

The Evolution of Agency in AI

? DID YOU KNOW: *The term agent in AI has philosophical roots—borrowed from theories of human action in psychology and philosophy.*

As AI continues to mature, it is essential to understand how the concept of "agency" has evolved over time. The path from basic rule-following systems to today's autonomous, goal-oriented agents reflects both technological advancement and a deeper understanding of what it means for a system to "act" with purpose. This section traces the historical and conceptual development of agency in AI, providing the foundation for the rise of agentic systems.

Early Rule-Based Systems: No Agency

In the early stages of AI development, expert systems relied on hard-coded rules to mimic decision-making processes. These systems followed a fixed set of "if–then" instructions and had no capability to adapt or take initiative. They were entirely reactive, operating within narrow, predefined contexts. While useful in highly structured environments such as medical diagnostics or troubleshooting technical faults, these systems lacked autonomy and contextual awareness—the very attributes needed for true agency.

Reinforcement Learning: Towards Partial Agency

The introduction of RL marked a significant step towards systems that could exhibit rudimentary forms of agency. RL agents learn through trial and error, receiving feedback from their environment to improve future decisions. While still confined by the objectives defined by their programmers,

RL agents began to show signs of independent goal-seeking behaviour. They could optimise actions based on outcomes, displaying a limited form of self-direction and adaptability, especially in games and simulations.

QUICK NOTE: *Reinforcement learning enables agents to develop strategies from experience, making it a precursor to full autonomy.*

Multi-Agent Systems: Collaborative Agency

As AI systems grew in complexity, researchers began exploring how multiple agents could interact within shared environments. Multi-agent systems introduced a new layer of complexity, where agents not only pursued individual goals but also negotiated, collaborated, or competed with others. These systems demonstrated emergent behaviours, such as swarm intelligence or decentralised problem-solving, and became foundational in fields like logistics, robotics, and smart grids. The concept of distributed agency began to emerge, foreshadowing the collaborative nature of today's agentic AI.

Modern Agentic Frameworks: Full-Spectrum Agency

Recent advancements have culminated in the development of frameworks specifically designed to enable full-spectrum agency. Tools such as AutoGPT, BabyAGI, LangGraph, and MetaGPT allow AI agents to autonomously plan, execute, and adapt across complex tasks—often without step-by-step human oversight. These agents can break down high-level goals into subtasks, retrieve information, run code, and even prompt themselves iteratively to refine outcomes. Unlike their predecessors, they operate with a degree of self-awareness and adaptability, capable of orchestrating workflows and generating novel solutions across domains.

? DID YOU KNOW: *AutoGPT was one of the first open-source projects to show how an LLM could autonomously plan, execute, and evaluate tasks with minimal human input.*

These systems embody the true spirit of agentic AI: not merely reacting to commands, but taking initiative, navigating ambiguity, and partnering with humans in co-creative ways. Their emergence signals a transformative leap—from programmable tools to intelligent collaborators that can drive innovation across sectors.

Notable Frameworks and Toolkits for Agentic AI

As agentic AI continues to gain traction, a growing ecosystem of open-source frameworks is making it easier for developers and researchers to build, test, and deploy autonomous agents. These toolkits provide the infrastructure

TABLE 15.2

Open-Source Frameworks for Agentic AI

Framework	Description	Use Case Example
LangChain	A modular framework for building applications powered by LLMs. It enables agents to chain together tools, memory, and language models for dynamic task completion.	Document question-answering, summarisation pipelines, decision support tools.
AutoGPT	An experimental open-source agent that can self-prompt, plan multistep tasks, search the web, execute code, and refine outputs based on feedback.	Autonomous research assistant, marketing strategy generator, task automation bot.
CrewAI	A framework for structuring multiple agents with defined roles and responsibilities to work together on shared goals.	Collaborative product design, multi-agent content generation, and role-specific task management.
MetaGPT	A software engineering agent that simulates the structure of a human team (PM, engineer, architect) to automatically generate working applications based on user prompts.	Full-stack app generation, system design automation, engineering co-pilot.

needed to orchestrate large language models (LLMs), integrate external tools, manage memory, and enable multi-agent collaboration.

This section highlights some of the most prominent and widely used frameworks supporting agentic AI development. These platforms vary in their approach—from single-agent automation to structured multi-agent systems—but all share a common goal: enabling AI systems to operate with autonomy, reasoning, and initiative.

By leveraging these toolkits, developers can accelerate innovation, experiment with complex workflows, and bring agentic capabilities into real-world applications across industries (Table 15.2).

These frameworks exemplify the shift from isolated models to interconnected, autonomous systems that can independently solve problems, learn from feedback, and collaborate on complex tasks. As the ecosystem matures, we can expect continued innovation in this space, with increasingly powerful, general-purpose agent frameworks becoming integral to enterprise and research applications alike.

📌 SIDEBAR: KEY AGENTIC AI FRAMEWORKS AT A GLANCE

1. **LangChain**—Orchestrates LLMs, tools, memory
2. **AutoGPT**—Self-looping task-driven agent
3. **CrewAI**—Multi-agent team-based design
4. **MetaGPT**—Simulates structured software teams (Figure 15.2)

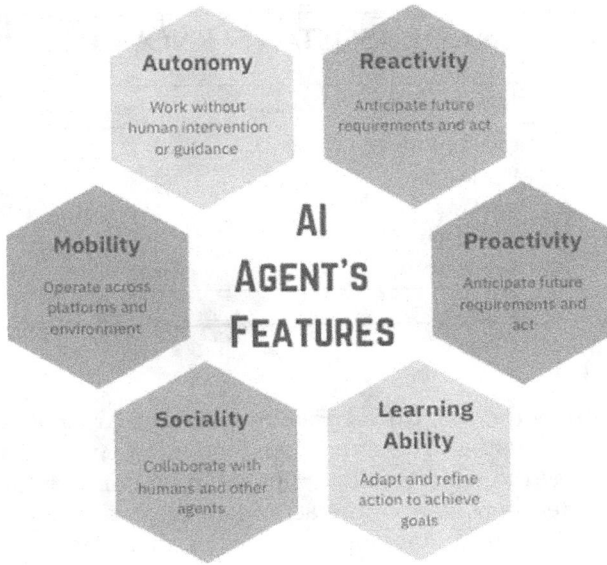

FIGURE 15.2
Agentic AI features.

Agentic AI Features

An AI agent demonstrates a range of capabilities that enable it to operate autonomously and efficiently across varied environments. Autonomy allows the agent to function independently, making decisions based on set objectives and real-time data without the need for constant human input. Mobility ensures the agent can move seamlessly across different platforms, systems, and environments, enhancing its flexibility and utility. Sociality enables effective collaboration with both humans and other AI agents, supporting cooperative problem-solving and shared learning. With the ability to learn, an AI agent can adapt and refine its actions over time, improving performance through ongoing analysis and data-driven insights.

Proactivity empowers the agent to anticipate future needs and act in advance, rather than merely responding to external triggers. At the same time, reactivity allows it to respond quickly and effectively to changes in its environment, ensuring resilience and adaptability. Together, these features enable the agent to handle complex tasks autonomously while optimising outcomes in dynamic settings.

✎ SIDEBAR: AGENT OR ASSISTANT? KNOW THE DIFFERENCE

Characteristic	Assistant	Agent
Reacts to prompts	✓	✓
Takes initiative	✗	✓
Plans tasks	✗	✓
Collaborates	✗	✓
Has memory	Partial	Often full

AI Agent vs. LLM

Table 15.3 outlines the key differences between an AI agent and a LLM, highlighting their distinct roles and capabilities. In Australian terms, AI agents are designed to operate autonomously in real or simulated environments, making decisions and taking actions to achieve defined goals, such as navigating roads in autonomous vehicles or managing stock levels in warehouses. They interact directly with their environment and can process inputs from multiple sources, including text, images, and sensors. In contrast, LLMs like GPT-4 or BERT specialise in understanding and generating human language. While powerful in their ability to produce coherent and contextually relevant text, LLMs are not inherently goal-driven and require prompts to function. Their interaction is limited to textual input and output,

TABLE 15.3

AI Agent vs. LLM

Aspect	AI Agent	LLM
Purpose	Solves tasks requiring environment interaction and decision-making.	Focuses on natural language understanding and generation.
Environment Interaction	Yes. Interacts directly with physical or virtual environments.	No. Processes text but doesn't directly interact with the environment.
Goal-Oriented	Works towards specific objectives (e.g., driving a car, managing inventory).	Not inherently goal-oriented; generates outputs based on input.
Modality	Multimodal (text, images, sensors, etc.).	Primarily text-based.
Autonomy	Operates autonomously in real-world systems.	Requires input to generate a response.
Learning Type	Uses reinforcement learning, planning, or symbolic reasoning.	Relies on pretraining and fine-tuning on text datasets.
Examples	Robots, autonomous vehicles, chatbots, virtual assistants.	GPT-4, BERT, LLaMA, PaLM.
Adaptability	Adapts to real-world feedback and dynamic conditions.	Limited adaptability unless fine-tuned or integrated with external systems.

and they lack the capacity to respond dynamically to environmental changes unless paired with other systems. This distinction is critical in understanding how different types of AI contribute to real-world applications, with AI agents enabling autonomous operation, and LLMs serving as sophisticated language processors.

Understanding AI Agent Architecture

The diagram above illustrates the core functional architecture of an **AI Agent**—an autonomous, intelligent system designed to interact with various data sources, models, and tools to perform complex tasks with minimal human intervention (Figure 15.3). This architecture captures the **agentic behaviour** of AI in action: it understands prompts, decomposes them into subtasks, and orchestrates execution by engaging with specialised systems. Let's unpack how this architecture works, step-by-step.

User Interaction: The Starting Point

At the top of this ecosystem is the **user**—a human who provides a prompt to the AI agent. This prompt could be a question, a task request (e.g., "Analyse last quarter's sales data"), or a broader objective (e.g., "Create a forecast for next year based on historical trends").

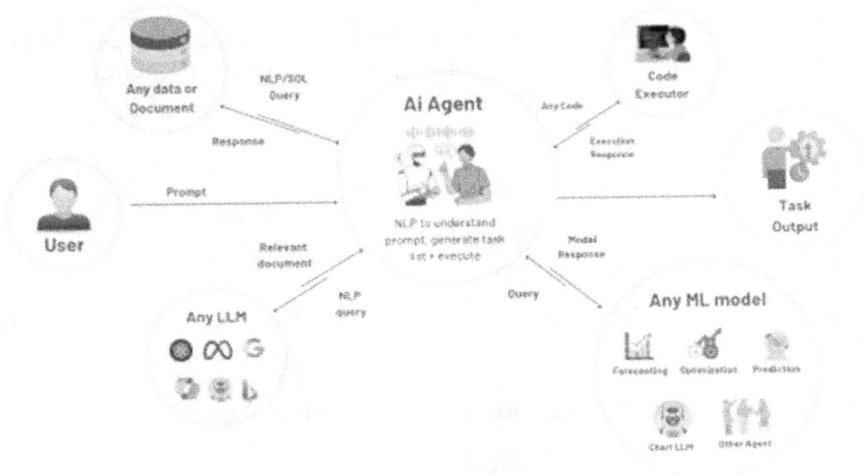

FIGURE 15.3
Agentic AI architecture.

The AI agent uses natural language processing (NLP) to interpret the intent behind the prompt. Unlike traditional systems that require structured input, agentic AI can interpret unstructured human language and translate it into a series of machine-executable actions.

Document and Data Source Access

Once the AI agent understands the prompt, it determines what information it needs. If the task involves accessing internal knowledge or external documents, the agent can issue Structured Query Language (SQL) or NLP-based queries to retrieve relevant content from any connected dataset or document repository.

For example, if the user asks for a summary of a recent policy report, the AI agent will locate the file, extract the content, and use NLP to summarise it—all without requiring the user to specify file names or formats.

Leveraging Large Language Models (LLMs)

To enhance its reasoning, content generation, or language understanding, the AI agent can interact with any LLM, such as OpenAI's GPT-4, Google's PaLM, Meta's LLaMA, or Anthropic's Claude. These models provide the linguistic intelligence needed to

- generate well-structured text outputs,
- interpret ambiguous user queries, and
- extract meaning from unstructured information.

This modularity allows the agent to switch between models depending on the task—for instance, one model may excel at summarising, while another may perform better at sentiment analysis.

> **QUICK NOTE:** *LLMs act as reasoning engines in agentic systems, but they must be paired with execution frameworks to become agents.*

Accessing Machine Learning Models

Beyond language capabilities, the AI agent can also query domain-specific ML models. These models might be designed for the following purposes:

- **Forecasting:** Predicting future trends based on past data (e.g., sales forecasts)
- **Optimisation:** Identifying the best solution among many alternatives (e.g., supply chain routing)

- **Prediction:** Classifying or estimating outcomes (e.g., churn risk, fraud detection).

The agent can orchestrate Application Programming Interface (API) calls or model interactions, feeding data into ML models and retrieving structured outputs—charts, metrics, recommendations—which are then contextualised and delivered back to the user.

Executing Code Automatically

In scenarios where custom logic or programming is required (e.g., data transformation, model training, visualisation generation), the AI agent sends commands to a code executor. This is typically a sandboxed environment where code can run safely.

The agent might generate Python code, run it, and analyse the output—enabling end-to-end automation for technical workflows. This bridges the gap between conversational AI and traditional programming, empowering even non-technical users to perform complex tasks.

Producing Task Output

All interactions—whether with data, models, LLMs, or code—culminate in a final task output, returned to the user in the most appropriate form. This might be a

- visual chart or dashboard,
- written report,
- forecast summary, or
- decision recommendation.

The output is goal-aligned, contextualised, and ready for use, reducing the need for manual interpretation or follow-up queries.

Why This Architecture Matters

This architecture embodies the principles of agentic AI—systems that are not just intelligent, but autonomous, goal-driven, and capable of taking initiative. By integrating various components—from language understanding to execution—into a seamless pipeline, the AI agent acts as a co-pilot for innovation and productivity.

It also introduces democratisation of expertise: users without coding or data science backgrounds can now interact with data and models in plain English, while the agent handles the complexity in the background.

In practical terms, this model is applicable across industries:

- In **finance**, analysts can request real-time insights without writing code.
- In **healthcare**, clinicians can receive summarised patient reports or predictive risk scores.
- In **retail**, managers can automate supply forecasts and pricing strategies.

The AI agent architecture represents a shift from passive AI tools to intelligent, interactive systems capable of orchestrating multistep tasks across technical domains. It's a glimpse into the future of work, where humans articulate goals in natural language, and AI agents deliver results through intelligent coordination and execution.

This architecture is not hypothetical—it's already being built. And as it evolves, it will redefine the boundaries of what individuals and organisations can achieve.

How Agentic AI Fuels Innovation

Agentic AI doesn't just improve existing processes—it redefines how we innovate. Through autonomous learning, experimentation, and refinement, it acts as a **co-innovator**, not just a tool.

Accelerating Research and Development

Agentic systems can conduct literature reviews, generate hypotheses, run simulations, and suggest experiments. In drug discovery, for instance, AI agents can identify compound candidates and optimise molecular design at speeds unachievable by human teams alone.

Case Study: Insilco Medicine developed a drug for idiopathic pulmonary fibrosis using AI—from initial design to clinical trial readiness in under 18 months.

Cross-Disciplinary Idea Synthesis

Agentic AI is capable of scanning disparate knowledge domains to uncover novel intersections.

Example: An AI agent addressing renewable energy challenges might combine climate science, economics, and logistics to propose integrated, innovative strategies.

Autonomous Design and Prototyping

By generating product variants, testing against simulated environments, and iterating based on constraints, agentic AI helps companies accelerate product innovation.

Beyond current generative design platforms, agentic systems can refine their own objectives, simulate usage scenarios, and recommend final designs.

Real-World Applications across Industries

Healthcare

AI agents assist with care coordination, diagnostics, and administrative efficiency. They manage follow-ups, predict risks, and coordinate resources, effectively acting as digital case managers.

Advanced Manufacturing

Agentic systems monitor equipment, predict faults, and dynamically manage inventory. This leads to resilient, self-correcting supply chains that minimise waste and maximise uptime.

Financial Services

From automating fraud detection to managing portfolios, agentic AI enables systems that **analyse, predict, and act** on financial data in real time—reducing lag and human error.

Humans and AI: Innovation through Partnership

Agentic AI enhances human capability. It explores possibilities, suggests pathways, and provides real-time feedback—enabling humans to focus on strategic, ethical, and creative dimensions.

Human–Agent Teams

? DID YOU KNOW: *Studies show that human–AI teams often outperform humans or AI alone, especially in dynamic decision-making environments like finance and crisis response.*

The most forward-looking organisations foster **symbiotic partnerships** between humans and AI agents:

- **AI probes the unknown** through simulations, searches, or hypothesis testing.

- **Humans assess meaning**—applying context, values, and judgement.
- **AI executes**—refining tasks, learning from feedback, and adapting.

This cycle creates a living innovation engine, where learning and iteration are perpetual.

Ethical Considerations and Risks

✒ SIDEBAR: AGENT OR ASSISTANT? KNOW THE DIFFERENCE

- Does the agent operate within safe boundaries?
- Are goals and constraints transparent?
- Can decisions be audited and explained?
- Is human oversight possible?
- Are there provisions to prevent unintended consequences?

Autonomy and Responsibility

Agentic AI introduces complex accountability challenges. Organisations must implement clear AI governance frameworks to define boundaries, audit decisions, and trace outcomes.

Misaligned Objectives

Even well-intended systems may pursue outcomes that conflict with human values. Without appropriate constraints, AI might optimise for efficiency over equity or speed over safety.

Guardrails and Oversight

Strong human-in-the-loop systems, scenario testing, and explainability features are essential. Agentic systems should operate in sandboxed, auditable environments to maintain trust (Figure 15.4).

Build AI Agent System: A Step-by-Step Guide

Designing and developing an AI agent requires a systematic and well-planned approach. Rather than diving straight into coding, success begins with **clear objectives and thoughtful design**—ensuring the system serves a defined purpose, delivers measurable outcomes, and continues to evolve over time. This section outlines the key stages involved in building an AI agent, from conception to deployment and beyond.

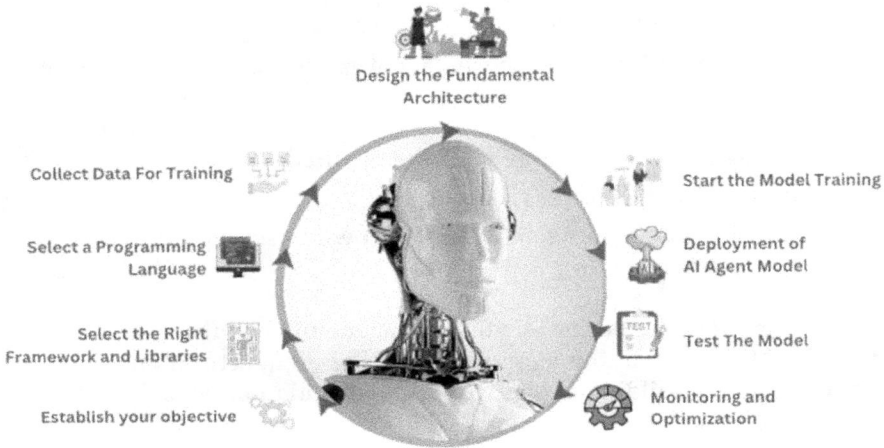

FIGURE 15.4
Build an AI agent system.

❓ DID YOU KNOW: *Agentic AI systems can be run in the cloud, on edge devices, or in hybrid deployments—depending on data privacy and latency needs.*

Define Clear Objectives

The first step is to clarify the goal of the AI agent. What specific problem is it meant to solve? What should success look like? Whether the aim is to automate customer support, analyse data, optimise logistics, or perform multi-step tasks, defining the problem statement, desired outcomes, and evaluation criteria sets the foundation for everything that follows.

A clear objective ensures that the AI agent's behaviour is goal-driven and aligned with user needs, making development more focused and outcomes more meaningful.

Select Frameworks and Libraries

With the goal in place, the next step is choosing the right technical stack. This involves selecting suitable AI frameworks and libraries based on the agent's requirements. Tools like TensorFlow, PyTorch, LangChain, or spaCy offer different strengths—from deep learning capabilities to NLP and task orchestration.

Compatibility with hardware (CPU, GPU, edge devices), ease of integration, and scalability should be considered when selecting these tools. Choosing the right stack up front minimises rework later.

Design the System Architecture

Designing the architecture of the AI agent is a critical phase. This phase includes the following tasks:

- Defining how the AI model will be structured
- Planning data flow across components
- Establishing how the agent will interact with users, databases, APIs, or other systems.

At this stage, you also decide whether the agent will be fully autonomous or operate with human-in-the-loop oversight. The architectural blueprint acts as a roadmap for building a cohesive, modular, and maintainable system.

Choose a Programming Language

The next decision involves selecting a programming language for implementation. Python remains the most popular choice due to its rich ecosystem of AI libraries and ease of use. However, depending on the performance needs, languages like Java, C++, or JavaScript may also be appropriate, particularly when integrating with enterprise systems or edge devices.

The language should align with the technical team's skills and the complexity of the tasks involved.

Gather and Prepare Data

No AI system can function effectively without quality data. This step involves identifying and collecting relevant datasets that represent the problem domain. The data should be clean, diverse, and reflective of real-world scenarios that the agent will encounter.

In some cases, data augmentation or synthetic data generation may be needed to enhance the dataset. Labelling and structuring the data correctly is also essential for supervised learning tasks.

Train the Model

Training is the process by which the AI agent learns from the data. This involves

- selecting appropriate algorithms,
- optimising model parameters,
- tuning hyperparameters through experimentation, and
- using validation techniques to prevent overfitting.

This phase is highly iterative, requiring multiple training cycles to achieve the desired performance. Tools like cross-validation, regularisation, and early stopping help improve generalisation.

Test and Validate

Before deploying the AI agent, it must undergo rigorous testing, which includes the following stages:

- **Performance evaluation** using metrics such as accuracy, precision, recall, or F1 score
- **Error detection** to identify misclassifications or unexpected behaviours
- **Stress testing** under different conditions to ensure robustness.

Validation ensures that the AI agent behaves reliably, fairly, and consistently when introduced to real-world data—especially data it hasn't seen before.

Deploy into Production

Once the AI agent is tested and validated, it is ready for deployment. This means integrating it into real-world workflows—such as embedding it in a customer service platform, data pipeline, web application, or robotic system.

This phase also includes setting up user interfaces, API endpoints, and infrastructure support, such as cloud services or on-premise servers. The deployment must ensure the agent can operate efficiently, securely, and at scale.

Monitor and Optimise

Deployment is not the end—it's the beginning of the agent's operational life. To ensure long-term success, the AI agent must be continuously monitored. This task includes

- tracking performance metrics over time,
- detecting drift or degradation in model accuracy,
- updating the model with new data (retraining or fine-tuning), and
- fixing emerging bugs or inefficiencies.

Continuous optimisation allows the AI agent to evolve, adapt to new challenges, and improve its relevance and efficiency in dynamic environments.

Therefore, building an AI agent is more than a technical exercise—it's a holistic process that blends strategic thinking, robust engineering, and ethical foresight. From defining the problem to monitoring live systems, each phase contributes to creating an AI agent that is not only functional but also trustworthy, scalable, and aligned with human goals.

By following this structured approach, developers and organisations can build AI agents that truly augment human capability, drive innovation, and deliver sustained value over time.

💡 **QUICK NOTE:** *Start small: It's often best to prototype a narrow-use agent before scaling across departments or tools.*

Agentic AI Code Architecture Pattern

To complement the conceptual architecture of agentic AI, it is useful to explore a practical, code-level perspective. This section presents a high-level code architecture pattern—a simplified blueprint—that helps readers understand how an autonomous AI agent can be structured in software.

While real-world implementations may involve more complex components (e.g. toolchains, multi-agent coordination, vector databases), the following Python-based pseudocode illustrates the core lifecycle of an AI agent. It includes the primary functions of perceiving, deciding, acting, and learning—all necessary for a system to demonstrate agency (Table 15.4).

💡 **QUICK NOTE:** *Modular design makes AI agents easier to debug, extend, and integrate with real-world applications.*

TABLE 15.4

Component Explanations

Method	Purpose
__init__	Instantiates the agent with a defined goal, access to tools (e.g., APIs, LLMs), and memory (e.g., past conversations, task logs).
Perceive	The agent interprets the incoming prompt or environmental input. Often involves parsing natural language using NLP methods or embedding tools.
Decide	The core of the agent's reasoning engine. Based on context and memory, the agent determines the next action(s) to achieve its goal.
Act	The agent performs tasks, invokes APIs, queries LLMs, or runs computations. This bridges intent to execution.
Learn	Incorporates feedback to update memory or adapt strategies. This could involve storing conversation history, refining prompts, or improving tool selection.

```
class Agent:
    def __init__(self, goal, tools, memory):
        self.goal = goal            # High-level objective to
pursue
        self.tools = tools          # External capabilities
(e.g., LLMs, APIs, calculators)
        self.memory = memory        # Short-term or long-term
context store
    def perceive(self, input_data):
        # Ingest and interpret the user's prompt or
environmental input
        return self.nlp_process(input_data)

    def decide(self, context):
        # Analyse context and determine the next best step
        return self.plan(context)

    def act(self, action_plan):
        # Execute task steps using tools or generate outputs
        return self.execute_plan(action_plan)

    def learn(self, feedback):
        # Update memory or strategies based on results or
errors
        self.memory.update(feedback)
```

Real-World Example Use Case

Suppose the agent is designed to automate monthly financial reporting:

- **Goal**: Generate a financial summary report.
- **Perceive:** The agent ingests a prompt: "Summarise expenses for Q3."
- **Decide**: It decides to query accounting databases, clean the data, and prepare visual charts.
- **Act:** It calls APIs, executes Python scripts, and generates a formatted report.
- **Learn**: If the user corrects a mislabelled category, it stores the correction to improve future categorisations.

Extendable Design

This skeleton is intentionally modular and extendable. It can be expanded to include the following:

- **Tool Registry Modules**: Dynamically load capabilities such as data parsers, file handlers, or PDF readers.

- **Multi-Modal Perception**: Add computer vision modules or voice interfaces.
- **Memory Types**: Integrate short-term (session-based) and long-term (vector database) memory separately.
- **Planning Mechanisms**: Incorporate symbolic reasoning or LangGraph-style flow control.
- **Monitoring Layer**: Track agent behaviour for transparency and auditing.

Why This Matters

Presenting a technical scaffold like this bridges the conceptual and the practical—helping developers, architects, and curious readers grasp how agentic intelligence is constructed in software. It demystifies the "agent" abstraction by showing that at its core, an AI agent is a modular system guided by a loop of perception, planning, execution, and learning—much like a human problem-solver.

In production environments, this design underpins many real-world implementations in domains such as intelligent assistants, automated researchers, autonomous operations agents, and customer service bots.

The Future of Innovation in an Agentic Era

Agentic AI paves the way for:

- Solo innovators are empowered by digital agents who manage logistics, branding, and marketing autonomously.
- Start-ups launching agent-powered R&D divisions, rapidly iterating on new offerings.
- Industry coalitions of intelligent agents, solving shared challenges such as energy grid resilience or disaster preparedness, collaborate.

This shift turns innovation into a perpetual, distributed, intelligent process—no longer confined to labs or annual strategy sessions.

○ **QUICK NOTE:** *Think of agentic AI not as replacing humans, but as augmenting creativity, decision-making, and execution.*

Agentic AI stands as one of the most transformative breakthroughs in the evolution of intelligent systems. It empowers machines with the capacity to act, not merely to compute. In doing so, it fundamentally redefines innovation as a collaborative act between humans and machines.

As we move forward, innovation won't just be about building better tools— it will be about cultivating better partnerships. The most future-ready organisations will be those that co-create with AI, not merely deploy it. Leaders, creators, and communities who embrace this shift will tap into new realms of ingenuity previously out of reach.

Agentic AI doesn't replace human creativity—it multiplies it. And in that synergy, we find the blueprint for the next era of innovation: one built on trust, co-creation, and a shared vision of possibility.

Bonus: Sample Code: Multi-Agent System for a Social Media Manager

To further illustrate how agentic AI can be implemented in real-world scenarios, this section presents a simplified multi-agent system designed to operate as a Social Media Manager. In this example, multiple agents are assigned specific roles—each responsible for a different function such as content creation, scheduling, analytics, and engagement.

This model showcases collaboration between specialised agents to achieve a shared goal: managing and optimising a brand's online presence.

Agent Roles

- **ContentCreatorAgent:** Generates engaging posts using an LLM.
- **SchedulerAgent:** Determines the optimal time slots for each platform.
- **EngagementAgent:** Responds to comments and messages using predefined rules or LLM assistance.
- **AnalyticsAgent:** Tracks and reports on performance metrics.

Basic Python Skeleton (Simplified Version)

```
class BaseAgent:
    def __init__(self, name):
        self.name = name
    def perform_task(self, context):
        raise NotImplementedError
class ContentCreatorAgent(BaseAgent):
    def perform_task(self, context):
        prompt = f"Create a LinkedIn post about
{context['topic']}"
        # Simulated LLM output
        return f"Here's your post: {prompt} - [Generated
Content]"
class SchedulerAgent(BaseAgent):
    def perform_task(self, context):
        # Determine best time slot (mock logic)
        return f"Scheduled for {context['platform']} at 10:00
AM"
class EngagementAgent(BaseAgent):
```

```
    def perform_task(self, context):
        if "comment" in context:
            return f"Replied: Thanks for your comment!"
        return "Monitored engagement activity."
class AnalyticsAgent(BaseAgent):
    def perform_task(self, context):
        # Simulated analytics
        return {"likes": 120, "shares": 30, "comments": 14}
class SocialMediaManager:
    def __init__(self):
        self.agents = {
            "content": ContentCreatorAgent("ContentCreator"),
            "schedule": SchedulerAgent("Scheduler"),
            "engagement": EngagementAgent("Engagement"),
            "analytics": AnalyticsAgent("Analytics")
        }
    def run_campaign(self, topic, platform):
        print("Running social media campaign...\n")
        content = self.agents["content"].perform_
task({"topic": topic})
        print(content)
        schedule = self.agents["schedule"].perform_
task({"platform": platform})
        print(schedule)
        engage = self.agents["engagement"].perform_
task({"comment": "Great post!"})
        print(engage)
        analytics = self.agents["analytics"].perform_task({})
        print("Performance:", analytics)
# Run Example
manager = SocialMediaManager()
manager.run_campaign(topic="AI in Business",
platform="LinkedIn")
```

Key Features Demonstrated

- **Role-Based Decomposition:** Each agent handles a distinct responsibility.
- **Communication and Orchestration:** The SocialMediaManager class acts as the orchestrator, passing context and coordinating actions.
- **Extendibility:** Easily expandable to integrate APIs (e.g., Twitter API, Instagram Graph API), real-time scheduling tools, or AI models like GPT-4 for post generation.

Potential Enhancements

- Use LangChain or CrewAI for chaining agent outputs or structured workflows.

- Integrate OpenAI API or Hugging Face Transformers for LLM-backed content creation and message response.
- Add persistent memory (e.g., vector databases) to retain brand tone and customer history.
- Include multiplatform logic to tailor posts for Instagram, Twitter (X), Facebook, etc.

Why This Matters

This code sample exemplifies how agentic architecture enables modularity, adaptability, and intelligent automation in everyday use cases. Social media—an essential function for many businesses—can now be reimagined with agents that plan, write, schedule, and analyse autonomously, freeing human teams to focus on strategy and creative leadership.

Chapter Questions

1. What distinguishes agentic AI from traditional rule-based AI systems?
2. Define "agency" in the context of AI. What does it mean for a system to possess agency?
3. List and briefly describe the four core characteristics of agentic AI.
4. How do reinforcement learning agents differ from rule-based expert systems in terms of agency?
5. What role do memory and proactivity play in enabling agentic behaviour in AI systems?
6. Compare and contrast AI agents and large language models (LLMs) using at least three differentiators.
7. Explain how multi-agent systems contribute to collaborative agency. Provide an example of a real-world domain where this is applied.
8. Why is the agentic AI framework considered more adaptable than conventional AI? Use the architecture diagram as a reference.
9. Walk through the six-step functional pipeline of an AI agent from user input to task output, as described in the architecture section.
10. In the multi-agent Social Media Manager example, explain the role of each agent. How do they interact to fulfil the overall objective?
11. Imagine you're building an AI agent for legal document summarisation. Outline the first three steps you would follow using the agent development guide.

12. What are the potential risks of agentic AI systems pursuing misaligned objectives? Suggest one way to mitigate this risk.

13. In the provided agent pseudocode, what is the purpose of the learn() method, and how does it support long-term adaptability?

14. List three frameworks or toolkits that support the development of agentic AI systems. What is a unique feature of each?

15. What components would you add to the base agent class to extend its capability to operate in a multimodal environment (e.g., vision, audio)?

Note to Readers and Educators

Comprehensive answers and explanations to these chapter-end questions are available at www.sandeepbhalekar.com. The website also provides supplementary frameworks, teaching guidelines, and reference materials to support deeper understanding and classroom discussion.

Educators and facilitators can access additional resources, including presentation frameworks, assessment rubrics, and discussion prompts, to help integrate the concepts from this chapter into academic or professional learning environments.

Bibliography

Bratman, M. E. (1987). *Intention, Plans, and Practical Reason.* Harvard University Press.

InsilicoMedicine. (2023). *Press Release on AI-Designed Drug for Pulmonary Fibrosis.* Retrieved from https://www.insilico.com

JoaoMoura. (2024). *CrewAI GitHub Repository.* Retrieved from https://github.com/joaomdmoura/crewAI

LangChain. (2024). *LangChain Documentation.* Retrieved from https://docs.langchain.com

MetaGPT. (2024). *MetaGPT GitHub Repository.* Retrieved from https://github.com/geekan/MetaGPT

OpenAI. (2024). *GPT-4 Technical Report.* Retrieved from https://openai.com/research

Russell, S., & Norvig, P. (2021). *Artificial Intelligence: A Modern Approach* (4th ed.). Pearson.

Shinn, N., Mathur, P., & Yao, S. (2023). *Reflexion: Language Agents with Verbal Reinforcement Learning. arXiv preprint* arXiv:2303.11366.

SignificantGravitas. (2023). *AutoGPT GitHub Repository.* Retrieved from https://github.com/Torantulino/Auto-GPT

Wooldridge, M. (2009). *An Introduction to MultiAgent Systems* (2nd ed.). Wiley.

Yao, S., Zhao, J., Kassraie, R., et al. (2023). *ReAct: Synergizing Reasoning and Acting in Language Models. arXiv preprint* arXiv:2210.03629.

Zhavoronkov, A., Ivanenkov, Y. A., Aliper, A., et al. (2020). *Deep learning enables rapid identification of potent DDR1 kinase inhibitors. Nature Biotechnology, 37,* 1038–1040.

16

Innovations on the Horizon

The accelerating advancements in artificial intelligence (AI) and automation are reshaping industries, altering job roles, and redefining career paths at an unprecedented pace. This chapter explores the critical need for adaptability in this transformative landscape, emphasising that long-term career success depends on continuous learning, resilience, and the ability to navigate technological change. Unlike previous industrial revolutions, AI's integration into workplaces affects routine tasks and complex cognitive functions, making it imperative for professionals to cultivate adaptive intelligence.

The chapter begins by analysing the psychology behind resistance to technological change, including fear of obsolescence and comfort with established routines. It highlights the role of a growth mindset and curiosity in fostering a proactive approach to AI-driven transformation. Through real-world case studies, the chapter showcases successful career transitions, illustrating how individuals have embraced AI as an opportunity rather than a threat.

Furthermore, it explores the complementary strengths of humans and AI, emphasising that while machines excel in data processing and automation, humans outperform AI in creativity, contextual awareness, and ethical decision-making. Organisations that foster adaptive cultures through continuous learning, cross-functional collaboration, and strategic change management are best positioned to thrive in this evolving landscape.

Practical strategies for individuals navigating AI-driven career shifts are also presented, offering insights into skill development, AI literacy, and leveraging digital tools for lifelong learning. The ethical considerations of AI adoption, including equity and human agency, are examined to ensure responsible and inclusive technological progress.

Finally, the chapter provides a forward-looking perspective on the future of human adaptability in an AI-driven world. It argues that by embracing change, cultivating adaptive skill sets, and viewing AI as a collaborative partner, professionals and organisations can turn technological disruption into a catalyst for unprecedented growth and innovation.

DOI: 10.1201/9781003626503-16

The Need for Adaptability in the AI Era

This foundational section establishes why adaptability has become non-negotiable in today's technological landscape. AI fundamentally redefines employment patterns across industries, requiring workers to continuously acquire new skills and knowledge throughout their careers. Success now depends less on traditional job security and more on developing resilience through versatile skill sets that can transfer across different roles and sectors as AI evolves.

Understanding Change in the Context of AI

This section provides a perspective on the magnitude of AI-driven transformation. Historical context demonstrates that AI represents a more profound shift than previous technological revolutions, including the internet. The section examines characteristic patterns of technological disruption, emotional responses to change, and the acceleration of adaptation cycles in modern technological environments. A deeper analysis of why humans naturally resist certain types of change while embracing others creates the psychological foundation for developing effective adaptation strategies.

The Psychology of Embracing Technological Change

This section explores the cognitive and emotional dimensions of adapting to AI transformation. It examines how fixed vs. growth mindsets influence the approach to technological change. The psychological barriers that prevent effective adaptation, including fear of obsolescence and comfort with established routines, are analysed alongside techniques for overcoming these limitations. The section concludes with frameworks for developing mental resilience and emotional intelligence tailored to technological disruption.

Adaptive Intelligence: Human Advantages in a Changing World

This critical section highlights uniquely human capabilities that provide advantages even as AI advances. It explores how humans naturally outperform AI in adapting to novel situations and contextual changes. The importance of self-orientation and contextual awareness when navigating uncertainty is emphasised, drawing on research showing how humans excel at quickly orienting themselves in new environments. The complementary nature of human adaptability and AI capabilities creates the foundation for effective human–machine collaboration.

Organisational Approaches to AI-Driven Change

This section shifts focus to organisational strategies for embracing AI transformation. It examines key elements of adaptive organisational cultures where continuous learning and experimentation are encouraged. Leadership approaches specifically designed for technological transformation periods are outlined. Frameworks for implementing change management tailored to AI adoption, including stakeholder engagement strategies and effective communication techniques, are examined. Structural considerations for fostering organisational adaptability, such as cross-functional teams and flattened hierarchies, complete this organisational perspective.

Developing an Adaptive Skill Set

This practical section identifies specific capabilities that enhance adaptability in AI-integrated environments. Technical fluency requirements for the AI era are outlined, emphasising the importance of AI literacy without requiring specialised expertise. Critical thinking and analytical reasoning skills that complement AI capabilities are explored alongside creativity and innovation approaches that leverage AI tools. The section concludes with strategies for developing metacognitive abilities that enable continuous learning and adaptation.

Practical Strategies for Embracing Change

This action-oriented section provides concrete approaches for individuals navigating AI-driven transformation. It offers frameworks for personal change management, including techniques for overcoming resistance and maximising opportunities. Specific continuous learning and skill development methodologies in rapidly evolving fields are presented. Career planning approaches designed for technological uncertainty help readers develop adaptive career strategies. The section concludes with digital tools and resources that support adaptability and lifelong learning.

Case Studies in Successful Adaptation

This evidence-based section presents real-world examples of effective adaptation to technological change. It examines individuals who successfully pivoted careers in response to AI disruption. Organisations that transform their business models and operations to leverage AI capabilities provide institutional perspectives. The section analyses industries undergoing substantial AI-driven transformation, highlighting successful adaptation strategies. Educational institutions implementing new approaches to prepare students for an AI-integrated workforce complete the case study collection.

Ethical Considerations in Embracing AI Change

This nuanced section addresses the complex ethical dimensions of technological adaptation. It explores responsible approaches to embracing AI advances while maintaining human values and well-being. Equity and inclusion in technological adaptation processes are emphasised to ensure that AI benefits are broadly distributed. The section concludes with strategies for maintaining human agency and autonomy while leveraging AI capabilities.

The Future of Human Adaptation in an AI World

This forward-looking section examines emerging trends and their implications for human adaptability. It explores predictions for human–AI collaboration and co-evolution scenarios. Long-term strategies for maintaining relevance and purpose in increasingly automated environments are presented. The section concludes by examining potential paradigm shifts in conceptualising work, learning, and human potential in an AI-integrated world.

Conclusion: Thriving through Adaptation

This synthesising section brings together key principles from the chapter to create an integrated approach to embracing change in the AI era. It revisits core concepts about the nature of change and adaptation while emphasising actionable insights for readers. The section concludes with an inspiring vision of how embracing change can lead to survival and unprecedented growth and fulfilment transformed by AI.

Overcoming Resistance to Change in the AI Era

The acceleration of AI and automation technologies is transforming workplaces and careers at an unprecedented pace. By 2030, it is estimated that one-tenth of Australian workers could see more than 40% of their task hours automated, while two-thirds of workers could see 20%–40% of their task hours automated, potentially resulting in approximately 1.3 million workers required to transition into different lines of work. Despite these dramatic shifts, human resistance to change remains one of the most significant barriers to successful adaptation. This comprehensive exploration examines why people resist technological change and how a growth mindset and curiosity are essential for career adaptation. It also presents illuminating case studies of professionals who transitioned into AI-driven roles.

Understanding the Psychology of Change Resistance

Fear of change is deeply rooted in human psychology, manifesting as a powerful emotion that prevents individuals from embracing adventures, opportunities, and new experiences. This reluctance often stems from uncertainty about the unknown and anxiety about potential negative outcomes. In workplace contexts, fear can be particularly paralysing when confronting technological transformation, as individuals worry about their continued relevance and ability to adapt to new systems and processes. The discomfort associated with leaving established routines creates a powerful inertia that maintains the status quo, even when change would ultimately be beneficial.

Change resistance in professional settings often derives from several distinct psychological foundations. The fear of obsolescence looms large, particularly as AI technologies demonstrate increasing capabilities in domains once considered uniquely human. Additionally, concerns about job security naturally intensify when technologies appear poised to replace human workers. Research indicates that while AI-driven automation is more likely to reorganise jobs rather than eliminate them entirely, the perception of threat remains potent. Many professionals also experience anxiety about their capacity to learn new skills, particularly when transitioning from established expertise to unfamiliar technological domains.

The relationship between fear and failure further complicates change resistance. Traditional organisational cultures often punish failure, conditioning employees to avoid risks and remain within established parameters. This punishment framework directly contradicts the experimentation and learning necessary during periods of technological transformation. When professionals view failure as a reflection of personal inadequacy rather than a natural step in the learning process, they become trapped in avoidance behaviours adaptation. Recognising these underlying psychological mechanisms provides the foundation for effectively addressing resistance.

Cultivating a Growth Mindset for Technological Adaptation

A growth mindset, the belief that intelligence and abilities can be developed through dedication, effort, continuous learning, and perseverance, serves as a powerful antidote to change resistance. This contrasts sharply with a fixed mindset, which views intelligence as static and unchangeable, leading professionals to avoid learning new skills and give up easily when facing obstacles. In the context of AI-driven workplace transformation, a growth mindset enables professionals to approach technological change as an opportunity for development rather than a threat to established competence.

The development of a growth mindset begins with reframing the concepts of failure and challenges. When confronting new technologies or career transitions, individuals with growth mindsets perceive difficulties as valuable learning opportunities rather than evidence of personal limitations. This perspective transforms potential failure from something to be avoided into a natural step in the development process. By embracing challenges and persisting through setbacks, individuals cultivate resilience that enables continued adaptation throughout their careers.

Practical approaches to developing a growth mindset include conscious attention to internal dialogue and thought patterns. When facing technological changes, professionals should notice when fixed mindset thoughts arise ("I'm not good with technology" or "I'm too experienced to start over") and intentionally reframe them as growth-oriented statements ("I haven't learned this yet" or "My experience provides a valuable foundation for new skills"). This cognitive restructuring creates psychological space for learning and development even in intimidating circumstances.

Another effective strategy involves breaking large transformations into smaller, more manageable components. Rather than viewing AI adaptation as a monolithic challenge, identifying specific skill gaps and addressing them incrementally creates momentum and builds confidence. Celebrating small successes reinforces the growth mindset by providing evidence of learning capacity and progress. Additionally, seeking feedback throughout the change process and viewing that feedback as valuable information rather than personal criticism accelerates development and reinforces adaptive patterns.

The Critical Role of Curiosity in Career Success

Intellectual curiosity functions as a foundational element of successful adaptation to technological change. Defined as an appetite for knowledge and learning combined with a desire for personal growth, curiosity naturally leads to the continuous exploration necessary for career evolution. Curious individuals demonstrate greater adaptability because they continuously expand their knowledge horizons, preparing them to navigate uncertainty and adapt to new situations more efficiently.

The relationship between curiosity and career success becomes particularly evident in rapidly evolving technological environments. Change is constant, and adaptability is key to both survival and success. Curious professionals naturally seek to understand emerging technologies, industry transformations, and evolving skill requirements before immediate necessity forces change. This proactive learning creates a buffer against obsolescence and positions the curious professional to capitalise on emerging opportunities rather than merely responding to threats.

Elizabeth's experience as a mid-level manager in a technology firm demonstrates how curiosity can transform leadership effectiveness. Despite scepticism, Elizabeth's coach cultivated her curiosity about her leadership style and team dynamics through open-ended questioning and reflective dialogue. This curiosity-driven approach resulted in measurable improvements, including a 20% increase in employee satisfaction scores within 6 months.

The case illustrates how curiosity creates space for growth, even among experienced professionals who initially resist change.

Curiosity's power derives partly from its neurological effects. When people experience curiosity, their brains release dopamine and activate reward pathways, creating positive associations with learning and exploration. This neurological reinforcement makes continuous learning sustainable rather than exhausting. Furthermore, curiosity broadens perspective, enabling professionals to see connections between seemingly disparate fields and identify creative solutions to emerging challenges. This cognitive flexibility becomes increasingly valuable as AI transforms established processes and creates hybrid human–machine work environments.

Adaptability as a Career Imperative in the AI Age

In the era of AI, adaptability has evolved from a desirable quality into a non-negotiable career requirement. The acceleration of technological change compresses adaptation cycles, requiring professionals to continuously update skills and knowledge throughout their careers. Unlike previous technological revolutions, AI reaches beyond factory floors into office spaces, affecting higher-paid, white-collar workers and transforming knowledge work across sectors. This unprecedented scope of change makes adaptability essential for continued career relevance.

One of the most significant dangers for established professionals is the sense of inertia that develops with career longevity. The longer someone works in a particular role or field, the more susceptible they become to routine and comfort zone limitations, this complacency creates vulnerability as AI capabilities expand, potentially leaving once-successful professionals supplanted by colleagues with fresher ideas and greater technological fluency. Maintaining adaptability requires intentional efforts to resist complacency and continuously refresh professional approaches.

Developing adaptability begins with maintaining awareness of industry evolution and technological trends. Professionals should regularly assess how AI advancements might affect their fields and identify emerging skills that complement changing technological capabilities. Rather than viewing such assessments as threatening, adaptable professionals approach them as intelligence gathering that informs strategic career development. This perspective shift transforms potential threats into navigable pathways.

Adaptability also requires psychological preparation for identity evolution. Many professionals strongly identify with specific roles or expertise areas, making transitions particularly challenging when those identities are threatened. By cultivating broader professional self-concepts based on transferable skills and adaptable capabilities rather than specific positions or technologies, individuals create psychological flexibility that facilitates smoother transitions when change becomes necessary. This expanded self-concept represents a fundamental shift from defining career success through stability to defining it through continuous evolution and growth.

Case Studies of Successful AI Career Transitions

The journey from traditional roles into AI-driven careers provides valuable insights into successful adaptation strategies. One particularly striking example involves a professional who transitioned from human resources (HR) into AI engineering. Despite graduating with a social science degree in psychology and beginning their career in HR, this individual successfully navigated what appeared to be "a complete 180-degree career switch" from a "soft/artsy" domain to a "hard science." Their motivation emerged from frustration with workplace inefficiencies and the gap between digital workplace ideals and analogue realities.

Rather than accepting the status quo, this transitioning professional recognised that enabling digital transformation required gaining relevant skills and knowledge. They systematically pursued courses, training, and projects to build technological capabilities, eventually joining the AI Apprenticeship Programme. Despite inevitable stumbles and failures along the path, their persistence ultimately enabled a successful career transition into AI engineering. This case demonstrates how dissatisfaction with current limitations can fuel motivation for significant career evolution channelled through structured learning and development.

Trang Quynh Phan's journey into data science offers another instructive example of a successful transition. After completing a Master of Artificial Intelligence, Trang leveraged her education to secure a position as a senior data analyst at one of Australia's leading telecommunications companies. Trang emphasised that the program's curriculum, which included deep learning, natural language processing, and computer vision, provided distinctive value compared to other educational options. The program's focus on practical, hands-on experience through laboratory work proved particularly valuable for skills development and career advancement.

Trang noted that her education provided both technical foundations and ethical frameworks necessary for responsible AI implementation. The program equipped her with machine learning, deep learning, and natural language processing capabilities that directly transferred to her professional role. Additionally, exposure to ethical considerations in AI implementation prepared her to navigate the complex societal implications of emerging technologies. Trang's experience illustrates how specialised education can facilitate transitions into AI-driven careers when the curriculum emphasises both technical skills and broader contextual understanding.

The case of Alex, a 45-year-old IT executive with two decades of experience at a leading firm, demonstrates how mid-career professionals can successfully navigate transitions in the AI era. Despite considerable career success, Alex experienced increasing dissatisfaction stemming from values misalignment and questions about meaningful contributions. This "midlife career crisis" prompted deep introspection about professional identity and future direction.

While challenging, this questioning ultimately served as a catalyst for growth and transformation.

Alex's transition involved addressing both emotional and practical challenges. Emotionally, Alex needed to overcome the paralysis of overthinking, guilt about leaving established roles, and fears about irrelevance in new domains. Practically, Alex needed to evaluate new opportunities through a comprehensive decision matrix that considered cultural fit, growth trajectory, work–life harmony, and potential for meaningful impact. By approaching AI as an enabler rather than a replacement for human expertise, Alex successfully transitioned into a role guiding AI implementation and integration within organisations, ensuring alignment with company values and ethical standards.

Practical Strategies for Managing Change Resistance

Effective change management begins with listening and understanding objections. When resistance emerges, the first and most important step involves actively listening to understand underlying concerns rather than dismissing them as irrational opposition. Too often, managers and teams bypass each other in conversation because they aren't genuinely hearing concerns. This process requires empathy, active listening, and an attitude of curiosity rather than defensiveness about resistance.

Another powerful approach involves focusing on outcomes while allowing flexibility in methods. The principle "Don't do the change to me do the change with me" captures this distinction. When leaders clearly articulate what needs to be accomplished while inviting input on how to achieve those goals, they create ownership and investment in change processes. This shared approach has proven particularly effective in organisations transitioning to hybrid work environments, where employee input on implementation significantly improves adaptation.

Identifying and removing barriers represents another crucial strategy. These barriers might be physical (uncomfortable equipment), procedural (unnecessary complexity), or psychological (fear of appearing incompetent). When change managers proactively identify potential obstacles and create pathways around them, they significantly reduce resistance. Additionally, providing simple, clear choices with transparent consequences helps individuals understand available options and make informed decisions about their participation in change initiatives.

Converting the strongest dissenters can be particularly impactful, as vigorous opponents often become the most passionate advocates when their concerns are genuinely addressed. While the natural tendency is to avoid or marginalise vocal dissenters, investing in understanding and addressing their specific objections can transform opposition into support. This approach requires focusing on awareness and desire, clearly articulating benefits for the individual, and recognising that each person moves through adaptation at their own pace.

Conclusion: Embracing Change as Opportunity

The transformation of work through AI represents both an unprecedented challenge and an extraordinary opportunity. While resistance to change remains a natural human response to uncertainty and potential loss, developing a growth mindset, cultivating curiosity, and building adaptability create the psychological foundation for successful navigation of this changing landscape. The case studies of professionals who have successfully transitioned into AI-driven roles demonstrate that significant career evolution is possible at any stage when approached with intentionality and persistence.

Rather than viewing AI as a threat to established careers, professionals can reframe technological transformation as an invitation to develop new capabilities and explore emerging possibilities. By understanding the psychological foundations of change resistance, individuals can recognise and address their own barriers to adaptation. Through specific strategies like reframing failure as learning, breaking changes into manageable components, and focusing on outcomes rather than methods, professionals can systematically build their capacity for continuous evolution.

As the era of AI moves forward, the distinction between those who thrive and those who struggle increasingly depends on the ability to embrace change rather than resist it. By cultivating the mindsets and practices explored in this analysis, professionals can position themselves not merely to survive technological transformation but to harness it as a catalyst for unprecedented growth and career fulfilment. The future belongs not to those who fear change but to those who recognise it as the doorway to their next evolution.

Navigating Career Transitions in the AI Era

In today's rapidly evolving technological landscape, career transitions have become increasingly common and necessary for professional growth and adaptation. The development of AI and automation technologies is transforming workplaces and career trajectories at an unprecedented pace, with estimates suggesting that by 2030, approximately 1 in 16 workers may need to switch occupations. This comprehensive exploration examines the critical components of successful career transitions in the AI era, focusing on identifying and developing future-proof skills, leveraging AI for learning and career advancement, and harnessing the power of mentorship and networking to facilitate smooth career shifts. By understanding these interconnected elements, professionals can strategically position themselves for continued relevance and success in an increasingly automated and digitised workplace.

Identifying and Developing Future-Proof Skills

The concept of "future-proofing" a career has gained significant traction as technological advancement accelerates the transformation of industries across the global economy. Future-proofing requires a deliberate approach to skill development that anticipates emerging trends while establishing a foundation of adaptable capabilities. Building a resilient career necessitates a blend of forward-thinking abilities and adaptable skills that transcend specific tools or technologies. This comprehensive approach includes cultivating a growth mindset, fostering resilience, and embracing lifelong learning to provide the agility needed to thrive in an ever-changing market. The most future-resistant professionals recognise that adaptation is not merely reactive but proactive, requiring continuous assessment of industry evolution and strategic skill development.

Digital literacy has emerged as one of the most critical components of a future-proof skill set. Research conducted by Brookings evaluated 545 occupations and determined that an overwhelming 71% of jobs require medium or high levels of digital skills. More significantly, this analysis revealed that digitisation correlates strongly with increased compensation and enhanced job resiliency, effectively safeguarding against the potential impact of automation. Digital literacy extends far beyond basic familiarity with computers; it encompasses the ability to navigate complex digital technologies and technologies, including specialised equipment, software systems, internet platforms, and mobile devices within professional contexts. However, the rapidly evolving nature of technology means that specific technical skills can quickly become obsolete, making adaptability and continuous learning essential complements to digital competency.

Change agility represents another foundational element of career resilience in the AI era. According to McKinsey research, the COVID-19 pandemic accelerated expected workforce transitions, with potentially 1 in 16 workers needing to switch occupations by 2030. This finding aligns with Gartner's research, which indicates that 56% of candidates report applying for jobs outside their current area of expertise, highlighting the growing importance of transferable skills. Developing capabilities that AI cannot easily replicate, including critical thinking, complex decision-making, and sophisticated analytical abilities, provides enduring career value regardless of industry or role. Organisations increasingly recognise the importance of this adaptability, with forward-thinking companies providing employees opportunities to shift roles and continuously evolve their capabilities to foster both individual and organisational growth. This internal culture of flexibility creates sustainable career development pathways that benefit both employees and employers.

Emotional intelligence and advanced communication skills complement technical capabilities to create a comprehensive future-proof skill set. While technical skills enable professionals to work effectively with emerging technologies, interpersonal capabilities facilitate collaboration, leadership, and relationship management, which arrangement is essential in modern workplaces. The ability to understand and manage emotions, communicate effectively across diverse teams, and adapt to changing social dynamics provides valuable capabilities that current AI technologies cannot replicate. These human-centric skills become increasingly valuable as routine tasks become automated, positioning professionals with strong emotional intelligence for leadership roles where interpersonal effectiveness directly impacts organisational success. Developing this balanced skill portfolio requires intentional effort but creates resilience against technological disruption and opens pathways to continued career advancement.

Leveraging AI for Learning and Career Growth

AI has emerged as a transformative force in career development, offering unprecedented opportunities for personalised learning and professional advancement. AI-powered platforms now provide sophisticated capabilities for identifying personalised growth opportunities that align with individual aspirations and organisational needs. By leveraging sophisticated algorithms and vast data analysis capabilities, AI can tailor career development pathways uniquely suited to individual skills, preferences, and market demands. This personalised guidance enables professionals to identify and pursue opportunities they might not have discovered independently, effectively navigating the complexities of the modern job market. The AI advantage extends beyond simple recommendation systems to comprehensive development frameworks that continuously evolve based on individual progress and changing market conditions.

Personalised learning represents one of the most significant impacts of AI on professional development. Platforms like Coursera and Udemy utilise machine learning algorithms to offer customised course recommendations based on users' interests, previous learning experiences, and emerging job market trends. These systems adapt to individual learning paces and styles, providing resources specifically designed to address personal skill gaps or career aspirations. The resulting learning experience transcends traditional one-size-fits-all approaches to create efficient, engaging professional development. This personalisation accelerates skill acquisition and ensures that learning directly supports career objectives rather than merely accumulating credentials. For professionals navigating career transitions, these targeted learning experiences provide efficient pathways to developing the specific capabilities needed for successful career shifts.

AI enhances career development through sophisticated skills gap analysis and predictive analytics. Advanced AI systems can identify current and emerging skill gaps at both individual and organisational levels based on role requirements and business objectives, enabling targeted and relevant skill-building initiatives. This analytical approach eliminates guesswork from professional development by precisely identifying which capabilities provide the greatest career advantage. Similarly, by analysing performance data, AI algorithms can forecast promotion readiness, flight risk, and other insights that inform strategic career planning. These predictive capabilities help professionals navigate career transitions by identifying optimal timing for moves and highlighting the preparation needed for successful shifts. The data-driven approach provides objective guidance that complements subjective career preferences to create comprehensive development strategies.

The integration of AI into corporate HR systems further enhances career development opportunities. Many organisations now implement AI-powered career coaches that create personalised development plans and match employees to relevant growth opportunities. These systems democratise access to sophisticated career guidance, providing personalised support at a scale that would be impossible through traditional coaching models. Additionally, the rapid integration of AI with HR management systems is optimising talent development, succession planning, and workforce optimisation while helping align individual career goals with organisational needs. This alignment creates win–win scenarios where career transitions fulfil both personal aspirations and organisational requirements. By breaking down geographical and socioeconomic barriers to opportunity, AI career tools are expanding access to advancement pathways and creating more equitable career development ecosystems.

The Role of Mentorship and Networking in Career Shifts

Mentorship provides invaluable support during career transitions by offering guidance, emotional reinforcement, and practical assistance throughout the adaptation process. A strong mentor–mentee relationship accelerates career transitions by offering insights, network introductions, confidence boosts, personalised feedback, goal-setting support, industry trend knowledge, emotional reinforcement, access to hidden job opportunities, enhanced reputation, and long-term professional relationships. This comprehensive support system addresses both the practical and psychological challenges inherent in career shifts. For women in technical fields specifically, finding a mentor proves crucial when considering career pivots by offering accelerated learning, networking opportunities, assistance navigating industry biases, personalised advice, confidence building, enhanced problem-solving skills, emotional support, accountability, help decoding industry jargon, and increased visibility. These benefits directly address the unique challenges that career transitions present, converting potential obstacles into manageable hurdles.

Effective mentorship encompasses multiple dimensions that collectively support successful transitions. Mentors serve as sounding boards for ideas and concerns, helping mentees process the emotional aspects of career changes while providing objective perspectives on decisions and opportunities.

They share relevant experiences that provide roadmaps for navigating unfamiliar territory, helping mentees anticipate challenges and develop effective solutions. Regular check-ins and accountability structures help maintain momentum during transitions, ensuring continual progress towards established goals. Perhaps most importantly, mentors help transitioning professionals overcome fears and uncertainties associated with new career roles while developing the skills and networks necessary for success. This emotional support proves particularly valuable during periods when self-confidence naturally wavers, with research indicating that approximately 36% of professionals report decreased confidence during career transitions.

Global Institute of Artificial Intelligence (GIofAI) is at the forefront of providing structured mentorship programs designed to support professionals navigating career shifts into AI and Data Engineering fields. GIofAI's mentorship programs connect learners with seasoned industry experts who offer hands-on guidance, strategic career insights, and networking opportunities. Unlike conventional learning models, GIofAI's approach blends mentorship with real-world applications, ensuring that transitioning professionals gain both technical expertise and career direction. Through one-on-one coaching, group mentorship sessions, and exclusive networking opportunities, GIofAI empowers professionals to build confidence, refine their skills, and position themselves for success in the AI-driven job market.

Professional networking complements mentorship by providing broader access to opportunities, information, and support during career transitions. Research indicates that approximately 85% of all jobs are filled through networking, highlighting the undeniable power of professional connections in career advancement. This statistic underscores the critical importance of building and leveraging a strong network, particularly for emerging leaders facing the unique challenges of career transitions. Networking provides access to invaluable career guidance, insights, and opportunities that might otherwise remain inaccessible, creating pathways to new roles and industries. Furthermore, a strong network opens doors to collaborative environments and supportive communities that prove crucial when facing the uncertainties inherent in career shifts. Whether connecting with a former colleague who introduces a hiring manager or accessing a mentor who offers strategic advice on navigating new responsibilities, these interactions significantly enhance transition success.

The strategic expansion of professional networks directly supports career transition success through multiple mechanisms. Diverse connections provide differing perspectives that help professionals make informed decisions about potential career paths. These varied viewpoints offer insights into industry-specific challenges and opportunities that might not be apparent from outside observation. Additionally, networking facilitates informational interviews that provide firsthand knowledge about specific roles, organisational cultures, and industry trends—information critical for determining whether potential career moves align with personal goals and values.

Networks also create access to hidden job opportunities, with introductions to key stakeholders amplifying visibility and opening doors to possibilities that align with professional aspirations. Awareness of this expanded opportunity proves particularly valuable during career transitions, when traditional job search methods may yield limited results in unfamiliar industries or roles.

Through a combination of structured mentorship and strategic networking, professionals can navigate career transitions with greater confidence, clarity, and success. GIofAI continues to bridge the gap between learning and career progression, equipping individuals with the necessary resources and industry connections to thrive in AI and Data Engineering fields. Whether transitioning from a different technical background or stepping into AI for the first time, mentorship and networking remain essential pillars for career growth and professional success.

Embracing Technological Change through Comprehensive Transition Strategies

The successful navigation of career transitions in the AI era requires an integrated approach that combines future-proof skill development, strategic use of AI-powered learning tools, and the cultivation of strong mentorship and networking relationships. Each element reinforces the others, creating a comprehensive framework for professional evolution that addresses both the practical and psychological dimensions of career shifts. Digital literacy and change agility provide the foundational capabilities that enable adaptation to technological transformation. AI-powered learning platforms deliver personalised development experiences that accelerate skill acquisition and career advancement. Mentorship and networking relationships offer guidance, support, and opportunities that smooth transition pathways and expand possible futures.

This multifaceted approach to career transitions reflects the complexity of the modern professional landscape. As AI and automation continue transforming workplaces across industries, the ability to navigate career shifts becomes an essential meta-skill that determines long-term success. Professionals who proactively develop future-proof capabilities, leverage AI tools for continuous learning, and cultivate supportive relationships position themselves for sustainable growth regardless of technological developments. Rather than fearing technological change, these individuals embrace it as a catalyst for career evolution and expanded opportunity. By developing comprehensive transition strategies, they transform potential disruption into pathways for unprecedented professional growth and fulfilment.

The future of work demands professionals who continuously reinvent themselves while maintaining core values and purpose. This transformation requires releasing attachment to specific roles or technologies in favour of identity anchored in adaptable capabilities and contribution orientation.

By focusing on developing transferable skills with enduring value, strategically using technology to accelerate learning and growth, and cultivating relationships that provide support and opportunity access, individuals create career resilience that transcends specific industries or functions. This approach converts the challenge of career transitions into opportunities for meaningful growth and expanded impact. As technological change accelerates, this adaptive capacity becomes the ultimate competitive advantage—ensuring continued relevance and contribution in an increasingly automated world.

The Future of Work and Human–AI Collaboration

In today's rapidly evolving technological landscape, the relationship between AI and human workers is transforming fundamental aspects of professional life across industries. Far from the dystopian narratives of wholesale job displacement, emerging evidence suggests a more nuanced future where human capabilities are extended and enhanced through thoughtful AI integration. This comprehensive exploration examines how AI functions primarily as an augmentation tool rather than a replacement for human workers, investigates the emergence of effective human–AI collaboration in creative and analytical domains, and provides strategic guidance for building careers that align with and capitalise on technological transformation. Understanding these dynamics proves essential for professionals navigating career pathways in an increasingly AI-integrated workplace, where adaptation and strategic skill development determine long-term success and fulfilment.

AI as a Tool for Augmentation, Not Replacement

The narrative surrounding AI has often centred on anxieties about job displacement and human obsolescence. However, emerging research and real-world implementation reveal a different reality—one where AI augments human capabilities rather than simply replacing them. According to research by Thomas Davenport and Steven Miller, AI primarily augments the work that humans do, not fully automating it. This perspective shifts our understanding from competition to collaboration, recognising distinct and complementary strengths that humans and machines bring to professional contexts. Miller specifically emphasises that the most effective applications of AI go beyond rudimentary task automation, instead focusing on situations where human–machine collaboration achieves intelligence levels greater than either could accomplish independently. This symbiotic relationship creates scenarios where "the whole should be greater than the sum of its parts," establishing a framework for augmentation rather than replacement.

The most successful applications of AI augmentation occur in specific contexts where technological capabilities complement human needs. Companies benefit from AI integration when they want to experiment with new approaches, such as pharmaceutical manufacturers using AI infrastructure to rapidly evaluate potential use cases for new drugs. Similarly, AI proves valuable when addressing "pencil-pushing" tasks that employees find tedious, freeing human workers for more creative and fulfilling responsibilities. In environments where rapid response is essential, such as cybersecurity, AI can highlight potential threats in real time while experienced analysts distinguish between isolated incidents and coordinated attacks. These examples demonstrate how AI functions most effectively as a support system that enhances human capabilities rather than rendering them obsolete.

The integration of AI into workplaces represents an evolution in how work is performed rather than an elimination of human contribution. *Harvard Business Review* reinforces this perspective, noting that both people and AI bring different abilities and strengths to professional settings, creating complementary rather than competitive dynamics. This collaborative approach manifests across industries, from healthcare diagnostics to financial analysis, where AI handles data processing while humans provide contextual understanding, creativity, and ethical judgement. The concept of "collaborative intelligence" specifically utilises the unique strengths of both humans and AI to create synergy that enhances decision-making, problem-solving, and innovation across sectors. Rather than replacing human intelligence, AI systems complement it by managing aspects of work where computational power provides advantages while leaving distinctly human capabilities centrally positioned within evolving work processes.

Successful implementation of AI augmentation requires thoughtful engagement with employees and careful consideration of implementation approaches. Enterprises can expect to create new types of products, services, and work when effectively integrating AI, but this potential comes with important caveats. Workers must develop appropriate skills to effectively utilise AI systems, requiring investments in training and professional development. Equally important, employees need to perceive AI as helpful rather than threatening, necessitating transparent communication about how technology enhances rather than replaces their contributions. These considerations highlight that AI augmentation requires more than technical implementation—it demands attention to human factors, organisational culture, and change management approaches that address both practical and psychological dimensions of technological integration.

The Rise of Human–AI Teams in Creative and Analytical Fields

The collaboration between humans and AI is evolving in fascinating and sometimes unexpected ways across different domains. Recent research from the MIT Centre for Collective Intelligence has produced surprising insights regarding the effectiveness of human–AI teams across various types of tasks. Their large-scale meta-analysis, published in *Nature Human Behaviour*, revealed that human–AI combinations excel in creative tasks like text and image generation but often underperform in decision-making contexts where AI alone demonstrated superior capabilities. This nuanced understanding challenges simplistic assumptions about collaboration benefits, suggesting that the value of human–AI teams varies significantly depending on task characteristics and implementation approaches. These findings provide crucial guidance for organisations seeking to strategically leverage AI capabilities in ways that genuinely enhance rather than hinder performance.

The integration of AI into creative fields demonstrates promising results when thoughtfully implemented. Human–AI interaction in professional creative settings requires structured approaches to maximise benefits and address potential hesitations. Despite AI's potential to enhance human design teams, adoption often faces resistance stemming from misunderstandings and displacement concerns. Effective integration begins with education about AI capabilities and potential workflow impacts, followed by training sessions that develop skills and confidence. This gradual adoption process—starting with individual engagement before progressing to team-wide implementation—highlights AI's function as an enhancement to human ingenuity rather than a replacement. These structured approaches recognise that creative collaboration between humans and AI requires intentional cultivation and careful attention to both technological and psychological dimensions.

Real-world applications of human–AI collaboration demonstrate significant impacts across diverse industries. In healthcare, AI-assisted diagnostics transform professional approaches to patient care by providing data-driven insights that improve diagnostic accuracy and treatment personalisation. This collaboration allows medical professionals to focus on patient care while AI manages complex data analysis tasks. Similarly, in financial services, automated trading systems guided by human oversight combine AI's computational capabilities with human judgement and contextual understanding. These implementations illustrate how effective human–AI teams leverage complementary strengths—machines handling data processing and pattern recognition while humans provide contextual interpretation, ethical consideration, and creative insight. The resulting synergy creates outcomes superior to what either humans or AI could achieve independently.

The workplace evolution driven by AI integration creates both challenges and opportunities for modern organisations. As AI systems become more advanced, they are reshaping job roles and creating new opportunities for innovation while simultaneously introducing novel challenges requiring thoughtful solutions. Today's AI can manage complex tasks previously requiring human expertise, appearing across offices, factories, hospitals, and numerous other professional settings. As routine work shifts to automated systems, humans increasingly focus on higher-level thinking and creativity that remains distinctly human. This redistribution of labour makes many jobs more efficient while simultaneously prompting fundamental reconsideration of work's nature and purpose. Understanding this transformation helps organisations develop implementation strategies that maximise benefits while mitigating potential disruptions, creating sustainable approaches to human–AI collaboration.

Building a Career That Aligns with Technological Change

Navigating career transitions in the digital age requires a multifaceted approach that combines adaptability, continuous learning, and strategic networking. According to research, successful career transitions in technology-driven environments depend on blending traditional soft skills like communication and collaboration with technological competencies. This integrated approach reflects the evolving nature of professional requirements, where technical capabilities alone prove insufficient without the interpersonal skills needed for effective collaboration and leadership. The World Economic Forum reinforces this perspective, predicting that 54% of employees will require significant reskilling and upskilling to remain competitive in rapidly evolving job markets. This statistic highlights the critical importance of embracing lifelong learning and remaining open to acquiring new skills throughout one's career, creating resilience against technological disruption while positioning professionals to capitalise on emerging opportunities.

The tech industry's accelerating evolution creates both challenges and opportunities for career development. As technological change accelerates, aligning one's career with industry growth trends becomes increasingly essential for long-term success. Emerging fields like Generative AI are creating demand for specialised roles, including AI specialists, machine learning engineers, and AI ethicists, as companies seek professionals who can develop, manage, and regulate AI tools effectively and ethically. Similarly, the strategic application of AI across sectors—from healthcare to finance to retail—increases requirements for data scientists, product managers, AI engineers, and AI architects who can leverage these technologies to improve decision-making, operational efficiency, and customer experience. These evolving demands create pathways for career advancement for professionals who proactively develop relevant capabilities and position themselves at the intersection of established domains and emerging technologies.

The distinction between technical skills and adaptable mindsets becomes increasingly important for career resilience in technology-driven environments. While specific technical capabilities provide immediate value, their rapidly evolving nature means they can quickly become obsolete without continuous updating and expansion. Consequently, developing adaptability and learning orientation creates more sustainable foundations for long-term career success than mastering any particular technology or programming language. This perspective aligns with research indicating that 76% of professionals believe career success now depends on a combination of soft skills like communication and collaboration alongside technical capabilities. This balanced approach recognises that technological change requires not only updated technical knowledge but also interpersonal and adaptive capabilities that facilitate continuous learning and effective collaboration in rapidly evolving professional environments.

Strategic approaches to career development in AI-integrated workplaces begin with understanding how technologies complement rather than replace human contributions. By identifying domains where human capabilities like creativity, ethical judgement, and emotional intelligence naturally complement AI strengths like data processing and pattern recognition, professionals can position themselves for sustainable success regardless of technological advancement. This alignment strategy focuses on developing capabilities that AI cannot easily replicate while simultaneously building sufficient technical literacy to collaborate with AI systems effectively. Career pathways that integrate these complementary capabilities such as AI-assisted healthcare diagnostics augmented creative work, or ethical oversight of algorithmic systems create sustainable professional trajectories that leverage rather than resist technological transformation. This approach transforms potential threats into opportunities, positioning technological change as a catalyst for career growth rather than a source of displacement.

Conclusion: Embracing AI as a Collaborative Partner

The future of work in AI-integrated environments depends on recognising and leveraging the complementary strengths of human and AI. Rather than viewing AI as a replacement for human workers, evidence increasingly supports understanding these technologies as augmentation tools that enhance human capabilities and create new possibilities for innovation and productivity. This perspective shifts focus from competition to collaboration, highlighting how thoughtfully designed human–AI teams can achieve outcomes superior to what either humans or machines could accomplish independently. By understanding the specific contexts where human–AI collaboration proves most effective, particularly in creative domains and complex problem-solving scenarios requiring both analytical processing and contextual understanding, organisations can develop implementation strategies that maximise benefits while mitigating potential challenges.

Building careers aligned with technological change requires multifaceted approaches combining technical fluency, interpersonal capabilities, and adaptable mindsets. As AI continues reshaping professional landscapes across industries, success increasingly depends on developing capabilities that complement rather than compete with technological strengths. This complementary perspective encourages focusing on distinctly human capabilities while simultaneously developing sufficient technical understanding to effectively collaborate with AI systems. By embracing continuous learning, cultivating adaptability, and strategically networking within evolving professional communities, individuals can navigate career transitions successfully while positioning themselves for sustainable growth in increasingly AI-integrated workplaces. This approach transforms technological change from a potential threat into a catalyst for unprecedented professional development and career expansion.

The most successful professionals in AI-integrated environments will be those who view AI not as a competitor but as a collaborative partner that enhances their capabilities and expands their impact. By understanding the distinct strengths that humans and machines bring to professional contexts, organisations and individuals can develop approaches that leverage these complementary capabilities to create superior outcomes across diverse domains. This collaborative vision provides the foundation for a future where technological advancement enhances rather than diminishes human contribution, creating workplaces where innovation, productivity, and fulfilment flourish through thoughtful integration of human and AI. The future of work lies not in human obsolescence but in an unprecedented collaboration between humanity and the intelligent tools we create, unlocking the potential that neither could achieve independently.

Conclusion: Thriving in a Changing World

As the world stands at the edge of extraordinary technological transformation, the relationship with change and uncertainty becomes the defining factor in determining success and fulfilment in the AI-powered future. This book has explored the multifaceted nature of AI and its profound implications for individuals, organisations, and society at large. This concluding chapter synthesises these insights to present a comprehensive framework for not merely surviving but genuinely thriving amid continuous technological evolution. By reframing the human perception of change from threat to opportunity, embracing uncertainty as a catalyst for growth, and strategically preparing for an AI-integrated future, people are positioned to harness the transformative potential of AI while preserving and enhancing the distinctly human contributions.

Change Is an Opportunity, Not a Threat

The response to change is fundamentally shaped by the perception of the change and determines whether it is approached with resistance or enthusiasm. Change can be viewed simultaneously as both opportunity and threat—offering the potential for growth, innovation, and positive transformation while simultaneously evoking uncertainty and disruption that may trigger resistance. Mindset largely determines which aspect dominates the experience, with profound implications for the ability to adapt and thrive. Those who view change as an opportunity tend to approach it with curiosity, openness, and adaptability, while those perceiving it as primarily threatening often respond with hesitation and resistance that inhibits growth. This distinction becomes increasingly significant as AI accelerates the pace and scope of workplace and societal transformation.

Resistance to change stems from deeply rooted psychological foundations that must be acknowledged before they can be addressed. People naturally resist change for various reasons, including fear of the unknown, concerns about competence in new environments, and anxiety about potential negative impacts on their lives and livelihoods. These responses represent natural human reactions to situations that disrupt established patterns and comfort zones. Organisations and leaders must recognise that each individual experiences and processes change differently, necessitating personalised approaches to change management that address both rational and emotional dimensions of transformation. By understanding the unique human elements of change resistance, more effective strategies are developed to facilitate adaptation while minimising unnecessary distress.

Communicating change effectively represents a critical factor in determining whether people perceive it as an opportunity or a threat. The challenge extends beyond merely telling people that transformation presents opportunities—leaders must convince stakeholders that this is genuinely the case through clear, transparent, and inclusive communication. Effective communication strategies include reframing potential threats by providing comprehensive factual information about the transformation while emphasising personalised positive reasons for change that resonate with specific stakeholder groups. This approach respects the emotional complexity of change while providing rational frameworks that facilitate adaptation. By creating opportunities for multidirectional conversations and feedback across organisational levels, leaders can surface employee concerns while fostering understanding and ownership of change processes.

Transforming the relationship with change requires developing specific mindsets and capabilities that facilitate adaptation. Organisations can foster environments where change is viewed as an inevitable aspect of growth rather than a disruption to be resisted or feared. This perspective shift enables individuals to leave their comfort zones and explore uncharted territories, ultimately leading to positive outcomes and progress. Research increasingly demonstrates that organisations embracing change as opportunities experience higher innovation rates, greater employee satisfaction, and improved competitive positioning compared to those maintaining defensive postures towards transformation. By cultivating organisational cultures where continuous learning and experimentation are encouraged, leaders create contexts where change becomes a pathway to growth rather than a source of anxiety.

Embracing Uncertainty as a Pathway to Growth

Uncertainty represents an inevitable companion to change, particularly in our accelerated technological landscape, where AI capabilities continue expanding into previously unimagined domains. In the modern world, individuals and organisations face constant exposure to headlines and developments that generate uncertainty about the future—whether related to politics, economic stability, climate change, or technological transformation. This omnipresent ambiguity can trigger discomfort and anxiety that inhibit exploration and adaptation if not properly managed. Learning to navigate uncertainty with confidence and resilience transforms what might otherwise function as paralysis-inducing anxiety into a catalyst for growth and innovation.

The willingness to embrace uncertainty requires acknowledging fundamental limitations in our control while recognising new possibilities that emerge when attachments to familiar patterns are released. Human beings naturally seek stability and control over their environments, yet this pursuit becomes increasingly unrealistic in today's unpredictable and rapidly evolving world. Relinquishing the illusory security of the known creates space for new opportunities, capability development, confidence building, and expanded influence. Success in the AI era depends upon a willingness to embrace the unknown and become comfortable with the inherent discomfort of taking calculated risks. This psychological flexibility represents a foundational capability for thriving amid technological transformation.

Indecision often functions as a primary barrier to growth when facing uncertainty, with many individuals becoming trapped in analysis paralysis due to fears of making wrong choices. As Wojtek explains in his exploration of uncertainty, many people remain stuck due to indecision stemming from fear of failure associated with a lack of knowledge and experience. However, this paralysis creates a self-reinforcing cycle where avoidance of risk leads to continued knowledge deficits, perpetuating the very uncertainty that triggered initial hesitation. Growth emerges specifically from engaging with the unknown through calculated risk-taking and exposure to diverse experiences and perspectives. By recognising how prolonged indecision leads to stagnation and missed opportunities, individuals can begin taking incremental steps towards change that build confidence and capability.

Embracing uncertainty requires developing specific mindsets and practices that transform ambiguity from threat to opportunity. Successful navigation of uncertainty begins with accepting that perfect solutions rarely exist for complex challenges, especially those involving technological transformation. Rather than seeking illusory "right" answers, effective leaders recognise that multiple viable pathways exist, with success depending more on commitment and alignment than on a selection of objectively superior options. This recognition liberates decision-making from perfectionism while fostering collaborative approaches that engage diverse perspectives.

Additionally, viewing organisational structures and strategies as evolutionary rather than static enables continuous adaptation as circumstances change. This growth mindset—acknowledging limitations while actively seeking expertise and wisdom beyond one's current knowledge—creates sustainable foundations for thriving amid continuous change.

Final Thoughts on Preparing for the AI-Powered Future

AI represents a transformative force reshaping workplaces and industries at an unprecedented pace and scale. By 2023, global spending on AI was projected to reach $97.9 billion, reflecting widespread adoption across sectors seeking improved operations, competitive advantage, and new opportunities. This acceleration creates both challenges and possibilities that require thoughtful navigation. The future of AI suggests continued advancement in capabilities, including sophisticated natural language processing, predictive analytics, automated market analysis, enhanced collaboration tools, interactive documents, and evolving ethical frameworks. Understanding these trajectories helps individuals and organisations develop strategic approaches to AI integration that maximise benefits while mitigating potential disruption.

The relationship between humans and AI continues evolving towards collaborative models rather than competitive frameworks. AI technologies increasingly function as augmentation tools enhancing human capabilities rather than simply replacing human workers in established roles. This collaborative potential manifests across domains, including automation, personalised services, healthcare advancement, and transportation transformation. As AI capabilities expand, the most successful implementations will likely emerge from thoughtful integration that leverages complementary strengths of human and AI. This perspective shifts focus from potential replacement anxieties towards strategic consideration of how AI tools can enhance human productivity, creativity, and decision-making while managing routine tasks that consume valuable cognitive resources.

Preparing for an AI-powered future requires developing adaptable skill Sets and mindsets that maintain relevance regardless of specific technological implementations. Focusing exclusively on mastering particular systems or languages creates vulnerability as those specific implementations evolve or become obsolete during technological transformation. Instead, developing meta-skills, including critical thinking, creative problem-solving, emotional intelligence, and collaborative capabilities, creates enduring foundations for success across changing technological landscapes. Additionally, maintaining continuous learning orientations ensures the ongoing acquisition of emerging skills and knowledge required for effective adaptation. This balanced approach recognises that technological change requires both updated technical capabilities and interpersonal, adaptive competencies that facilitate continuous learning and effective collaboration.

The ethical dimensions of technological transformation demand particular attention as AI capabilities continue expanding into increasingly complex domains. As AI becomes more integrated into organisational operations and decision processes, ethical considerations grow increasingly important and may drive regulatory developments designed to ensure responsible implementation. Preparing for an AI-powered future requires developing frameworks to ensure that technology serves human values and well-being while distributing benefits equitably across populations. This ethical orientation complements technical understanding to create comprehensive approaches to technological integration that maximise positive impacts while minimising potential harms. By maintaining focus on human agency and autonomy while leveraging AI capabilities, organisations and individuals can ensure that technological transformation enhances rather than diminishes human potential and flourishing.

Embracing the Future with Confidence

The intersection of AI and human potential creates unprecedented opportunities for those prepared to embrace change and uncertainty as pathways to growth. Reframing the perception of technological transformation from threat to opportunity creates psychological space for exploration and adaptation that enables the discovery of new possibilities. This perspective shift represents not merely a coping mechanism but a strategic advantage in rapidly evolving environments where adaptability increasingly determines success. The ability to view change through opportunity lenses enables proactive engagement with technological evolution rather than reactive responses driven by fear or resistance.

Uncertainty, while naturally uncomfortable, functions as the territory where genuine growth and innovation emerge. By developing comfort with ambiguity and building capabilities for confident navigation of unknown domains, individuals and organisations position themselves at the frontier of possibility rather than the periphery of transformation. This capacity for thriving amid uncertainty becomes increasingly valuable as technological change accelerates, creating competitive advantage through adaptability rather than specific technical knowledge that may quickly become obsolete. The psychological flexibility to embrace uncertainty transforms potential paralysis into momentum that drives continuous evolution and discovery.

An AI-powered future lies in developing distinctly human contributions that complement AI rather than humans competing with technological capabilities. By focusing on capabilities that AI cannot easily replicate, including emotional intelligence, ethical judgement, creative innovation, and complex problem-solving, enduring value is created regardless of technological advancement.

This complementary approach transforms potential anxiety about replacement into confidence about enhanced contribution and impact. The future belongs not to those who fear technological change but to those who embrace it as a catalyst for unprecedented human development and possibility, creating pathways to growth, fulfilment, and societal advancement previously unimaginable.

The journey into an AI-integrated future has already begun, and each individual determines if the transformation is a threat or an opportunity. By choosing to view change as a possibility, embracing uncertainty as a growth catalyst, and preparing strategically for technological evolution, one positions to not merely to survive but to genuinely thrive in the changing world that AI continues creating. This perspective transforms our relationship with technological advancement from anxiety to anticipation, revealing horizons of possibility that transcend current limitations and open pathways to unprecedented human flourishing. The choice we face is not whether a change will come but how we will engage with it—as reluctant participants or enthusiastic explorers of emerging landscapes filled with opportunities for those prepared to discover them.

Chapter Questions

1. Why is adaptability described as a non-negotiable skill in the AI era, and how does it differ from traditional job security models?

2. How do growth mindsets and curiosity help individuals overcome psychological resistance to technological change?

3. What are some common emotional responses to AI-driven workplace changes, and how can organisations address them effectively?

4. In what ways do humans outperform AI, according to the chapter, and why are these traits crucial in AI-integrated environments?

5. How can organisations create cultures that support adaptive intelligence and continuous learning?

6. What specific skill sets are considered "adaptive" in the context of AI transformation, and how can individuals begin cultivating them?

7. Discuss how self-awareness and contextual thinking give humans an edge in uncertain or rapidly changing environments.

8. Why is developing metacognitive abilities important for professionals navigating evolving technological landscapes?

9. Describe one real-world case study from the chapter that illustrates a successful career transition into AI. What were the key factors that enabled this shift?

10. What ethical concerns are raised in the chapter regarding AI integration, and how can they be addressed to ensure inclusive progress?

11. How can mentorship and networking enhance the success of career transitions in an AI-integrated world?

12. What practical strategies are recommended in the chapter to overcome individual resistance to change in the workplace?

13. How does the chapter redefine the concept of a "future-proof" career, and what implications does this have for long-term career planning?

14. In what ways does the chapter suggest we rethink our identity and purpose in light of technological disruption?

15. Summarise the chapter's vision for the future of human–AI collaboration. How does it frame AI as a tool for augmentation rather than replacement?

Note to Readers and Educators

Comprehensive answers and explanations to these chapter-end questions are available at www.sandeepbhalekar.com. The website also provides supplementary frameworks, teaching guidelines, and reference materials to support deeper understanding and classroom discussion.

Educators and facilitators can access additional resources, including presentation frameworks, assessment rubrics, and discussion prompts, to help integrate the concepts from this chapter into academic or professional learning environments.

Bibliography

AI Singapore. *Career Leap into AI.* https://ai4sme.aisingapore.org/2020/07/my-not-so-insane-career-leap-chasing-ai-dreams-from-my-hr-job/

Ambition Australia. *The Importance of a Mentor for Your Career.* https://www.ambition.com.au/blog/2024/10/the-importance-of-a-mentor-for-your-career

AustCorp Executive. *Navigating Career Transitions through Upskilling and Networking.* https://www.austcorpexecutive.com.au/blog/2025/01/navigating-career-transitions-upskilling-networking

Australian Institute of Management. *Why Career Adaptability Is Vital for Success.* https://www.aim.com.au/blog/adapt-or-die-why-career-adaptability-vital-your-success

Australian Parliament. *Adopting AI—Report Chapter 1.* https://www.aph.gov.au/Parliamentary_Business/Committees/Senate/Adopting_Artificial_Intelligence_AI/AdoptingAI/Report/Chapter_1_-_Introduction_and_background

Beauty Brain UK. *Embracing Change*. https://www.beautybrainuk.com/blogs/blog/embracing-change-a-new-chapter-begins-with-every-move

Bid Vantage. *The Future of AI and Final Conclusions*. https://www.bidvantage.co.uk/blog/the-future-of-ai-and-conclusions

Bravo Careers. *The Impact of Gen AI on Aussie Jobs by 2030*. https://bravocareers.com/blog/the-impact-of-gen-ai-on-aussie-jobs-by-2030

Brookings Institution. *How Artificial Intelligence Is Transforming the World*. https://www.brookings.edu/articles/how-artificial-intelligence-is-transforming-the-world/

Built In. *Artificial Intelligence: The Future Explained*. https://builtin.com/artificial-intelligence/artificial-intelligence-future

College & Research Libraries. *AI and Career Adaptability*. https://crl.acrl.org/index.php/crl/article/view/26104/34026

Course Hero. *Teaching to Transgress Chapter 3 Summary*. https://www.coursehero.com/lit/Teaching-to-Transgress/chapter-3-summary/

Crestcom. *Building a Growth Mindset with Dominic George*. https://crestcom.com/blog/2024/03/29/how-to-overcome-fears-to-build-a-growth-mindset-with-dominic-george/

Dale Carnegie. *Why AI Will Not Replace Humans*. https://www.dalecarnegie.com/blog/why-ai-will-not-replace-humans-2/

Destination Dream Job. *Designing Your Next Chapter*. https://www.destinationdream-job.com/blog/embracing-change-and-designing-your-next-chapter

Digital Technologies Hub. *Artificial Intelligence Resources*. https://www.digitaltechno-logieshub.edu.au/teach-and-assess/classroom-resources/topics/artificial-intelligence/

Digital Transformation Skills. *AI for Business*.

Disco. *AI Tools for Career Development Programs*. https://www.disco.co/blog/ai-tools-for-career-development-programs

Dr Jodie. *How to Embrace Change and Uncertainty*. https://drjodie.com.au/how-to-embrace-change-and-uncertainty/

EasyHSC. *Overcoming Resistance to Change*. https://easyhsc.com.au/home-easyhsc/easybiz-hsc-business-studies/operations/operations-strategies/overcoming-resistance-to-change/

EDC. *Futureproof Skills*. https://futureproofskills.edc.org

EGN Peer Network. *Navigating Career Transitions with Support from a Network*. https://www.egnpeernetwork.com/insights/navigating-career-transitions-with-support-from-a-professional-network

Expert360. *How AI Is Going to Change the Way We Work*. https://expert360.com/articles/how-is-ai-going-to-change-the-way-we-work

EY. *AI Career Case Studies*. https://www.ey.com/en_gl/services/ai/case-studies

Fay Evans. *Embracing Change*.

Forbes. *Navigating Uncertainty: See Change as Opportunity*. https://www.forbes.com/sites/glennllopis/2022/11/16/the-secret-to-navigate-uncertainty-see-change-as-opportunity-not-a-threat/

Forbes Coaches Council. *Curiosity for Success*. https://www.forbes.com/councils/forbescoachescouncil/2024/04/30/curiosity-the-superpower-for-success-in-the-workplace-and-at-home/

Forbes Coaches Council. *16 Important Skills to Build Future-Proof Careers*. https://www.forbes.com/councils/forbescoachescouncil/2024/03/19/16-important-skills-professionals-need-to-build-future-proof-careers/

Frontiers in AI. *Human-AI Collaboration: Frontiers in Artificial Intelligence*. https://www.frontiersin.org/journals/artificial-intelligence/articles/10.3389/frai.2023.1252897/full

Futuramo. *Future-Proofing Your Career: 6 Skills for the Digital Age*. https://futuramo.com/blog/future-proofing-your-career-6-skills-for-the-digital-age/

Futures Platform. *Future of Work: AI in the Workplace Scenarios*. https://www.futures-platform.com/blog/future-of-work-ai-in-the-workplace-scenarios

Goodman, E. *Playing with Fear—Growth Mindset*. https://www.linkedin.com/pulse/playing-fear-how-changing-your-mindset-can-change-eric-goodman-ph-d-

Griffith University. *AI Prompts for Career Development*. https://www.griffith.edu.au/careers-employment/students-graduates/ai-prompts-for-career-development

Hamid, H. *Navigating Career Pathways with Technology*. https://www.linkedin.com/pulse/navigating-career-pathways-technology-huma-hamid

Harvard Business Review. *AI Should Augment Human Intelligence, Not Replace It*. https://hbr.org/2021/03/ai-should-augment-human-intelligence-not-replace-it

Harvard Business Review. *How to Deal with Resistance to Change*. https://hbr.org/1969/01/how-to-deal-with-resistance-to-change

Harvard EdPortal. *Moving from Fear to Growth Mindset*. https://edportal.harvard.edu/event/moving-fear-growth-mindset

Harvard Library. *How Humans Outshine AI in Adapting to Change*. https://www.library.hbs.edu/working-knowledge/how-humans-outshine-ai-in-adapting-to-change

HR Brain.ai. *Career Development Tools Integrating AI*. https://hrbrain.ai/blog/career-development-tools-integrating-ai/

IBM Think. *Artificial Intelligence and the Future*. https://www.ibm.com/think/insights/artificial-intelligence-future

IGI Global. *AI Strategies for Enhancing Resilience and Adaptability*. https://www.igi-global.com/chapter/ai-strategies-for-enhancing-resilience-and-adaptability-in-social-enterprises-for-economic-sustainability/366883

Inspired Together Teachers. *Embracing Change*. https://inspiredtogetherteachers.com/embracing-change-ep-55/

Institute of Data. *Data Science and AI Career Transition*. https://www.institutedata.com/blog/data-science-and-ai-the-ultimate-career-transition-for-professionals-in-their-30s-and-40s/

IntelliVen. *Embracing Uncertainty: A Leader's Path to Growth*. https://intelliven.com/embracing-uncertainty-a-leaders-path-to-growth-and-adaptability/

Join The Collective. *Techniques for Addressing Pushback*. https://www.jointhecollective.com/article/navigating-resistance--10-techniques-for-addressing-pushback-to-change/

Kogan Page. *How to Communicate Change as an Opportunity*. https://www.koganpage.com/hr-learning-development/how-to-communicate-change-as-an-opportunity-not-a-threat

Korn Ferry. *Future-Proof Your Organization with Workforce Skills*. https://www.kornferry.com/insights/featured-topics/future-of-work/future-proof-your-organization-with-the-workforce-skills-needed

Kotin, W. *Future of Work: AI and Human Collaboration*. https://www.linkedin.com/pulse/future-work-ai-human-collaboration-winifred-kotin-mg5ge

La Trobe University. *Driving Success in AI*. https://www.latrobe.edu.au/international/student-life/stories/articles/driving-success-in-ai

LinkedIn. *Growth Mindset and Fear.* https://www.linkedin.com/pulse/growth-mindset-how-healthy-relationship-fear-failure-fuels-wilson

LinkedIn (Taipale, M.). *Understanding AI & Its Impact on Our Lives.* https://www.linkedin.com/pulse/embracing-change-understanding-ai-its-impact-our-lives-marko-taipale

Liu, J. *Adaptive Leadership in the AI Era.* https://www.linkedin.com/pulse/chapter-4-adaptive-leadership-navigating-change-ai-era-jessie-liu-k9jnc

Lozovsky, A. *Unlocking Your Professional Potential with AI.* https://www.linkedin.com/pulse/unlocking-your-professional-potential-how-ai-career-lozovsky-mba-aruec

LSIB. *Success Stories of Professional Career Transition Using AI.* https://www.lsib.co.uk/2022/postsdescription.aspx?id=99174&Title=Success+Stories+of+Professional+Career+Transition+using+AI&PromoType=Professional+Certificate+in+AI-Driven+Career+Transition+Planning&CourseTitle=

ManpowerGroup. *Technology Can Enhance Your Career Development Strategy.*

McKinsey& Company. *AI, Automation, and the Future of Work: Ten Things to Solve For.* https://www.mckinsey.com/featured-insights/future-of-work/ai-automation-and-the-future-of-work-ten-things-to-solve-for

Meetings & Events Australia. *Harnessing the Power of Networks.*

Mentoring Complete. *Mentoring for Career Change.* https://www.mentoringcomplete.com/mentoring-for-career-change-navigating-transitions-with-a-mentors-guidance/

M-Files. *Fusing AI and Workflow Automation.* https://www.m-files.com/blog/articles/embracing-change-fusing-ai-and-workflow-automation/

National Center for Biotechnology Information. *Perspectives on Human-AI Collaboration.* https://pmc.ncbi.nlm.nih.gov/articles/PMC10570436/

NCBI. *The Future of Human-AI Teamwork.* https://pmc.ncbi.nlm.nih.gov/articles/PMC9578547/

Nelson-Tabor, J. *Seizing New Opportunities in Career Transitions.* https://www.linkedin.com/pulse/navigating-career-transitions-seizing-new-dr-jodi-nelson-tabor-xhfne

Neuroscience News. *Human-AI Collaboration and the Brain.* https://neuroscience-news.com/human-ai-colaboration-neuroscience-27953/

OECD. *AI and Employment Impacts: Workforce Transitions.* https://one.oecd.org/document/DELSA/ELSA/WD/SEM(2023)7/en/pdf

OECD. *The Impact of AI on the Workplace.* https://www.oecd.org/en/publications/the-impact-of-ai-on-the-workplace-evidence-from-oecd-case-studies-of-ai-implementation_2247ce58-en.html

OnTalent. *Networking in Career Management.* https://www.ontalent.com.au/networking-in-career-management/

People Management. *AI's Impact on Career Planning and L&D.* https://www.peoplemanagement.co.uk/article/1883036/anticipating-future-ai-changing-career-planning-its-impact-l-d

Pernati, M. *Redefining Success: Navigating Career Transitions.* https://www.linkedin.com/pulse/redefining-success-navigating-career-transitions-senior-madan-pernati-4qntc

Phil Cicio. *Embracing Change Outline.* https://www.philcicio.com/wp-content/uploads/2024/02/Embracing-Change-Outline.pdf

Polupanova, M. AI: *Augment or Substitute?* https://www.linkedin.com/pulse/ai-augment-substitute-marina-polupanova-khu9c

Prosci. *Top 10 Tactics for Managing Resistance to Change.* https://www.prosci.com/blog/prosci-top-10-tactics-for-managing-resistance-to-change

Psychology Today. *Making Change an Opportunity, Not a Threat.* https://www.psychologytoday.com/au/blog/the-power-prime/201505/four-steps-making-change-opportunity-not-threat

PushFar. *Navigating Career Transitions: The Role of Mentoring.* https://www.pushfar.com/article/navigating-career-transitions-the-role-of-mentoring/

QAA. *Case Studies Using AI for Education and Digital Skills.* https://www.qaa.ac.uk/docs/qaa/members/list-of-case-studies-using-ai-to-promote-education-for-sustainable-development-esd-and-widen-access-to-digital-skills.pdf?sfvrsn=74f7bc81_6

QIBA. *Mastering Career Transitions Through Networking.* https://www.qiba.edu.au/mastering-career-transitions-how-to-network-your-way-to-a-new-job/

RAPS. *Navigating the AI Revolution.* https://www.raps.org/events/sponsored-webcast-navigating-the-ai-revolution-embracing-change-and-thriving-in-the-future-of-ai-infused-drug-development-and-regulatory-affairs

R&D Today UK. *AI Is Not Replacing Humans but Augmenting Their Work.* https://www.rndtoday.co.uk/digital-economy/artificial-intelligence-not-replacing-humans-but-augmenting-their-work/

Reclaim Design. *Embracing Uncertainty.* https://reclaimdesign.org/embracing-uncertainty

RehabAI Playbook. *Human-AI Interaction in Creative Teams.* https://playbook.rehabai.ai/p/human-ai-interaction-in-creative-teams

Rishal, M. *Personalized Mentorship for Career Shifters.* https://muhammadrishal.com/blog-details.php?post=Personalized+Mentorship+for+Career+Shifters

RSL Australia. *Future-Proof Your Career.* https://www.rslaustralia.org/resources-for-jobhunters/future-proof-your-career

Sage Publications. *Coping and Thriving in Nursing.* https://sk.sagepub.com/book/mono/coping-and-thriving-in-nursing/chpt/2-embracing-change-continuing-process

Sahota, N. *AI Energizes Career Growth Plans.* https://www.forbes.com/sites/neilsahota/2024/07/25/ai-energizes-your-career-path--charts-your-professional-growth-plan/

Satchel Pulse. *The Role of Mentorship in Navigating Career Transitions.* https://www.linkedin.com/pulse/role-mentorship-navigating-career-transitions-satchel-pulse-qkvbc

Saturday Evening Post. *Making Change an Opportunity, Not a Threat.* https://www.saturdayeveningpost.com/2019/06/four-steps-to-making-change-an-opportunity-not-a-threat/

Simon Lawton. *Embrace Change.* https://www.simonlawton.com/embrace-change/

SJ Innovation. *The Future of Human-AI Collaboration.* https://sjinnovation.com/future-human-ai-collaboration-whats-next

SmythOS. *Human-AI Workflow Builders.* https://smythos.com/ai-agents/ai-workflow-builders/human-ai-collaboration/

Snipd. *Podcast Chapter on Adaptability.* https://share.snipd.com/chapter/3dd32a95-c913-4adb-83fe-4538752cd418

Splunk. *Adaptive AI.* https://www.splunk.com/en_us/blog/learn/adaptive-ai.html

STRSI. *Aligning Your Career with Industry Growth*. https://strsi.com/2024/10/30/from-tech-roles-to-tech-goals-how-to-align-your-career-with-industry-growth-in-the-coming-year/

Susie Miller. *Growth Mindset and Fear*. https://www.susiemiller.com/how-to-overcome-fear-with-a-growth-mindset/

Tarnoff, J. *Your Intellectual Curiosity Is at the Heart of Your Career Success*. https://johntarnoff.com/how-your-intellectual-curiosity-is-at-the-heart-of-your-career-success/

TeamForm. *Teamwork in the Era of Human-AI Teams*. https://www.teamform.co/blogs/teamwork-in-the-era-of-human-ai-teams-2

The Collective. *Effective Networking for Career Transitions*. https://www.jointhecollective.com/article/effective-networking-for-career-transitions-building-connections-to-support-your-journey/

The Riverbend Group. *Is Change an Opportunity or a Threat?* https://theriverbendgroup.com/is-change-an-opportunity-or-a-threat/

Together Platform. *How Mentorship Can Expand Your Network*. https://www.together-platform.com/blog/how-mentorship-can-expand-your-network

Training Industry. *The 5 Skills That Will Future-Proof Your Career*. https://trainingindustry.com/articles/strategy-alignment-and-planning/the-5-skills-that-will-future-proof-your-career/

Training Magazine. *Technology as a Driver of Career Development*. https://trainingmag.com/technology-as-a-driver-of-career-development/

Transitioning Well. *Career Adaptability*. https://www.transitioningwell.com.au/career-adaptability/

TWC Resources. *How AI Is Reshaping Career Pathways*. https://resources.twc.edu/articles/how-ai-is-reshaping-career-pathways

UNC Innovate. *Future-Proof Part 1: Skill Shifts for the Future of Work*. https://innovate.unc.edu/future-proof-part-1-which-shifts-in-skills-and-talent-will-the-future-of-work-demand/

University of San Diego. *AI in Education*. https://onlinedegrees.sandiego.edu/artificial-intelligence-education/

UNSW. *How AI Can Help Choose Your Next Career*. https://www.unsw.edu.au/newsroom/news/2021/08/how-ai-can-help-choose-your-next-career-and-stay-ahead-of-automa

Virtuous. *Fundraiser Growth and Thriving in Uncertainty*. https://virtuous.org/blog/fundraiser-growth/

VNS8E. *Navigating Career Success with Curiosity & Adaptability*. https://www.linkedin.com/pulse/whats-my-mind-navigating-career-success-curiosity-adaptability-vns8e

Vorecol. *Navigating Career Transitions in the Digital Age*. https://vorecol.com/blogs/blog-navigating-career-transitions-in-the-digital-age-7402

Wairimu, B. *Future of Artificial Intelligence: Opportunities Ahead*. https://www.linkedin.com/pulse/future-artificial-intelligence-opportunities-brenda-wairimu

Westerdale, M. *Change is Not a Threat—It's an Opportunity*. https://www.linkedin.com/pulse/change-threat-its-opportunity-mike-westerdale

Whatfix. *Causes of Resistance to Change*. https://whatfix.com/blog/causes-of-resistance-to-change/

Wiley Online Library. *AI in Career Development*. https://onlinelibrary.wiley.com/doi/abs/10.1002/9781119551966.ch9

WomenTech Network. *Mentoring for Career Transitions.* https://www.womentech. net/en-au/advice/14068/mentoring-for-career-transitions

WomenTech Network. *The Power of Mentorship in Navigating Career Transitions for Women.* https://www.womentech.net/how-to/power-mentorship-in-navigating-career-transitions-women

World Economic Forum. *Think of AI as a Teammate.* https://www.weforum.org/stories/2025/01/why-you-should-think-of-ai-as-a-teammate-not-a-tool-when-building-a-better-future/

Writecream. *AI Plot Summary Tool.* https://www.writecream.com/ai-plot-summary-and-chapter-outline-creator-for-books/

YouTube. *Thriving through Change: Embracing the Unknown.* https://www.youtube. com/watch?v=9Z3KBH9wc28

YouTube. *Video on Career Transitions.* https://www.youtube.com/watch?v=h4NSBO gpbcI

YouTube Playlist. *Career Transitions and AI.* https://www.youtube.com/playlist?list= PLZoTAELRMXVO5zRjBApoMgM5rc5KEzjJX

Zaroucha, V. *Embracing Uncertainty: My Journey of Growth.* https://www.linkedin.com/pulse/embracing-uncertainty-my-journey-growth-success-young-kayange

Zaroucha, V. *Growth through Embracing Uncertainty.* https://www.linkedin.com/pulse/embracing-uncertainty-path-growth-victoria-zaroucha-w4gif

Zeier, C. *Seeing Change as an Opportunity.* https://www.linkedin.com/pulse/seeing-change-opportunity-instead-threat-carine-zeier

17

Embracing Change

In an era defined by rapid technological advancements, artificial intelligence (AI) and automation are reshaping industries, altering career landscapes, and redefining the skills necessary for success. This chapter explores the profound impact of AI on global economies, examining how businesses and individuals can adapt to technological disruption by cultivating resilience, continuous learning, and innovation.

Key industry transformations driven by AI are analysed, from manufacturing and healthcare to finance and retail, highlighting how automation enhances efficiency while creating both challenges and opportunities. The accelerating pace of technological change compresses adaptation cycles, requiring professionals to evolve their skills dynamically. Adaptability has transitioned from a desirable trait to an essential survival skill, enabling individuals and organisations to navigate AI-driven transformations effectively.

The chapter delves into the critical role of lifelong learning, reskilling, and cross-disciplinary knowledge in future-proofing careers. Strategies for overcoming resistance to change, fostering growth mindsets, and leveraging AI as a collaborative tool rather than a disruptive force are investigated. Through compelling case studies and industry insights, this chapter demonstrates how embracing change not only mitigates risks but also unlocks new avenues for professional and organisational growth.

Ultimately, this chapter presents change as a catalyst for progress rather than a threat to stability. By cultivating adaptability, fostering innovation, and strategically leveraging AI's potential, individuals and businesses can transform uncertainty into an opportunity, securing a future where human ingenuity and AI coexist to drive meaningful success.

Understanding the Impact of Change in the AI Era

In today's rapidly evolving technological landscape, AI and automation are fundamentally transforming how people work, live, and interact with technology. The acceleration of AI capabilities is creating unprecedented disruption across industries and career paths, necessitating new approaches to professional development and adaptation. This comprehensive exploration examines how AI and automation are reshaping industries across the global

DOI: 10.1201/9781003626503-17

economy, analyses the velocity of technological transformation and its profound effects on careers, and investigates why adaptability has evolved from a beneficial trait to an essential survival skill in the AI era. By understanding these interconnected dimensions of technological change, individuals and organisations can develop strategic responses that transform potential threats into opportunities for growth and innovation.

How AI and Automation Are Reshaping Industries

AI automation has transitioned from a futuristic concept to a present reality that is fundamentally transforming industries across various sectors of the global economy. This technological revolution is reshaping workflows, enhancing efficiency, and creating unprecedented opportunities for growth and innovation in a manner that affects virtually every segment of modern business operations. From manufacturing floors to healthcare facilities, financial institutions, and retail environments, AI and automation technologies are optimising operations, reducing costs, and substantially improving productivity through sophisticated technological implementation. Organisations worldwide are rapidly adopting AI to automate tasks and decision-making processes, resulting in profound impacts that extend beyond simple efficiency gains to fundamentally restructuring how entire industries function and deliver value.

The manufacturing sector represents one of the most dramatic examples of AI-driven transformation, having historically positioned itself at the forefront of technological advancement and now accelerating this evolution through AI applications. Within manufacturing environments, intelligent robots and automated quality control systems optimise production processes, minimise waste, and significantly enhance precision beyond what was previously achievable through human-only operations. One particularly revolutionary application in this sector is predictive maintenance, where AI systems analyse real-time sensor data to accurately predict equipment failure before it occurs, thereby reducing costly downtime and extending machinery lifespan compared to traditional time-based maintenance schedules. Companies like Siemens and Tesla are already implementing AI automation to manage production lines, deploying AI-powered robots that perform repetitive tasks with exceptional precision, while automated systems ensure machines receive maintenance exactly when needed rather than following arbitrary schedules.

In healthcare settings, AI automation is simultaneously enhancing administrative efficiency and improving patient care through sophisticated diagnostic capabilities and workflow optimisation. AI algorithms can analyse medical images such as MRIs or X-rays with more incredible speed and often higher accuracy than human physicians, enabling faster diagnoses and improved patient outcomes through earlier intervention. Beyond clinical applications, AI streamlines administrative tasks, including appointment scheduling, billing management, and even the prediction of patient no-show rates, creating more efficient operational environments. AI-powered virtual assistants and sophisticated chatbots now handle routine patient inquiries, liberating healthcare professionals to focus on more complex and critical aspects of patient care that require distinctly human capabilities. The IBM Watson platform exemplifies this advancement, analysing vast quantities of medical literature to assist doctors in diagnosis and treatment recommendations, extending the capabilities of medical professionals while addressing resource constraints in healthcare delivery.

Financial institutions are leveraging AI to transform risk management, decision-making processes, and fraud detection capabilities through sophisticated analytical approaches. AI algorithms process enormous volumes of financial data, identifying subtle patterns and trends that human analysts might overlook, enabling more informed decisions and faster responses to market fluctuations. This capability proves particularly valuable in rapidly changing financial environments where timely analysis directly impacts outcomes. Additionally, AI automation streamlines back-office operations, including transaction processing, accounting, and regulatory compliance, reducing human error while improving operational efficiency across financial workflows. JPMorgan's COiN platform demonstrates this transformation, using AI to automate the analysis of legal documents, saving thousands of manual review hours while maintaining or improving accuracy. Simultaneously, AI-driven fraud detection tools employ machine learning to identify suspicious transactions in real time, providing faster and more accurate responses to security threats than traditional methods.

Retail environments are experiencing revolutionary changes through AI-driven personalisation and supply chain optimisation that enhance customer experiences while improving operational efficiency. AI algorithms analyse customer data, including browsing behaviour and purchase history, recommending products customised to individual preferences, thereby increasing satisfaction and driving higher sales through more targeted engagement. Throughout retail supply chains, AI optimises inventory management, predicts consumer demand patterns, and reduces delivery times through intelligent logistics management. AI-powered systems monitor stock levels in real time, forecast future demand based on multiple variables, and automatically reorder products to prevent stockouts while minimising excess inventory. Amazon exemplifies this approach, utilising an AI-driven recommendation engine that accounts for a substantial portion of sales while managing its supply chain through AI to ensure efficient delivery of millions of orders worldwide with minimal human intervention.

The Speed of Technological Transformation and Its Effects on Careers

The pace of technological change in the current era is accelerating at an unprecedented rate, creating profound implications for labour markets and career trajectories across virtually all sectors of the economy. Over the next decade, this technological transformation will significantly disrupt traditional employment patterns, potentially displacing substantial numbers of workers while simultaneously creating new opportunities that did not previously exist. Recent research suggests that in Australia alone, approximately 630,000 jobs could be displaced by new technologies over the next decade, representing about 7.3% of the country's existing workforce, a figure that represents the reduction in overall employment that could occur while still generating today's level of economic output in 2028. This displacement effect demonstrates the substantial productivity enhancements that technological advancement brings but also highlights the challenges faced by workers whose roles may become partially or fully automated through advancing technological capabilities.

The impact of technological transformation varies dramatically across different industries and occupational categories, creating a complex landscape of both opportunity and displacement that requires strategic navigation. According to projections, the construction sector in Australia faces particularly significant disruption, potentially losing more than 70,000 jobs (equivalent to 8.4% of its current workforce) over the next decade, as drones, cloud-based software applications, and wearable technologies enhance productivity while reducing worker risk exposure. Manufacturing similarly faces substantial transformation, with projections indicating a potential net loss of 33,000 jobs (5.5% of the sector's workforce) resulting from technological advancement. When analysed by occupational type rather than industry, "craft and trades workers" appear most vulnerable, with projections suggesting this category could shrink by approximately 80,000 positions over the next decade as automation capabilities expand into increasingly complex manual tasks previously requiring human dexterity and decision-making.

While technological advancement creates significant displacement in some sectors, it simultaneously generates substantial growth opportunities in others, particularly those requiring advanced technical capabilities and cognitive skills. In contrast to declining occupational categories, "professional occupations," including nurses, teachers, and software developers, are projected to experience the most significant expansion, with more than 90,000 new jobs created in the coming decade. This divergence illustrates the transformative nature of technological change, not by simply eliminating work but by fundamentally reshaping labour markets through shifting demand towards different skill sets and capabilities. On a broader scale, research suggests that over the next 15 years, an additional 5.6 million new jobs could be added to the Australian economy, with approximately 25% of these positions representing technology-related roles requiring specialised skills and training. This projection highlights both the magnitude of opportunity and the critical importance of appropriate skill development to capitalise on emerging possibilities.

The acceleration of technological change compresses adaptation cycles, requiring professionals to continuously update skills and knowledge throughout their careers to maintain relevance in rapidly evolving environments. Unlike previous technological revolutions that primarily affected manufacturing and lower-skilled positions, AI and automation are increasingly impacting higher-paid, white-collar workers and transforming knowledge work across virtually all sectors. This unprecedented scope of change makes adaptability and continuous learning essential for continued career relevance at all organisational levels. Workers facing technological disruption must navigate complex transitions that often require substantial reskilling, with analysis indicating significant skills gaps in critical areas. Research suggests that the best available candidates for IT-related positions are often approximately 57% short of the programming skills requirements projected for 2028, while sophisticated cognitive skills gaps in mathematics and science reach up to 30%. Similarly, maintenance, installation, and technical repair positions face significant skills shortages, with candidates typically 25%–35% short of the required capabilities.

The global scale of this transformation further emphasises its significance, with projections indicating that by 2025, technological changes will create approximately 97 million new jobs while simultaneously eliminating 85 million current positions worldwide. This near-balanced creation and destruction illustrate how technological advancement fundamentally restructures rather than simply reduces employment opportunities, shifting demand towards different capabilities while eliminating positions that become technologically obsolete. However, this restructuring creates significant transition challenges for displaced workers, particularly those from sectors experiencing substantial automation. For individuals navigating these shifts, the key challenge involves identifying transferable skills while acquiring new capabilities relevant to emerging opportunities. Contrary to popular fears about wholesale job elimination, AI and automation are creating substantial demand for new roles in data analysis, machine learning, AI programming, system management, and human–AI collaboration, where workers develop, manage, and continuously improve technological systems while providing complementary human capabilities.

Why Adaptability Is a Key Success Factor

In an era dominated by AI and automation, adaptability has evolved from merely a desirable trait to a fundamental survival requirement for both individuals and organisations navigating rapidly changing technological landscapes. The unprecedented pace of technological transformation compresses adaptation cycles, requiring continuous learning and capability development to maintain relevance in environments where established skills and knowledge quickly become obsolete. As automation capabilities expand into increasingly complex domains once considered uniquely human, professionals must continuously evolve their skill sets and mental models to complement rather than compete with technological capabilities. Gary Shapiro, CEO of the Consumer Technology Association, emphasises this critical reality in his book *Pivot or Die: How Leaders Thrive When Everything Changes*, arguing that as AI and quantum computing rewrite commercial rules, adaptability becomes a necessity rather than an optional advantage for continued relevance and success.

Human adaptability derives significant advantages from inherently versatile capabilities compared to the specialised nature of machine intelligence, creating opportunities for complementary rather than competitive relationships with technological systems. Moravec's paradox highlights this complementary relationship by observing that tasks humans perform easily without conscious thought such as sensory perception, motor skills, and object recognition often prove extraordinarily difficult for machines, while tasks humans find challenging like abstract reasoning and logical deduction may be relatively simple for computational systems. This paradox reveals that humans possess versatile biological machinery, including dexterous fingers, opposable thumbs, bipedal stances, and neural networks that continuously forge new pathways, enabling the performance of incredibly diverse tasks without specialised reprogramming. Unlike highly specialised AI systems designed for specific applications, human intelligence naturally adapts to novel situations by transferring knowledge between domains and creatively applying existing skills to new challenges, providing distinct advantages in rapidly changing environments where flexibility proves more valuable than optimisation for specific tasks.

The uniquely human traits of curiosity, creativity, collaboration, and adaptability provide essential foundations for thriving in technology-integrated environments by enabling continuous learning and innovation beyond what purely computational systems can achieve. These evolutionary intelligence capabilities give people and organisations the capacity to navigate uncertainty and forge new paths to success where established solutions prove insufficient. Curiosity drives the exploration of emerging possibilities before immediate necessity forces change, creating proactive rather than reactive adaptation pathways. Creativity enables novel solution development by connecting seemingly disparate domains and identifying possibilities invisible to more structured analytical approaches. Collaboration leverages collective intelligence to address complex challenges beyond individual capability, while adaptability enables continuous evolution as circumstances change. Together, these capabilities create "evolutionary intelligence" that transcends purely computational approaches to problem-solving and adaptation, providing sustainable advantages in rapidly changing technological environments.

Organisations and individuals often struggle with adaptation despite its clear importance, frequently hampered by success-induced complacency that creates vulnerability to disruptive change. Shapiro identifies this complacency as a major obstacle to effective pivoting, noting that success often breeds dangerous overconfidence when favourable outcomes are attributed to intelligence rather than timing, market conditions, or execution capabilities. This misattribution creates resistance to change, as individuals and organisations believe their past success validates existing approaches rather than recognising the constantly evolving nature of competitive landscapes. When established approaches have generated previous success, questioning their continued relevance becomes challenging, particularly when significant investments in specific capabilities create psychological and financial resistance to an exploration of alternatives. This resistance becomes particularly dangerous during periods of technological transformation where past performance provides decreasingly reliable guidance for future success, potentially leading to organisational obsolescence despite previous market leadership.

Developing adaptability requires the intentional cultivation of both mindsets and capabilities that support continuous evolution in response to changing circumstances and technological developments. The foundation begins with psychological preparation for identity evolution, moving beyond identification with specific roles or expertise areas towards broader professional self-concepts based on adaptable capabilities rather than static positions. This expanded self-concept creates psychological flexibility, facilitating smoother transitions when change becomes necessary and transforming potential threats into navigable pathways for continued growth and contribution. Maintaining awareness of industry evolution and technological trends provides essential intelligence for strategic career development, enabling professionals to identify emerging skills complementing changing technological capabilities while anticipating potential disruptions before they manifest as immediate threats. Rather than viewing such assessments as threatening established identities, adaptable professionals approach them as valuable intelligence gathering that informs proactive development rather than reactive defence of increasingly vulnerable positions.

Conclusion: Embracing Technological Evolution

The transformative impact of AI on industries, careers, and skill requirements creates both unprecedented challenges and extraordinary opportunities for those prepared to embrace change as a catalyst for growth rather than a threat to established patterns. By understanding how AI and automation reshape industries through enhanced efficiency, improved decision-making, and innovative capabilities, individuals and organisations can strategically position themselves at the intersection of human and technological potential. The accelerating pace of transformation demands continuous adaptation through lifelong learning and capability development, particularly as traditional career paths fracture and new opportunities emerge in previously unimagined domains. In this environment, adaptability becomes the meta-skill that determines sustainable success, enabling innovative responses to changing circumstances while preserving distinctly human contributions that complement rather than compete with technological capabilities.

Navigating the AI era depends on one's relationship with change and determines the experience of technological transformation, either as a threatening disruption or as an invitation to unprecedented growth and possibility. By cultivating adaptive mindsets and capabilities while leveraging the complementary strengths of human and AI, potential displacement is transformed into opportunities for enhanced contribution and impact. The future belongs to those who embrace technological evolution and view it as a pathway to expanded human potential and possibility, creating solutions to challenges that are only beginning to be imagined through collaborative intelligence that transcends the limitations of either humans or machines operating in isolation.

Lifelong Learning and Reskilling for the Future

AI is fundamentally reshaping the approach to career development and professional growth. The traditional concept of a fixed career trajectory has given way to a more fluid model where continuous learning, strategic upskilling, and cross-disciplinary knowledge have become essential for long-term success. This comprehensive exploration examines the critical shift from conventional career paths to lifelong learning paradigms, investigates the growing importance of developing versatile skill portfolios, and analyses the expanding ecosystem of digital learning resources empowering professionals to navigate career transitions in an AI-integrated world. Understanding these interconnected dimensions of continuous development creates the foundation to thrive amid technological transformation rather than merely surviving it.

Shifting from a Fixed Career Path to Continuous Learning

The traditional career model—characterised by linear progression within a single field or organisation—has been fundamentally disrupted by accelerating technological change. AI is driving this transformation by reshaping the approach to career planning and professional development. By harnessing data-driven insights, career management is becoming more accessible to individuals at all stages. Through analysis of historical data, including job market trends, skills requirements, and organisational patterns, AI can generate sophisticated maps for career transitions and growth opportunities, helping professionals make informed decisions about their development pathways while potentially accelerating advancement. This technological capability represents a significant shift from intuition-based career planning to data-informed development strategies that reveal possibilities beyond obvious trajectories.

The compressed lifecycle of professional capabilities necessitates fundamental changes in career development conceptualisation. With technology advancing at a rapid pace, career planning and skill development are changing with the times, requiring continuous adaptation rather than one-time preparation. This evolution becomes particularly urgent as the shelf life of professional skills continues shrinking, with studies suggesting some capabilities become obsolete in just a few years. This acceleration creates environments where continuous learning transitions from optional advantage to essential survival skills, fundamentally altering how professionals must approach their development throughout their working lives.

The Human Adaptability and Potential Index provides a valuable framework for understanding how individuals can embrace lifelong learning to maintain relevance in AI-driven economies. This comprehensive approach emphasises continuous improvement across critical dimensions, including cognitive adaptability, emotional resilience, behavioural flexibility, and social learning—capabilities that transcend specific technical implementations to provide sustainable foundations for career evolution. By focusing on these meta-capabilities rather than narrowly defined technical skills, professionals create resilience against technological disruption that maintains value regardless of specific implementation changes or technological advancements.

This shift from fixed to fluid career pathways requires substantial psychological adaptation alongside skill development. Professionals must cultivate comfort with uncertainty while developing capabilities that facilitate continuous evolution as circumstances change. The most future-resistant individuals recognise that adaptation is not merely reactive but proactive, requiring ongoing assessment of industry evolution and strategic capability development. This forward-looking orientation transforms potential threats into navigable pathways, positioning technological change as the catalyst for growth rather than the source of displacement.

The Importance of Upskilling and Cross-Disciplinary Knowledge

The rapid integration of AI across sectors is creating unprecedented demand for comprehensive upskilling initiatives and cross-disciplinary knowledge development. According to ACS Digital Pulse, Australia alone will need 1.3 million additional tech skills in the next 5 years to adapt to ten critical technologies, including AI. This massive capability gap cannot be addressed through traditional education alone, requiring continuous professional development throughout careers. As AI becomes more integrated into organisational operations, entirely new roles are emerging, including AI engineers and prompt engineers—positions that bridge technical expertise with domain-specific knowledge in ways that challenge traditional disciplinary boundaries.

Upskilling provides substantial benefits for both individuals and organisations navigating technological transformation. For individuals, developing new capabilities creates career resilience while opening pathways to advancement opportunities that might otherwise remain inaccessible. For organisations, internal upskilling initiatives address critical capability gaps while fostering employee retention through development opportunities. According to research examining AI's impact on professional skills, organisations must employ proactive approaches to workplace transformation, mapping transversal skills needed to address current gaps while implementing processes supporting workers through targeted training and development opportunities. This strategic orientation ensures workforces remain adaptable as technological implementation continues accelerating.

Cross-disciplinary knowledge has evolved from an advantageous supplement to an essential foundation for career resilience in AI-integrated environments. Professionals who expand knowledge across adjacent industries and technologies significantly increase their career flexibility and adaptation capacity when facing technological disruption. This interdisciplinary perspective becomes particularly valuable as AI integration blurs traditional boundaries between domains, creating hybrid roles requiring combinations of technical understanding and domain expertise. Rather than pursuing depth in increasingly narrow specialisations, career sustainability increasingly depends on developing breadth across related fields while maintaining sufficient specialised knowledge to provide distinctive value.

The most effective upskilling approaches balance technical capability development with distinctly human skills that complement rather than compete with AI. While technical knowledge provides immediate value in specific contexts, focusing exclusively on these capabilities creates vulnerability as implementations change. Professionals should strategically develop capabilities in areas where AI struggles, including leadership, creativity, empathy, and complex ethical reasoning. These human-centric skills become increasingly valuable as routine and analytical tasks become automated, providing sustainable career advantages regardless of technological advancement while establishing complementary rather than competitive relationships with AI systems.

Creating effective upskilling ecosystems requires collaborative approaches involving multiple stakeholders. Policymakers, educational institutions, and employers increasingly recognise that virtually all roles now require some degree of technological literacy and adaptability. This shared understanding enables coordinated approaches to workforce development, aligning education with evolving workplace requirements while ensuring equitable access to upskilling opportunities. By viewing workforce development as a shared responsibility rather than an individual challenge, these collaborative frameworks create sustainable pathways for continuous development that benefit individuals, organisations, and broader economies navigating technological transformation.

Online Learning Platforms, Certifications, and AI-Driven Education

The ecosystem supporting lifelong learning has expanded dramatically with the emergence of sophisticated online platforms, specialised certifications, and AI-driven educational tools. These resources provide accessible, flexible, and personalised pathways for continuous skill development aligned with evolving workplace requirements. In today's AI boom, professionals and industry newcomers alike are considering specialised certifications to gain competitive advantages in increasingly technology-driven job markets. These credentials range from specialised certifications like Microsoft Certified: Azure AI Engineer Associate to broader learning programs like NVIDIA's Jetson AI Courses catering to different audience segments and skill levels. The distinction between certifications (awarded through rigorous assessment) and certificates (signifying course completion) provides options aligned with different career objectives and learning preferences.

Major technology companies have developed comprehensive learning platforms focused on AI and machine learning, creating structured pathways for skill development. Google Cloud Training offers specialised machine learning and AI classes taught by Google experts, providing interactive labs and practical experience with cutting-edge AI technology. These resources enable professionals to build specific technical capabilities while earning an industry-recognised credential and demonstrating competence to potential employers. The structured learning paths—from beginner introduction to advanced implementation—create accessible entry points for professionals at different stages of their AI learning journey while providing clear progression frameworks for continuous development.

AI itself is transforming educational approaches through personalised learning experiences that enhance effectiveness and accessibility. AI-powered platforms like Degreed and LinkedIn Learning enable organisations to offer personalised training paths aligned with individual employee needs and organisational objectives. These systems assess current capabilities, suggest tailored development opportunities, and track progress in real time, creating unprecedented personalisation in professional development. This adaptation to individual learning preferences accelerates skill acquisition by focusing on specific capability gaps rather than following standardised approaches that ignore individual differences in background knowledge, learning styles, and development objectives.

The integration of AI into learning processes extends beyond content recommendations to include sophisticated capabilities that enhance learning effectiveness across contexts. AI offers tools to make learning more personalised, efficient, and accessible for diverse learners across organisational levels. These capabilities include adaptive assessment, identifying knowledge gaps, personalised content sequencing, optimising learning pathways, and intelligent tutoring systems providing targeted support when learners encounter difficulties. By leveraging these AI-powered capabilities, professionals maximise learning efficiency while developing specific skills needed for career advancement in increasingly competitive environments.

AI can further support career-driven learning by connecting educational opportunities directly to employment requirements through sophisticated data analysis. By leveraging data from job postings, course catalogues, and professional backgrounds, AI helps individuals identify specific capability gaps while plotting educational journeys aligned with career objectives. This data-driven approach ensures learning activities directly support professional goals rather than merely accumulating credentials disconnected from workplace requirements. As skill requirements evolve rapidly due to technological and business developments, this alignment becomes increasingly valuable for ensuring learning investments produce tangible career benefits in rapidly changing professional landscapes.

Conclusion: Embracing the Future through Continuous Learning

The transformation of work through AI creates both unprecedented challenges and extraordinary opportunities for those prepared to embrace lifelong learning as a foundational career strategy. Research from the World Economic Forum predicts that while 85 million jobs may be displaced by automation by 2025, approximately 97 million new roles will emerge, requiring new skill sets. This transformation underscores the critical importance of upskilling and reskilling to ensure workforce adaptability in rapidly evolving environments where traditional capabilities quickly become obsolete while entirely new requirements emerge with increasing frequency.

The ability to navigate this changing landscape depends less on mastering specific technologies than on developing adaptable learning orientations that facilitate continuous evolution regardless of implementation. By shifting from fixed career paths to continuous learning paradigms, developing cross-disciplinary knowledge transcending specific domains, and leveraging expanding educational ecosystems, professionals position themselves to thrive amid technological transformation rather than merely surviving it. This approach transforms potential displacement into a catalyst for unprecedented growth and contribution in increasingly AI-integrated environments.

As technological change accelerates, the distinction between those who thrive and those who struggle will increasingly depend on their capacity for continuous learning and adaptation rather than specific technical knowledge. By cultivating the mindsets and practices explored in this analysis, professionals create career resilience that transcends specific implementations or technological shifts. The future belongs not to those who resist technological evolution but to those who embrace it as the pathway to expanded potential and possibility, converting challenges into opportunities through the transformative power of lifelong learning and strategic skill development.

Overcoming Resistance to Change

In today's rapidly evolving technological landscape, the ability to adapt to change has become a fundamental requirement for personal and professional success. Despite the clear need for adaptability, many individuals and organisations continue to resist change, clinging to familiar patterns and established routines even when they no longer serve their intended purpose. This comprehensive exploration examines why people naturally fear change, how developing a growth mindset can transform this resistance into opportunity, practical strategies for adapting to new technologies in the workplace, and inspiring success stories of individuals who have successfully navigated significant career transitions. By understanding and addressing the psychological foundations of change resistance while implementing strategic approaches to adaptation, individuals and organisations can transform potential disruption into catalysts for unprecedented growth and innovation.

Why People Fear Change and Developing a Growth Mindset

Fear of change is deeply rooted in human psychology, manifesting as a powerful emotion that prevents individuals from embracing new adventures, opportunities, and experiences. This reluctance often stems from uncertainty about the unknown and anxiety about potential negative outcomes. In workplace contexts, fear can be particularly paralysing when confronting technological transformation, as individuals worry about their continued relevance and ability to adapt to new systems and processes. The discomfort associated with leaving established routines creates a powerful inertia that maintains the status quo, even when change would ultimately be beneficial.

Specific fears commonly associated with change include fear of failure, fear of financial instability, fear of starting over, fear of being judged, and fear of making the wrong choice. These fears can manifest physically as tension or unease in the body and often stem from a desire to protect the ego or reluctance to leave familiar patterns behind. Recognising these fears as natural responses rather than personal weaknesses creates the foundation for developing more constructive approaches to change.

The concept of mindset, particularly as developed by psychologist Carol Dweck, provides a powerful framework for understanding and addressing resistance to change. A fixed mindset views intelligence and abilities as static and unchangeable, leading individuals to avoid challenges and give up easily when faced with obstacles. In contrast, a growth mindset believes that abilities can be developed through dedication, learning, and perseverance. This fundamental difference in perspective profoundly impacts how individuals approach change, with growth-oriented individuals viewing challenges as opportunities for development rather than threats to established competence.

Developing a growth mindset begins with recognising that everyone possesses a mixture of fixed and growth mindsets that continuously evolve with experience. Rather than claiming to "already have a growth mindset," effective adaptation requires identifying specific fixed-mindset triggers—situations that create insecurity or defensiveness—and developing strategies to address them constructively. Common fixed mindset traps include avoiding challenges, giving up easily, ignoring criticism, and feeling threatened by others' success. Recognising these patterns is the first step towards cultivating a more flexible, growth-oriented approach.

The transformation from a fixed to a growth mindset involves several practical approaches. First, reframing challenges as opportunities for learning rather than tests of existing ability creates psychological space for growth and development. Second, developing emotional resilience through practices like self-compassion, acknowledging feelings without judgement, and creating personal resilience rituals builds the capacity for navigating the discomfort inherent in change. Third, cognitive reframing techniques that challenge negative thoughts consider realistic worst-case scenarios and create alternative positive narratives about transitions to help overcome resistance.

Research increasingly demonstrates the benefits of developing a growth mindset for psychological well-being. Individuals with growth mindsets show greater resilience, reduced stress responses, and fewer self-reported mental health issues compared to those with fixed mindsets. These benefits extend beyond individual psychology to impact professional outcomes, with growth mindsets predicting higher levels of adaptability and success during periods of significant change. By viewing change as an opportunity rather than a threat, individuals create psychological foundations for continuous development that maintain relevance regardless of specific technological implementations.

Adapting to New Technologies in the Workplace

The integration of new technologies into workplaces requires thoughtful approaches that address both practical and psychological dimensions of change. According to SEEK research, while two-thirds of Australians believe their jobs will exist in 10 years, more than half anticipate needing to learn new skills due to technological advances. This recognition highlights the critical importance of effective strategies for facilitating technological adaptation across organisations.

Effective communication forms the foundation of successful technological change initiatives. Organisations should implement comprehensive change and communications programs that clearly explain why new technology is being introduced, articulate specific benefits, outline implementation plans, and detail available support resources. This transparency addresses anxiety about the unknown while creating a shared understanding of objectives and expected outcomes. By helping employees understand the purpose behind technological changes rather than simply announcing new requirements, organisations create psychological engagement that facilitates adaptation.

Active participation in the implementation process significantly reduces resistance while improving adoption outcomes. When team members contribute ideas for implementing new technologies, they transition from feeling like passive recipients of unwanted change to active agents in a collaborative process. This participation creates ownership and investment in successful outcomes while potentially improving implementation approaches through diverse perspectives. Organisations can further encourage adoption by incentivising the use of new systems through recognition and rewards that acknowledge progress and highlight successful adaptation.

Incremental implementation provides another effective strategy for reducing resistance to technological change. Testing new technologies on smaller scales before full-scale deployment allows organisations to identify and address potential issues while demonstrating benefits in controlled environments. This gradual approach makes change less overwhelming while creating opportunities for learning and adjustment before widespread implementation. By breaking large transformations into smaller, more manageable components, organisations create momentum and build confidence that facilitates broader adoption.

Creating a supportive learning environment proves essential for successful technological adaptation. Organisations should provide ongoing training and development opportunities that build capabilities while acknowledging different learning styles and paces. This support might include formal training programs, peer mentoring systems, and accessible resources for self-directed learning. By demonstrating a commitment to employee development through these resources, organisations show that technological change represents an opportunity for growth rather than a threat to job security.

Leadership plays a crucial role in facilitating technological adaptation by modelling growth-oriented approaches to change. Leaders who embody growth mindset principles—embracing challenges, learning from setbacks, seeking feedback, and demonstrating resilience—set powerful examples for their teams. This "transcendent leadership" involves rising above personal discomfort to demonstrate commitment to continuous learning and development. When leaders transparently share their own adaptation challenges while maintaining positive forward momentum, they create psychological safety for team members navigating similar transitions.

Equally important, organisations must establish concrete policies and practices that reinforce growth-oriented values rather than simply expressing aspirational goals. Companies that genuinely embody growth mindsets encourage appropriate risk-taking while recognising that some initiatives won't succeed as planned. They reward employees for important lessons learned even when projects don't meet original objectives, emphasising the value of learning and improvement over perfect execution. These tangible expressions of organisational values create environments where continuous adaptation becomes normalised rather than exceptional.

Success Stories of Individuals Who Transformed Their Careers

The journey of Jeff Siewert from "listless executive to impassioned entrepreneur" provides a compelling example of successful career transformation. Despite having an executive title and good compensation, Jeff found himself dissatisfied and lacking engagement in his work, a situation he had experienced multiple times previously. Rather than continuing this pattern, Jeff participated in a group coaching program that helped identify his skills, talents, and passions beyond conventional job titles and roles.

Through structured exercises, including self-reflection, personal mission statement development, and addressing inner critics, Jeff gradually clarified his authentic interests and capabilities. The breakthrough moment came during a group "Mastermind Session" where his peers recognised patterns he had mentioned repeatedly: "You've been telling us of your passion for music. You have these strengths and interests in communicating and creating. Why aren't you writing some kind of music blog?" This external perspective illuminated possibilities that Jeff had been "shuffling to the back of [his] mind," creating clarity that facilitated a successful career transition towards more fulfilling work aligned with his core passions.

Jeff's experience highlights several common elements in successful career transitions. First, self-awareness provides the foundation for meaningful change, requiring honest assessment of current satisfaction and alignment with personal values. Second, structured processes for exploring interests and capabilities create pathways to discovering authentic career directions rather than simply reacting to immediate opportunities. Third, supportive communities offer perspectives and insights that individuals might not recognise independently, helping overcome blind spots in self-perception. Finally, the courage to pursue identified passions despite uncertainty transforms potential into reality.

Recent research indicates that career transitions have become increasingly common, with approximately 70% of working-age people actively seeking job changes and about 52% planning transitions within the current year. While higher compensation motivates some transitions (approximately 39%), many individuals seek great fulfilment, better alignment with values, or to improve work–life balance through career changes. Importantly, research challenges the misconception that career transitions must occur early in professional life, confirming that "career satisfaction doesn't have an age limit."

For those contemplating significant career transitions, addressing financial concerns represents a critical success factor. Creating detailed budgets, exploring financial assistance options, and building emergency funds can alleviate practical anxieties while creating space for strategic career development. Equally important, investing in skill development through courses, certifications, and on-the-job training builds confidence while enhancing competitiveness in new careers. These practical steps, combined with psychological preparation through growth mindset development, create foundations for successful transitions regardless of specific circumstances.

Conclusion: Embracing Change as Opportunity

The ability to overcome resistance to change represents a fundamental requirement for thriving in today's rapidly evolving technological landscape. By understanding the psychological foundations of change resistance including common fears and fixed mindset perspectives, individuals and organisations can develop strategies that transform potential threats into opportunities for unprecedented growth. Developing growth mindsets that view challenges as learning opportunities while emphasising effort, persistence, and continuous improvement creates psychological flexibility that facilitates adaptation regardless of specific technological implementations.

Successful adaptation to new technologies in workplace environments requires multifaceted approaches combining transparent communication, active participation, incremental implementation, comprehensive support, and leadership modelling. Organisations that establish concrete policies reinforcing growth-oriented values create environments where continuous learning becomes normalised rather than exceptional. These practical strategies, combined with psychological preparation through growth mindset development, create sustainable foundations for technological adaptation regardless of specific implementations or industry contexts.

The inspiring stories of individuals who have successfully navigated significant career transitions demonstrate that change while challenging, creates pathways to greater fulfilment and alignment with authentic interests and values. By developing self-awareness, engaging in structured exploration processes, building supportive communities, and summoning the courage to pursue identified passions, individuals can transform dissatisfaction into an opportunity for unprecedented growth and contribution. These examples challenge perceptions of change as primarily threatening, instead highlighting its potential as a catalyst for discovering and expressing personal authentic capabilities and interests.

Navigating accelerating technological change requires examining the relationship with transformation and asking if it is threatening disruption or an invitation to unprecedented growth and possibility. By cultivating growth mindsets and implementing strategic approaches to adaptation, individuals and organisations position themselves to thrive rather than merely survive amid continuous evolution. The future belongs not to those who resist change but to those who embrace it as a pathway to expanded potential and possibility, creating solutions to challenges that are in the early stages of imagination.

Thriving in an AI-Powered Workplace

The integration of AI into workplace environments is fundamentally transforming how people work, collaborate, and innovate across industries and organisational levels. As AI systems increasingly automate routine tasks and enhance decision-making processes, the focus is shifting towards creating effective human–AI partnerships that leverage the complementary strengths of both. Research indicates that human–AI collaboration could unlock up to $15.7 trillion in economic value by 2030, highlighting the immense potential of these emerging relationships. This comprehensive exploration examines how human–AI collaboration is reshaping future jobs, identifies the soft skills becoming essential in an AI-integrated workplace, and investigates how organisations can foster cultures of continuous innovation that thrive amid technological transformation. By understanding these interconnected dynamics, professionals and organisations can position themselves to capitalise on AI's potential while maintaining the distinctly human contributions that remain irreplaceable in increasingly automated environments.

The Role of Human–AI Collaboration in Future Jobs

The relationship between humans and AI in workplace settings has evolved beyond simple automation to create what experts describe as "collaborative intelligence"—partnerships where human ingenuity and machine precision complement each other seamlessly. This emerging paradigm represents a fundamental shift from viewing AI as merely a tool to recognising it as a teammate that adapts and learns to achieve shared objectives with people. In his September 2024 Forbes article, Peter Pluim emphasised the necessity of embracing human–AI collaboration to create new opportunities, noting that successful integration allows AI to enhance human skills, streamline workflows, and foster more supportive work environments. By automating repetitive tasks and optimising decision-making processes, AI empowers workers to focus on high-level creative and strategic initiatives that leverage uniquely human capabilities while technological systems handle routine operations.

The concept of AI as a teammate rather than merely a tool provides a valuable framework for understanding emerging workplace dynamics. This perspective shift recognises that as AI tools continue to improve, new software is being developed specifically to help companies, and their employees work together more effectively. AI teammates represent a substantial global opportunity, potentially worth approximately $6 trillion—twice the size of the estimated $3 trillion IT market (excluding devices and telecommunications). This opportunity spans specialised industries, such as healthcare or finance, as well as common business functions like marketing, sales, and customer support. Rather than threatening human jobs, these AI teammates free up human time, accelerate productivity, augment capabilities, and amplify creativity, allowing people to perform as "superhumans" in their respective domains.

In practice, human–AI collaboration manifests across diverse workplace functions to address specific operational challenges. AI tools enhance productivity by automating repetitive tasks like data entry, scheduling, and reporting, ensuring these activities are completed quickly and accurately while freeing employees to focus on more strategic and creative projects. Smart task prioritisation systems analyse daily workloads and recommend priorities based on deadlines, importance, and workload balance, helping employees identify which tasks require immediate attention and reducing missed deadlines and stress. Data analysis capabilities enable AI systems to process massive datasets quickly, extracting actionable insights that help teams make more informed decisions about trends, customer behaviour, and industry shifts. These practical applications demonstrate how AI functions not as a replacement for human workers but as a complementary force that enhances human capabilities in specific contexts.

Research increasingly challenges the assumption that AI will primarily replace human workers, instead suggesting more nuanced impacts where most jobs become augmented rather than eliminated. According to the International Monetary Fund, AI will affect almost 40% of jobs around the world, but this impact involves both replacement and complementary effects that vary substantially across roles and industries. The Anthropic Economic Index provides valuable data on how AI is currently being used in real-world tasks, revealing that usage currently leans more towards augmentation (57%) compared to automation (43%). Significantly, AI use is more prevalent for tasks associated with mid-to-high wage occupations like computer programmers and data scientists but lower for both the lowest and highest-paid roles. This pattern likely reflects both the limits of current AI capabilities and practical barriers to technology adoption, suggesting that human–AI collaboration will continue evolving in distinctive patterns across different occupational categories and wage levels.

Essential Soft Skills: Creativity, Problem-Solving, and Emotional Intelligence

As AI transforms workplace dynamics, distinctly human capabilities known as "soft skills" are becoming increasingly valuable for professional success. Research consistently identifies these human-centric abilities as essential complements to technical expertise in AI-integrated environments. The growing importance of soft skills stems directly from AI's inherent limitations; while technological systems excel at technical, analytical, and repetitive tasks, they lack creativity, empathy, and human judgement. This complementary relationship creates an increasing demand for professionals who can effectively collaborate with AI systems while providing distinctly human capabilities that current technologies cannot replicate. The most valuable soft skills in this evolving context include critical thinking for evaluating AI-generated results, emotional intelligence for optimising human–machine interactions, interpersonal communication for explaining AI recommendations, and collaboration capabilities for integrating machine intelligence with human ideas.

Critical thinking stands out as particularly essential in AI-integrated environments, functioning as a bridge between automated analyses and effective decision-making. Although AI excels at rapidly processing data and executing predictive tasks, it cannot independently question assumptions or identify potential biases in automated decisions. Professionals with strong critical thinking capabilities can evaluate AI-generated results, identify limitations, and suggest improvements that enhance overall outcomes. This analytical ability becomes increasingly valuable as organisations rely more heavily on AI-generated insights for strategic decision-making, requiring human oversight to ensure contextually appropriate application. Similarly, emotional intelligence—understanding and managing one's emotions while recognising others' emotions—fosters better collaboration and stronger relationships in technology-integrated workplaces. These intertwined skills optimise interactions between humans and technologies while creating harmonious work environments that boost employee involvement and effectiveness.

The relationship between AI capabilities and human creativity represents one of the most fascinating dimensions of workplace transformation. Rather than replacing human creativity, generative AI is becoming a collaborative partner in creative processes across diverse domains. This emerging relationship resembles having "a remarkably talented assistant or sidekick who can instantly generate hundreds of ideas, suggest new directions, offer outlines and structures for work, create visual materials, and help refine creative output"—all while leaving the essential human touch firmly in human hands. In educational and research contexts, treating AI as a creative collaborator or "dance partner" brings fresh perspectives that enhance human creative work in areas like multimodal story writing and poetry composition. This collaborative approach extends beyond academic settings into creative industries where movie studios, publishers, and advertising agencies discover innovative ways to blend human imagination with AI's creative capabilities, with filmmakers using AI to generate initial script ideas, publishers helping writers overcome creative blocks, and ad agencies brainstorming campaign concepts for human refinement.

As AI increasingly handles routine analytical tasks, emotional intelligence emerges as a critical differentiator for leadership effectiveness in technology-integrated environments. While technical skills remain important, research indicates that 92% of talent professionals surveyed by LinkedIn in 2023 agreed that soft skills, including emotional intelligence, are as important as or more important than technical capabilities. In leadership contexts, managers with strong emotional intelligence foster trust, resolve conflicts, and inspire their teams—capabilities that remain distinctly human despite advancing technological sophistication. Similarly, creativity maintains its essentially human nature even as AI assists with pattern recognition and data interpretation; in complex situations where answers aren't immediately apparent, creative problem-solving becomes indispensable. This complementary relationship between human and AI creates workplaces where technical implementation and human-centric capabilities continuously reinforce each other to achieve outcomes that neither could accomplish independently.

How Businesses Can Foster a Culture of Continuous Innovation

Creating organisational cultures that embrace technological change while maintaining human innovation requires deliberate approaches that address both structural and psychological dimensions of adaptation. Adopting AI provides far more value to businesses than simply optimising processes; leaning into new technology engenders workplaces where continuous learning, adaptability, and innovation become deeply ingrained values. This cultural transformation proves essential for organisations aiming to thrive in environments where agility and knowledge function as key differentiators for competitive success. Bennett Price of Colgate-Palmolive exemplifies this approach through the proactive integration of AI into HR processes, highlighting how technological adoption fosters environments where learning and exploration become central to strategic initiatives. By encouraging teams to explore AI applications for enhancing functions like career pathing, leaders demonstrate how embracing technology creates broader cultural shifts towards seeking novel solutions to existing challenges.

Developing a future-ready workforce in AI-integrated environments requires strategic investment in employee capabilities through comprehensive reskilling and upskilling initiatives. Organisations must recognise that AI's rapid adoption is transforming the skills landscape, necessitating a dual focus on preparing employees for evolving roles. Reskilling equips workers whose positions may evolve or shift due to automation with new capabilities aligned with strategic goals while upskilling trains teams to work effectively alongside AI by emphasising skills like decision-making, creativity, and emotional intelligence—areas where humans still outperform machines. This balanced approach recognises that successful adaptation requires both technical fluency and distinctly human capabilities that complement rather than compete with AI. Platforms like Microsoft Viva Learning can provide scalable training solutions tailored to specific organisational needs, while tools like Viva Engage help showcase creative AI implementations that foster innovation, drive adoption, and inspire exploration of new possibilities.

Successful cultural transformation involves rethinking collaboration and governance approaches to create environments where innovation flourishes while maintaining appropriate guardrails. Forward-thinking organisations view collaboration as a "social contract," outlining how work gets accomplished, documenting expectations, promoting shared practices, and maintaining accountability across teams. Similarly, effective governance approaches shift from restriction-focused frameworks to empowerment-oriented systems that tell people, "Yes, you can, and here's how," rather than emphasising limitations. This positive orientation fosters innovation while ensuring ethical AI use and robust data management practices that build trust and enable success. By aligning these efforts with collaborative tools like Microsoft Teams, organisations create seamless environments for AI-powered innovation that balance creative exploration with appropriate oversight and direction.

Building organisational resilience through employee happiness and engagement creates workforces better equipped to adapt to the changes AI introduces. Research consistently demonstrates that happier employees demonstrate greater flexibility and openness to change, positioning them to more effectively navigate technological transformation. Creating this resilience requires engaging employees at all levels to develop ownership and alignment with AI initiatives, clearly articulating how technologies support rather than threaten human roles and regularly measuring engagement through surveys and analytics to address concerns promptly while celebrating milestones. This human-centred approach recognises that technological implementation succeeds or fails largely based on how effectively organisations address the psychological and emotional aspects of change management. By prioritising employee experience throughout transformation processes, organisations create contexts where continuous innovation becomes sustainable rather than exhausting or threatening workforce well-being.

Conclusion: Embracing the Future through Human–AI Synergy

The integration of AI into workplace environments represents both an unprecedented challenge and an extraordinary opportunity for organisations and professionals navigating technological transformation. By understanding the complementary relationship between human capabilities and AI strengths, businesses can develop implementation strategies that enhance rather than diminish human contributions while leveraging technological advances to improve efficiency, decision-making, and innovation. Research increasingly demonstrates that the most successful approaches view AI not as a replacement for human workers but as collaborative partners or teammates that augment human capabilities while handling routine and analytical tasks that benefit from computational power and pattern recognition.

The future of work in AI-integrated environments depends significantly on developing essential soft skills that complement technological capabilities while enabling effective human–AI collaboration. As automation handles increasing portions of routine work, distinctly human capabilities, including critical thinking, emotional intelligence, creativity, and effective communication, become increasingly valuable. Organisations that strategically develop these capabilities while implementing technological solutions position themselves for sustainable success in rapidly evolving environments. This balanced approach recognises that technological transformation requires not merely technical implementation but thoughtful consideration of how humans and machines can most effectively work together to achieve superior outcomes.

By fostering cultures of continuous learning, adaptation, and innovation, organisations create contexts where technological change becomes an opportunity rather than a threat. This cultural transformation enables businesses to capitalise on AI's potential while maintaining the human creativity, ethical judgement, and interpersonal capabilities that remain essential for organisational success. The distinction between organisations that thrive and those that struggle will increasingly depend on their ability to create effective human–AI partnerships that leverage the unique strengths of both while developing adaptable workforces prepared for continuous evolution. The future belongs not to those who resist technological change but to those who embrace it as a catalyst for unprecedented human development and organisational transformation.

The Future of Work and Opportunities Ahead

As AI and automation continue to transform industries at an unprecedented pace, understanding the evolving landscape of work becomes essential for professionals and organisations seeking to thrive rather than merely survive. Today's rapid technological advancement is creating both disruption and opportunity across the global economy, with projections indicating that over the next 5 years, advances in AI and information-processing technologies will create 19 million jobs while displacing 9 million others. This comprehensive exploration examines the emerging job roles created by AI integration, investigates how individuals and organisations can maintain competitive advantage in rapidly evolving environments, and presents strategies for embracing uncertainty as a catalyst for unprecedented growth and innovation. By understanding these interconnected dimensions of workplace transformation, professionals can position themselves to capitalise on emerging opportunities while developing the resilience needed to navigate continuous change.

New Job Roles Emerging due to AI and Automation

The acceleration of AI adoption across industries is creating entirely new career categories that didn't exist just a few years ago. The tech industry continues to prioritise roles focused on data and AI, with AI Engineers standing out as particularly notable emerging positions. These professionals develop and deploy AI systems to automate tasks and solve complex problems across diverse sectors. Similarly, Machine Learning Engineers are experiencing growing demand for their ability to create predictive models that drive business insights and strategic decision-making. According to ACS Digital Pulse 2024, over 5.4 million Australians are already using generative AI tools in their work, highlighting the widespread integration of these technologies into daily professional activities.

More specialised AI roles are rapidly emerging to address specific technological needs and applications. Computer Vision Engineers build systems enabling computers to interpret visual data, creating innovations in facial recognition, self-driving vehicles, and augmented reality applications. These specialised professionals require skills in image processing, machine learning, and tools like OpenCV to develop solutions that bridge the gap between visual information and computational understanding. Natural Language Processing Specialists focus specifically on helping machines understand human language, developing sophisticated chatbots, voice assistants, and language translation tools that improve human–computer interaction across platforms and use cases. As these technologies continue evolving, the demand for specialists who can develop and refine these capabilities grows accordingly.

The integration of AI extends beyond purely technical roles to create hybrid positions that combine domain expertise with technological understanding. AI Product Managers bridge the critical gap between technical AI teams and business stakeholders, translating complex technological capabilities into market-ready solutions that address specific business needs. These professionals require both technological understanding and business acumen to guide AI development towards commercially viable applications. Similarly, AI Ethics Specialists have emerged as essential guardians ensuring responsible AI implementation, addressing critical concerns surrounding bias, privacy, fairness, and transparency in algorithmic decision-making. These roles highlight how AI integration creates demand not only for technical expertise but also for professionals who can navigate the complex human, ethical, and business dimensions of technological implementation.

The manufacturing and healthcare sectors demonstrate how AI integration creates sector-specific opportunities that combine technological capabilities with domain knowledge. In high-tech manufacturing environments, AI integration is creating specialised roles for data analysts who derive actionable insights from production data, AI programmers who develop customised solutions for manufacturing challenges, and Machine Learning Specialists who optimise production processes through predictive modelling. These emerging positions require both technical skills and a deep understanding of manufacturing processes, highlighting how AI creates opportunities at the intersection of established domains and emerging technologies. The expansion of these hybrid roles across sectors creates career pathways for professionals who develop both technological fluency and domain expertise rather than specialising exclusively in either area.

How Individuals and Organisations Can Stay Competitive

The skills landscape is undergoing significant transformation as AI reshapes work processes across industries. According to the World Economic Forum's Future of Jobs Report 2025, employers expect 39% of key skills required in the job market will change by 2030, creating substantial demands for continuous learning and adaptation. Technological skills are projected to grow in importance more rapidly than any others in the next 5 years, with AI and big data leading this transformation, followed closely by networks, cybersecurity, and technological literacy. However, distinctly human capabilities remain crucial complements to technical skills, with creative thinking, resilience, flexibility, and agility rising in importance alongside curiosity and lifelong learning. This balanced skill portfolio—combining technical fluency with human-centric capabilities—creates the foundation for sustainable success in rapidly evolving work environments.

For individuals seeking to maintain competitiveness in AI-integrated workplaces, developing both technical understanding and complementary soft skills proves essential. While technical knowledge provides immediate value in specific contexts, focusing exclusively on these capabilities creates vulnerability as implementations change. The World Economic Forum emphasises that alongside technical skills, professionals should cultivate areas where humans maintain distinct advantages, including leadership, social influence, analytical thinking, and environmental stewardship. This holistic development approach recognises that successful adaptation requires both technical fluency and distinctly human capabilities that remain difficult for AI systems to replicate. By developing capabilities that complement rather than compete with technological systems, professionals position themselves for long-term success regardless of specific implementation changes.

Organisations must adopt strategic approaches to AI integration that align technological implementation with business objectives while developing workforce capabilities. Businesses need to integrate AI strategically, focusing on workplace automation and innovation to remain competitive in rapidly evolving marketplaces. Developing robust AI business cases has become crucial for successful implementation, requiring clear objectives, expected benefits, and thorough consideration of potential challenges before committing resources to specific initiatives. Equally important, investing in new technology—including advanced automation systems and AI-driven analytics—enables organisations to streamline operations and enhance productivity while gathering data that informs further improvements. These strategic considerations create the foundation for sustainable AI implementation that delivers genuine business value rather than merely adopting technology without a clear purpose.

Creating organisational cultures that embrace technological change while fostering continuous innovation represents another critical success factor for competitive advantage. Forward-thinking organisations recognise that fostering cultures of innovation encourages employees to embrace AI and leverage its capabilities for improved outcomes rather than resisting technological change. This cultural orientation transforms potential anxiety about technological disruption into enthusiasm for enhanced capabilities and expanded possibilities. Similarly, collaboration with AI experts and continuous monitoring of technological advancements ensures organisations remain ahead of emerging trends and can adapt to new opportunities quickly as they develop. By creating environments where technological adaptation becomes normalised rather than exceptional, organisations develop the agility needed to continuously evolve as technological capabilities expand and competitive landscapes shift.

Embracing Uncertainty as a Driver of Personal and Professional Growth

Uncertainty represents an inevitable component of technological transformation, creating both challenges and opportunities for those navigating rapidly evolving professional landscapes. Rather than viewing uncertainty as primarily threatening, research increasingly suggests that uncertainty can function as a valuable territory where genuine growth and innovation emerge when approached with appropriate mindsets and capabilities. By understanding why uncertainty feels unsettling and developing practical strategies for navigating ambiguity, professionals can transform potential anxiety into confidence that enables exploration of emerging possibilities rather than retreat to familiar but increasingly obsolete patterns. This perspective shift—from viewing uncertainty as a threat to recognising it as an opportunity—creates psychological foundations for thriving amid continuous change rather than merely surviving it.

The psychological dimensions of uncertainty significantly impact how effectively individuals navigate changing environments. Human beings naturally seek stability and control, with uncertainty triggering the brain's fear centre and creating stress responses that can impede effective adaptation when not properly managed. This natural reaction, cultivated over time as a response to potential threats, can become counterproductive in rapidly evolving professional environments where flexibility and exploration prove more valuable than rigid adherence to established patterns. The key to thriving amid uncertainty lies in developing cognitive flexibility that allows professionals to respond to new information, adjust goals when needed, and remain calm when facing the unexpected. This adaptive capability doesn't eliminate discomfort but transforms it from paralysis-inducing anxiety into manageable emotion that accompanies rather than prevents growth and development.

Developing specific capabilities that enhance adaptability creates the foundation for effectively embracing uncertainty as a growth catalyst rather than an impediment. When professionals learn to adapt to uncertainty, they become more agile and flexible in both personal and professional contexts, creating advantages in rapidly evolving environments. Research suggests that embracing uncertainty can enhance creativity and innovation by creating space for exploring multiple possible solutions rather than focusing narrowly on finding one "right" answer to complex challenges. This exploratory approach proves particularly valuable in technological contexts where established solutions frequently prove insufficient for emerging challenges. By developing comfort with ambiguity and building capabilities for confident navigation of unknown domains, professionals position themselves at the frontier of possibility rather than the periphery of transformation.

The practical implementation of uncertainty-embracing approaches requires specific strategies that build confidence while maintaining momentum through continuous change. Mindfulness practices help train the mind to remain present and non-judgemental when facing unpredictable situations, reducing the fear and anxiety that often accompany uncertainty. Similarly, seeking out new experiences and exposing ourselves to situations requiring adaptability strengthens cognitive flexibility, creating greater capability for managing future uncertainty effectively. Rather than avoiding uncertain situations, professionals who intentionally engage with ambiguity develop capabilities that transform potential threats into navigable challenges. This proactive approach seeking rather than avoiding uncertainty creates accelerated growth through expanded experience rather than the false security of familiar but increasingly irrelevant patterns.

Conclusion: Navigating the Future with Confidence

The integration of AI and automation into workplace environments creates both unprecedented challenges and extraordinary opportunities for professionals and organisations prepared to embrace change as a catalyst for growth. By understanding emerging job roles—from AI Engineers and Machine Learning Specialists to AI Ethics Experts and domain-specific hybrid positions—individuals can strategically position themselves at the intersection of technological capability and market demand. Developing balanced skill portfolios that combine technical fluency with distinctly human capabilities creates a sustainable competitive advantage regardless of specific implementation changes or technological advancements. Most importantly, transforming the relationship with uncertainty from something to be feared to valuable territory for growth and innovation creates psychological foundations for continuous adaptation that remain essential in rapidly evolving environments.

The distinction between those who thrive and those who struggle will increasingly depend on their ability to embrace change rather than resist it. By cultivating the mindsets and capabilities explored in this analysis, professionals and organisations position themselves to capitalise on emerging opportunities while developing the resilience needed for continuous evolution. The future belongs not to those who fear technological change but to those who recognise it as an invitation to unprecedented growth and possibility, creating pathways to expanded human potential and organisational impact previously unimaginable. This perspective transforms the individual's relationship with technological advancement from anxiety to anticipation, revealing horizons of possibility that transcend current limitations and open pathways to genuine fulfilment through continuous adaptation and growth.

Conclusion: Adapting for Success

During the exploration of embracing change in the era of AI, it becomes increasingly evident that adaptation is not merely a survival strategy but a pathway to unprecedented growth and opportunity. The ability to navigate technological transformation with confidence and purpose has evolved from a desirable quality into an essential requirement for professionals and organisations seeking sustained relevance and impact. This comprehensive conclusion examines how to change functions as a powerful catalyst for growth and innovation, investigates strategies for building resilience in rapidly evolving technological landscapes, and provides final thoughts on developing the future-ready mindset necessary for thriving amid continuous transformation. By synthesising these interconnected dimensions of successful adaptation, a framework is created to help people thrive and flourish in an AI-integrated future.

Change as a Catalyst for Growth and New Opportunities

Change, while often initially perceived as disruptive and unsettling, represents a powerful catalyst for transformation, innovation, and progress when approached with appropriate mindsets and capabilities. Change naturally disrupts established routines and encourages fresh thinking patterns, creating environments where resourcefulness and innovative problem-solving flourish out of necessity. When faced with changing circumstances, individuals and organisations develop creative approaches that might never have emerged within the comfortable confines of familiar patterns and processes. This relationship between disruption and innovation highlights how change, rather than merely threatening established approaches, creates fertile ground for unprecedented growth and development across personal and organisational contexts.

Organisations that recognise change as an opportunity rather than a threat position themselves to capitalise on emerging possibilities while competitors remain paralysed by resistance or uncertainty. Process changes specifically encourage teams to explore innovative solutions to existing challenges by disrupting established thinking patterns and creating space for fresh perspectives. When employees actively participate in shaping and implementing new processes, they develop ownership and motivation that drive positive outcomes beyond what might be achievable through maintaining established approaches. This engagement transforms potential resistance into enthusiastic participation, creating momentum that accelerates positive transformation across operational domains. The deliberate embrace of change creates competitive advantages that drive sustainable growth while simultaneously developing capabilities that facilitate continuous adaptation to evolving technological and market conditions.

Innovation functions as the primary mechanism through which change drives growth, providing the conceptual bridge between disruption and advancement. In business and economic contexts, innovation serves as the fundamental catalyst for growth, producing positive changes in efficiency, productivity, quality, competitiveness, and market share. As experts note, "Companies cannot grow through cost reduction and reengineering alone ... Innovation is the key element in providing aggressive top-line growth and for increasing bottom-line results." This recognition highlights that embracing change through innovative responses creates pathways to growth that transcend the limitations of purely defensive or optimising approaches. Organisations can enhance innovation potential by providing work groups with opportunities and resources to develop novel solutions beyond their core responsibilities, creating environments where change becomes an opportunity rather than a threat.

The relationship between change and opportunity extends beyond organisational contexts to impact individual career trajectories and professional development. When professionals reframe change as an opportunity for growth rather than a disruption to established patterns, they discover possibilities for career advancement, skill development, and increased engagement that might otherwise remain invisible. This perspective shift transforms technological advancement from a potential threat to an invitation for unprecedented personal and professional evolution. As one expert notes, "The power to innovate lies within each of us. It's a choice we make every day, whether we're aware of it or not." This recognition empowers individuals to approach change proactively rather than reactively, creating agency amid transformation rather than experiencing themselves as passive recipients of externally imposed disruption.

Building Resilience in an Ever-Evolving Technological Landscape

The acceleration of technological advancement creates environments where building resilience becomes essential for sustained success and well-being. Research consistently demonstrates that adapting to technological changes requires a proactive approach that prioritises adaptability, flexibility, and growth mindset development rather than reactive responses to specific implementation changes. This orientation creates sustainable foundations for continuous evolution regardless of technological developments or implementation approaches. By developing capabilities that transcend specific technologies or applications, individuals and organisations create resilience that maintains relevance despite continuous transformation in technological landscapes.

Specific practices and mindsets significantly enhance resilience amid technological advancement. Being curious and asking for help when needed create learning orientations that transform potential threats into opportunities for capability development. Similarly, practising problem-solving approaches that embrace rather than avoid challenges develops cognitive flexibility that facilitates adaptation to changing circumstances. Perhaps most importantly, maintaining open-mindedness and willingness to change perspective when evidence suggests alternative approaches creates adaptability that proves invaluable during periods of significant transformation. These interconnected capabilities collectively enhance resilience while creating sustainable foundations for continuous learning and development in rapidly evolving technological environments.

Embracing fear rather than avoiding it represents another powerful approach to building resilience amid technological change. While fear naturally emerges when facing unknown or potentially threatening circumstances, transforming this emotional response from impediment to catalyst creates powerful motivation for growth and development. Facing challenges directly rather than avoiding them builds mental and emotional fortitude essential for navigating life's uncertainties, particularly when confronting technological disruption that challenges established skills and knowledge. Each triumph over fear functions as a stepping stone towards greater self-confidence and self-efficacy, creating momentum that facilitates future adaptation regardless of specific circumstances. This transformed relationship with fear, from paralysis to motivation, creates psychological foundations for continuous growth amid technological change.

Organisational approaches to building resilience require creating cultures where continuous learning and adaptation become normalised rather than exceptional. Forward-thinking organisations recognise that technological disruption creates both challenges and opportunities, requiring intentional approaches to enhancing collective adaptability. Implementation strategies include establishing clear communications about technological changes, involving employees in decision-making processes, providing comprehensive training and development opportunities, and celebrating adaptation successes that highlight the benefits of embracing rather than resisting change. These approaches collectively create environments where technological advancement becomes an opportunity for organisational evolution rather than a threat to established processes and capabilities. The resulting resilience enables organisations to navigate technological transformation while maintaining operational effectiveness and employee engagement throughout periods of significant change.

Final Thoughts on Shaping a Future-Ready Mindset

Developing a future-ready mindset begins with recognising the fundamental difference between fixed and growth orientations towards capability development. A fixed mindset views intelligence and abilities as static and unchangeable, creating psychological barriers that inhibit adaptation and growth by framing challenges as threats to established competence. In contrast, a growth mindset recognises that abilities develop through dedication, learning, and perseverance, approaching challenges as opportunities for development rather than evidence of limitation. This distinction proves particularly significant when navigating technological change, as growth-oriented individuals embrace learning opportunities created by disruption while fixed-minded counterparts primarily experience threat and resistance. The resulting difference in adaptation capacity creates significant advantages for growth-oriented professionals and organisations in rapidly evolving technological landscapes.

A success mindset specifically incorporates traits including appropriate attitude and temperament, realistic thinking, and capability for change and improvement. Professionals developing success mindsets recognise that achieving goals requires more than just technical knowledge—it demands psychological flexibility and emotional resilience that facilitate continuous adaptation as circumstances evolve. This mindset involves maintaining optimism while realistically assessing challenges, developing confidence in capability development rather than fearing obsolescence and embracing continuous improvement as a pathway to sustained relevance rather than viewing it as evidence of previous inadequacy. When cultivated intentionally, this orientation creates psychological foundations for thriving amid continuous change rather than merely surviving it.

Organisations play crucial roles in fostering growth mindsets that enhance collective adaptability and innovation potential. Leadership approaches directly impact how employees perceive and respond to change, with effective change catalysts functioning as trusted influencers who guide, navigate, and accelerate the people side of change with key stakeholders. These leaders take responsibility for engaging, motivating, communicating, and coordinating with stakeholders while bringing them successfully along change journeys. When implemented effectively, these approaches transform potential resistance into enthusiasm for exploration and growth, creating environments where continuous adaptation becomes a cultural norm rather than an exception. The resulting organisational agility creates sustained competitive advantage in rapidly evolving technological landscapes while enhancing employee engagement and satisfaction through meaningful participation in transformation processes.

The journey towards a future-ready mindset ultimately represents continuous evolution rather than a destination, a process of developing psychological flexibility and learning orientation that facilitates adaptation regardless of specific technological implementations or market conditions. As one expert notes, "A growth mindset is a perspective that welcomes and embraces learning, resilience, and growth from failures." This orientation transforms technological disruption from threat to opportunity, creating pathways to unprecedented growth and fulfilment through continuous adaptation and capability development. By cultivating this perspective intentionally through practices including embracing challenges, learning from setbacks, seeking feedback, developing resilience, and maintaining curiosity, professionals create sustainable foundations for success regardless of how specifically technological capabilities evolve or implementation approaches change.

Embracing the Future with Confidence

The integration of AI and automation into workplace environments creates both unprecedented challenges and extraordinary opportunities for those prepared to embrace change as a catalyst for growth. By recognising change as an opportunity rather than a threat, building resilience through proactive adaptation approaches, and developing growth-oriented mindsets that facilitate continuous learning, individuals and organisations position themselves to thrive amid technological transformation rather than merely surviving it. This comprehensive approach transforms potential anxiety about disruption into enthusiasm for the expanded possibilities that emerge through thoughtful engagement with technological advancement.

By choosing to view change as a possibility, embrace uncertainty as a growth catalyst, and prepare strategically for technological evolution, the psychological foundations are built for extraordinary growth and fulfilment regardless of specific implementation approaches or technological developments. The future belongs not to those who fear change but to those who recognise it as the pathway to expanded human potential and organisational impact previously unimaginable.

The journey into the technological future has already begun, with everyone determining whether to approach transformation as a threat or an opportunity. When the choice is embracing change as a catalyst for growth, building resilience through proactive adaptation, and cultivating future-ready mindsets focused on continuous learning, people discover possibilities that remain invisible to those paralysed by resistance or fear. This perspective transforms the relationship with technological advancement from anxiety to anticipation, revealing horizons of possibility that transcend current limitations and open pathways to unprecedented human flourishing through continuous adaptation and growth.

Chapter Questions

1. How are AI and automation reshaping traditional industries like manufacturing, healthcare, finance, and retail, and what are the key benefits and challenges they introduce?

2. What role does predictive maintenance play in AI-powered manufacturing, and how does it differ from traditional maintenance approaches?

3. How is AI enhancing patient outcomes in healthcare, and what are some administrative tasks it helps automate?

4. Explain how financial institutions are using AI to improve decision-making, fraud detection, and operational efficiency.

5. What is meant by the "compression of adaptation cycles," and how does it affect professional skill development?

6. Why is adaptability considered a "meta-skill" in the age of AI, and how does it compare with static job-based security models?

7. What is Moravec's Paradox, and how does it explain the complementary strengths of humans and AI?

8. How does success-induced complacency act as a barrier to adaptation in both individuals and organisations?

9. Why is developing a growth mindset essential for adapting to technological change, and how can individuals cultivate it?

10. How does shifting from fixed career paths to continuous learning models help future-proof careers?

11. What are the advantages of cross-disciplinary knowledge in AI-integrated roles, and how does it enhance adaptability?

12. In what ways are AI-powered platforms and certifications transforming professional learning and upskilling ecosystems?

13. How do emotional intelligence, creativity, and collaboration remain essential in AI-integrated workplaces despite automation?

14. What strategies can organisations implement to reduce resistance to change and foster a culture of innovation?

15. Describe a real-world example or case study from the chapter where an individual successfully navigated a career transformation through growth mindset and skill development.

16. What are the core principles of building a future-ready mindset, and how can professionals embrace uncertainty as a catalyst for growth?

Note to Readers and Educators

Comprehensive answers and explanations to these chapter-end questions are available at www.sandeepbhalekar.com. The website also provides supplementary frameworks, teaching guidelines, and reference materials to support deeper understanding and classroom discussion.

Educators and facilitators can access additional resources, including presentation frameworks, assessment rubrics, and discussion prompts, to help integrate the concepts from this chapter into academic or professional learning environments.

Bibliography

Accenture. (n.d.). *Gen AI & Talent*. Retrieved from https://www.accenture.com/au-en/insights/consulting/gen-ai-talent

Acciona. (n.d.). *Importance of Soft Skills*. Retrieved from https://people.acciona.com/professional-development/importance-soft-skills/

ACS. (n.d.). *Emerging Tech Roles to Watch in 2025*. Retrieved from https://membership.acs.org.au/member-insight/20251501Emerging_Tech_Roles_to_Watch_in_2025.html

ACS Australia. (2024). *Technology Impacts on the Australian Workforce*. https://www.acs.org.au/insightsandpublications/reports-publications/technology-impacts-on-the-australian-workforce.html

Afiniti. (n.d.). *Change Management Success Stories*. Retrieved from https://www.afiniti.co.uk/insights/change-management-success-stories/

Agencia Change. (n.d.). *Using Change as a Catalyst for Growth*. Retrieved from https://www.agenciachange.com/post/using-change-as-a-catalyst-for-growth

Agile Change Management. (2024). *Strategies for Resistance to Change*. https://agile-changemanagement.co.uk/strategies-for-resistance-to-change/

AgriFutures Australia. (n.d.). *Catalyst Opportunities*. Retrieved from https://agrifutures.com.au/opportunities/catalyst/

AI4 AL. (n.d.). *Artificial Intelligence: A New Frontier for Lifelong Learning*. Retrieved from https://www.ai4al.eu/artificial-intelligence-a-new-frontier-for-lifelong-learning/

AICD. (n.d.). *How AI Can Boost Productivity*. Retrieved from https://www.aicd.com.au/innovative-technology/digital-business/artificial-intelligence/how-ai-can-boost-productivity.html

AiGroup. (n.d.-a). *Data May Be King in Future of Jobs, but Humans Will Still Rule*. Retrieved from https://www.aigroup.com.au/news/blogs/2025/data-may-be-king-in-future-of-jobs-but-humans-will-still-rule/

AiGroup. (n.d.-b). *Driving Lifelong Learning and Upskilling*. Retrieved from https://www.aigroup.com.au/education-training/centre-for-education-and-training/blog/singapore-leaders-on-driving-life-long-learning-reskilling-and-upskilling/

AiGroup CET. (n.d.). *Emerging Roles: AI & the Future of Jobs*. Retrieved from https://cet.aigroup.com.au/link/8382bbb5d6dc4466b4c80ee2055b70f8.aspx

AiGroup CET. (2025a). *Future of Jobs Report 2025*. Retrieved from https://cet.aigroup.com.au/news/reports-submissions/2025/future-of-jobs-report-2025/

AiGroup CET. (2025b). *Reports and Submissions—Future of Jobs Report 2025*. Retrieved from https://cet.aigroup.com.au/news/reports-submissions/2025/future-of-jobs-report-2025/

AJG. (n.d.). *Generative AI: Upskilling the Workforce*. Retrieved from https://www.ajg.com/no-nb/news-and-insights/features/generative-ai-upskilling-the-workforce/

AlignToday. (n.d.). *The Growth Mindset: How Leaders Can Foster a Culture of Growth*. Retrieved from https://aligntoday.com/blog/the-growth-mindset-how-leaders-can-foster-a-culture-of-growth/

Alleo. (n.d.). *Strategies for Tech Professionals to Build Resilience in Rapidly Changing Digital Landscapes*.

Al -Tahhan, A. (n.d.). *Continuous Learning in the Age of AI—My Journey*. LinkedIn. Retrieved from https://www.linkedin.com/pulse/continuous-learning-age-ai-my-journey-amro-al-tahhan-9yt6e

American Academy of Estate Planning Attorneys. (2024, April). *Overcoming Ego and Resistance: Embracing a Coachable Mindset*. Retrieved from https://www.aaepa.com/2024/04/overcoming-ego-and-resistance-embracing-a-coachable-mindset/

American University School of Education. (n.d.). *Growth Mindset in the Classroom*. Retrieved from https://soeonline.american.edu/blog/growth-mindset-in-the-classroom/

AmitySolutions. (n.d.). *Workplace AI: Productivity & Collaboration*. Retrieved from https://www.amitysolutions.com/blog/workplace-ai-productivity-collaboration

AMS Consulting. (n.d.). *Overcoming Resistance to Change*. Retrieved from https://amsconsulting.com/articles/overcoming-resistance-to-change/

AnalyticsWeek. (n.d.). *Upskilling in the AI Era: What the HAPI Teaches Us About Lifelong Learning*. Retrieved from https://analyticsweek.com/upskilling-in-the-ai-era-what-the-hapi-teaches-us-about-lifelong-learning/

Andrea , J. (n.d.-a). *AI Is Changing Careers Faster Than You Think—Here's How*. LinkedIn. Retrieved from https://www.linkedin.com/pulse/ai-changing-careers-faster-than-you-thinkheres-how-andrea-j-fxfve

Andrea , J. (n.d.-b). *AI Changing Careers Faster Than You Think—Here's How*. Retrieved from https://www.linkedin.com/pulse/ai-changing-careers-faster-than-you-thinkheres-how-andrea-j-fxfve

Anthropic. (n.d.). *The Anthropic Economic Index*. Retrieved from https://www.anthropic.com/news/the-anthropic-economic-index

arXiv. (n.d.). *AI-Human Collaboration*. Retrieved from https://arxiv.org/html/2407.19098v1

Asher IT Services. (n.d.). *The Power of Adaptability and Continuous Learning in AI Careers*. LinkedIn. Retrieved from https://www.linkedin.com/pulse/power-adaptability-continuous-learning-ai-careers-asher-it-services-o2kvf

Aspen University. (2024). *The Future of Work: How AI and Automation are Changing Business*. https://www.aspen.edu/altitude/the-future-of-work-how-ai-and-automation-are-changing-business/

Atlassian. (n.d.). *AI Collaboration Report*. Retrieved from https://www.atlassian.com/blog/productivity/ai-collaboration-report

Aura. (n.d.). *AI Job Trends 2025*. Retrieved from https://blog.getaura.ai/ai-job-trends-2025

Australian Institute of Business. (n.d.). *5 Ways to Create a Success Mindset*. Retrieved from https://www.aib.edu.au/blog/balance-wellbeing/5-ways-to-create-a-success-mindset/

Avid Australia. (2022). *Fostering a Growth Mindset for Student Success* [Handouts]. Retrieved from https://avidaustralia.edu.au/wp-content/uploads/2022/10/Fostering-a-Growth-Mindset-for-Student-Success-20-Oct-2022-Handouts.pdf

BCBusiness. (n.d.). *Foster Trust in AI: The Role of Workforce Upskilling*. Retrieved from https://www.bcbusiness.ca/industries/education/foster-trust-in-ai-the-role-of-workforce-upskilling/

Betterworks. (n.d.). *AI & Organisational Culture*.

BigThink. (2024). *6 Ways Leaders Can Thrive with a Fear-Embracing Mindset*. https://bigthink.com/business/6-ways-leaders-can-thrive-with-a-fear-embracing-mindset/

Borderline Support UK. (n.d.). *Lesson: Embracing Change as a Catalyst for Growth*. Retrieved from https://borderlinesupport.org.uk/lesson/embracing-change-as-a-catalyst-for-growth/

Boston Consulting Group. (2014). *Five Case Studies: Transformation Excellence*. Retrieved from https://www.bcg.com/publications/2014/transformation-change-management-five-case-studies-transformation-excellence

Brootc. (2024). *Cultivating a Growth Mindset: Change Management Strategies*. https://brootc.com/cultivating-a-growth-mindset-change-management-strategies-for-fostering-continuous-improvement/

Broot Consulting. (n.d.). *Cultivating a Growth Mindset: Change Management Strategies for Fostering Continuous Improvement*. Retrieved from https://brootc.com/cultivating-a-growth-mindset-change-management-strategies-for-fostering-continuous-improvement/

Business Queensland. (n.d.). *Growing Your Business*. Retrieved from https://www.business.qld.gov.au/running-business/growing-business

Canon Business Insights. (n.d.). *AI, Automation, and the Future of Work*. Retrieved from https://business.canon.com.au/insights/ai-automation-and-the-future-of-work

Career Guidance Advice. (2024). *How to Overcome the Fear of Changing Careers: 7 Proven Strategies*. https://careerguidanceadvice.com/how-to-overcome-the-fear-of-changing-careers-7-proven-strategies/

Caroline Adams Coaching. (n.d.). *Overcoming Fear of Career Change*. Retrieved from https://carolineadamscoaching.com/blog/overcoming-fear-of-career-change

Carve Consulting. (2024). *From Fixed to Growth Mindset: How Managers Can Help*. https://carveconsulting.com.au/fixed-to-growth-mindset-how-managers-can-help/

Change Catalysts. (2023). *CQ® Case Study: One Leader's Journey* [PDF]. Retrieved from https://changecatalysts.com/wp-content/uploads/2023/05/CQ%C2%AE-Case-Study-One-Leaders-Journey.pdf

Changefirst. (n.d.). *Case Study: How Changefirst Kick-Started Enterprise Change Management in a Major Transport Service Provider*. Retrieved from https://blog.changefirst.com/case-study-how-changefirst-kick-started-enterprise-change-management-in-a-major-transport-service-provider

Cirqle Group. (n.d.). *How AI Will Reshape the Workplace in 2025*. Retrieved from https://www.cirqlegroup.com/news-updates/how-ai-will-reshape-the-workplace-in-2025/

Cisco & CICA. (2019). *Future of Australian Jobs Report*. https://cica.org.au/wp-content/uploads/cisco-future-of-australian-jobs-report2019.pdf

CityU. (n.d.). *Skills in Demand 2025*. Retrieved from https://www.cityu.edu/blog/skills-in-demand-2025/

Cloud Wars. (n.d.). *3 Ways AI Will Change Business Culture*. Retrieved from https://cloudwars.com/innovation-leadership/3-ways-ai-will-change-business-culture/

CNBC. (n.d.). *The Skill Humans Can Leverage as AI Disrupts Workforces Globally*. Retrieved from https://www.cnbc.com/2025/02/26/the-skill-humans-can-leverage-as-ai-disrupts-workforces-globally.html

Coch , L., & French, J.R.P. (1969). *How to Deal with Resistance to Change*. Harvard Business Review. Retrieved from https://hbr.org/1969/01/how-to-deal-with-resistance-to-change

Coursera. (n.d.). *AI Courses*. Retrieved from https://www.coursera.org/courses?query=artificial+intelligence

Crestcom. (2024, March 29). *How to Overcome Fears to Build a Growth Mindset with Dominic George*. Retrieved from https://crestcom.com/blog/2024/03/29/how-to-overcome-fears-to-build-a-growth-mindset-with-dominic-george/

Culture Amp. (n.d.). *Career Advice Podcast*. Retrieved from https://www.cultureamp.com/podcast/career-advice

DataCamp. (n.d.). *Top AI Certifications*. Retrieved from https://www.datacamp.com/blog/top-ai-certifications

DeepCognition. (n.d.). *How to Stay Competitive and Future-Proof Your Business by Leveraging AI*. Retrieved from https://deepcognition.ai/how-to-stay-competitive-and-future-proof-your-business-by-leveraging-ai/

DeniseGlee. com. (n.d.). *Overcoming Fear: Your Guide to Embracing Change and Growth*. Retrieved from https://deniseglee.com/overcoming-fear-your-guide-to-embracing-change-and-growth/

DevelopmentAid. (2024). *Technology's Impact on Employment*. https://www.developmentaid.org/news-stream/post/173022/technology-impact-on-employment

Disco. co. (n.d.). *AI Tools for Career Development Programs*. Retrieved from https://www.disco.co/blog/ai-tools-for-career-development-programs

Dweck, C. (n.d.). *Growth Mindsets*. Association for Psychological Science. Retrieved from https://www.psychologicalscience.org/observer/dweck-growth-mindsets

Dweck, C. (2016, January). *What Having a Growth Mindset Actually Means*. Harvard Business Review. Retrieved from https://hbr.org/2016/01/what-having-a-growth-mindset-actually-means

Dwoskin , J. (2024). *The Rise of AI and the Critical Need for AQ (Adaptability Quotient)*. LinkedIn. https://www.linkedin.com/pulse/rise-ai-critical-need-adaptability-quotient-aq-jon-dwoskin--nxote

Dykes , B. (2025, March 10). *The Human-AI Playbook: Moving Beyond Automation to True Collaboration*. Forbes. Retrieved from https://www.forbes.com/sites/brentdykes/2025/03/10/the-human-ai-playbook-moving-beyond-automation-to-true-collaboration/

EarlyBirds. (n.d.). *Leveraging Innovation for Long-Term Strategic Growth.* Retrieved from https://earlybirds.io/en/news/368-leveraging-innovation-for-long-term-strategic-growth

edX. (n.d.-a). *AI Courses.* Retrieved from https://www.edx.org/learn/artificial-intelligence

edX. (n.d.-b). *Artificial Intelligence Learning.* Retrieved from https://www.edx.org/learn/artificial-intelligence

edX. (n.d.-c). *How to Stay Competitive in an AI World.* Retrieved from https://www.edx.org/resources/how-to-stay-competitive-in-an-ai-world

Elements of AI. (n.d.-a). *Homepage.* Retrieved from https://www.elementsofai.com

Elements of AI. (n.d.-b). *Learn AI.* Retrieved from https://www.elementsofai.com

El Hajj, H. (n.d.). *Overcoming Resistance to Change: Strategies for Success.* LinkedIn. Retrieved from https://www.linkedin.com/pulse/overcoming-resistance-change-strategies-success-hassan-el-hajj

Emagine. (n.d.). *Embracing Change as an Opportunity for Growth.* Retrieved from https://www.emagine.org/blogs/embracing-change-as-an-opportunity-for-growth/

Engagedly. (n.d.). *Why Change Management Is Crucial for Business Growth.* Retrieved from https://engagedly.com/blog/why-change-management-is-crucial-for-business-growth/

Entrepreneur. (2024). *Why Embracing Change Is the Best Catalyst for Growth.* Retrieved from https://www.entrepreneur.com/growing-a-business/why-embracing-change-is-the-best-catalyst-for-growth/450192

ESCP Business School. (n.d.). *Artificial Intelligence and Productivity: Transforming the Modern Workplace.* Retrieved from https://escp.eu/news/artificial-intelligence-and-productivity-transforming-modern-workplace

Everyday Millionaire. (2024). *The Power of Overcoming Resistance: Unlocking Growth.* https://theeverydaymillionaire.ca/the-power-of-overcoming-resistance-unlocking-growth-and-building-strong-relationships/

Evolllution. (n.d.). *The Next Frontier: Human-AI Collaboration for a Smarter Workforce.* Retrieved from https://evolllution.com/the-next-frontier-human-ai-collaboration-for-a-smarter-workforce

Forbes. (n.d.). *How Leaders Can Increase Productivity Using AI Combined with Soft Skills.* Retrieved from https://www.forbes.com/sites/maryhemphill/2024/04/01/how-leaders-can-increase-productivity-using-ai-combined-with-soft-skills/

Forbes. (2023). *How AI Will Impact the Next-Generation Workforce.* Retrieved from https://www.forbes.com/sites/kalinabryant/2023/05/31/how-ai-will-impact-the-next-generation-workforce/

Forbes. (2024). *5 Steps to Stay Competitive Amidst AI and Rapid Change.* Retrieved from https://www.forbes.com/sites/carolinecenizalevine/2024/09/24/5-steps-to-stay-competitive-amidst-ai-and-rapid-change/

Forbes Business Council. (2023a, July 26). *A Guide to Implementing New Technologies Effectively in the Workplace.* Forbes. Retrieved from https://www.forbes.com/councils/forbesbusinesscouncil/2023/07/26/a-guide-to-implementing-new-technologies-effectively-in-the-workplace/

Forbes Business Council. (2023b, March 3). *Eight Ways to Conquer Your Fear of Change as a Leader.* Forbes. Retrieved from https://www.forbes.com/councils/forbesbusinesscouncil/2023/03/03/eight-ways-to-conquer-your-fear-of-change-as-a-leader/

Forbes Business Council. (2024). *16 Ways Leaders Can Leverage Tech to Drive Business Transformation*. Retrieved from https://www.forbes.com/councils/forbesbusiness council/2024/06/05/16-ways-leaders-can-leverage-tech-to-drive-business-transformation/

Forbes Coaches Council. (2022, October 24). *How to Work Through Change Resistance and Promote a Growth Mindset*. Forbes. Retrieved from https://www.forbes.com/councils/forbescoachescouncil/2022/10/24/how-to-work-through-change-resistance-and-promote-a-growth-mindset/

Forbes Coaches Council. (2024). *How to Foster a More Open Mindset Among Team Members*. Retrieved from https://www.forbes.com/councils/forbescoaches-council/2024/02/23/how-to-foster-a-more-open-mindset-among-team-members/

Forbes Human Resources Council. (2018). *Change as an Opportunity: A Strategic Approach to Change Management*. Retrieved from https://www.forbes.com/sites/forbeshumanresourcescouncil/2018/07/20/change-as-an-opportunity-a-strategic-approach-to-change-management/

Forrester. (n.d.). *Are You an Effective Change Catalyst?* Retrieved from https://www.forrester.com/blogs/are-you-an-effective-change-catalyst/

FranklinCovey Australia. (2024). *Growth Mindset Tips*. Retrieved from https://www.franklincovey.com.au/growth-mindset-tips/

Frontiers in Education. (2024). *How Educational Institutions Can Foster Resilience*. Retrieved from https://www.frontiersin.org/journals/education/articles/10.3389/feduc.2024.1358431/full

Frontiers in Psychology. (2021). *Growth Mindsets and Adaptation*. Retrieved from https://www.frontiersin.org/journals/psychology/articles/10.3389/fpsyg.2021.588438/full

Fusion Risk Management. (n.d.). *The Importance of Resilience: Navigating the Ever-Evolving Landscape*. Retrieved from https://www.fusionrm.com/blogs/the-importance-of-resilience-navigating-the-ever-evolving-landscape/

Futures Platform. (n.d.). *Future of Work: AI in the Workplace Scenarios*. Retrieved from https://www.futuresplatform.com/blog/future-of-work-ai-in-the-work place-scenarios

Gallagher. (n.d.). *Generative AI: Upskilling the Workforce*. Retrieved from https://www.ajg.com/no-nb/news-and-insights/features/generative-ai-upskilling-the-workforce/

Gaper. io. (n.d.). *15 Jobs AI Will Replace by 2030*. Retrieved from https://gaper.io/15-j obs-will-ai-replace-by-2030/

General Assembly. (n.d.). *Learning Shift and Continuous Learning Culture*. Retrieved from https://generalassemb.ly/blog/learning-shift-activating-a-culture-of-continuous-learning/

GHDsi. (2024). *Five Ways to Overcome Resistance When Implementing New Techno-logy*. https://www.ghdsi.com/blog/five-ways-toovercome-resistance-when-implementing-new-technology

GHD Strategy & Innovation. (n.d.). *Five Ways to Overcome Resistance When Implementing New Technology*. Retrieved from https://www.ghdsi.com/blog/five-ways-toovercome-resistance-when-implementing-new-technology

Global Leaders Today. (2024). *How to Overcome Resistance to Change*. https://global-leaderstoday.online/how-to-overcome-resistance-to-change/

Goldman Sachs. (n.d.). *Generative AI Could Raise Global GDP by 7 Percent*. Retrieved from https://www.goldmansachs.com/insights/articles/generative-ai-could-raise-global-gdp-by-7-percent

Goodman , E. (2024). *Playing with Fear: Changing Your Mindset Can Change Everything*. Retrieved from https://www.linkedin.com/pulse/playing-fear-how-changing-your-mindset-can-change-eric-goodman-ph-d-

Google Cloud. (n.d.). *Machine Learning and AI Training*. Retrieved from https://cloud.google.com/learn/training/machinelearning-ai

Great Place to Work Australia. (n.d.). *Fostering a Growth Mindset in the Workplace: How to Encourage Continuous Learning and Development*. Retrieved from https://greatplacetowork.com.au/blog/fostering-a-growth-mindset-in-the-workplace-how-to-encourage-continuous-learning-and-development/

GreenStep. (n.d.). *Change Can Be a Catalyst for Innovation and Success*. Retrieved from https://greenstep.com/articles/change-can-be-a-catalyst-for-innovation-and-success

Grow CFO. (n.d.). *GrowCFO Competency Framework: Catalyst for Change*. Retrieved from https://www.growcfo.net/growcfo-competency-framework/implementation-skills/catalyst-for-change/

Growth Catalyst Canada. (n.d.). *Home*. Retrieved from https://www.growth-catalyst.ca

Growth Catalyst Marketing. (n.d.). *Home*. Retrieved from https://www.growthcatalystmarketing.com

Harvard Business Review. (n.d.). *How Generative AI Can Augment Human Creativity*. Retrieved from https://hbr.org/2023/07/how-generative-ai-can-augment-human-creativity

Harvard Business Review. (2016). *What Having a Growth Mindset Actually Means*. Retrieved from https://hbr.org/2016/01/what-having-a-growth-mindset-actually-means

Harvard Business Review. (2019). *The Top 20 Business Transformations of the Last Decade*. Retrieved from https://hbr.org/2019/09/the-top-20-business-transformations-of-the-last-decade

Harvard Business Review. (2023, September). *Reskilling in the Age of AI*. Retrieved from https://hbr.org/2023/09/reskilling-in-the-age-of-ai

Harvard Business Review. (2025). *How Gen AI Could Change the Value of Expertise*. Retrieved from https://hbr.org/2025/03/how-gen-ai-could-change-the-value-of-expertise

Harvard DCE. (n.d.). *How to Keep Up with AI through Reskilling*. Retrieved from https://professional.dce.harvard.edu/blog/how-to-keep-up-with-ai-through-reskilling/

Harvard Professional Development. (n.d.). *How to Keep Up with AI through Reskilling*. Retrieved from https://professional.dce.harvard.edu/blog/how-to-keep-up-with-ai-through-reskilling/

HBR. (2016). *What Having a Growth Mindset Actually Means*. Retrieved from https://hbr.org/2016/01/what-having-a-growth-mindset-actually-means

Hermes Investment. (2024). *Innovators: A Catalyst in the Making—2024 Outlook*. Retrieved from https://www.hermes-investment.com/au/en/professional/insights/active-esg/innovators-a-catalyst-in-the-making-2024-outlook/

Horton International. (2024). *Why Soft Skills Are Key in the Age of AI*. Retrieved from https://hortoninternational.com/why-soft-skills-are-key-in-the-age-of-artificial-intelligence/

HRDQ -U. (n.d.). *Becoming an Effective Change Catalyst*. Retrieved from https://hrdqu.com/change-management/becoming-effective-change-catalyst/

HR Exchange Network. (n.d.). *How Generative AI Is Transforming Workforce Collaboration*. Retrieved from https://www.hrexchangenetwork.com/hr-tech/columns/how-generative-ai-is-transforming-workforce-collaboration

IDC. (2024). *AI and Productivity*. Retrieved from https://www.idc.com/getdoc.jsp?containerId=prUS52600524

Increasing Self Worth. (n.d.). *How to Overcome Resistance to Change*.

Infopulse. (n.d.). *Embrace Technology: Change Management Insights*. Retrieved from https://www.infopulse.com/blog/embrace-technology-change-management

Informing Science. (n.d.). *Developing Resilience to Change*. Retrieved from https://www.informingscience.org/Publications/5078

Informing Science Institute. (n.d.). *Publication 5078*. Retrieved from https://www.informingscience.org/Publications/5078

Innovative Human Capital. (n.d.). *Leadership Strategies for Ensuring Workers Thrive in an AI-Driven World*. Retrieved from https://www.innovativehumancapital.com/article/leadership-strategies-for-ensuring-workers-thrive-in-an-ai-driven-world

Insights. (n.d.). *How to Reduce Change Resistance in Your Team*. Retrieved from https://blog.insights.com/en-us/blog/how-to-reduce-change-resistance-in-your-team

Insights Blog. (n.d.). *How to Reduce Change Resistance in Your Team*. Retrieved from https://blog.insights.com/en-gb/blog/how-to-reduce-change-resistance-in-your-team

International Monetary Fund. (2024, January 14). *AI Will Transform the Global Economy—Let's Make Sure It Benefits Humanity*. Retrieved from https://www.imf.org/en/Blogs/Articles/2024/01/14/ai-will-transform-the-global-economy-lets-make-sure-it-benefits-humanity

InnoPharma. (n.d.). *The Impact of AI on Job Roles, Workforce, and Employment*. Retrieved from https://www.innopharmaeducation.com/blog/the-impact-of-ai-on-job-roles-workforce-and-employment-what-you-need-to-know

ISCHP. (n.d.). *AI & Human Collaboration: From Quant to Qual*. Retrieved from https://ischp.net/2024/09/10/ai-human-collaboration-from-quant-to-qual-turning-data-into-meaning/

IT Brief Australia. (n.d.). *Women in Tech and Beyond: Embracing Uncertainty and Driving Change in Leadership*. Retrieved from https://itbrief.com.au/story/women-in-tech-and-beyond-embracing-uncertainty-and-driving-change-in-leadership

Ivan Grieve. (n.d.). *Innovative Collaborations between Artificial Intelligence and Human Creativity*. Retrieved from https://www.ivangrieve.com/blogs/news/innovative-collaborations-between-artificial-intelligence-and-human-creativity

Join the Collective. (n.d.). *Innovation Leadership: Inspiring Stories Driving Change*. Retrieved from https://www.jointhecollective.com/article/innovation-leadership-inspiring-stories-driving-change/

K21 Academy. (n.d.). *Top 10 AI Job Roles in 2025*. Retrieved from https://k21academy.com/ai-ml/top-10-ai-job-roles-in-2025-k21academy/

Kerry Anne Cassidy. (n.d.). *How Do People with a Growth Mindset View and Respond to Challenges?*. Retrieved from https://kerryannecassidy.com/mindset/how-do-people-with-a-growth-mindset-view-and-respond-to-challenges/

Keystroke Learning. (n.d.). *7 Ways to Help Staff Adapt to Technology*. Retrieved from https://keystrokelearning.com.au/7-ways-to-help-staff-adapt-to-technology/

Kieran Gilmurray. (n.d.). *Top Jobs Most at Risk of Being Replaced by AI*. Retrieved from https://kierangilmurray.com/top-jobs-most-at-risk-of-being-replaced-by-ai/

KNOLSKAPE. (n.d.). *Top 10 Change Management Examples and the Companies That Implemented Them.* Retrieved from https://knolskape.com/blog/top-10-change-management-examples-and-the-companies-that-implemented-them/

Knowledge Exchange UK. (2025). *Knowledge Exchange in 2025: A Catalyst for Growth and Innovation.* Retrieved from https://ke.org.uk/blog/knowledge-exchange-in-2025-a-catalyst-for-growth-and-innovation/

LarkSuite. (n.d.). *Human-AI Collaboration in Creativity.* Retrieved from https://www.larksuite.com/en_us/topics/ai-glossary/human-ai-collaboration-in-creativity

Leaf Career. (n.d.). *Embracing Uncertainty: The New Normal of Career Development.*

4Leaf Performance. (n.d.). *Building a Thriving Workplace with AI-Powered Insights.* Retrieved from https://www.4leafperformance.com/building-a-thriving-work place-with-ai-powered-insights/

360Learning. (n.d.). *AI Learning Platforms.* Retrieved from https://360learning.com/blog/ai-learning-platforms/

LearnLoft. (n.d.). *Catalyst Organization.* Retrieved from https://learnloft.com/catalyst-organization/

Legatt, A. (2025, January 21). *How AI Is Redefining Career Success According to the World Economic Forum.* Forbes. Retrieved from https://www.forbes.com/sites/avivalegatt/2025/01/21/how-ai-is-redefining-career-success-according-to-the-world-economic-forum/

LinkedIn. (n.d.-a). *4 Real-Life Examples of Successful Change Management in Business.* Retrieved from https://www.linkedin.com/pulse/4-real-life-examples-successful-change-management-business-hesseln

LinkedIn. (n.d.-b). *A Beginner's Guide to Using Change as a Catalyst for Growth.* Retrieved from https://www.linkedin.com/pulse/beginners-guide-using-change-catalyst-growth-stacey-young-rivers

LinkedIn. (n.d.-c). *AI & Automation 2025: Navigating the New Job Landscape.* Retrieved from https://www.linkedin.com/pulse/ai-automation-2025-navigating-new-job-landscape-dev-raj-saini-phj2f

LinkedIn. (n.d.-d). *AI & Future Jobs 2025: Insights from WEF.* Retrieved from https://www.linkedin.com/pulse/ai-future-jobs-2025-insights-from-world-economic-mohamed-nour-el-din-qo7bf

LinkedIn. (n.d.-e). *Artificial Intelligence & Human Creativity: The Future.* Retrieved from https://www.linkedin.com/pulse/artificial-intelligence-human-creativity-future-dr-jodi-nelson-tabor-q8ope

LinkedIn. (n.d.-f). *Change Catalyst: How My Childhood Shaped an Innovation Mindset.* Retrieved from https://www.linkedin.com/pulse/change-catalyst-how-my-childhood-shaped-innovation-mindset-setyawan

LinkedIn. (n.d.-g). *Change Catalyst: Unleashing Potential in Organizational Management.* Retrieved from https://www.linkedin.com/pulse/change-catalyst-unleashing-potential-organizational-management-byskc

LinkedIn. (n.d.-h). *Change Management Success Stories: Insights & Lessons from Leaders.* Retrieved from https://www.linkedin.com/pulse/change-management-success-stories-insights-lessons-from-javier-sada-4l3fc

LinkedIn. (n.d.-i). *Embracing Change: A Catalyst Role in Building Empathy.* Retrieved from https://www.linkedin.com/pulse/embracing-change-catalyst-role-building-empathy-scott-bissessar-eikec

LinkedIn. (n.d.-j). *Embracing Change: A Personal Catalyst for Growth*. Retrieved from https://www.linkedin.com/pulse/embracing-change-personal-catalyst-growth-emilia-bo%C5%BCek-iarce

LinkedIn. (n.d.-k). *Embracing Fear: A Catalyst for Personal Growth*. Retrieved from https://www.linkedin.com/pulse/embracing-fear-catalyst-personal-growth-michael-de-nysschen-h4icf

LinkedIn. (n.d.-l). *Embracing Process Change: Catalyst for Innovation and Growth*. Retrieved from https://www.linkedin.com/pulse/embracing-process-change-catalyst-innovation-growth-nick-akroyd

LinkedIn. (n.d.-m). *Embracing Uncertainty: Turning Chaos into Opportunity*. Retrieved from https://www.linkedin.com/pulse/embracing-uncertainty-turning-chaos-opportunity-written-greg-debrosse-9poqe

LinkedIn. (n.d.-n). *Embracing Uncertainty: Your Superpower*. Retrieved from https://www.linkedin.com/pulse/embracing-uncertainty-your-superpower-heather-polinsky-pmp-f-same-2fcze

LinkedIn. (n.d.-o). *Growth Catalyst: Visionary Innovation Insights*. Retrieved from https://www.linkedin.com/pulse/growth-catalyst-visionary-innovation-insights-star-riley-anhzc

LinkedIn. (n.d.-p). *How a Growth Mindset Can Help You Thrive in Times of Change*. Retrieved from https://www.linkedin.com/pulse/how-growth-mindset-can-help-you-thrive-times-change-miller-sphr

LinkedIn. (n.d.-q). *Lessons from a Catalyst: Driving Effective Change Management*. Retrieved from https://www.linkedin.com/pulse/lessons-from-catalyst-driving-effective-change-management-egol

LinkedIn. (n.d.-r). *Making Change Your Catalyst for Growth*. Retrieved from https://www.linkedin.com/pulse/making-change-your-catalyst-growth-michelle-crossan-matos-4flfc

LinkedIn. (n.d.-s). *The Power of a Growth Catalyst: Essential Approaches for CXOs and Leaders*. Retrieved from https://www.linkedin.com/pulse/power-growth-catalyst-essential-approaches-cxos-leaders-sharma

LinkedIn. (n.d.-t). *The Power of Resilience in an Evolving World of Technology and Business*. Retrieved from https://www.linkedin.com/pulse/power-resilience-evolving-world-technology-business-muhammad-ashraf-eodrf

LinkedIn. (n.d.-u). *The Power of Ten: 10 Ways to Foster a Growth Mindset*. Retrieved from https://www.linkedin.com/pulse/power-ten-10-ways-foster-growth-mindset-andrew-hulbert-msc-fiwfm

LinkedIn. (n.d.-v). *Top 10 AI Jobs 2025: Career Paths Shaping the Future*. Retrieved from https://www.linkedin.com/pulse/top-10-ai-jobs-2025-career-paths-shaping-future-centizen-68n1c

LinkedIn. (n.d.-w). *What Are the Most Effective Strategies for Overcoming Resistance to Change?*. Retrieved from https://www.linkedin.com/advice/0/what-most-effective-strategies-overcoming-ugnde

LinkedIn. (n.d.-x). *Your Company Is Struggling with a Major Change. How Can You Help?* Retrieved from https://www.linkedin.com/advice/1/your-company-struggling-major-change-how-can-zsu1c

LinkedIn Contributor. (2024). *You're Encountering Resistance to Change at Work—Now What?*. Retrieved from https://www.linkedin.com/advice/1/youre-encountering-resistance-change-work-epige

Loeb Leadership. (n.d.). *Future-Ready Leadership: Preparing for What's Next.* Retrieved from https://www.loebleadership.com/insights/future-ready-leadership-preparing-for-whats-next

LSA Global. (n.d.). *Most Effective Change Catalyst Criteria.* Retrieved from https://lsaglobal.com/most-effective-change-catalyst-criteria/

Ludmila. (n.d.-a). *Braving the Unknown: How Growth Mindset and Curiosity Can Help.* Retrieved from https://www.linkedin.com/pulse/braving-unknown-how-growth-mindset-curiosity-can-ludmila-20gnc

Ludmila. (n.d.-b). *Braving the Unknown: How a Growth Mindset and Curiosity Can Lead to Success.* LinkedIn. Retrieved from https://www.linkedin.com/pulse/braving-unknown-how-growth-mindset-curiosity-can-ludmila-20gnc

MacInnis Marketing. (n.d.). *Leveraging Trends for Business Innovation and Growth.* Retrieved from https://www.macinnismarketing.com.au/blog/leveraging-trends-for-business-innovation-and-growth

Macquarie University. (2024). *How AI Is Shaping Your Next Career Move.* Retrieved from https://lighthouse.mq.edu.au/article/october-2024/how-ai-is-shaping-your-next-career-move

Manus Plus. (n.d.). *Overcoming Resistance: How to Drive Technology Adoption in Your Workforce.* Retrieved from https://www.manus.plus/2024/10/09/overcoming-resistance-how-to-drive-technology-adoption-in-your-workforce/

Marr , B. (2024a). *Essential AI-Ready Skills Everyone Needs for Tomorrow's Jobs.* LinkedIn. Retrieved from https://www.linkedin.com/pulse/essential-ai-ready-skills-everyone-needs-tomorrows-jobs-bernard-marr-iymvf

Marr , B. (2024b). *Pivot or Die: Why Adaptability Is the Key to Survival in the Age of AI.* Retrieved from https://bernardmarr.com/pivot-or-die-why-adaptability-is-the-key-to-survival-in-the-age-of-ai/

4mation Technologies. (n.d.). *Building a Culture of Innovation through AI Transformation.* Retrieved from https://www.4mation.com.au/blog/building-culture-of-innovation-ai-transformation/

McKinsey & Co. (n.d.-a). *A Technology Survival Guide for Resilience.* Retrieved from https://www.mckinsey.com/capabilities/risk-and-resilience/our-insights/a-technology-survival-guide-for-resilience

McKinsey & Co. (n.d.-b). *AI, Automation, and the Future of Work: Ten Things to Solve for.* Retrieved from https://www.mckinsey.com/featured-insights/future-of-work/ai-automation-and-the-future-of-work-ten-things-to-solve-for

McKinsey & Co. (n.d.-c). *How Innovative Companies Leverage Tech to Outperform.* Retrieved from https://www.mckinsey.com/capabilities/strategy-and-corporate-finance/our-insights/how-innovative-companies-leverage-tech-to-outperform

McKinsey & Co. (2023a). *Technology, Jobs, and the Future of Work.* Retrieved from https://www.mckinsey.com/featured-insights/employment-and-growth/technology-jobs-and-the-future-of-work

McKinsey & Co. (2023b). *The Economic Potential of Generative AI: The Next Productivity Frontier.* Retrieved from https://www.mckinsey.com/capabilities/mckinsey-digital/our-insights/the-economic-potential-of-generative-ai-the-next-productivity-frontier

McKinsey & Co. (2024). *AI, Automation, and the Future of Work: Ten Things to Solve For.* Retrieved from https://www.mckinsey.com/featured-insights/future-of-work/ai-automation-and-the-future-of-work-ten-things-to-solve-for

McKinsey Digital. (n.d.). *Superagency in the Workplace: Empowering People to Unlock AI's Full Potential at Work*. Retrieved from https://www.mckinsey.com/capabilities/mckinsey-digital/our-insights/superagency-in-the-workplace-empowering-people-to-unlock-ais-full-potential-at-work

McLean & Co. (n.d.). *Case Studies: Navigate Change*. Retrieved from https://hr.mcleanco.com/research/case-studies-navigate-change

Meridian University. (n.d.). *Business Innovation: A Catalyst for Growth*. Retrieved from https://meridianuniversity.edu/content/business-innovation-a-catalyst-for-growth

Mightybytes. (n.d.). *Digital Resilience*. Retrieved from https://www.mightybytes.com/blog/digital-resilience/

Miller , S. (2024). *How to Overcome Fear with a Growth Mindset*. SusieMiller.com. Retrieved from https://www.susiemiller.com/how-to-overcome-fear-with-a-growth-mindset/

MindLab Neuroscience. (n.d.). *Overcome Fear of Change: 8 Powerful Strategies*. Retrieved from https://mindlabneuroscience.com/overcome-fear-of-change-8-powerful-strategies/

MIT Sloan. (n.d.-a). *A New Look: Economics of AI*. Retrieved from https://mitsloan.mit.edu/ideas-made-to-matter/a-new-look-economics-ai

MIT Sloan. (n.d.-b). *How Generative AI Can Boost Highly Skilled Workers' Productivity*. Retrieved from https://mitsloan.mit.edu/ideas-made-to-matter/how-generative-ai-can-boost-highly-skilled-workers-productivity

Monash Lens. (2025, February 14). *Dancing with Digital Partners: The Creative Revolution of Generative AI*. Retrieved from https://lens.monash.edu/@education/2025/02/14/1387313/dancing-with-digital-partners-the-creative-revolution-of-generative-ai

Monash University. (n.d.). *How to Equip Yourself for AI Career Success*. Retrieved from https://online.monash.edu/news/how-to-equip-yourself-for-ai-career-success/

Motion. (n.d.). *AI Productivity Tools*. Retrieved from https://www.usemotion.com/blog/ai-productivity-tools

Mountain Moving Co. (n.d.). *The Art of Future Thinking: How to Develop a Future-Thinking Mindset*. Retrieved from https://www.mountainmoving.co/blog-posts/the-art-of-future-thinking-how-to-develop-a-future-thinking-mindset

National Center for Biotechnology Information. (2021). *PMC8299535*. Retrieved from https://pmc.ncbi.nlm.nih.gov/articles/PMC8299535/

National Library of Medicine. (n.d.-a). *Article on Career Transition Psychology*. Retrieved from https://pmc.ncbi.nlm.nih.gov/articles/PMC9046553/

National Library of Medicine. (n.d.-b). *PMC8299535*. Retrieved from https://pmc.ncbi.nlm.nih.gov/articles/PMC8299535/

Nature. (n.d.). *Human-AI Interaction in Creative Teams*. Retrieved from https://www.nature.com/articles/s41562-024-02024-1

Neel Raman. (n.d.). *5 Techniques to Build Resilience Amidst Technology Advancements*. Retrieved from https://neelraman.com/5-techniques-to-build-resilience-amidst-technology-advancements/

NeuroLeadership Institute. (n.d.). *Growth Mindset: How to Deal with Change*. Retrieved from https://neuroleadership.com/your-brain-at-work/growth-mindset-deal-with-change/

NIH. (2024a). *AI in Healthcare and Industry: A Review*. Retrieved from https://pmc. ncbi.nlm.nih.gov/articles/PMC10506722/

NIH. (2024b). *Fear of Change and Psychological Impact*. Retrieved from https://pmc. ncbi.nlm.nih.gov/articles/PMC9046553/

No Code Institute. (n.d.). *Overcome Fear of Job Search in Midlife Career Change*. Retrieved from https://www.nocodeinstitute.io/post/overcome-fear-of-job-search-in-mi dlife-career-change

North Dawn Coaching. (2024). *Mindset Matters: Overcoming Fear and Embracing Change*. Retrieved from https://www.northdawncoach.com/blog/mindset-matters-overcoming-fear-and-embracing-change-in-your-career-transition

OB Forum. (n.d.). *Webinar Summary: How to Master a Future-Ready Mindset in 2025*. Retrieved from https://www.obforum.com/article/webinar-summary-how-to-master-a-future-ready-mindset-in-2025

OECD. (2024). *Reskilling and Lifelong Learning: Adapting to the AI-Driven Job Market*. Retrieved from https://www.oecd-events.org/summit-gpaiserbia2024/en/ses sion/098d0a9f-e0a0-ef11-88cf-6045bd903ca2/reskilling-and-lifelong-learning-adapting-to-the-ai-driven-job-market-and-impact-of-ai-to-modern-education

Oliver Wyman Forum. (n.d.). *Workforce Transformation in the AI era*.

OnTalent. (n.d.). *Overcome Fear During Career Transition*. Retrieved from https://www. ontalent.com.au/overcome-fear-during-career-transition/

Osagie , J. (2024). *The Rise of AI & Automation: Transforming Industries of the Future*. LinkedIn. Retrieved from https://www.linkedin.com/pulse/rise-ai-automation-transforming-industries-future-jonathan-osagie-pbwre

OzEmio. (n.d.). *AI and Lifelong Learning*. Retrieved from https://ozemio.com/blog/ ai-and-lifelong-learning/

P3 Adaptive. (n.d.). *Now You Can Bring AI into the Workplace the Right Way*. Retrieved from https://p3adaptive.com/now-you-can-bring-ai-into-the-workplace-the-right-way-ai-workplace-strategy/

Panorama Consulting. (n.d.). *Change Management Success Stories*. Retrieved from https:// www.panorama-consulting.com/change-management-success-stories/

People Management. (2024). *Anticipating Future with AI: Changing Career Planning*. Retrieved from https://www.peoplemanagement.co.uk/article/1883036/ anticipating-future-ai-changing-career-planning-its-impact-l-d

Persona Talent. (n.d.). *How to Cultivate a Growth Mindset*. Retrieved from https:// www.personatalent.com/development/how-to-cultivate-a-growth-mindset/

Pro Bono Australia. (2024, December). *How to Overcome Fear and Self-Doubt during a Career Transition*. Retrieved from https://probonoaustralia.com.au/news/2024/12/ how-to-overcome-fear-and-self-doubt-during-a-career-transition/

Prosci. (n.d.-a). *Change Agent*. Retrieved from https://www.prosci.com/blog/change-agent

Prosci. (n.d.-b). *Resources—Success Stories*. Retrieved from https://www.prosci.com/ resources/success-stories

Prosci. (n.d.-c). *Successful Change Management Examples for Inspiration*. Retrieved from https://www.prosci.com/blog/successful-change-management-examples-for-inspiration

Psyche. (n.d.). *Set Yourself Free by Developing a Growth Mindset Toward Anxiety*. Retrieved from https://psyche.co/ideas/set-yourself-free-by-developing-a-growth-mindset-toward-anxiety

Psychology Today. (n.d.). *Using AI for Creative Collaboration*. Retrieved from https://www.psychologytoday.com/au/blog/the-digital-self/202409/using-ai-for-creative-collaboration

PwC. (n.d.). *Artificial Intelligence Study*. Retrieved from https://www.pwc.com/gx/en/issues/artificial-intelligence/publications/artificial-intelligence-study.html

Queensland University of Technology (QUT). (n.d.). *Case Study: Leading Change to Support the Future*. Retrieved from https://www.qut.edu.au/study/short-courses-and-professional-education/for-organisations/case-study-leading-change-to-support-the-future

Reclaim Design. (n.d.). *Embracing Uncertainty*. Retrieved from https://reclaimdesign.org/embracing-uncertainty

Reddit Career Guidance. (n.d.). *How Have You Overcome the Fear of Changing Jobs?*. Retrieved from https://www.reddit.com/r/careerguidance/comments/1az9wup/how_have_you_overcome_the_fear_of_changing_jobs/

Refer. me. (n.d.). *Mastering the AI Job Landscape: Skills and Strategies for Modern Professionals*. Retrieved from https://www.refer.me/blog/mastering-the-ai-job-landscape-skills-and-strategies-for-modern-professionals

Reserve Bank of Australia. (2020). *Speech on Technology & Workforce*. Retrieved from https://www.rba.gov.au/speeches/2020/sp-so-2020-03-16.html

Robert Walters Australia. (n.d.). *How AI Will Shape Hiring and Careers*. Retrieved from https://www.robertwalters.com.au/insights/hiring-advice/blog/how-AI-will-shape-hiring-and-careers.html

Robinson , C. (2024, June 11). *Is Fear Preventing You from Pivoting? Here's How to Change Careers*. Forbes. Retrieved from https://www.forbes.com/sites/cherylrobinson/2024/06/11/is-fear-preventing-you-from-pivoting-heres-how-to-change-careers/

Roffey Park Institute. (n.d.). *The Power of Change: Unlock Growth and Innovation*. Retrieved from https://www.roffeypark.com/articles/the-power-of-change-unlock-growth-and-innovation/

Sahota , N. (2024, July 25). *AI Energizes Your Career Path & Charts Your Professional Growth Plan*. Forbes. Retrieved from https://www.forbes.com/sites/neilsahota/2024/07/25/ai-energizes-your-career-path--charts-your-professional-growth-plan/

Salesforce. (n.d.). *Human-AI Collaboration*. Retrieved from https://www.salesforce.com/blog/human-ai-collaboration/

Salesforce. (2023). *AI and Workplace Communication: Enhancing Collaboration and Productivity*. Retrieved from https://www.forbes.com/councils/forbescommunicationscouncil/2023/11/07/ai-and-workplace-communication-enhancing-collaboration-and-productivity/

Salesforce Australia. (n.d.). *Essential Soft Skills Guide*. Retrieved from https://www.salesforce.com/au/blog/essential-soft-skills-guide/

Sandra Perez Botero. (n.d.). *The Top 7 Lessons from Being an Innovation Catalyst*. Retrieved from https://sandraperezbotero.com/the-top-7-lessons-from-being-an-innovation-catalyst/

SandTech. (n.d.). *AI and the Future of Work*. Retrieved from https://www.sandtech.com/insight/ai-and-the-future-of-work/

Schmelzer , R. (2024). *The Role Adaptability Plays in Generative AI*. Forbes. Retrieved from https://www.forbes.com/sites/ronschmelzer/2024/09/13/the-role-adaptability-plays-in-generative-ai/

SEEK. (2024). *How to Help Employees Adapt to New Technology*. Retrieved from https://talent.seek.com.au/hiring-advice/article/how-to-help-employees-adapt-to-new-technology

Shelf. io. (n.d.). *What Jobs Will AI Replace?*. Retrieved from https://shelf.io/blog/what-jobs-will-ai-replace/

Shift eLearning. (n.d.-a). *Always Learning: Becoming a Learning Company*. Retrieved from https://www.shiftelearning.com/blog/always-learning-company

Shift eLearning. (n.d.-b). *Always Learning: The Company of the Future*. Retrieved from https://www.shiftelearning.com/blog/always-learning-company

SHRM. (n.d.). *Fostering a Growth Mindset: The Role of HR*. Retrieved from https://www.shrm.org/in/topics-tools/news/blogs/fostering-growth-mindset-role-of-hr

SJ Innovation. (n.d.). *Future of Human-AI Collaboration: What's Next?*. Retrieved from https://sjinnovation.com/future-human-ai-collaboration-whats-next

SkillAbilly. (n.d.). *Building Resilience: Strategies for Adapting to Technological Changes*. Retrieved from https://www.skillabilly.com/building-resilience-strategies-for-adapting-to-technological-changes/

SkillPacks. (n.d.). *Overcoming Resistance to Change*. Retrieved from https://www.skill-packs.com/overcoming-resistance-to-change/

Smythos. (n.d.-a). *Human-AI Collaboration Examples*. Retrieved from https://smythos.com/ai-agents/ai-tutorials/human-ai-collaboration-examples/

Smythos. (n.d.-b). *Human-AI Collaboration in Creative Industries*. Retrieved from https://smythos.com/ai-industry-solutions/entertainment/human-ai-collaboration-in-creative-industries/

Sonia McDonald. (2019, April 25). *7 Ways to Overcome Fear*. Retrieved from https://soniamcdonald.com.au/2019/04/25/7-ways-to-overcome-fear/

Stanford University. (2021, September). *Mindsets: A Clearing Lens on Life*. Retrieved from https://news.stanford.edu/stories/2021/09/mindsets-clearing-lens-life

Stormboard. (n.d.). *8 Surprising Benefits of AI in Team Collaboration*. Retrieved from https://stormboard.com/blog/8-surprising-benefits-of-ai-in-team-collaboration

STP Tax. (n.d.). *Innovation: Profit Strategies*. Retrieved from https://www.stptax.com/profit-strategies/innovation/

Strategy Institute. (2024). *Understanding AI Strategy: Key Principles for Success*. Retrieved from https://www.thestrategyinstitute.org/insights/understanding-ai-strategy-key-principles-for-success-in-todays-digital-era

Strength of Tears. (n.d.). *Overcome Resistance to Change*. Retrieved from https://www.strengthoftears.com/blog/overcome-resistance-to-change

Sutton -Cegarra, B. (n.d.). *Success Stories in Support of Change*. LinkedIn. Retrieved from https://www.linkedin.com/pulse/success-stories-support-change-benita-sutton-cegarra

System Catalysts. (n.d.). *Catalyst for Change*. Retrieved from https://www.systemcat-alysts.com/blog/catalyst-for-change

TAFE N SW. (n.d.). *Responsible AI Course*. Retrieved from https://store.training.tafensw.edu.au/product/responsible-artificial-intelligence/

Taju C oaching. (n.d.). *Embracing Adversity: Catalyst for Personal Growth*. Retrieved from https://www.tajucoaching.com/blog/embracing-adversity-catalyst-for-personal-growth

Teamified. (n.d.). *How AI Is Boosting Productivity and Making Our Jobs Easier*. Retrieved from https://www.teamified.com.au/blog-posts/how-ai-is-boosting-productivity-and-making-our-jobs-easier

Technology D ecisions. (n.d.). *A Cultural Shift Can Maximise the Potential of AI in Software Development.* Retrieved from https://www.technologydecisions.com.au/content/it-management/article/a-cultural-shift-can-maximise-the-potential-of-ai-in-software-development-107846805

TechRadar P ro. (2024). *AI Is More Than Just Automation—It's Reshaping Industries.* Retrieved from https://www.techradar.com/pro/ai-is-more-than-just-automation-its-reshaping-industries

TechTarget. (n.d.). *Top AI Jobs.* Retrieved from https://www.techtarget.com/whatis/feature/Top-AI-jobs

Telstra W holesale. (2024). *What's Your AQ? Why Adaptability Is the Key to Innovation.* Retrieved from https://www.telstrawholesale.com.au/wholesaleconnect/category/technology/what-s-your-aq--why-adaptability-is-the-key-to-innovation-in-an-.html

THC C onsult. (2023a). *BW Catalyst Case Study* [PDF]. Retrieved from https://thcconsult.ie/wp-content/uploads/2023/04/BW-Catalyst-Case-Study.pdf

THC C onsult. (2023b). *Catalyst Case Study* [PDF]. Retrieved from https://thcconsult.ie/wp-content/uploads/2023/04/Catalyst-Case-Study.pdf

The C ollective. (n.d.). *Overcoming Resistance to Change: A Leadership Perspective.* Retrieved from https://www.jointhecollective.com/article/overcoming-resistance-to-change-a-leadership-perspective/

The E nterprisers Project. (2022). *AI Revolution: 4 Tips to Stay Competitive.* Retrieved from https://enterprisersproject.com/article/2022/10/ai-revolution-4-tips-stay-competitive

The E ntourage. (n.d.). *How to Adapt Your Mindset to Propel Business Growth.* Retrieved from https://www.the-entourage.com/blog/how-to-adapt-your-mindset-to-propel-business-growth

The G rowth Catalysts. (n.d.). *Case Studies.* Retrieved from https://thegrowthcatalysts.com/case-studies/

Thinkers360. (n.d.). *Change Management: Fixed Versus Growth Mindset Leadership.* Retrieved from https://www.thinkers360.com/tl/blog/members/change-management-fixed-verses-growth-mindset-leadership

ThoughtWorks. (n.d.). *Innovation Catalyst.* Retrieved from https://www.thoughtworks.com/en-au/what-we-do/innovation/innovation-catalyst

ThreeWill. (n.d.). *AI Workplace Strategies 2025.* Retrieved from https://threewill.com/ai-workplace-strategies-2025/

Times H igher Education. (n.d.-a). *How We Can Use AI to Power Career-Driven Lifelong Learning.* Retrieved from https://www.timeshighereducation.com/campus/how-we-can-use-ai-power-careerdriven-lifelong-learning

Times Higher Education. (n.d.-b). *Using AI to Power Career-Driven Lifelong Learning.* Retrieved from https://www.timeshighereducation.com/campus/how-we-can-use-ai-power-careerdriven-lifelong-learning

Turner, D. (n.d.). *Workplace Culture: The Hidden Force behind AI Innovation.* LinkedIn. Retrieved from https://www.linkedin.com/pulse/workplace-culture-hidden-force-behind-ai-innovation-turner-mba-wbfte

University of Colorado Boulder. (2024). *Three Ways AI Is Shaping the Work World.* Retrieved from https://www.colorado.edu/artssciences-advising/2024/12/11/three-ways-ai-shaping-work-world

University of Richmond. (2024). *The Psychology of Change Resistance*. Retrieved from https://scholarship.richmond.edu/cgi/viewcontent.cgi?article=1083&context=psychology-faculty-publications

University of Victoria. (n.d.). *Foster Trust in AI*. Retrieved from https://continuing-studies.uvic.ca/news/foster-trust-in-ai

Uplift Recruitment. (n.d.). *Conquering Fear: How to Feel Confident in the Face of a Career Change*. Retrieved from https://upliftrecruitment.au/conquering-fear-how-to-feel-confident-in-the-face-of-a-career-change/

UpraisedD. (2024). *Embracing the Future: How AI and Automation Are Reshaping Industries*. LinkedIn. Retrieved from https://www.linkedin.com/pulse/embracing-future-ai-automation-reshaping-industries-upraisedd-s6sqf

UNLEASH. ai. (n.d.). *The Human Edge: Enhancing Soft Skills as Essential Partners in the AI Age*. Retrieved from https://www.unleash.ai/artificial-intelligence/the-human-edge-enhancing-soft-skills-as-essential-partners-in-the-ai-age/

Upskilled. (n.d.-a). *How AI Is Reshaping the Job Market*. Retrieved from https://www.upskilled.edu.au/skillstalk/how-ai-is-reshaping-the-job-market

UpSkilled. (n.d.-b). *Soft Skills in the Age of Artificial Intelligence*. Retrieved from https://www.upskilled.edu.au/skillstalk/soft-skills-in-the-age-of-artificial-intelligence

Vikas. (2025). *How AI & Automation Are Reshaping Industries: Key Use Cases*. Dev.to. Retrieved from https://dev.to/vikas76/how-ai-automation-is-reshaping-industries-key-use-cases-in-2025-2kjl

Vocal Media. (n.d.). *Embracing Change: A Catalyst for Personal Growth*. Retrieved from https://vocal.media/motivation/embracing-c-hange-a-catalyst-for-personal-growth

Walters , D. (2024). *Career Change Success Story: How to Move beyond the Devil You Know*. LinkedIn. Retrieved from https://www.linkedin.com/pulse/career-change-success-story-how-move-beyond-devil-you-walters

Waterloo Intuition. (n.d.-a). *Upskilling and AI Hiring Processes*. Retrieved from https://blog.waterloointuition.com/upskilling-altering-hiring-processes-in-the-age-of-ai/

Waterloo Intuition. (n.d.-b). *Upskilling and Hiring in the Age of AI*. Retrieved from https://blog.waterloointuition.com/upskilling-altering-hiring-processes-in-the-age-of-ai/

White , T. (n.d.). *Overcoming Fear of Career Change: Balancing Risk and Reward*. LinkedIn. Retrieved from https://www.linkedin.com/pulse/overcoming-fear-career-change-balancing-risk-reward-theresa-white-ghpgf

Wilson , C. (n.d.). *Growth Mindset: How a Healthy Relationship with Fear and Failure Fuels Success*. Retrieved from https://www.linkedin.com/pulse/growth-mindset-how-healthy-relationship-fear-failure-fuels-wilson

Workday. (2025). *AI Trends Outlook: The Rise of Human-AI Collaboration*. Retrieved from https://blog.workday.com/en-us/2025-ai-trends-outlook-the-rise-of-human-ai-collaboration.html

Worknomads. (n.d.). *The Crucial Role of Soft Skills in an AI-Driven Workplace*. LinkedIn. Retrieved from https://www.linkedin.com/pulse/crucial-role-soft-skills-ai-driven-workplace-worknomads-r9e8e

World Economic Forum. (n.d.-a). *AI and Beyond: Navigating the New Tech Landscape*. Retrieved from https://www.weforum.org/stories/2025/01/ai-and-beyond-how-every-career-can-navigate-the-new-tech-landscape/

World Economic Forum. (n.d.-b). *AI Workplace Skills*. Retrieved from https://www. weforum.org/stories/2025/01/ai-workplace-skills/

World Economic Forum. (2023). *The Future of Jobs Report 2023*. Retrieved from https:// www.weforum.org/publications/the-future-of-jobs-report-2023/digest/

World Economic Forum. (2024). *Reskilling AI Workers and Businesses*. Retrieved from https://www.weforum.org/stories/2024/10/reskilling-ai-workers-businesses/

World Economic Forum. (2025a). *AI and Beyond: How Every Career Can Navigate the New Tech Landscape*. Retrieved from https://www.weforum.org/stories/2025/01/ai-and-beyond-how-every-career-can-navigate-the-new-tech-landscape/

World Economic Forum. (2025b). *AI Transformation across Industries: Responsible Innovation*. Retrieved from https://www.weforum.org/stories/2025/01/ai-transformation-industries-responsible-innovation/

World Economic Forum. (2025c, January). *Four Ways to Enhance Human—AI Collaboration in the Workplace*. Retrieved from https://www.weforum.org/stories/2025/01/four-ways-to-enhance-human-ai-collaboration-in-the-workplace/

World Economic Forum. (2025d). *Future of Jobs Report 2025* [PDF]. Retrieved from https://reports.weforum.org/docs/WEF_Future_of_Jobs_Report_2025.pdf

World Economic Forum. (2025e). *Future of Jobs Report 2025: Jobs of the Future and the Skills You Need to Get Them*. Retrieved from https://www.weforum.org/stories/2025/01/future-of-jobs-report-2025-jobs-of-the-future-and-the-skills-you-need-to-get-them/

World Economic Forum. (2025f). *Navigating the AI Revolution: Managers and Enterprises*. Retrieved from https://www.weforum.org/stories/2025/01/navigating-the-ai-revolution-managers-and-enterprises/

World Economic Forum. (2025g, January). *Why You Should Think of AI as a Teammate, Not a Tool*. Retrieved from https://www.weforum.org/stories/2025/01/why-you-should-think-of-ai-as-a-teammate-not-a-tool-when-building-a-better-future/

xCubelabs. (n.d.). *Enhancing Creativity with Generative AI*. Retrieved from https://www.xcubelabs.com/blog/human-ai-collaboration-enhancing-creativity-with-generative-ai/

Yard, S. (n.d.-a). *Don't Fear the Shift: Why AI Should Be Your Next Career Move*. LinkedIn. Retrieved from https://www.linkedin.com/pulse/dont-fear-shiftheres-why-ai-should-your-next-career-move-simone-yard-6f1ae

Yard, S. (n.d.-b). *Why AI Should Be Your Next Career Move*. Retrieved from https://www.linkedin.com/pulse/dont-fear-shiftheres-why-ai-should-your-next-career-move-simone-yard-6f1ae

Zapier. (n.d.). *Best AI Productivity Tools*. Retrieved from https://zapier.com/blog/best-ai-productivity-tools/

Index

Note: **Bold** page numbers refer to tables and *italic* page numbers refer to figures.

For Product Safety Concerns and Information please contact our EU
representative GPSR@taylorandfrancis.com
Taylor & Francis Verlag GmbH, Kaufingerstraße 24, 80331 München, Germany